BOSIE

The Story of Lord Alfred Douglas

At the age of 24.

BOSIE

Lord Alfred Douglas, His Friends and Enemies

RUPERT CROFT-COOKE

THE **BOBBS-MERRILL** COMPANY, INC.
A SUBSIDIARY OF HOWARD W. SAMS & CO., INC.
Publishers • INDIANAPOLIS • NEW YORK

CONTENTS

ILLUSTRATIONS

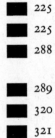

Please let us hear no more of the tragedy of Oscar Wilde. Oscar was no tragedian. He was the superb comedian of his century, one to whom misfortune, disgrace, imprisonment were external and traumatic. His gaiety of soul was invulnerable: it shines through the blackest pages of his *De Profundis* as clearly as in his funniest epigrams. Even on his deathbed he found in himself no pity for himself, playing for the laugh with his last breath, and getting it with as sure a stroke as in his palmiest prime. Not so the young disciple whose fortunes were poisoned and ruined through their attachment. The tragedy is his tragedy, not Oscar's.

George Bernard Shaw

Introduction

ALFRED DOUGLAS has ceased to be a controversial figure, and in the general estimate is condemned, if not with execration at least with a shrug. In the many books which describe his friendship with Wilde, even in those which profess to be concerned primarily with Douglas, an image has been created which must fill the reader with antipathy, and two fairly recent films have done nothing to modify it. Douglas is shown as petulant and wilful, coercing Wilde to attack Queensberry, abandoning him in distress, disloyal to his memory, an egotist monstrous in his vanity and fatal in his personal beauty. This image is a false one, but it is not my object to destroy it by an impassioned polemical defence of the man in all his actions or a denunciation of his enemies. I shall rely on evidence, much of which has never hitherto been brought to light, to erase the crude lines of caricature and substitute a portrait.

My friendship with Douglas was unbroken during the last twenty-five years of his life, so that although I had opportunities of hearing from him and those about him a certain amount of past history, I have been dependent for most of it on research, in which I have received the most generous assistance. In spite of my affection for Douglas, I had more than a suspicion that this research would reveal weaknesses and perhaps demerits in his behaviour at the time of the Wilde scandal to justify the popular and persistent abuse of him which, initiated by Robert Ross, has continued ever since the publication of Arthur Ransome's book and the libel action which followed it in 1913.

I have found, though, that all the evidence shows that Douglas's conduct at the time, however impulsive and ill-advised, was honourable and courageous in a degree scarcely to be expected of a young man of twenty-four, faced with a tragic and dangerous situation and having only his own initiative, his own sense of loyalty, his own idea of right and wrong, to guide him. The selfish youth who goaded Wilde to his doom, and afterwards abandoned him is an artfully created myth, for which, however, Douglas by his feverish protestations and his abominable book, *Oscar Wilde and Myself*, must be held partially to blame. The truth was that alone among Wilde's friends he took the very real risk of arrest to remain in England and visit Wilde (remanded in custody in Holloway) daily till the opening of the trial and thereafter tried, with tactless loyalty, to defend him in print and to identify himself with him in his views and misfortune.

Later, in spite of what one friend called Wilde's 'gaol fever' of rancour against him, Douglas remained constant, as well as imaginatively sympathetic, during the next two difficult years. Even when I was coming to the end of my researches and (through the kindness of H. Montgomery Hyde) read the letters Douglas wrote to More Adey at this time, manly and unflinching in acceptance of Wilde's hysterical outbursts against him, I was not prepared for anything so contrary to the generally accepted notion of the man.

To me one of the most absorbing parts of the story has been not so much the friendship itself, but the night of long knives among Wilde's friends and associates which followed it. The intrigue which started as soon as Wilde and Douglas met continued for twenty-seven years, and in the popular view of its treacheries it is always Douglas who used the poisoned blade. To demonstrate this, I have only to quote Mr. Vyvyan Holland, Wilde's son, who wrote to me of Douglas when I told him of this book, "Don't forget that he practically murdered my greatest friend, Robert Ross". This attitude has been adopted by many people with less right to their prejudices, and adopted without much thought or reason, as a study of events will show. There have been grudging admissions that Douglas was a fine poet, but for the man there has been no apologist. There has, in fact, been no serious attempt to study his career and character, his achievements and misfortunes.

Everything published about the Wilde affair, with one or two notable exceptions, has been written to prove something, if it is only that there is nothing of *that* kind about the writer. This does not exclude what Douglas and Wilde wrote about one another, for both Wilde's grandiloquently resentful *De Profundis* and Douglas's scurrilous *Oscar Wilde and Myself* were written in periods of stress and disillusionment and their authors recanted, either by action or words, after writing them. Robert Sherard's books were written to prove that Wilde was a blameless and noble man, Frank Harris's book to prove that Frank Harris was. There has been much to whiten Douglas at the expense of Ross, more to whiten Ross at the expense of Douglas. It is only in recent years that any impartiality has been attempted and that rarely, and only by writers and editors like Hesketh Pearson, Rupert Hart-Davis and H. Montgomery Hyde.

What nearly all the books about the Wilde affair and its aftermath have in common is their authors' attitude to homosexuality. They speak with a shudder of Wilde's 'extraordinary practices' and even H. Montgomery Hyde, who writes with scholarly detachment of the *Trials of Oscar Wilde*, adds a learned Appendix on *The Problem of Wilde's Inversion*. The thing has been viewed, either authoritatively or not, from the medico-legal standpoint rather than with naturalness, humour or understanding. For this attitude of awe towards 'strange sins', Wilde himself was partly responsible, for he dramatized his relationships with stable-boys and blackmailers as he dramatized everything else. Yet they were paltry and everyday affairs and Alfred Taylor and his circle and 'Uncle' Burton and his gang or their counterparts exist as openly in London today as in the 'nineties. Even their vocabulary has changed little and their way of living scarcely at all.

In Wilde's time the ridiculous word 'homosexual' was almost unheard-of outside the textbooks of sexual psychology and the silly attempts at categorization which have been a feature of modern research were unknown and unimaginable. No one tried to pretend that all men and women belonged to one of three categories—'heterosexual', 'bi-sexual' and 'homosexual'; all that was uncomfortably realized was that in large cities there often existed—and had existed since large cities were built—a nucleus of obsessed pederasts and a body of male prostitution which depended on it. Decent and discreet sexual relationships between men were disregarded by the majority or taken for granted by the knowledgeable. The police had not realized what a gift to the ambitious prosecution-seeker was Section 2 of the Criminal Law Amendment Act of 1885 and it was not only the academically minded who spoke (inaccurately) of 'the Greek Ideal'.

Most writers on Wilde have treated the whole thing as larger than life, a fantastic abnormality, instead of a commonplace of urban life. It is only dealt with in this book in so far as it affected Douglas and the Wilde-Douglas friendship, but to that degree it is discussed without mystery or wonder and without fear on my part of what inferences may be drawn from this familiarity. I employ the word 'homosexuality' under protest, as it were. Like other textbook terms, it is misused in popular speech, but it indicates to the modern reader something otherwise explicable only by cumbrous phraseology. I do not mean it to suggest some exotic or ultramontane form of life. Thus when I record that Douglas passed through a period of homosexuality, I intend to convey that for a time he was involved in the promiscuity and viciousness which were revealed in the trials of Wilde, not that his essential character changed. He became a Catholic and accepted the Church's teaching on sexual morality, and did so with a whole-heartedness and severity with himself which made the last thirty years of his life chaste. But he was not 'homosexual' at one time, 'hetero-sexual' at another, or 'bi-sexual' throughout, and his life showed the futility of such classifications.

Again, inevitably I employ the terms now in common usage, 'queers' and 'queens' for example, with their special connotations. To say of some of the sissily intellectual friends of Wilde, like Ross and Reggie Turner, that they were 'inverts' seems to me pompous and discriminating; to call them 'queers' is to use a lighter term as familiar to the modern reader and far more expressive. Wilde himself used such terms and wrote to Douglas of being 'rented by every black-mailer in London'. The whole story seems to need extricating from the spell of capital letters and pseudo-scientific terminology. There was nothing very extraordinary about the case against Wilde except that it became a *cause célèbre*.

What interests me most about Douglas himself is his development. How the hard-riding and athletic young man with a taste for poetry became the friend if not the disciple of Oscar Wilde, and in turn the litigious pamphleteer of the middle period, and finally the urbane and humorous poet whom I knew, is a story which I have always found absorbing, and most of all now, when I see it, I believe, in its natural proportions. It is a story in which the incidental characters refuse to play minor rôles, and Wilde, Harris, Queensberry, Ross, Crosland and others insist on being heard and seen, sometimes creditably, sometimes not. It is not all tragedy, as Shaw suggests, and in his last years Douglas achieved gaiety and serenity though he never became complacent.

He was his own worst advocate. The fact, for instance, that after Wilde's arrest, when Ross and the others had fled to France, he risked arrest by remaining with Wilde and saw him in prison every day until his trial would have impressed many people if they had not heard it so often from Douglas. The sacrifice he made of good opinion and the goodwill of his family and friends when he lived with Wilde after his imprisonment would have been a more noble thing if he had not boasted of it. He did so, it is true, under provocation and as a counter-attack to the far more subtle strategy of Robert Ross, but he protested too much and lost the sympathy which, with time, would have come to him.

This is what renders valueless the little that has been written about him since his death. His own autobiographical books were turgid and self-justifying. He was incapable of writing about himself, or anything else, with coolness or detachment. No master of prose he could not, in his books, communicate the lightness and humour with which, in conversation, he recalled the incidents of his life. Those who know him only from his *Autobiography* have a painfully false conception of him, and those who write about him on the strength of this, sometimes shamelessly paraphrasing whole passages from the book, misrepresent him. They are writing of the autobiographer, not of the man. They miss the basic paradox—that as a public figure and as an apologist for himself Douglas was crude and arrogant while as a man he was lovable and modest.

I found a particular problem when I came to consider his letters. The smallest impulse, the most casual enquiry, the least inaccuracy observed, or the most trivial letter received, caused him to write, sometimes at great length, to persons known or unknown, hostile or friendly to himself. At a rough and not over-generous calculation, I would say that from the age of twenty till his death at seventy-five he wrote an average of a letter a day, or in his whole life some twenty thousand letters, of which probably more than a third have been preserved. The William Andrews Clark Memorial Library in California has a vast collection of these, the Royal Society of Literature another, H. Montgomery Hyde another, while there are many collections in private hands. In the twenty-five years during which I knew him he wrote to me alone some hundred and thirty letters while similar or greater numbers were received by W. Sorley Brown, George Bernard Shaw, Marie Stopes, A. J. A. Symons, John Betjeman, R. H. Sherard, and other friends and acquaintances. Many hundreds of them are of little or no biographical interest, others reflect sincere but ephemeral opinions and prejudices, yet others are trivial and commonplace notes. I have therefore quoted from them sparingly, using them as a means of interpreting his point of view or fixing the dates of events, and have made exceptions of only a few which seem to me too important historically to print otherwise than in their entirety.

In the body of this book I have referred to Douglas by his universally-used nickname 'Bosie', which has many advantages in transcription, including the avoidance of the clumsy apostrophe 's' after Douglas. I have done so for the better reason that this is not an 'official biography', or anything of the sort, but a familiar study of the man and his life not primarily concerned with critical consideration of his work. It suits the tone of the book better than surname or title. For Wilde I have used 'Wilde' or 'Oscar' as they have occurred to me in the context. In writing even of living persons, I have omitted the pompous 'Mr' or 'Mrs' and most titles. This does not indicate that these persons are known to me personally.

People mentioned in the story, whose lives are not recounted in it, and not generally known, are in a short biographical index. I have forborne to mark them with an asterisk in the text, supposing that the reader who, like me, cannot resist chasing an asterisk to its lair, will not wish to be so frequently interrupted and can turn up those about whom he may feel curiosity. I have added a few bibliographical notes to show my great, though numerically few, obligations.

As to acknowledgements of a more personal kind, I express them here with fervour. I have found, like other biographers before me, extraordinary unselfishness in those who have taken trouble and devoted time to helping my researches, and recalling details. My debt in some cases is heavy and has involved my informant in long correspondence, but as this will be apparent in the text I need not try here to distinguish in any detail, between my benefactors.

Mr. Edward Colman, Douglas's literary executor, has not only allowed me to quote from his work, but has given me much information about his last years which would otherwise have been denied to me. Mr. John Betjeman, whose friendship with Douglas was long-standing and intimate, has supplied many personal details, and Lord Birkenhead, against whom Douglas made his last attempt at litigation, has been at pains to dig up details of the affair. Captain E. W. Brook, the present owner of Kinmount, the former home of the Queensberry family, has given me information about it and its purchase from the eighth Marquess by his grandfather. Mr. W. Sorley Brown, the son of Douglas's old friend and supporter, has given me the freedom of his father's papers, and Mr. Brian Fothergill, who was himself preparing to write a biography, when he heard that mine was almost completed, has helped me in several ways. Mr. Rupert Hart-Davis has given me endless help and encouragement and Mr. H. Montgomery Hyde the benefit of his unique collection of Wildeana. Mr. Hesketh Pearson has not only allowed me to quote from his—incomparably the best— Life of Wilde, but given me information about his own and Hugh Kingsmill's acquaintance with Douglas, besides sending me, for quotation, letters from Douglas and others. The present Lord Queensberry,

Douglas's great-nephew, has allowed me to quote the letters of the eighth Marquess and given me information, Mr. Martin Secker has gone to great trouble to give me the benefit of his knowledge, after being Douglas's friend and publisher for more than thirty years, and Mr. Julian Symons has helped me from his knowledge of his brother's long friendship with Douglas. My old friend F. G. B. Wills has done a great deal of research and made a number of exciting discoveries.

I also have to thank for their patience under epistolary questioning, for information or other help, Mr. Hector Bolitho, Mr. Keith Briant (whose *Marie Stopes: A Biography* has been invaluable), Mr. Lincoln Torrey Brown, Mr. Richard Blake Brown, Sir Terence Creagh-Coen, Lord Horder, Mr. Derek Ingram, Sir Shane Leslie, Captain Anthony Ludovici, Mr. Franklin Matthiason, Mr. William Plomer and Mrs. Hilda Young.

My secretary, Joseph Susei Mari, has typed and re-typed this book and dealt with the endless correspondence it has entailed.

CHAPTER I

Family Background and Boyhood

I

THE Douglases of history whose pennons flew in so many savage battles from Bannockburn to Halidon Hill became in time the licentious grandees whose passions for pugilism, horseflesh and adultery were notorious in the eighteenth and nineteenth centuries.

The name derives from the Gaelic *dubh glas*, 'dark water', which Scott rendered as 'dark grey', for in *The Abbot* he refers to an eighth-century Douglas, a semi-mythical figure who fought against a contemporary Lord of the Isles, as 'the Dark-Grey Man'. From this hero to the Black Douglas, who terrorized the Border and fought for King Bruce, and from him to the immediate predecessors of that disreputable 'Old Q', who lived through the reigns of three Georges, the Douglases were almost continuously involved in bloodshed, treachery and reckless heroism.

Their history is interspersed with those curious, familiar terms, sometimes grotesquely affectionate, which the soldiers of all ages have given to people, places and events with bitter associations for them. Roman centurions called their most bloodthirsty Emperor, Caligula, from the sandals he wore in the Army, and there are 'Boney', 'Little Willie', 'Wipers', 'Cœur de Lion', with a score of nicknames for regiments and a thousand terms that must have been lost with ancient armies. Those associated with Douglas history are sufficient to indicate the course and nature of it.

One of the most ruthless raids of the "Black Douglas" (Sir James de Douglas, 1286-1330) on the English garrison at Douglas Castle on Palm Sunday, 1307, was followed by such barbarities that it was given the sinister name of "Douglas's Larder"; another of his guerrilla victories over the English under the Archbishop of York at Mitton-on-Swale in 1319 was called "the Chapter of Myton", while his reward for forcing the English army to retreat at the Pass of Byland in Yorkshire was to be granted "The Emerald Charter", by which

King Bruce gave him and his successors powers of life and death in his domains. In 1316 he fought in single combat Sir Robert de Neville, "The Peacock of the North", and killed him.

His half-brother's nephew, William the first Earl, murdered his kinsman, William Liddesdale, known as "the Flower of Chivalry", and William's successor, Robert, defeated "Hotspur" Percy and died at the Battle of Otterburn. Sixty years later, a part of the Douglas territory was given to Margaret, "the Fair Maid of Galloway", who married her cousin, William Douglas. Although under safe conduct at the time, this Douglas was murdered by the Scottish King with his own hands in Stirling Castle in 1451 when he refused to break his alliance with the Earl of Crawford, known as "the Tiger".

Even at this period most of the cadets of the family were sent to Paris for their education, and several of them returned to France in manhood with soldiers to aid the French against English invaders. The French found them too fond of wine and mutton.

Nicknames given to members of the Douglas clan also have point, and recall some illuminating scraps of their history. "Black Douglas" was applied to two of the chieftains, the James already mentioned and Sir William of Nithsdale. James was also called "The Good Douglas". "Douglas the Hardy" joined Wallace's rising and died a prisoner in the Tower of London, "Douglas the Grim" was the third Earl and a bastard of the Black Douglas, who, during the weak kingship of Robert III of Scotland, imposed feudal law on the border chieftains and ruled as a king. "Douglas the Dull" was a churchman who surrendered his lands to the King, and "Douglas the Gross" was the seventh Earl. The Red Douglases were a collateral branch of the clan of which the Earls of Angus were the heads, "the Great Earl of Angus", also known as "Bell-the-Cat Angus", being the father of Gavin Douglas, the poet and Bishop who was prominent in the "Clear-the-Causeway" incident in 1517 and died of the plague in London.

The clan Douglas has given to this century, it sometimes seems, a fair proportion of its peerage. Apart from the present (twelfth) Marquess of Queensberry, who is also Viscount Drumlanrig, Baron Douglas and Earl of Queensberry, there are the Earls of Home (Douglas-Home), the Dukes of Hamilton (Douglas-Hamilton), the Dukes of Buccleuch and Queensberry (Montagu-Douglas-Scott), the Earls of Morton (Douglas), the Earls of Wemyss (Wemyss-Charteris-Douglas), the baronets, Douglas of Cau, Douglas of Springwood, Douglas of Glenbervie, and so on.

It has also given us, directly and indirectly, a good deal of our literature. Gavin Douglas, the first translator of the *Aeneid* into English, William Douglas, who wrote *Annie Laurie*, and the poet who is the subject of the present book are represented in most anthologies, but the *Oxford Dictionary of Quotations* shows no less than ten references to the name in prose and verse, which vary from Wordsworth's "Degenerate Douglas! Oh, the unworthy Lord!" to the fifteenth-century Sir Richard Holland's "O Dowglas, O Dowglas, tendir and trewe!" and John Home's "Like Douglas conquer, or like Douglas die". Scott was several times inspired by the name, and *The Douglas Tragedy* is in his *Border Minstrelsy*.

All this balladry and bravado, all the ferocity of feudal potentates at war from motives of self-advancement, from hatred of the English or from loyalty to their own Kings, degenerated after Stuart times to mere prosperity and eccentricity under Queen Anne and the Hanoverians. The first Earl of Queensberry got his title from Charles I, and the second supported his monarch in the Civil War, to be mulcted of a quarter of a million pounds by Cromwell and the Parliament party. But the third Earl, who was also made the first Marquess, deserted James II for Dutch William, and was rewarded under Anne with another couple of dukedoms or marquisates, those of Dover and Beverley.

All these, and many other lavishly dispensed titles came eventually to William, the fourth Duke, the notorious indeed the legendary monster known as "Old Q". He earned this nickname in his last years when after a life devoted to the pleasures of gaming, the turf, the table and the bed, he tottered round, deaf and one-eyed, still looking for gratifications till he died in his eighty-seventh year in 1810. Such lecherous old despots with the money to buy appeasement for their appetites were as common in the eighteenth century in England as they were in France, though the English did not find in them cause for revolution, but treated them with scandalized affection. Of "Old Q" they retailed or invented many anecdotes—of the fantastic bets he made as a young man for huge purses of gold sovereigns (one of them was that he could deliver a letter fifty miles away within an hour; he won this by having the letter stitched in a cricket ball thrown from hand to hand by a picked team), of his innumerable mistresses and offspring, of his skill in youth as a boxer and steeplechaser, of his prowess at cards and his luck at dice. Thackeray is supposed, on no very certain authority, to have portrayed him as the Marquess of

Steyn; he must certainly have been in Aldous Huxley's mind when he wrote *After Many a Summer*.

"Old Q" was the first of the Queensberrys to interest himself in the prize-ring and the stables, but thereafter a passion for these seems to have been hereditary. The marquisate passed to "Old Q's" Cousin Charles, who, with Byron, was among the boxing pupils of 'Gentleman Jackson' and joined with the Dukes of York and Clarence and Byron himself to form the Pugilistic Club. Charles was succeeded by his brother John, who was the first Master of the Dumfriesshire Hounds. His son was a gambler whose losses drove him to what was almost certainly suicide. It is *his* son who chiefly interests us here, for he was the father of Bosie and the mouthpiece of his time against Wilde.

2

John Sholto Douglas, the eighth Marquess of Queensberry, heir to this long line of brave and despotic chieftains who had become in recent centuries rich and wilful noblemen, was born in 1844.

The family home, Kinmount, which is four miles from Annan, might have been a feudal castle, for it stood in thirty thousand acres of valuable land which produced a rent roll of £20,000 a year, and the great Georgian house was like a township, peopled by scores of retainers who observed the elaborate protocol of a Victorian nobleman's staff. The boy rode, shot and fished, but was given little education and was encouraged in the philistine, indeed, contemptuous, attitude towards the arts which was considered proper at that time in a child of his class. At the age of twelve years he entered the Navy.

He had received two years' training as a naval cadet when his father was found dead beside his gun. So the boy succeeded at fourteen, not only to the Kinmount estate, but to Torthowald Castle and several other holdings. His grandson, writing of this nearly a century later, believed that his fortune on succession was 'in the neighbourhood of £780,000'.

At nineteen he left the Navy and returned to his estates, a remarkable horseman and a good shot who cared nothing for books. Almost at once he was prevailed upon to go up to Cambridge and spent two years at Magdalene College. He matriculated, but there is no evidence that he took any interest in the scholastic life of the University, though in later life he could write powerfully phrased and not illiterate letters in a good, strong hand.

His whole life was given to the sports he loved—hunting, steeple-chasing and boxing. He was a small, sinewy young man, barely five foot eight, hirsute and horsy, reckless in the saddle and not yet given to the excesses and vices of his later years.

At Cambridge he became friends with a man named John Graham Chambers, who had come from Eton to Trinity College. Chambers was a fine all-round athlete and oarsman who joined young Queensberry in his interest in boxing. In 1866 when they were twenty-two and twenty-three respectively, they founded the Amateur Athletic Club to combat the brutality and unfair practices of the professional bruisers which had caused the laws against prize-fighting to be more rigidly enforced. They also drew up fourteen rules for the sport of boxing which are still known as the Queensberry Rules. In 1867 young Queensberry presented cups for the British amateur championships at all weights.

He was still only twenty-one when in 1865 he married Sybil, one of the two daughters of Alfred Montgomery. It is curious to find that in their unfortunate book, *Oscar Wilde and the Black Douglas*, the late Marquess of Queensberry and the late Percy Colson have conferred a knighthood (or is it a baronetcy?) on Mr. Montgomery. One would have thought that even from the most narrowly Debrettish point of view this was unnecessary for Montgomery was a notable figure in Victorian society, a close personal friend of the Prince of Wales and a man of considerable culture. Bosie in his books never referred to his grandfather as anything but Mr. Alfred Montgomery, though his grandmother, a daughter of the first Lord Leconfield, was the Hon. Mrs. Alfred Montgomery.

It was a marriage which was in some ways a challenge to fate. Bosie wrote of it:

It is an interesting fact that my mother, who, on her father's (the late Mr. Alfred Montgomery) side, comes from the Scottish Montgomeries of Eglinton (a princely Norman family, nearly as old in Scotland as the Douglas family), on her mother's side can trace her descent back to Jocelyn, the thirteenth and last Earl of Northumberland. Thus, when my father married my mother, the direct descendant in the male line of the Douglas killed at Chevy Chase married a descendant of the Percy who was taken prisoner by the Douglases at the same historic battle.

It was not only in these somewhat fanciful historical grounds that it might have been thought ill-fated but in its personal incongruities.

Queensberry, hard-riding and probably hard-drinking (though there is no record of this in his young manhood), was Master of the Dumfriesshire Hounds, rode his own or his friends' horses over jumps and several times competed in the Grand National. He was a patron of the Fancy, a sporting peer in the narrowest sense of the word. He was very much in love with Sybil Montgomery, but she was of an entirely different tradition.

The Montgomerys were patrons of the arts and there is an exquisite portrait by Watts of the two daughters of Alfred Montgomery. But although Bosie remembered his maternal grandfather kindly, the old man was something of a tyrant in religious matters, and when his wife became a Catholic (she was a convert of Manning's) he succeeded in separating her from her daughters. Moreover, the Montgomery family was popular in what were still called 'Court circles', which the Queensberrys were not. Bosie remembered later how when staying with his grandfather Montgomery at Homburg they dined *à la belle franquette* with the Prince of Wales (later Edward VII) on several occasions, and how he went with his grandfather to the house of the Duke of Cambridge in Piccadilly.

Sybil Montgomery was beautiful—so beautiful, said both her son and her grandson, that when she and her sister went driving in Hyde Park people stood on chairs to look at them. She was fair and her sister dark. "She had angels' beauty", wrote Bosie, "a gentle, sad, proud, tiny flower-like face and head, with a slim figure like a Tanagra statuette." She kept her beauty till late middle life, and when she became an 'old lady' she did so with such grace that in the last twenty years of her life (she died in 1935 at the age of ninety-one) she had an exquisite porcelain beauty rarely seen in the very old.

But not only was she a famous beauty when Queensberry met her, she was a highly talented, carefully educated young woman who had spent her winters in Florence, spoke Italian and French, and had read a great deal, from Greek and Roman history to the poems of Tennyson and Browning. She did all the things that well-finished Victorian girls did—painted, played the piano and talked without eagerness, but well.

Queensberry took her at once to Kinmount, which must have seemed a somewhat forbidding place to her. The house was magnificent, with the stark dignity, the rows of long windows, the careful setting of a great house built at the turn of the eighteenth century, but no Queensberry had much knowledge of beautiful things, and although there were, more by chance than judgement, some fine paintings and furniture in the large, tall rooms, the effect was grim. The young Marchioness had known too many great houses to be much impressed by the huge ill-organized staff of lowland Scots, and she was not interested in the stables.

But they were young, (both were just twenty-one,) and sincerely in love, and at first the disparity of their interests did not matter. A year after the marriage their first son, Francis, was born and a year later Percy, who was to become the ninth Marquess. Then Queensberry began to show restlessness. He sold the Torthowald estate, which had been in the family for centuries, as later he was to sell Kinmount, but at first there were no marked signs of the eccentricity in money matters which was a characteristic of his later life. He was much away from home, and when he was at Kinmount he entertained his sporting friends to the exclusion of people who might have interested his wife. He began to adopt atheism, at first as a gesture of arrogance, a pose to show his contempt for conventional religion, but later with noisy conviction. He was cantankerous and given to tirades which were at once self-righteous and self-pitying, and before he had been married five years the gross and vicious sadism which was a part of his nature (or perhaps the mainspring of it) began to show itself.

Home life at Kinmount had the stuff of Victorian melodrama, the sporting peer rising at dawn to hunt with his own pack, or gambling with the local squirearchy, or boxing with professional bruisers, his wife growing more remote, spending her time with her children and her books. There were scenes, departures, reconciliations, in the pattern of 'high life' fiction, but the fiery little man was losing his never very strong self-control and his wife her patience.

He gave up the mastership of the Dumfriesshire Hounds for reasons which are unknown. He was for a time a Lord Lieutenant of the county and commanded the 1st Dumfriesshire Rifle Volunteers, and these two offices he also relinquished. He left Kinmount for a time and bought Ham House near Worcester in order to become Master of the Worcestershire Foxhounds.

It was in this house on October 22nd, 1870, that his third son, Alfred, was born.

3

He was christened Alfred Bruce Douglas, the first after his maternal grandfather, the second after his godfather, Lord Robert Bruce, who had been in the Royal Navy with Queensberry. But from babyhood his mother called him Boysie, which became Bosie, a name which followed him through the seventy-five years of his life.

His father kept the Mastership of the Worcestershire Foxhounds only two years, after which he moved his family back to Kinmount, where they remained for ten years, and where two more children were born, Sholto in 1872 and Edith in 1874. Queensberry, however, was seldom at home. He was at Melton, where his brother-in-law, George Finch, who was Member for Rutland, had a place, Burley-on-the-Hill, from which Queensberry hunted with the Quorn and Cottesmore. (George Finch had married the elder of the beautiful daughters of Alfred Montgomery.) Or he was riding in the Grand National or other cross-country races. He was prouder of his success as a gentleman-jockey than of his part in drawing up the Queensberry Rules of boxing. Bosie remembered in after years that as a boy at Winchester he spent hours looking up in old numbers of the *Field*, of which there was a bound set in his house library, Queensberry's many successes. This pride in his father's prowess Bosie never quite lost even in the days of hatred.

From the first Bosie seems to have been his mother's favourite. "After Bosie's birth", wrote Queensberry and Colson, "virtually no one else mattered to her." He was an exquisitely beautiful child, as a pastel portrait which hung in his flat in Hove sixty years later showed. There is, however, a suggestion, in one of his father's infuriated mad letters during the Wilde trials, that Bosie as a small child suffered from that favourite device of the surgeons in those days, an 'iron leg', a framework designed to straighten the limbs of knock-kneed or bandy-legged children. "When he was a child swathed in irons to hold him together it used to make me sick to look at him and think he could be called my son", wrote Queensberry in May 1895 to an unfortunate solicitor named Stoneham, who received a series of insanely abusive letters. But the detail here can scarcely have been invented, and though Bosie was to become a fine cross-country runner he missed getting his half Blue because of a knee weakness badly treated.

It must have been a strange home in which he grew to a boy of ten. It was 'kept up', in a term of the time, with a lavish contempt for economy which eventually caused Queensberry to sell it, for although in later years he developed a habit of speaking of himself as a poor man and became in many ways a stingy one, at this time he was spending a good deal of the £400,000, by which he left his family impoverished.

The retinue was feudal. In after years Bosie remembered many of the governesses and personal servants, the grooms and gardeners, the builders and carpenters, the huntsmen and indoor servants who lived as an isolated community on the estate, doubtless with intrigue and invidiousness, but on the whole, in his recollection, very happily. Such great households were still common in the 1870's and 1880's and some persisted till the outbreak of the First World War and even, in a broken and difficult way, after it. To visualize them one must read Jane Austen rather than visit such houses which are Open to the Public today.

The young mother with her five children, all born in the first eight years of her marriage, may have felt herself neglected afterwards by her husband, but she was entirely wrapped up in her four fine sons and her daughter. They were closely united, as the father on his rare visits must have realized with something like jealousy. In those years at Kinmount they saw little of other children, and, thrown together, they developed family mannerisms. They all called one another 'darling', an endearing habit which lasted into later life. They adored their mother and among themselves there was a facile and demonstrative love which was pleasant to see.

For the rest, there are only Bosie's own recollections in his *Autobiography* of those years at Kinmount, and these have already been more or less paraphrased by other writers on him. He has some sharp personal touches, but scarcely enables us to picture life in that doomed household during its last decade.

Kinmount House (which under that name is now marked as a village in the *Times Atlas*) was built by John Douglas, the sixth Marquess and the successor to 'Old Q' in about 1812 on estates which had belonged to his family for seven centuries. It stands near the site of the former Queensberry home, Kelhead House, which was burnt down in 1800. It is built of grey sandstone, quarried in Cumberland. Though it would probably have gone the way of all such family properties in the seventy odd years since then, Queensberry's disposal of it seemed wilful and philistine to his generation, for there was little economic compulsion for it. The first ten years of Bosie's life were the last of the Queensberrys as a landed family, of his parents as a married couple and of a large number of men and women as hereditary servants of a great house. He can have had no perception of this as a little boy, and his brief lucid account of his life at Kinmount shows no foreknowledge of disaster. In after years he felt no self-pity about it and spoke only lightly of his lost inheritance, but I think it cut more deeply than he showed. "It is a fairly satisfactory proposition to be the younger son of a marquis who possesses a large landed property, a stable full of horses, a big income, a huge circle of wealthy relatives and friends, and a large crowd of more or less devoted dependents and henchmen. The proposition begins to lose a good deal of its bright colour when the landed property goes."

At Kinmount, he said, he passed the happiest days of his childhood, "and to this day", he wrote fifty years after the house was lost, "I sometimes dream that we are going back there". He writes of his father's brief visits, when to his sons that increasingly vicious and opinioned little man was generally good-natured and kindly, though he taught Bosie nothing—not even to ride. It was his father, however, who gave him his first pony when Bosie was six years old, a "rattling good pony" which had cost £60 at Tattersalls. It was called "The Rat" and although this name had been given to it before it reached Kinmount it would be amusing to think that it commemorated 'Old Q', who voted for the Regent during George III's insanity and was called "a Rat who had deserted his Master to hobble after a young Prince".

It was on The Rat that Bosie would ride with his elder brother, Percy, their favourite objective being Ecclefechan, Carlyle's birthplace, five miles away. (Carlyle was buried there a year after the Queensberry family had left the district.)

Their mother took the boys to church on Sunday at Cummertrees when they could not manage to get out of it, but she never gave her sons any definite religious teaching and their father had already begun to voice his anti-Christian prejudices.

Apart from his mother and brothers and sister, Bosie's warmest recollections were of the staff. There was no family Nanny, (though for the younger children there were 'nurses, nursemaids, schoolroom-maids and so forth'), and her place in the children's hearts was taken by "dear Lizzie, my mother's maid, the most faithful, loving soul that ever inhabited a mortal body, and who, though she never was our nurse, takes in our family the place of the 'Nannie' of tradition". He adds touchingly (he is writing when a man of sixty):

Needless to say she also reposes in my prayers, with her sister Ruthie. One of the advantages of being a Catholic is that when anyone you love dies you "put him into your prayers" and keep him there ever afterwards.

There was also Joe Graham, his grandfather's and father's huntsman, who retired to a cottage at Cummertrees after the estate was sold and recognized Bosie when he went to see him years later because, he said, Bosie had his father's smile.

The estate carpenter was named Dunkeld. He was the 'kindest of men' and used to make the boys wooden spears and shields on which the 'Douglas Heart' was painted. This heart had been in the Douglas arms since the thirteenth century, when, after the death of King Bruce, his heart in a silver casket was entrusted to James, one of those known as the Black Douglas, to carry to Palestine. Bruce had vowed to go on a Crusade, but his wars with the English had kept him at home. Douglas set out, but became involved in fighting in Spain and was killed by the Moors in 1330. What became of the heart in its casket is unknown, but it has since been represented in the Douglas coat of arms. So with wooden swords and gold-leaf paper from a shop at Ecclefechan and with other warlike equipment made by Dunkeld, the small Douglas boys made forays and fought battles.

There was a dignified butler who was remembered for years afterwards in a family joke which is no more amusing than most jokes in other people's families. An 'odd man' was engaged to clean the boots and knives and to wait on the upper servants in the housekeeper's room. When he had been in the house a few days, the stately butler approached Lady Queensberry: "If your Ladyship has no objection, we propose to call the new man 'the Usher of the Hall'."

There was also a series of governesses who captured the affections of the children.

The earliest recollection I have of them takes the shape of a somewhat dour and formidable Scotswoman, Miss MacCormick; but fortunately (or perhaps unfortunately) for me I did not come under her *régime* except for a very short time. She belonged to the old-fashioned school, and went in for "old-fashioned schoolroom discipline" (ranging from the back of a hairbrush to a cane, inflicted "on the raw"). I have distinct recollections of the first-named form of correction, but I was too young during her reign to experience the second. My two elder brothers, on the other hand, had the full benefit of her Spartan system for several years (my mother, of course, not being aware of it). It certainly did them no harm, and as they were both quite devoted to Miss Mac-Cormick I don't imagine they would ever have given her away. She went, not unwept by her victims. Others followed; and I particularly remember Miss Smelt, whom I adored, and on whose lap I used to sit while she told me the most wonderful fairy stories, which she invented as she went on, and which lasted for days and days. There was also poor Miss Holland, who took a gloomy view of life, and mistakenly took our mischievous pranks for hostility to herself (and in some ways we must have been very trying, for, with all our sentimentality and our "darlings" and facile tears we were distinctly rough and occasionally violent boys). There was a French governess to whom we were devoted, Mademoiselle de Soubeiran, and I also remember a Miss Humphrey, whom I loved deeply.

4

It is probable that Queensberry vacated Kinmount because he resented the expense of its upkeep for the benefit of his wife and children, who, he felt, were united against him. But although for five years he had been only an occasional visitor there it was he who suffered most from his wilful act. Without the house in which he and his immediate forebears had been born and the land which had belonged to his family for centuries he lost what little stability was left to him. He no longer made any pretence of living at home, but took rooms in James Street, Buckingham Gate, while for his family he rented 67 Cromwell Road and after a time moved them to 18 Cadogan Place. So although the boys did not know it, when they left Kinmount in 1880 it was for good, though the place was not sold for some years.*

It was in the year in which the family left Kinmount that there was a public event which influenced Queensberry in a ridiculous and eventually rather tragic way. Charles Bradlaugh, a notorious free-thinker who had gallantly risked prison in defence of a principle, was elected as Member of Parliament for Nottingham, but was not permitted to take his seat. He claimed to be allowed to 'affirm' under the Parliamentary Oaths Act, and, although he afterwards expressed his willingness to take the oath, this was refused him. There were sensational scenes in the House and in July, 1880, Bradlaugh was unseated. The next year he was again elected and attempted to force his way into the House, but was ejected. After another year, at the opening of the Session, he walked up the floor of the House and, pulling a Bible from his pocket, he administered the oath to himself. He was again excluded and re-elected, and not until six years later did a new Speaker allow him to take the oath.

* There was some confusion in Bosie's mind about when it was sold. He said, "By the time I was seventeen it had passed out of the possession of the family", but in 1895, when Bosie was twenty-five, Queensberry wrote to his daughter-in-law, "should Kinmount be sold I should feel bound to increase Percy's income if I got a profit myself". It was in fact sold on November 9th, 1896, to the grandfather of the present owner, Captain E. W. Brook. The Queensberry family retain an area of about two acres, which is their private burial ground.

The Press of 1880 and 1881 was full of these shocking events and all Queensberry's combative atheism and love of publicity was aroused. A Scottish peer did not sit in the House of Lords as a natural right, but Queensberry, like his father and grandfather, had as a matter of course been elected one of the sixteen Representative peers of Scotland. In 1881, while Bradlaugh was being ejected from the Commons, Queensberry made a scene in the Lords, called the oath of allegiance to the Crown "Christian tomfoolery" and was described by the *Annual Register* as "a supporter of Bradlaugh". He thus became violently unpopular, not only with his fellow peers who had elected him, but with the whole Establishment and with the middle classes, who could not forgive atheism and an 'insult to the Queen', as it was called, even in the inventor of the Queensberry Rules.

Public opprobrium went to his head and he set out to invite it in various ways. In 1882 Tennyson's unsuccessful play, *The Promise of May*, was produced at a London theatre and Queensberry, told that an agnostic would be unfavourably presented on the stage by an actor called Herman Vezin, went to the theatre with a bouquet of vegetables, and not only flung this at the cast, but made a rather vulgar speech in defence of atheism. He made no secret of what was considered at that time a highly scandalous life—rather, he advertised himself as above the law and above convention.

But he had not the stamina for the running fight with society which he had deliberately provoked. As a horseman and pugilist, he had immense courage, but as a rebel he lacked staying power and nerve and would relapse into self-pity and morbid attempts at self-justification, as his letters a few years afterwards plainly show.

There is no one more bigoted than a thorough-paced atheist and Queensberry had become not only a bigot, but a bore. His whims and prejudices were often adopted only to exasperate his wife. When, for instance, she wanted him to send his heir, Lord Drumlanrig, now a boy of thirteen, to Harrow, he insisted for a long time that he must go to a Scottish school, though none of his family had done so and he was breaking all his ties with Scotland. Only at the last moment and after pressure from other members of his family did he agree, and Francis became a Harrovian while the second son Percy went to a naval school at Portsmouth in preparation for the *Britannia*. Bosie was sent to school in the same year, for governesses were left behind at Kinmount. He went to a preparatory school called Lambrook, at which his eldest brother, Drumlanrig, known as Francie in the family, was in his last term. All this in the year in which the family moved south from Kinmount, 1880.

5

Queensberry did not want his sons with him and they spent their holidays with their mother in London, or at her country house, The Hut, three miles from Bracknell in Berkshire. Bosie's description of this has a pleasantly dated touch, recalling the ducal extravagances of the time.

The Hut was a picturesque, rambling ranch of a house, larger than its name might imply (at a pinch it would hold quite twenty-five people), which had been run up by Lord Downshire in the pine woods as a temporary abode while his big place, Easthampstead, was being built.

At Easthampstead lived Lady Downshire and her son 'Artie', who was a boy of about Bosie's age. He was amiable but stolid and given to driving farm-carts. Bosie's particular crony in that household was 'Artie' Downshire's cousin, Wellington Stapleton-Cotton, who came frequently to stay there. This was the first recorded friend whom Bosie adored, "and I think he adored me", he added in recalling him half a century later. They were "tremendous friends", and though Bosie afterwards went to Winchester and Wellington to Wellington College they spent together as much of their school vacations as they could. Once when Bosie had been to Zermatt for the summer he returned with only a week of the holiday left in which to be with his friend and developed a most untimely attack of mumps. Bosie was isolated at The Hut and Wellington was forbidden to visit him, but a note was sent from Bosie who pointed out that the only solution was for his friend to come and catch the disease so that they could spend the next three weeks together. Wellington came in the early morning and, climbing in by the window, joined Bosie in bed, this being the surest way, the boys decided, to pass the infection. Unhappily, it did not 'take'.

Wellington Stapleton-Cotton was a year younger than Bosie and their friendship continued after he was sent to Sandhurst, for he would come over from there to dine and sleep at The Hut. He would have become the third Viscount Combermere, but was killed at Spion Kop. "I have never forgotten to pray for him every day since his death", wrote Bosie "and I look forward to being a boy again with him in Paradise."

Bosie's first preparatory school, Lambrook, was the 'Cheam' of the

At the age of 8, by the Hon. Henry Richard Graves.

ALFRED BRVCE DOVGLAS

W S.
NOV.
1895

Aged 21, at Oxford.

Aged 24.

time. Queen Victoria used to drive over to it from Windsor to see her grandsons, Prince Victor and Prince Albert of Schleswig-Holstein. But after Bosie had been there a year a row took place of the kind which breaks out at even the most discreet preparatory schools and the reputation of Lambrook declined. Bosie was removed and sent to Wixenford, which was under a kindly but rather frightening bearded man called Arnold, who found him—as he certainly was—a spoilt child, and made fun of him, using that most merciless weapon for attacks on small boys, a sarcastic tongue. Nor was Arnold guiltless of the kind of diplomacy common among proprietors of small schools, a diplomacy which sees that the right parents are gratified on prize-giving day, for Bosie remembered all his life that a prize for Classics which was his by right of marks was diverted to young Lord Leveson, the son of the Earl of Granville.

But Bosie's chief friend at Wixenford, a boy of whom he was passionately fond, was an American called Shepherd. Shepherd fascinated him by his way of talking. He was older than Bosie, who hero-worshipped him in spite of the nickname of 'Puppy-dog' which he gave to Bosie, a nickname sarcastically dignified by Mr. Arnold into 'Italian Greyhound'. Bosie longed to follow Shepherd to Eton, for which the American left before Bosie's time at Wixenford was completed. He begged his mother to arrange this and she did her best, but when Queensberry discovered what he called 'this plot' he promptly entered the boy for Winchester. No son of his, he said, should be turned into a 'Belgravian loafer' and once he had enunciated this he could not be persuaded.

6

None of Bosie's family realized when they moved from Kinmount that they would never return there. Even his father had not at first decided to sell the place, or, if he had, he did not admit it. He had grown secretive and sullen with his wife and never discussed such things with his children, though Drumlanrig and Percy were old enough to understand. Nor did his mother ever criticize their father to the boys. As long as she possibly could, she kept up the appearance of a united family whose father was unfortunately away from home rather much. In spite of Queensberry's morbid suspicions, she was never in the least disloyal to her husband, and let the boys think him a hero.

By the time they had moved to The Hut the elder boys realized the

c

situation and Bosie was beginning to do so before he left his preparatory school. But in spite of it they were very happy in Berkshire. He certainly did not perceive then that among the people they knew, their countless relatives, the Downshires, the Granvilles and the rest, Lady Queensberry was greatly pitied and her husband's life was considered a scandal.

About himself he said ingenuously that he was an excessively spoilt and notably pretty little boy. In writing of the sarcastic Headmaster of Wixenford, he said:

Mr. Arnold's attacks on me were purely verbal, but I suffered agonies from them, being very sensitive and also (alas that I must say!) frightfully spoilt at home by my mother. I was a very pretty child and had captivating ways, and my mother could not, or did not, resist me. The consequence was, of course, that I suffered proportionately more at school.

He did not lose his 'prettiness' for twenty years and in some ways was a spoilt child all his life.

7

In a phrase all too commonly used of public schools, Winchester was in the process of being cleaned up, and when Bosie arrived there for the Christmas Term of 1884 only an aftermath of vice and bullying remained, but to the little spoilt boy, just under fourteen, it was frightening. "I remember thinking that my parents must be quite mad to send me to such an awful place." "There was a boy in our House who might have sat for a model of Flashman." "My first eighteen months there were pretty much of a nightmare." All this is commonplace stuff in the school memories of Victorians. What is unusual is Bosie's naïvety in saying of himself, the victim of it, that he had been brought up by his mother to love purity, truth and beauty, and was a sensitive, dreamy child, devoted to noble ideals. But there is no reason to suppose that he suffered more than other new boys and many public school men remember the torments of their first few terms.

In those moods of bigotry which are common in many converts to Catholicism he would put it all down to the 'Protestantism' of Winchester. When he had to educate his own son he decided that he would rather see him dead than in a Protestant public school and in spite of opposition from his father-in-law he sent him to a Catholic school (Ampleforth), "with the result that at twenty-five years of age he is as 'innocent' in the true sense of the word as I was when I first went to Winchester".

But the early terms passed, life was "pretty well rose-coloured all through" and became a "wild rag". He learned very little, but, neglecting the work he was supposed to be doing, indulged in a great deal of indiscriminate reading. He could not take team games seriously, was no good as a cricketer and only 'fairly good' at football, but he was then and thereafter a fine cross-country runner and won the school steeplechase of two and a half miles when he was sixteen in 1887, and would have won it again in his last year and perhaps the mile as well if he had not been laid up with influenza.

His school friendships he divided, again rather ingenuously, into three categories. There were those which were fine, perfectly normal, wholesome and quite unsentimental. Such was his friendship with Lord Encombe with whom he was later to share rooms at Oxford. There were those which were sentimental and passionate, but perfectly pure and innocent. And there were those which were "neither pure nor innocent".

Encombe, known at school as 'Jane' Encombe, was heir to the Earl of Eldon and a grandson to that notoriously conservative Lord Chancellor who for forty years fought every innovation and reform, including Catholic Emancipation. It was this first Lord Eldon (a Newcastle coal-broker's son who eloped with a banker's daughter and made a reputation for himself at the Bar) who drew up the Regency Bill which Bosie's ancestor, 'Old Q', opposed so strongly. The two boys may not have been aware of this coincidence; they were fast friends at Winchester and Oxford and until Encombe's early death at the age of twenty-nine. By another coincidence, Encombe during his year in college had the rooms in Magdalen which Wilde had occupied in the 'seventies and which were occupied later by H. Montgomery Hyde, editor of *The Trials of Oscar Wilde*. At the end of a year he and Bosie took rooms together in High Street. Their friendship at Winchester seems to have been a strong but conventional one.

Bosie did not write much in his books about his other friends at Winchester, perhaps lest they might be identified as those whose friendship was "neither pure nor innocent", but in his last term there he grew very fond of a boy in his house who was just four years younger than himself. This was Encombe's fag, George Montagu, afterwards the Earl of Sandwich.* He was "a fair-haired, blue-eyed, pretty boy with engaging manners" and although in later years he

---

* He died on June 15th, 1962, aged eighty-seven, while this book was being written.

claimed that Bosie used to "brock" him (a Wykehamist word for "bully"), this, Bosie thought, could only have been teasing, a sign of affection at school. Their mothers were great friends, too, and Bosie used to stay at the family home, Wherwell Priory on the River Test.

Religion 'simply did not exist' in his time at Winchester, or, rather, was treated with 'utter contempt, ridicule, and blasphemy', and he remembered how a popular Prefect in his house, whenever he came in to tea in the absence of masters, used to fling a piece of bread at the figure of Christ in a picture of The Last Supper hanging over the High Table in the dining-room.

There was a good deal of what Bosie called public-school nonsense at the school at the time—as at any public school at any time. In his first year he felt the usual repugnance and resisted, but later learned 'to do what everyone else did', and by the time he was in his last year was neither better nor worse than other boys in his house.

If it is to be assumed from this that I was "abnormal" or "degenerate" or exceptionally wicked, then it must also be assumed that at least ninety per cent. of my contemporaries at Winchester and Oxford were the same.

He was a gay, popular boy who avoided school games as much as possible, and to most of his fellow Wykehamists was remarkable as the winner of the school steeplechase. He was also known to have unaccountable literary leanings, and in his last year became editor of a successful independent magazine. His Housemaster, the Rev. John Trant Bramston, also seems to have liked him and took him and Encombe abroad for a summer.

There was at least one future poet at the school during Bosie's first two years. This was Lionel Johnson, who was to play a part in his later life. He was three years older than Bosie and was a scholar in College while Bosie was in a house. Bosie remembered no acquaintance between them at Winchester, though Johnson insisted that it was he who had to hold up Bosie's shirt when he was given a licking by the Headmaster, Dr. Fearon, known as the Bear. Johnson was a small, frail creature who afterwards became a much-anthologized poet and eventually an alcoholic who died at thirty-five after falling on a Fleet Street pavement and cracking his skull. His *By the Statue of King Charles at Charing Cross* is a poem which no collection of early twentieth-century verse could be without and his faultless little *Precept of Silence* is quoted to this day.

It was not Johnson who encouraged Bosie to start his school paper called *The Pentagram*, for he had already gone up to Oxford when its first issue appeared, but he certainly contributed to it.

The *Pentagram* was started in the summer of 1888 by Bosie with Edward Wadsworth Lidderdale of Morsehead's House and 'Sal' Phipps, who was in the same house as Bosie. It had, he wrote with pride in his *Autobiography*, a "tremendous success" and its circulation came to exceed a copy per head of the school because old Wykehamists took it. Bosie's contributions consisted chiefly of humorous verse, none of which he thought worth preserving. It was "the only literary or journalistic venture" out of which he ever made a profit. But it was the first of five he was to edit.

Bosie left Winchester at Christmas, 1888, after exactly four years. He was then eighteen years old.

Though his distorted notions of self-defence made him write some rather hard things about Winchester during the middle period of his life, he kept for it that reminiscent and sentimental affection which even the most unimaginative Englishmen are apt to feel for the schools in which they passed their teens.

"A Wykehamist!" he used to say with amused triumph when someone came favourably into the news.

I well remember his animation when he heard that the senior science master in his time was my great-uncle, William Bleadon Croft. (Winchester, in spite of its Classics tradition, was one of the first public schools to take Science seriously as a subject for study.) "We used to call him 'the Bleeder'," he said. "And Morsehead was 'the Doidge'."

8

Meanwhile, at his mother's home in London and at The Hut, what was left of his parents' married life was disintegrating. Queensberry came to The Hut for 'one or two nights at most' during the years his wife and children spent their summers there and 'hardly ever' turned up at their house in London, but when he did appear it was to cause trouble.

While Bosie was at Winchester his father took as mistress a particularly notorious woman whose reputation and history were such that when Lady Queensberry eventually brought an action for divorce the proceedings took only fifteen minutes. Just before Ascot Week, 1886, Queensberry turned up suddenly at The Hut and announced his intention of bringing this woman and a number of her friends to the house. Lady Queensberry had invited a party of her own and her children's friends for the race week, but was forced to send telegrams to put off her guests and, having only a day's notice of her husband's intentions, to pack up and take to London her young daughter and three of her sons who were then at home. It does not, perhaps, sound so heinous today, but a phrase that Bosie used in describing it shows how the conduct of Queensberry must have appeared at the time. He refers to his father's mistress as "a lady whom it was impossible for my mother to meet".

That was a bad year for Queensberry, who was finding himself past his best in the pigskin. He had been riding in gallops a horse called Old Joe, which his cousin, Arthur Johnstone Douglas of Lockerbie, had bought as a hunter for £150 and hunted for a season, but was now training for the Grand National. Queensberry, who had ridden several times in the race on his own horses, was anxious to ride Old Joe in that year, but the owner put up a professional jockey called Skelton. When the horse won at forty to one, 'on three legs', Queensberry felt he had been done out of his chance to fulfil one of the chief ambitions of his life. His misanthropy and self-pity increased, and in the following year 1887 he ironically suggested to his wife that, since she complained of his absences, he would come home to stay, *with* his mistress, so that the three of them would be together. On that his wife's patience gave way and, aided by her father and friends, she divorced him.

This made little or no difference to Bosie himself, since he had scarcely seen his father during the last three years, but it meant that Queensberry managed to become convinced that he had been rejected by his own children. From this time began his repetitions of "no son of mine" which eventually became: "I never believed he was my son."

CHAPTER II

Oxford and Meeting with Wilde

I

EARLY in the following year, 1889, Bosie was sent abroad with a tutor to fill in the time until the beginning of the university year in October. This was arranged by his mother and afterwards gave Queensberry occasion to voice his loudest 'I told you so'.

The job of travelling with and coaching Bosie was given to a young man called Gerald Campbell, who was a nephew of Mrs. Percy Wyndham, Bosie's beloved great-aunt. He may have thought his task a sedative one—if so, he was soon to be disillusioned. Bosie already had some acquaintance with fashionable foreign watering-places and after a little conscientious sight-seeing in France led his tutor to the *Côte d'Azur*.

Here the grand tour ended with an incident to which Bosie gave some importance. Though he recounted it flippantly enough, it made a deep impression at the time, as well it might for it was his first affair with a woman.

When he and his tutor arrived in the South of France they found staying in the hotel they had chosen a lady of whom Bosie tells us four things: she was a cousin of Gerald Campbell's, she was a celebrated beauty, she was the divorced wife of an earl who had run away with a lover from whom she was now separated, and she was at least twelve years older than Bosie. The affair "worked out very much on the lines of the first episode of Byron's Don Juan and Julia", but it must have caused considerable anxiety to the tutor, for one night, "very indiscreetly as I thought then and still maintain", he came to the lady's room and, knocking on the door, "demanded the restitution of his ravished ewe-lamb".

The ewe-lamb, reduced to tears and dressed in one of the lady's much-be-ribboned nightgowns, was duly handed out after a painful scene, and to the accompaniment of loud barks from the lady's pet dog.

There were repercussions. Mr. Campbell sent Bosie back to England in disgrace, and there was much indignation against the beautiful divorcée for having seduced "an innocent boy". This infuriated Bosie, who felt that it impugned his manliness, and he replied indignantly that after four years at Winchester he was *not* an innocent boy. He felt afterwards that if the two had been left together it might have saved him from "baser promiscuities" such as he and other undergraduates sought at the promenade of the Empire and the Corinthian Club. But he goes too far in suggesting that this conventional incident was an answer to those who in later years accused him of being "abnormal and degenerate from a sexual point of view". He was—and it has never been seriously doubted even by his detractors—a virile young male who, like many others, passed through a period of active homosexuality which came however, (perhaps because of his freakish physical youthfulness,) rather later in life than with most men. It needed no boyish love affair with a divorced countess to prove this.

Bosie never saw his tutor again though he followed his career. Writing in 1929 he said that Campbell was and had been for many years on the staff of *The Times*.

2

Bosie went up to Magdalen College Oxford in 1889, just twelve years before Compton Mackenzie, who has depicted it so lovingly as 'St. Mary's'. His first two years there were intensely but irresponsibly happy. His good, sound, cheerful friendship with Encombe continued and though he did not train hard for it he did a good deal of running. In his first year in Magdalen College Sports he came second in the two-mile race and in his second year won it, as well as the mile handicap. He entered for the three miles in the university sports and believed he had a fair chance of winning it and getting his half-blue, but on the day before the race he consulted a doctor about a slightly swollen vein behind his knee. The doctor said it was of no importance, but for safety's sake he would 'fix it with a bandage' and encased the knee in a stiff plaster. This, of course, shortened Bosie's stride and put a 'frightful' handicap on him so that, finding he could not keep his place and was twenty-five yards behind the leading runner, he dropped out and from that day gave up running. It was not, he admits, until years later that it occurred to him that 'this wretched bandage' was the reason for his discomfiture, and it was, it must be admitted, characteristic of Bosie to look for some outside cause, some piece of ill-luck or persecution to account for a defeat.

I do not of course say that I would certainly have won the race without the bandage, but I had run a trial three miles about a week before with a man who had his blue for three miles and I had beaten him very easily by quite a hundred yards; so, obviously, if I had run my true form I should have been "there or thereabouts" at the finish.

He wrote this, but it is as if I could hear him saying it today. Lightly, deprecatingly, with a smile, and yet with concealed earnestness he recalled the mischances, the perversities of Fate which robbed him of his victories.

If he was not a good loser he was still a very popular young man with the face of a schoolboy and a light-hearted rebelliousness which was endearing to his fellow undergraduates. He did very little work and amused his friends by printing a card:

> Lord Alfred Bruce Douglas presents his compliments to........
> ....and regrets that he will be unable to..............
> in consequence of.....................

Filled up, this ingenious document would read as follows:

> Lord Alfred Bruce Douglas presents his compliments to Professor Smith and regrets that he will be unable to show up an essay on the Evolution of the Moral Idea in consequence of not having prepared one.

This piece of impudence gained him some reputation and, he said optimistically, angered the Dons to the point of madness.

He went further. He was gated for going to the Derby and was rusticated for a term because he was ploughed in his examination for Greats. He nearly killed himself when leading a party of friends across the river which was choked with blocks of ice after one of the historic frosts of those years. The party succeeded in crossing by stepping from block to block of ice, but when Bosie started back a block on which he jumped dipped and pitched him into the water. This amused his friends on the bank until one of them, 'Tyler' Reid, realized that he was being held under by the ice and waded out to save him.

During the vacations he sometimes stayed at Burley-on-the-Hill, the 'glorious' house of his uncle, George Finch, and, as his father had done before him, from there hunted with the Cottesmore. He was fond of shooting, though he did not become a good shot till later, and he spent much time on the river without taking up rowing seriously. There was nothing in the least pansy about him and in these years his inherited love of sport and gambling occupied much of his time.

It was, as we have seen, with his grandfather, Alfred Montgomery, that he met the Prince of Wales, afterwards King Edward VII. One would think there could be little sympathy between the Prince and this young sprig of a younger son whose father had made himself unpopular, but they seem to have got on well and Bosie saw quite a lot of the Prince during summer vacations, which he spent with his mother and maternal grandparents in Homburg. He was also 'kindly taken to' by the old Duke of Cambridge, who, Bosie remembered, went fast to sleep at the table during a dinner party given by Alfred Montgomery at the Travellers' Club.

Bosie's eldest brother Drumlanrig was now in the Coldstream Guards and during Ascot Week would supply his family with tickets for the Guards' tent. Bosie recalled that tickets for the Royal Enclosure then cost a guinea for the whole week.

He used to go back to his old school whenever he had a chance and "made a bee-line" for the young friend of his last year there, George Montagu, whom he called 'Jidge'. A Wykehamist of the time remembers him playing the school brand of football for a team of Old Wykehamists, the game being 'sixes', a fast six-a-side affair. The ground was heavy after rain and Bosie had forgotten to bring his football boots, so was set to play 'hot watch', which needs a fast runner. He did this in patent leather boots, to the amusement and admiration of spectators.

He was, in other words, an eager, sporting, rather fast young man, generally liked for his gay and dashing personality.

There was, however, another side to his character which puzzled his heartier friends. In his second year there appeared in *The Oxford Magazine* a poem of his called *Autumn Days*, which he had written at The Hut in 1890. It is a wistful little lament for "a year that is past" such as any undergraduate with his brain full of Tennyson and Mathew Arnold might have written, but an earlier poem called *Apologia* is more defiantly pagan. "I will kiss the lips of the seraphim," cried the poet, and pluck flowers "in the infinite gardens of God".

His poem in *The Oxford Magazine* brought him a gushing letter from the President of his College, Mr. (later Sir) Herbert Warren. "I thought it really passionate and really fine", he wrote. "I had no idea you could do anything so good." Warren was a strange creature who has figured in many biographies as an arch-snob and prince of time-servers. He trimmed his sails so shrewdly to the winds of favour that he attracted much royalty, including the Prince of Wales (the

Duke of Windsor), to Magdalen College during the forty-two years of his presidency. He was clever at cultivating the right man and even cleverer at dropping the wrong one with a hand-washing air of innocence, as he showed later with Oscar Wilde who was his admired friend in the sunlit days, and with Bosie himself.

3

The friend with whom Bosie discussed poetry rather than athletics or hunting was Lionel Johnson. He had probably 'the finest head and the kindest heart in the University', a delicate tiny man and a brilliant talker. Bosie always had the greatest admiration for him as a scholar and poet and spoke of him with warmth in later years. Even at school and the university Shakespeare was Bosie's god, almost to the exclusion of other poets, and in the last years of his life he read little else. His mother read the plays to him before he could read them for himself and one of his earliest sonnets was *To Shakespeare* (1893). Lionel Johnson was as ardent a Shakespearean as Bosie, though a more scholarly and critical one, and the two would argue whole nights away, to the amusement of Bosie's philistine friends.

Lionel Johnson lived in London and, unlike Bosie, had decided to follow a literary career. During the vacations he was already boozing and talking with writers little older than himself, and at a pub in Charing Cross Road called The Crown he frequently met Ernest Dowson the poet and Charles Conder the artist.

The Crown was then a pub with a clientèle similar to many still existing in the area round Charlotte Street. Vociferous young writers and a good many literary charlatans, painters and would-be painters together with male prostitutes and Service men looking for an addition to their miserable wages from one or another of the richer and older men who came there. It was not by any means exclusively a 'queer' pub, but having once gained a reputation for being lively it was used by those who wanted to find a young sailor or an out-of-work stable boy, as well as by artists who may have been scarcely conscious of these activities. George Moore, for instance, then just forty and known chiefly for *A Mummer's Wife*, was still to be seen there and young men like Dowson, who had nothing in common with the male prostitutes about him, still came frequently. Lionel Johnson was delighted with the atmosphere.

Back at Oxford he told Bosie about it but did not rouse much curiosity. Though no respecter of persons and the least snobbish of

men, Bosie was not a Bohemian and in the years just before the first
world war when he used to be seen with Crosland among the noisy
cosmopolitan crowd in the downstairs room of the Café Royal (as
opposed to the dining-room upstairs to which he went with Wilde)
he was noticeably out of place. Nor had Bosie become familiar with
the brazen and vicious homosexuality he was to explore with Wilde
and if he had any understanding of his own proclivities he put them
down to the poet in him and talked of 'aestheticism'. Johnson, who
sincerely loved and respected Bosie, did not discuss the squalid world
he was discovering and described The Crown merely as a place in
which he met other writers and that strange, interesting young artist
Charles Conder. Stewart Headlam, the Christian-Socialist parson who
was to be a noble friend to Wilde in the time of crisis, also came to
The Crown, though he was older than most of the others, being born
in 1847.

Lionel Johnson had met Oscar Wilde during a visit Wilde made to
Oxford early in 1890. "I was determined to meet you before I left
Oxford", Wilde wrote to Johnson. "I hope you will let me know when
you are in town." Perhaps Johnson took Wilde to The Crown, or
perhaps they met there again by chance. They were certainly there
together during 1890 and 1891, after Johnson had come down from
Oxford. Wilde found Johnson charming and Johnson thought Wilde
remarkable and something of a monster but like almost everyone else
was seduced by the generosity with which he talked, giving his
hearers all the enchantments of his voice and wit, his touches of fantasy
and easy dismissal of pompous and tiresome things.

Johnson, in a phrase of seventy years later, could not wait to tell his
friend Bosie of this brilliant person, just as with undergraduate enthusiasm he spoke to Wilde of Bosie whom he described as the most
beautiful young man alive and a fine poet. He was not a silly, well-
meaning little man, but a creature of vision and intuition who believed that these two were made for one another. In his later years,
before and after the Wilde catastrophe, it was a grief to him that he
brought them together for he never lost his devotion to Bosie and
believed that Wilde was wrecking his friend's life. He directed at
Wilde a sonnet which is among his best, "I hate you with a necessary
hate", before the scandal had broken and regretted it after. But at this
time he saw only the older man, gay, sparkling and in search of young
friends, and the younger uncannily handsome and full of charm, and
believed that he was doing a kind act in arranging a meeting.

Having told each of them that he would *adore* the other, he arranged with Wilde that he should bring Bosie to his house in Tite Street on an afternoon in 1891 and Bosie, curious rather than interested, went with him to this meeting. Bosie was a month or two short of his twenty-first birthday and Wilde sixteen years older.

4

Oscar Wilde at thirty-seven was formidable. Some people claimed to find him ridiculous, others said that he made them shudder, but no one thought him commonplace.

His appearance at this period has been frequently described and there are many photographs. He had been, as a fellow-student recorded, 'an ungainly, overgrown, moping, awkward lad'. In his twenties in London he had worn the curious costume he invented for himself as an 'aesthete' and now as he approached his first success as a dramatist he appeared in clothes which though conventional enough, a frock coat and striped trousers, he contrived to make dressy and baroque. He was never without flowers in his button-hole, he wore a showy scarab ring and carried a gold-topped eighteenth-century walking-stick. These with his large frame, his long hair and his great expanse of face made him look, even in his formal dress, un-English and imposing but sometimes a little absurd.

Picture a tall, broad, thick-set slow-moving man [says Mr. Hesketh Pearson in an unforgettable passage of his *The Life of Oscar Wilde*] inclined to corpulence; with a large bloodless coarse-skinned face, clean-shaven at a time when moustaches were in vogue, a powerful well-shaped nose, thick purple-tinged sensual lips, long crowded uneven discoloured teeth, fleshy cheeks, heavy jaw, firm mouth, fine brow, long dark carefully-waved hair, and expressive heavy-lidded eyes. It was a proconsular face, masklike at moments of introspection, lit up in conversation by a smile which radiated good-will. The dominant expression was one of humour, and sometimes he appeared to be smiling ironically at himself, the critic in him being entertained by the actor. His hands were fat and flabby; his hand-shake lacked grip, and at a first encounter one recoiled from its plush limpness, but this aversion was soon overcome when he began to talk, for his genuine kindliness and desire to please made one forget what was unpleasant in his physical appearance and contact, gave charm to his manners, and grace to his precision of speech.

George Bernard Shaw, writing to Frank Harris in 1918, said:

You know that there is a disease called giantism, caused by "a certain morbid process in the sphenoid bone of the skull—viz., an excessive development of the anterior lobe of the pituitary body" (this is from the nearest encyclopedia). "When this condition does not become active until after the age of twenty-five, by which time the long bones are consolidated, the result is acromegaly, which chiefly manifests itself in an enlargement of the hands and feet." I never saw Lady Wilde's feet; but her hands were enormous, and never went straight to their aim when they grasped anything, but minced about feeling for it. And the gigantic splaying of her palm was reproduced in her lumbar region. Now Oscar was an overgrown man, with something not quite normal about his bigness—something that made Lady Colin Campbell, who hated him, describe him as "that great white caterpillar". . . . Well, I have always maintained that Oscar was a giant in the pathological sense, and that this explains a good deal of his weakness.

For at least six years before his meeting with Bosie he had been a familiar figure in three worlds. There is no way of naming these but by the silly and misleading terms usually applied to them—Society, Fleet Street and the homosexual underworld. His place in the stuffy society of the 1880's was a precarious one and depended almost entirely on his talent for being entertaining. He had begun to accept invitations sent to him alone rather than to him and his wife when Constance Wilde had her first baby and that such invitations were sent and accepted was significant. It is said in praise of his great gift for conversation that a London hostess, instead of putting 'Music' at the bottom of her invitations to show the entertainment she would offer, put 'Mr. Oscar Wilde'. If this is true it reveals mercilessly what was Wilde's place in great houses, something between a guest and a conjuror. He had few real friends in society, and none who gave him any support during or after his downfall. He had many satellites outside it and, again to quote Shaw—

The vulgar hated him for snubbing them; and the valiant men damned his impudence and cut him. Thus he was left with a band of devoted satellites on the one hand, and a dining-out connection on the other, with here and there a man of talent and personality enough to command his respect, but utterly without that fortifying body of acquaintance among plain men in which a man must move as himself a plain man, and be Smith and Jones and Wilde and Shaw and Harris instead of Bosie and Robbie and Oscar and Mister. This is the sort of folly that does not last forever in a man of Wilde's ability; but it lasted long enough to prevent Oscar laying any solid social foundations.

His place in Fleet Street was even more insecure, for here there was added an element of jealousy. Hard-working, hard-drinking and hard-boiled journalists felt very little warmth towards a man who made his living among them, but called the Press vulgar and impertinent. His dressiness, his name-dropping and his extravagance irritated them and they had little chance to perceive his more amiable qualities, his kind-heartedness, his easy-going nature free of personal malice, or the charm which was revealed in his conversation.

It was among homosexuals that he was most at home and like many of them he was obsessed with homosexuality not only in his life, but in his writing. *The Picture of Dorian Gray* has the peculiar stench of what was called 'unhealthy' in Victorian times as opposed to 'muscular christianity', (though both of these too often resulted in the same thing,) the half-repressed pederasty of donnish writers on ancient Greece, the girlish tittering about male beauty, the 'wickedness' of perfume and exotic drinks and colours among homosexuals which corresponded to the tara-de-boom-de-ay 'naughtiness' of hetero-sexuals in the 'nineties.

In his private life Wilde was indiscreet to a point of imbecility. He wrote, behaved and talked as a homosexual till his 'dining-out con-nection' became almost a chore from which he escaped to his circle of admirers with relief.

Frank Harris★ tells a story of him which has an air of horrible veracity such as the many inventions of Harris rarely achieved:

I was in a corner of the Café Royal one night downstairs, playing chess, and, while waiting for my opponent to move, I went out just to stretch my legs. When I returned I found Oscar throned in the very corner, between two youths. Even to my short-sighted eyes they appeared quite common: in fact they looked like grooms. In spite of their vulgar appearance, however, one was nice-looking in a fresh boyish way; the other seemed merely depraved. Oscar greeted me as usual, though he seemed slightly embarrassed. I resumed my seat, which was almost opposite him, and pretended to be absorbed in the game. To my astonishment he was talking as well as if he had had a picked audience; talking, if you please, about the Olympic Games, telling how the youths wrestled and were scraped with strigulae and threw the discus and ran races and won the myrtle wreath. His impassioned eloquence brought the sun-bathed palaestra before one with a magic of representment. Suddenly the younger of the boys asked: "Did you sy they was niked?" "Of course," Oscar replied, "nude, clothed only in sunshine and beauty." "Oh, my," giggled the lad in his unspeakable Cockney way. I could not stand it.

In an appendix to his *Trials of Oscar Wilde* Montgomery Hyde says: "There are strong grounds for believing that Wilde was initiated into

★ See Bibliographical Notes.

homosexual practices in 1886 by Robert Ross." There are no grounds for this, I think; what is far more probable is that Ross played Virgil to Wilde's Dante and led him into the underworld of shrill inverts, male prostitutes from the Services and elsewhere, 'drag' parties, scandal, promiscuous amours, blackmail, petty theft and hysteria which homosexuals created in all big cities then as today, but nowhere more noticeably than in London. That Wilde had long been at home in that underworld was obvious during the trials when some of his associates were dragged into the witness-box.

5

Robert Baldwin Ross was an amusing little queen when Wilde met him. It is difficult to determine his age at the time for in her Introduction to a collection of letters written to him* his niece says he was born in 1869, but was twenty when he met Wilde in 1886. He certainly had not come of age, but he was a frequenter of The Crown and other meeting-places for people of his kind. In October 1888 he went up to King's College Cambridge but was not popular. He caught pneumonia from being thrown into the Fountain and left Cambridge abruptly. He was a small kittenish creature born in Canada but brought up in London by his widowed mother, whom even Bosie cannot help calling a charming old lady. When Ross met Wilde he was living with her in Onslow Gardens but soon moved into rooms of his own in Church Street, Kensington. His mother made him a small allowance.

Montgomery Hyde has a footnote about him:

"Frank Harris told Lord Alfred Douglas, when after many years they renewed their acquaintance at Nice in 1925, that Ross had actually boasted to him that he was "the first boy Oscar ever had". And that their homosexual relationship had begun in about the year 1886. At that date Ross was 17 and Wilde 32. Arthur Ransome, who obtained the biographical details for his study of Wilde from Robert Ross, must be taken to confirm this when he writes that "in 1886 he (Wilde) began that course of conduct that was to lead to his downfall in 1895".

Hesketh Pearson says: "Though no one but his intimate friends was aware of it in the 'nineties, Robert Ross was also a pederast." This is surely using the word rather loosely for it means specifically a boy-lover whereas Ross, as might be gathered from the evidence many years later at the Old Bailey, was an invert who liked older men of

* *Robert Ross: Friend of Friends.* Letters edited by Margery Ross (Cape, 1952).

intelligence and social position and only later looked for soldiers to play male to him. "He was a small, slight, attractive man, with an affectionate, impulsive nature and considerable charm of manner," Mr. Pearson says. "Always unassuming he played up to those he wished to impress."

Where he and Wilde met is not recorded though Frank Harris used to say it was in a public lavatory. Little Ross ingratiated himself at once with Oscar and there was a brief affair between them which was not very serious as Ross was not Oscar's 'type'. Oscar actually preferred heterosexuals who were merely vicious and mercenary and he found Ross's feminine willingness facile and not at all like "feasting with panthers", as he described his associations. This is perhaps why later Wilde's merely sexual attraction to Bosie soon gave place to something which he considered more 'ideal'.

Through his elder brother Augustus, who had started a promising career as a writer, Ross met W. E. Henley, then literary editor and later editor of the *Scots*, later *National*, *Observer* and started a long career of usefulness to writers and artists. "I should like you, if you've time, to go to the Reading Room (B.M.) and do a bit of devilling for me and the Tudor Translations", wrote Henley in 1889 and in the following year spoke of him as a "young contributor—'the Youngest gentleman in the Company'". That 'bit of devilling' was repeated for a great number of writers over the next thirty years, and Ross's services to painters were no less painstaking and appreciated. Towards the end of his life he rivalled Sir Edward Marsh as an encourager of youth.

From the first he was immensely proud of his association with Wilde who was then approaching the zenith of his success. Ross longed, in an obliging, flattering and unassuming way, to appropriate him. Oscar was indulgent and if he was also a little patronizing it was with such affectionate good-nature that it only excited Ross to a more Boswellian devotion. He wanted to show off Oscar and show off his friendship with him and was rewarded when other writers and artists took that friendship for granted. "Do tell Oscar Wilde that last Monday I drew to the very doorstep of Babbacombe Cliff and then had less resolution than was needed to invade his retirement", wrote Edmund Gosse a year or two later. Ross became a friend of Beardsley and his mother and worked to keep the peace between Beardsley and Wilde.

His will to flatter and his attitude to Wilde as a writer may be gathered from a letter of his of 1890. "Dear Oscar", it opens and states

D

that even in the precincts of the Savile Club there is nothing but
praise of Dorian Gray, (which had just been published,) though it is
said to be "very dangerous"—a shrewd piece of praise for Wilde who
liked to see himself as a rebel. Eighty copies were sold in one day at a
Strand booksellers. Ross hopes Wilde will 'consent to speak' at the
Authors Club. Wilde's article in the *Nineteenth Century Review* "if
possible eclipses" his *Decay of Lying*. It is as well that Wilde should
be in every magazine to correct the tediousness of all other articles.
The trowel, it will be seen, is skilfully handled.

This attitude persisted through the last years of Wilde's life. Ross
(to his credit) was as proud of his discipleship after Wilde's conviction
as before, and with an assiduity which would have been praiseworthy
if it had been wholly disinterested he gradually insinuated himself into
the position of the faithful friend and finally the literary executor, but
he gained possession of Wilde only after his death. In those years
between the time of his meeting with Wilde and Bosie's appearance,
he made himself useful in a number of ways, (some rather questionable
though there is no evidence that he actually pimped for Wilde). He
flattered him, was seen with him, and introduced other friends of his
with similar sympathies like More Adey, Reginald Turner and
Arthur Clifton, all young queers with enough money to be idle and
give themselves up to admiration for Wilde. Ross was the most
single-minded in this exhibitionistic devotion, and, until Wilde met
Bosie, the most successful.

6

Wilde and Bosie met in 1891. Bosie says "as far as I can place it, (it)
must have been in the summer". He also says that he was not with
Wilde when he was writing *Lady Windermere's Fan* "except on isolated
occasions." Wilde wrote that play in the late summer of 1891 and
handed it to George Alexander in the autumn. Ross told Hesketh
Pearson that Wilde stayed with friends in the Lake District for a short
time and named his character after the lake as he named later characters
after places in which he wrote, like Lady Bracknell and Lord Goring,
but there is no other evidence of it. The meeting with Bosie took place
at the end of the Oxford term, in early July, and Wilde was probably
already writing *Lady Windermere's Fan* at the time and finished it
during the first months of the friendship. Rupert Hart-Davis★ tenta-
tively suggests that the meeting may have taken place in January but
this is contradicted by the fact, attested by Bosie and others, that at

★ See Bibliographical Notes.

their first meeting Wilde invited Bosie to dine at the Albermarle Club a few days later and on this, their second meeting, gave him a copy of *Dorian Gray*, published on July 1 1891, in which he wrote: "Alfred Douglas from his friend who wrote this book. July 91. Oscar." This copy is still in existence.

Having arranged time and place with both parties, Lionel Johnson called for Bosie at his mother's house in Cadogan Place and took him in a hansom to Tite Street. Though all three must have known that this was more than a casual introduction such as might be made in a club, the whole call was conducted with the greatest decorum. Bosie and Johnson were shown into the small sitting-room on the ground floor which had a Victorian bay window looking over iron railings to the street. This room was decorated in red and yellow—yellow walls and scarlet enamel—and there was a cast of the Hermes of Praxiteles. There were a few pictures, Beardsley's drawing of Mrs. Patrick Campbell, a Simeon Solomon and a Monticelli, but most of the wall space was taken up with bookshelves.

Wilde made his entrance, splendid in frock coat and button-hole. Bosie has recorded, as others have, that the first impression he had was of someone rather 'comic-looking' but this was soon dissipated as Wilde began to talk. The practised artist, with a range of modulations for his rich and plummy speaking voice and what Ross called "one of the hundred artificial manners which he has for every person and every occasion," soon mesmerized the undergraduate. When Wilde asked Bosie to dine with him during the next few days at the Albermarle Club, Lionel Johnson must have been delighted with the success of his introduction.

There have been several attempts to reconstruct the background and imagine the conversation at that first meeting. Harris, of course, weighs in with a hearsay picture of Bosie hanging on Oscar's lips 'with his soul in his eyes'. "Before he had listened long, I have been told, the youth declared his admiration passionately." That 'I have been told' is very Harris.

Harris [retorted Bosie in his *Autobiography*], in his book, invents a deliberately lying account of my first meeting with Wilde. What really happened, of course, at that interview was just the ordinary interchange of courtesies. Wilde was very agreeable and talked a great deal, I was very much impressed (much more so than I have admitted in my book, *Oscar Wilde and Myself*, which I wrote with Crosland), and, before I left, Wilde had asked me to lunch or to dinner at his club, and I had accepted his invitation.

Certainly both were dazzled, though by different qualities in the other. To Wilde, who was already surrounded by young men both of Ross's intelligent and artistic kind and the more sexually congenial ruffians he had begun to pick up, Bosie's combination of the poetic and athletic, his spectacular good looks and his title, must have been irresistible. To Bosie to be flattered and listened to by the bulky and assured Irishman who talked so confidently and brilliantly of life, which he saw as a splendid drama whose acts were the three hundred and sixty-five days of the year, was the most exciting experience he had known.

Conventions, however, were maintained to the end and Bosie was taken up to the drawing-room on the first floor to be introduced to Constance Wilde. Here there was a more oriental atmosphere— bulrushes in Japanese vases, bamboo chairs, and—Whistler's idea— huge coloured feathers let into the ceiling. Bosie and Wilde's wife met and there is no reason to doubt Bosie's statement, maintained consistently through all his phases, that they liked each other at once and continued to like each other till the crash, after which Ross and others were able to influence Constance Wilde against Bosie and she began to write and speak bitterly about him.

CHAPTER III

The Friendship: First Two Years
Summer 1891–Summer 1893

I

THE new friendship did not become a thing of sustained passion and inseparability in a few days or even months. Bosie went off to Homberg to stay with his Montgomery grandparents and Wilde, apart from the dubious visit to Windermere, remained in London, as his letters of July and August show. But Wilde and Bosie met again before Bosie went back to Oxford for the Michaelmas term, for during that term Wilde went down to Oxford for a week-end.

Bosie who in later life admitted that the love affair between them had some sexual expression, (though "of the sin which takes its name from one of the Cities of the Plain there was never the slightest question,") says tersely that this began 'at least six months' after he had met Wilde, was completely discontinued about six months before the final catastrophe and never resumed thereafter. This blunt statement of the facts deserves to be believed and is consistent with the characters of both men. Wilde, as can be gathered from the evidence against him in court, was addicted to roughs, criminals and male prostitutes, and though his promiscuous nature admitted at times affairs with young men of some refinement he felt a distaste, very common among intelligent homosexuals, for sexual relations with those of his own class or education. Moreover he took the male part and treated the young men he picked up, as one of them gratuitously stated, 'as if they were girls'. Bosie was aggressively masculine.

All my life, up till two or three years ago, I have angrily and violently resented the suggestion that I ever had anything feminine about me. If anyone wanted to "get a rise" out of me, at any time from my schooldays onwards, the way to do it was to make some such suggestion. When I was a schoolboy I was so determined to be "manly" that I deliberately went about insufficiently clothed in winter. I used to shiver without underclothing unless someone took the trouble to insist that I wore it, which of course did not happen at school. Although by nature rather nervous and apprehensive, I cultivated insensibility to pain, and whenever any danger appeared I trained myself to rush out to meet it more than half way.

Between these two the chief bond could not be a sexual one. Their friendship was passionate and some expression was given to their passion but it was almost incidental to their love. "I did with him and allowed him to do just what was done among boys at Winchester," Bosie told Montgomery Hyde in later years, adding "It was dead against my sexual instincts which were all for youth and beauty and softness." He confirmed all this in crude and telling detail in a letter to Frank Harris in 1925.

So during the rest of that year 1891, though Wilde may have been engaged in the 'long patient and strenuous siege' by which he achieved what he wanted, there was nothing between the two beyond happy meetings, hours spent over meals in delightful conversation and mutual exultation over their new-found friendship.

Early that winter Wilde went to Paris alone, and in circumstances which he described somewhat theatrically to Vincent O'Sullivan wrote most of *Salomé*. On his return he went to Oxford to stay a week-end in the rooms in the High Street which Bosie shared with Lord Encombe. This was an enchanting occasion for both of them. Bosie was at Magdalen, Wilde's old College, and Wilde took his protégé to see Dr. Warren the President whom he startled by facetiously threatening to present a colossal equestrian statue of himself to the College. They also called on Walter Pater whom Wilde regarded as the greatest living prose-writer. Bosie tried hard to appreciate both the man and his work but found the prose finnicking and the man a bore. "He had practically no conversation and would sit for hours without saying more than an occasional word."

It is hard to imagine which of the two friends was prouder of the other as they re-visited Oscar's haunts, Bosie of the famous writer and poseur or Oscar of the beautiful young man with the title 'like the name of a flower'.

Letters followed the visit which Bosie did not keep but one probably written about a month later survives, in which Wilde talked of 'strange and troubling personalities'. Though this is scarcely likely to refer to it, Wilde had just picked up his publisher's office-boy, a youth named Edward Shelley who later became one of the witnesses against him.

Bosie knew nothing of Shelley that winter—though he met him later—and it is interesting to speculate about this. Bosie may have been away for part of the time when Wilde was seeing Shelley for he and his mother had taken a house called St. Ann's Gate in the Close at Salisbury, but he was certainly in London for the first night of *Lady Windermere's Fan*. It may be that Wilde had not yet shown the complete frankness which came later about his curious acquaintances, but this can scarcely have been because Wilde supposed Bosie innocent, for his ready response to an appeal by Bosie during his next term at Oxford clearly suggests that he was very well aware of Bosie's hedonistic behaviour with youths rather younger than himself. Nor is it likely that Wilde was making a pretence of faithfulness to Bosie with whom he had not yet slept. It was probably a fastidious wish to keep the two apart. He did not mind Bosie seeing him 'feast with panthers' when he had begun to meet handsome and dangerous cockney youths, but this earnest and suburban worshipper of his talents was embarrassing. However, he introduced Shelley to a young man called Maurice Schwabe, an acquaintance of a very different kind though scarcely less fatal to him in the future. For Schwabe whom Wilde had met through Ross was in turn to introduce him to Taylor and his gang and acted as a link between those two sets of people.

Ross and his friends, More Adey, Reggie Turner, Maurice Schwabe and the rest, went to the first night of *Lady Windermere's Fan* on February 20 1892 and Richard le Gallienne remembered seeing Wilde with them in the theatre bar in the interval, towering head and shoulders over them. Bosie was with Wilde for Constance Wilde was unable to come. This was a pity for by her well-mannered conventionality she might have saved her husband from making one of his sillier gestures—congratulating the audience on their performance and their appreciation of his play. Bosie, as an undergraduate, probably thought this and Oscar's holding a lighted cigarette while he took his curtain, to be magnificent gestures. One can see him applauding, then, as they drove to Willis's Rooms for a triumphant supper later, congratulating Oscar on what the Press called his 'insolent effrontery'. Bosie loved that play and would never hear of its being a somewhat tawdry thing redeemed only by Wilde's effervescent wit. Half a century after its first night he wrote:

I do not profess to be a dramatic critic; I am only a poet, but I do venture to think that I am a fairly good judge of the merits of any play. I saw *Lady*

Windermere's Fan at least twenty times when it was first put on by George Alexander and loved every word of it every time.

A few nights later, as Bosie confessed to Frank Harris in a letter which is still preserved by Harris's American lawyer, Wilde took Bosie back to his empty house in Tite Street at two o'clock in the morning. This was the first occasion of what Harris called 'familiarities' between them.

2

During the term that followed Bosie was involved in some trouble at Oxford which Wilde helped to settle by calling in his friend and solicitor, Sir George Lewis. Precisely what form this trouble took or who was involved cannot be discovered but it is reasonably certain that Bosie was being blackmailed, for this is the only conclusion to be drawn from Wilde's references to the occasion in *De Profundis* and Queensberry's in letters to his family. As both *De Profundis* and the letters were written in violent emotion by men who at the time of writing were under great stress the evidence is not conclusive but the details given neatly correspond and are sadly convincing, even though the terms used sound uncontrolled. Wilde said:

Our friendship really begins with your begging me in a most pathetic and charming letter to assist you in a position appalling to any one, doubly so to a young man at Oxford: I do so, and ultimately through your using my name as your friend with Sir George Lewis I began to lose his esteem and friendship, a friendship of fifteen years' standing.

He returned to it later:

I would not, of course, have expected, nor indeed wished you to have stated how and for what purpose you had sought my assistance in your trouble at Oxford.

Queensberry wrote to his daughter-in-law some months before Wilde's action against him:

I am obliged to bring out more evidence about Alfred's character, and to speak about something I knew about. I have kept secret until now entirely to myself but I will do it no longer after this wretched accusation. I explained all this in my letter, Percy knows nothing of it. It is a horrible story, nothing to do with Oscar Wilde, and as it has been told me by a personal friend, an eminent lawyer who himself supplied the money, £100, to hush up the scandal, there can be no doubt of the truth of it.

In another letter to Percy's wife written eight days later:

Having now given Percy evidence of what his brother's character is by relating the Oxford incident, which has nothing to do with this brute Oscar Wilde.

And in a third, of three months later, to his son Percy's solicitor:

I know of his brother's infamous conduct at Oxford and how he had to pay £100 blackmail to get out of it, which ranked him before with this lot and showed me what he was long ago.

Bosie appealed to Wilde who asked Lewis to settle the matter and that clever lawyer did so for £100. Bosie probably obtained this sum from his family. It certainly was not paid by Wilde who in *De Profundis* was recalling every penny he had spent on Bosie and would not have missed this item. At the time he was delighted to offer the shield of his influence to his young friend and gain his lasting gratitude.

Bosie's homosexuality, while it lasted, was reckless and irresponsible, with no sense of sin or twinge of conscience. He was boastfully a pagan and full of popular misconceptions of the Greek Ideal. An aristocrat in what is now considered the worst sense, he was indifferent to bourgeois morality and felt himself privileged, as his forefathers had been for two centuries, to amuse himself as he pleased. It was one of his many phases and he was to grow out of it, but at this time he was frankly pleasure-loving, perhaps somewhat licentious.

Wilde, on the other hand, theatrical to the last flick of his gloves, saw in these 'strange sins' the fulfilment of a macabre destiny. He was conscious of the danger and delighted in it. Wholly lacking the common touch he found something romantic in the plebeian as he found it in the aristocratic. "Clibborn (Cliburn) and Atkins were wonderful in their infamous war against life. To entertain them was an astounding adventure" he was to write of two blackmailers after they had betrayed him. He had an intellectual and self-dramatizing approach to the whole thing and though he spoke scornfully of 'what are called sins', his vices would have lost half their attraction for him if they had not been generally frowned on.

Each influenced the other in this, though not very deeply. Bosie began to write poems about 'the love that dare not speak its name' and Oscar assumed some of Bosie's nonchalance in his dealings with the young men he favoured. But all through their friendship, till after Wilde's imprisonment, to Bosie homosexual adventures were thoughtless escapades which excited and delighted him while to Oscar they were beautiful guilty things through which he could show his defiance of the commonplace.

3

Malicious talk about the two friends was beginning to rage. With *Lady Windermere's Fan* filling the St. James's Theatre and its gags being repeated all over London, Wilde was more than ever a subject for gossip-writers and gossip-mongers, and as he and Bosie made a point of eating together in public whenever they were in town, introducing one another as 'my friend' to as many of their respective acquaintances as possible—each having an acquaintanceship of astonishing variety—and generally publicizing the fact, of which both were proud, that this was a great if not already immortal friendship, it was scarcely surprising that there was a good deal of talk.

This talk soon reached Queensberry who had been leading a raffish life since his divorce. He kept chambers of his own but travelled about a good deal for horse-racing and hunting, staying in one of the few country houses in which he was still welcome and in London publicly and defiantly entertaining his more disreputable mistresses. Compared with his anger and frustration over his heir, Drumlanrig, who had obtained a seat in the House of Lords from which Queensberry was excluded, his dissatisfaction with Bosie was as yet mild.

After I had known Wilde for a few months and been about a great deal with him, my father suddenly one day spoke to me about it, and told me that Wilde was not a fit man for me to associate with. I must do my father the justice to say that at this stage he was not unkind or offensive, as he became afterwards. He light-heartedly told me that I must give up knowing Wilde, and seemed to think that this would be quite enough.

It might have been, at least to make the friendship a more discreet one, if Queensberry had spoken to a less volatile and headstrong son. Bosie thought about that conversation and perhaps talked it over with his mother and with Wilde, then realizing that he was of age and free to choose his own friends, but not apparently realizing that he was a younger son living on an allowance of £350 a year which his father was quite voluntarily making him, he sat down to write one of those reckless letters which for many years gave him a peculiar satisfaction. It was, he says, a 'perfectly respectful and affectionate letter' which told his father that he saw no reason why he should give up his friend and that he would not think of it, 'begging' (his own word) his father not to interfere. There were further exchanges in which Bosie was called a fool and a baby and his father was doubtless called something equally 'respectful and affectionate'. But Queensberry, busy raging against Drumlanrig, Gladstone and Rosebery—he followed Rosebery to Homberg and threatened him with a horse-whip—did no more at this time about Bosie's scandalous association with the man whom Queensberry was later to call 'this brute Wilde', 'this hideous monster', 'this fellow Wilde', 'this villain Oscar Wilde'.

4

Another man watched the rapid growth of the Wilde and Douglas friendship with no more satisfaction than Queensberry, though more reticently and for different reasons. This was Robert Ross.

For some five years he had been privileged to produce Wilde in gatherings of his friends, to attend him in public, to be invited to Tite Street, and he now found himself treated with friendly but abstracted politeness. Apart from the young men—of a sphere almost as foreign to Ross as it was to Wilde—whom he picked up, Oscar seemed to have attention for no one but Bosie. There were no more little dinners such as Wilde was later to describe in *De Profundis*:

One of the most delightful dinners I remember ever having had is one Robbie and I had together in a little Soho café, which cost about as many shillings as my dinners to you used to cost pounds. Out of my dinner with Robbie came the first and best of all my dialogues. Idea, title, treatment, mode, everything was struck out at a 3 franc 50 c. *table d'hôte*.

Those occasions were left behind, for Bosie was taken to the Café Royal, Kettners or the Savoy and lived, as Wilde later maintained and Ross believed, almost exclusively on 'clear turtle soup', 'luscious ortolons wrapped in their crinkled Sicilian vine-leaves', 'amber-scented Champagne', 'pâtés procured directly from Strasburg', washed down with 'special cuvées of Perrier-Jouet'. There were no more gatherings at which Oscar scintillated for the benefit of Robbie, Reggie Turner, Arthur Clifton, More Adey, Maurice Schwabe and the rest of Ross's circle for he was now inseparable from Bosie. Ross had been kept in a particular compartment of Wilde's life, welcomed there and treated with kindness but never encouraged to emerge into the white lights of Wilde's social magnificence. He now watched while Bosie as by natural right was taken everywhere, introduced to every-one. Ross had been petted but patronized, Bosie was not only adored but revered. Ross had been a useful amanuensis, Bosie was a fellow-writer. Ross found himself taken for granted while Bosie walked over a ubiquitous red carpet laid by Oscar. While Bosie was introduced to the most distinguished people Wilde knew, Ross, to whom such things were of urgent importance, found himself being offered by Besant the unpaid sub-editorship of the house organ of the Society of Authors. While Bosie was to be given the distinction of translating *Salomé* into English, Ross was reduced to making himself useful to Edmund Gosse and receiving the anxious confidences of Aubrey Beardsley's mother. He cannot have been much pleased to receive from Oscar that summer a letter from the Royal Palace Hotel, Kensington saying, "Bosie is quite like a narcissus—so white and gold. He lies like a hyacinth on the sofa, and I worship him."

Ross was too shrewd to remonstrate or even to show the smallest sign of resentment. Perhaps he believed his day would come again and that the highly publicized friendship would blaze itself to ashes in a month or two. Or perhaps he felt for Bosie some of the awed devotion he felt for Wilde, in spite of his own eclipse. Certainly Bosie thought so.

Ross was by way of being devoted to me in those days. If I had followed his example, and kept the letters he wrote to me, I could have showed that he professed devotion and admiration for me in as extravagant terms as those used by Wilde.

Bosie liked Ross then. He took him about more than Wilde had ever done, inviting him to his mother's house in Cadogan Place and introducing him to people whom Ross thought important. Bosie, in fact, introduced him to the Glenconners through whom he met the Asquiths and it is ironical that these were his chief support in his life-and-death struggle with Bosie twenty years later.

5

During the Trinity term of that year (1892) Bosie wrote a couple of poems which were published in an undergraduate weekly called *The Spirit Lamp*. The first number of this appeared on May 6th and it continued throughout the term. 'Founded and Edited' by a Christ Church man named Sandys Wason it bore the sub-title *An Oxford Magazine Without News*. Sandys Wason seems to have been something of a wag for he printed a large *Second Edition* on the front cover of one number, a gesture which the publisher, Thornton of Oxford, called a 'little pleasantry'.

Towards the end of May Wason came to Bosie and said that he was going down that term and would pass *The Spirit Lamp* on to him.

Whether it had been a financial success or not Bosie does not record but he was delighted to become owner and editor of it and spent the last few weeks of the term preparing for its reappearance after the long vacation.

In June there was another burst of publicity for Wilde which he handled in a most unfortunate way. Sarah Bernhardt had agreed to appear at the Palace Theatre in *Salomé* and the play had already gone into rehearsal when the Lord Chamberlain withheld his licence on the grounds that it introduced biblical characters, a remnant of Puritan legislation to abolish Miracle Plays in the sixteenth century. Wilde lost his head and in an interview said that he would leave England and settle in France where he would take out letters of naturalization. He would not consent to call himself a citizen of a country that showed such narrowness in its artistic judgements. This sort of petulant arrogance brought nothing but a laugh from philistia and *Punch* appeared with a caricature showing Wilde in the uniform of a *legionnaire*.

Bosie finding Oscar in the middle of all this invited him to come with him to Homberg in which spa he would be staying as usual with his grandfather Montgomery. Wilde consented and a London paper reported that they were at 51 Kaiser-Friedrich Promenade. Wilde met the Prince of Wales (later Edward VII) and forgot his anglophobe outburst when he was smiled on by that genial little gentleman who came to the first night of *An Ideal Husband* two and a half years later. Wilde's meeting with Bosie's grandfather, Alfred Montgomery, was less successful, however, and though the statement is made in *Oscar Wilde and Myself* which is no more to be trusted than *De Profundis*, it is worth recording that Bosie said Montgomery "took a violent and invincible dislike to him and declined to meet him again."

6

When they returned Wilde took a farm-house, Grove Farm, Felbrigg, near Cromer, for his family and Bosie stayed with them there. Neither Wilde nor Bosie makes more than a passing reference to this unlikely holiday, so we are left to form our own pictures. Oscar cannot have been much at home in a Norfolk farm-house. His sons were now seven and five respectively and a good deal of the attention of the three highly incongruous grown-ups was devoted to them. Vyvyan Holland gives us an endearing picture of Wilde at the seaside, building sand-castles and manning them with tin soldiers pulled from his pockets, wearing a Norfolk jacket and knickerbockers, no shoes and stockings and a large grey hat which he had probably brought back with him from the United States. Bosie was far less a metropolitan than Oscar, and took his surroundings for granted. To the end of his life he kept the fondest recollections of Wilde's little sons and was greatly distressed when the surviving one, Vyvyan Holland, as a middle-aged man, refused his offer of friendship on the grounds that it was impossible for any friend of Ross's to be a friend of Douglas's. Vyvyan Holland tells me that he cannot remember in the faintest way ever having met Bosie as a small boy.

It does not seem to have been a long holiday and Bosie stayed for only ten days—'playing golf' Wilde said bitterly in *De Profundis*, though in a letter to Tree at the time he said: "I find Cromer excellent for writing and golf still better." Wilde's hospitality was returned at Lady Queensberry's house The Hut at which Wilde and his wife stayed a number of week-ends that spring and summer.

What Constance Wilde thought about it all, then or thereafter, is not without interest. She told Bosie about this time that she liked him better than any of Oscar's friends. She was a favourite with Lady Queensberry and went to a dance of hers that year which was probably given for Bosie's sister Edith. Wilde had asked young Shelley to come and stay at Cromer, which fortunately he was unable to do, but even that would have seemed no more to Constance Wilde, probably, than the fact that Oscar was being kind to a boy from his publisher's office who could not afford a holiday. At what point, if ever, before the crisis, she began to realize the reason for Wilde's long absences and insistence on the entertainment of young men, even Frank Harris never dared to guess.

7

It was when he returned to town that Wilde met Alfred Taylor and introduced him to Bosie. It was through Taylor that Wilde began to know the young blackguards who later testified against him.

Alfred Waterhouse Somerset Taylor himself was not a blackguard. Thirty-one years old when Wilde met him through Maurice Schwabe in September or the early part of October 1892, he was the son of a rich cocoa manufacturer and was educated (though for only about a year) at Marlborough. His father died when he was twelve and as a boy of eighteen he joined the 4th Battalion of the Royal Fusiliers, City of London Regiment. This, his Counsel maintained later, was with the idea of gaining a commission and making the Army his career but on the death of his uncle and his own coming of age in 1883 he inherited £45,000 and set about spending it with astonishing prodigality. In the nine years which followed he not only went through it but became bankrupt.

Taylor was superficial, musical, talkative, a bright and aimless queen. He was not exactly a professional procurer but he gave tea-parties at which 'gentlemen' could meet out-of-work roughs, and other amenable youths. Having had a good deal of money to spend, he was accustomed to entertaining and was now reduced to doing it in a semi-professional way. His brother made him a very small allowance but he had become unfitted for any serious work and lived a silly chattering life, picking up young men and bringing them to his home, entertaining them and introducing them, passing his days in vacuous incontinence.

The first young man Taylor produced for Wilde was Sidney Mavor, who was then about twenty years old, tall and rather handsome with 'perhaps a slight cast in one eye', whose ambition was the common one of the time, to go on the music-hall stage. Mavor was known to his friends as 'Jenny Mavor'. The introduction was actually made by Schwabe in Taylor's rooms and Wilde took an instant liking to Mavor in which he was justified, as later events showed. He at once asked Taylor to bring 'Sidney' (Christian names were used instantly at Taylor's) to dinner on the following evening at Kettner's and invited Bosie to make a fourth. It seems an odd thing to have done but Mavor's meeting Bosie then had a happy sequel when Wilde was on trial, for Bosie saw the young man in the corridor at Bow Street when he was waiting to give evidence against Wilde and, recognizing him from that night at Kettner's, tackled him at once.

This youth was a gentleman by birth and of an entirely different character and class to the other witnesses. He was terrorized into making a statement against Wilde (I am not suggesting that what he alleged may not have been true) by the same means as the other "victims". I happened to see him in the corridor at Bow Street Police Court while he was waiting to give evidence. I went up and shook hands with him, and said: "Surely you are not going to give evidence against Oscar?" He looked round in a frightened way, and then whispered: "Well, what can I do? I daren't refuse to give evidence now; they got a statement out of me." I said: "For God's sake, remember you are a gentleman and a Public School boy. Don't put yourself on a level with scum like —— and —— (two of the witnesses). When counsel asks you the questions, deny the whole thing, and say you made the statement because you were frightened by the police. They can't do anything to you." He grabbed my hand and said: "All right, I'll do what you say." He did (more power to him!). To the consternation of prosecuting counsel, he denied his own statement, and swore that Wilde had never been anything to him but a good friend. Counsel, of course, dropped him like a hot brick, he was told to "stand down", and walked out of the court, having inflicted a very nasty jolt to the Prosecution.

But at dinner on that October evening in a private room at Kettner's this was unimaginably far away. There was much laughter for Wilde talked irresistibly, Taylor and 'Jenny' Mavor added the tinsel wit of the male chorus and young Bosie found these new acquaintances of Oscar's novel and bizarre. Afterwards Mavor accompanied Wilde to the Albermarle Hotel, at which Wilde frequently booked rooms for the night. A week later Mavor received a cigarette-case—the first of many Wilde was to give to Taylor's young men—inscribed 'Sidney from O.W.'

8

Bosie's acquaintanceship with Taylor was a brief episode and a lark to which he never gave another thought. Wilde's was the beginning of a relationship which continued for nearly two years and was the direct cause of his conviction. But neither took it very seriously at the time, for that October they found their passionate friendship under the scrutiny of both of Bosie's parents.

Queensberry's anger seemed to have been dormant since his exchange of letters with Bosie in the spring. The story of his meeting with Wilde at the Café Royal that October has often been told. Oscar and Bosie were lunching together when Queensberry entered alone and sat at a nearby table.

Now one of the sorrier aspects of the whole calamitous story is that underneath their mutual abuse and recrimination, the hysterical epithets they flung to and fro and the hatred they both believed they felt, Bosie and his father had a kind of unwilling love for each other. Bosie hated his father partly because he loved his mother (whom Queensberry undoubtedly wronged,) partly because he loved Oscar, and partly because he believed his father hated him. Queensberry, the sour psychopathic misanthrope with an aching persecution mania, hated his son because he had once loved and now abhorred his wife, to whom Bosie was passionately devoted, because he believed that Bosie like all his children, indeed like all the world, was against him, and

The Marquess of Queensberry (1844–1900).
The Spy cartoon, from 'Vanity Fair', and an
engraving based on a photograph.

Kinmount House, where Bosie spent his childhood.

because he was the kind of man in whom love and hatred were always mixed. But underneath these twin hatreds was the shy and tortured love of father for son and son for father. It was something which Wilde could never perceive. If he had done so and known how to take advantage of it, it would have saved him.

That day, when Bosie saw his father across the restaurant, he may or may not have realized the full possibilities offered by a meeting between Queensberry and Wilde, his father and his friend, but he had enough faith in both to bring it about. He hurried across to Queensberry's table and begged him to come and meet Wilde. With surly unwillingness, Queensberry agreed. Wilde gave him all he had of charm, brilliance and courtesy and in ten minutes Queensberry was laughing and listening eagerly. At the end of lunch Bosie tactfully left them but he later heard from Oscar that they had remained together in friendly converse till past four o'clock and Queensberry had accepted an invitation to stay at Babbacombe early in the following year. This was confirmed by a letter which Bosie received from his father two days later. Queensberry wished to 'take back' all he had said of Wilde. He considered him charming and clever and did not wonder that Bosie was so fond of him. He had been told by his old friend Lord de Grey that Wilde was a friend of his and Lady de Grey's and was 'perfectly all right in every way'. Bosie was delighted.

Lady Queensberry, however, was not so easily won over. She had never liked Wilde and entertained him and his wife for Bosie's sake and because she was fond of Constance Wilde. She, too, had been disturbed by rumours and had grown so anxious about her son's extravagant friendship that she had written to the man whom she thought most able to advise her on the subject, the President of her son's College, Herbert Warren. He had sent her a long letter in reply, giving Wilde a very high character, praising his gifts and achievements in scholarship and literature and suggesting that Bosie might consider himself fortunate in Wilde's friendship.

But Lady Queensberry, who loved her son, was not altogether satisfied and when the Wildes spent a week-end at Bracknell that autumn she took Oscar for a walk through the woods one morning and tackled him. According to Wilde in *De Profundis*, she spoke of Bosie's vanity and extravagance; if this was so, it was a tactful way of reaching what she really wanted to convey but was too kind and gentle to state outright—that this hectic friendship between a public man nearing forty and an undergraduate was being adversely discussed and might be harmful to Bosie's future. She admitted that it was difficult to talk to Bosie himself, for he was headstrong and impatient of criticism even—or perhaps most of all—from people he loved. She was, in other words, with tact and diffidence appealing to Wilde not perhaps to give up the friendship but to moderate it and make it less ostentatious. Wilde thought she was criticizing Bosie. This was the kind of thing in which he had not much delicacy of feeling. He was prepared to neglect his wife to spend his time and money with Bosie and with Taylor's disreputable circle and perhaps did not see why Bosie in return should owe much consideration to his mother.

9

Back at Oxford, Bosie busied himself with his new toy, *The Spirit Lamp*. He changed the yellow wrappers in which it had been issued to glazed ones printed in blue and added a design of Magdalen College tower to rise beside the list of contents. Three numbers were issued that term at irregular intervals (November 4 and 18 and December 6) and the circulation began to increase. It was nominally a weekly but in the following summer term (his last at Oxford) Bosie increased its size, doubled its price (to a shilling) and issued it monthly. Altogether eight numbers appeared under his editorship, the last two bearing the sub-heading, *An Aesthetic, Literary and Critical Magazine*. During this time he obtained contributions from Wilde, John Addington Symonds and Lionel Johnson. The first article of Max Beerbohm's to appear in print, *The Incomparable Beauty of Modern Dress*, came out in it and there were numerous contributions from a friend of Bosie's, who afterwards edited *The Artist*, Charles Kains Jackson. Twenty years after Bosie had gone down from Oxford *The Morning Post* (March 7 1912) described *The Spirit Lamp* as "the best of Oxford's many momentary periodicals".

One night in a restaurant in London Wilde handed Bosie a sonnet called *The New Remorse* and to the end of his life Bosie believed it had been written specially for him though in fact it had appeared in an earlier form in *The Court and Society Review*, under the title, *Un Amant de nos Jours*. Bosie published it in *The Spirit Lamp* and thought it was the best sonnet Wilde ever wrote. 'The sin was mine; I did not understand;' was its first line and it can be found among Wilde's *Poems*. Bosie wrote verses that year and the next with the facility of a young man who has been given a medium of publication; they are full of heartbreaks over lost summers, laments for the wreck of a boat called

Happiness, cries for "one hour of golden June, In the heart of this chill November"—all the *Weltschmerz* that is the perennial theme of happy young poets with good appetites. They are not better or worse than the verses written by countless undergraduates before and since. Perhaps a skilled literary analyst could find in them promise of the poetry that was to come, could see that these were not the verses of a boy who would soon forget such gewgaws as he faced the realities of existence but the first essays of a poet who would never face those realities and write more perfectly and more profoundly as they assailed his tower. He certainly did not lack encouragement. Wilde, Lionel Johnson and all his young friends gave him to understand that he was a born singer. Wilde, that winter, writing to him the prose poem letter which gave such ammunition to the Prosecution, said: "Your sonnet is quite lovely."

Max Beerbohm and Reggie Turner were both at Oxford with Bosie, though Max was two years younger than the others. Bosie had met Reggie Turner through Ross in London and came to know Beerbohm through him. He liked Reggie as everyone did throughout that charming and easygoing creature's life. Turner was one of the illegitimate sons of the first Lord Burnham, who was the principal proprietor of the *Daily Telegraph*. Born Edward Levy, he changed his name to Lawson and became Lord Burnham in 1903. Reggie's half-brother, Frank Lawson, was left a wealthy man and shared his good fortune with Reggie, who remained a life-long friend of Beerbohm's. A charge against him under the Act which imprisoned Wilde failed some years after Wilde's conviction, and when it was over Turner preferred to remain abroad. He wrote several novels. He was in every sense one of Ross's circle.

Bosie had one interest which Oscar never shared, for he loved music. Wilde was entirely music-deaf and covered his ignorance with clever phraseology—"Dvořák writes passionate, curiously coloured things" being his only known reference to a composer. Bosie throughout his life was a good pianist. At Oxford he scarcely ever missed the evening service in Magdalen Chapel, whose choir, he used to say, was the finest in the world, adding: "It ought to be, for it is a separate foundation and has about £5,000 a year to spend." This led to his friendship which continued through all his vicissitudes with Frank Marshall, one of the 'Academical Clerks', who was a splendid pianist, and with another chorister named Tapsfield, who became a Canon of St. Paul's. Dr. Roberts, the organist, gave Bosie the free run of the

organ loft and he learned a great deal about church music. He also
saw much of Walter Pater's great friend at Brazenose, Dr. Bussell,
whose devotion to Handel and Bach endeared his memory to Bosie
long afterwards.

10

Since Bosie had left him in London, Wilde had been behaving irresponsibly. Maurice Schwabe had rooms in Margaret Street off Regent
Street and in October asked Wilde to dinner there to meet a boy
called Fred Atkins, whom Wilde immediately took to Paris for a
week-end.

On his return he rented from Lady Mount-Temple her house at
Babbacombe in Devon, paying £100 for three months. He moved
there with his family in November.

The house was called Babbacombe Cliff and it had been designed
by Ruskin. The decorations were by Morris and Burne-Jones and the
whole thing must have been a pleasant period piece with the rooms
named after the flowers in their William Morris wallpapers, each with
its name on the door. A woodland garden spread down the slope before
it to the sea.

Wilde never took kindly to life in the country. "Are there beautiful
people in London?" he wrote to Ross soon after moving. "Here there
are none; everyone is so unfinished." He added that he was doing no
work and wanted stirring up.

Just after Christmas he wrote to Bosie a letter which he himself
produced in Court later, perhaps because he had been blackmailed
over it.

My Own Boy,

Your sonnet is quite lovely, and it is a marvel that those red rose-leaf lips of
yours should have been made no less for music of song than for madness of
kisses. Your slim gilt soul walks between passion and poetry. I know Hyacinthus, whom Apollo loved so madly, was you in Greek days.

Why are you alone in London, and when do you go to Salisbury? Do go
there to cool your hands in the grey twilight of Gothic things, and come here
whenever you like. It is a lovely place—it only lacks you; but go to Salisbury
first.

Always, with undying love,

Yours,

Oscar.

The sonnet referred to was *In Sarum Close* and soon after receiving
it Bosie went to Salisbury, if not to 'cool his hands in the grey twilight

of Gothic things' at least to stay with his mother in her house, St. Ann's Gate. That phrase, by the way, was not as inane as it seems in the letter, for Wilde was paraphrasing Bosie's own sonnet—"I thought to cool my burning hands in this calm twilight of forgotten things". If Wilde in producing his letter had been content to show this for a piece of flippant quotation from a poor poem instead of trying to cover up (when Tree had been shown a copy of the letter) by saying it was a prose poem and getting Pierre Louÿs to do a French version to prove it, it might have been better for him. Louÿs rendered the line: "*Va! rafraichs tes mains dans le clair crepuscule Des choses ou descend l'âme antique.*"

From Salisbury Bosie went to Oxford during the vacation, especially, it would seem, to entertain a youth named Alfred Wood, whom he had met through Taylor. Wood was described as tall and fair-haired and at this time he was no more than seventeen years old. Wood stayed a week or two and Bosie gave him a suit of clothes, for the twenty-two-year-old man and seventeen-year-old boy were identical in build. In the pocket of the suit Bosie, by a characteristic piece of carelessness, left some ecstatic letters from Wilde, including the 'Hyacinthus' letter just quoted.

Bosie was sent down for a term for his failure to pass an exam., probably 'Greats', though Crosland called it 'Smalls'. He returned to his mother at Salisbury, where a tutor was to be found for him. While there he received, forwarded from London, a letter from Wood saying he had the letters and threatening blackmail.

At this point both the friends behaved with a want of discretion approaching idiocy. Bosie wrote to Wilde, who was in London, and gave him details of the case. Wilde, who was staying alone in Tite Street, (his wife was still at Babbacombe with the children), replied with a request that Wood should be sent to him to be dealt with. When Wood appeared Wilde, knowing all he did, took him back to his empty house and had an affair with him.

It all came out later, of course—how Bosie wired Wood to find Wilde in the downstairs room of the Café Royal and Wood had no difficulty in doing that, how Wood went about nine o'clock and found Wilde alone. "Are you Alfred Wood?" Wilde asked, and after a drink took him round to the Florence in Rupert Street for dinner in a private room. The dinner was 'very nice, one of the best to be got' and they drank champagne. They they drove to Tite Street, where Wilde let himself into the empty house with a latchkey. They went up to a bedroom, where they drank hock and seltzer and Wood remained for 'about an hour'. He had no difficulty in explaining to the Court later what took place. He was told to be on the corner of Tite Street at eleven o'clock on a night of the following week. Wilde came up in a cab and took him to the house again, where they raided the larder for a cold chicken and afterwards went to the bedroom.

Wood still had the letters, but Wilde was apparently undisturbed by this. There were occasions, Mr. Hesketh Pearson points out, "when it is difficult to think of Wilde as a responsible person at all, when he seems more like a schoolboy than a rational adult". More so when later he said of the episode that he was forced to take everything Bosie had done on his shoulders and answer for it.

Wood then got in touch with a pretty pair of rogues named Robert Cliburn (*alias* Harris, Collins, Stephenson, Robertson and Carew) and William Allen (*alias* Pea). Allen was then twenty-five and Cliburn somewhat older. Cliburn had already served a sentence for blackmail, having been convicted at Lewes Assizes in December 1890 in the name of Robert Henry Harris. Both eventually, but not till two or three years after the Wilde case, were given further sentences, though Allen, who informed against Cliburn, got only eighteen months' hard labour to Cliburn's seven years' penal servitude.

Alfred Wood told them of the letters from Wilde which he had found in Bosie's pocket. He wanted to go to America and proposed to get the fare from Wilde on the strength of these letters. Cliburn and Allen read them, no doubt to give an expert valuation, and the two persuaded or bribed or intimidated Wood into giving them one. "This one's quite hot enough," Cliburn said, for it was the 'Hyacinthus' letter.

Wood made an appointment with Wilde at Taylor's rooms, where he was now staying. He produced several letters and Wilde supposed these were all he had. Wilde had the clearest recollection of the event:

When he entered the room he said: "I suppose you will think very badly of me." I replied, "I hear that you have letters of mine to Lord Alfred Douglas which you certainly ought to have given back." He handed me three or four letters, and said they had been stolen from him "the day before yesterday" by a man named Allen, and that he (Wood) had had to employ a detective to get them back. I read the letters, and said that I did not think them of any importance. He said, "I am very much afraid of staying in London, as this man and other men are threatening me. I want money to go away to America." I asked what better opening as a clerk he could have in America than in England, and he replied that he was anxious to get out of London in order to escape from the man who had taken the letters from him. He made a very strong appeal to me. He said that he could find nothing to do in London. I paid him £15. The letters remained in my hand all the time.

Though it was afterwards stated that the sum was £30—a reasonable assumption, since it was to pay a fare to New York—this would seem an otherwise accurate account. But Wilde also invited Wood to a farewell lunch in a private room at the Florence next day and at this lunch stated, according to Wood, that £30 was very little for a journey to America. He promised to send Wood £5 more, and did so by special messenger that afternoon. Wood sailed for America and no more was heard of him for a year.

II

In February Bosie joined Wilde at Babbacombe. He had been staying with his mother at Salisbury and Lionel Johnson had been his guest. He needed a tutor and Johnson suggested a friend who had been with him at Winchester and New College. This was Campbell Dodgson, afterwards Keeper of Prints and Drawings, British Museum.

In a letter to Johnson, Dodgson leaves a most happy account of his adventures as tutor to Bosie and guest of Wilde. Improbable things have happened to him, he says. He arrived at Salisbury expecting to find Bosie but no, he was 'gadding about' and did not appear till the evening in a 'flutter of telegrams'. Next morning Bosie read Plato with great zeal for an hour and a half, but at lunch quietly informed poor Mr. Dodgson that they were leaving for Torquay that afternoon to stay with Oscar Wilde.

Our departure was dramatic; Bosie was as usual in a whirl; he had no book, no money, no cigarettes and had omitted to send many telegrams of the first importance. Then, with a minimum of minutes in which to catch our train, we were required to overload a small pony chaise with a vast amount of trunks while I was charged with a fox terrier and a scarlet morocco dispatch-box, a gorgeous and beautiful gift from Oscar. After hurried farewells to the ladies, we started on a wild career, Bosie driving.

He finds life at Babbacombe Cliff indolent, though anything but dull.

Our life is lazy and luxurious; our moral principles are lax. We argue for hours in favour of different interpretations of Platonism. Oscar implores me, with outspread arms and tears in his eyes, to let my soul alone and cultivate my body for six weeks. Bosie is beautiful and fascinating, but quite wicked.

Dodgson left before the end of February, to receive a gay letter from Wilde, describing Babbacombe as a school with himself as headmaster and Bosie as 'the boys'.

As Constance Wilde had gone away with the children Wilde and Bosie were alone together for a time. Bosie found Wilde's conversation more urbane and sincere than in London. He heard, and remembered in after years Wilde's opinions of contemporary writers and said that Oscar could be trusted to pick out 'good new stuff' when he saw it for the first time. He could admire the work of men he disliked personally, like Henley, and declared that he would rather have written Swinburne's *Poems and Ballads: First Series* than anything that had appeared in his lifetime. His taste ranged widely enough to include Dickens, Meredith, Huysmans, Stevenson, Tennyson, Kipling and Anatole France.

Literature was a frequent subject of conversation between them but when they were alone, as they often were, they—in a nasty but useful modern phrase—talked sex, and Bosie wrote of this forty years later.

Even before I met Wilde I had persuaded myself that "sins of the flesh" were not wrong, and my opinion was of course vastly strengthened and confirmed by his brilliantly reasoned defence of them, which may be said almost to have been the gospel of his life. He went through life preaching the gospel which he puts into the mouth of Lord Henry Wotton in *Dorian Gray*. Wilde was, in fact, a most powerful and convincing heresiarch. He preached that it was the duty of every man to "live his own life to the utmost", to "be always seeking for new sensations", and to have what he called 'the courage' to commit "what are called sins". I am trying to be fair to Wilde and not to make him responsible for "corrupting" me more than he did. All the same, I must say that it strikes me now that the difference between us was this: that I was at that time a frank and natural pagan, and that he was a man who believed in sin and yet deliberately committed it, thereby obtaining a doubly perverse pleasure. I was a boy and he was a *blasé* and very intellectual and brilliant man who had immense experience of life. Inevitably I assimilated his views to a great extent.

This is obviously written with a determination to be fair-minded and is probably true enough so far as it goes, but it leaves an impression of solemnity as though the two argued soberly over the rights and wrongs of their behaviour. Nothing could have been less like them. Both loved laughter, and though sexual experience to Oscar may have been drama, like one of his own plays it was not without comedy, while to Bosie it was a delightful extravaganza.

12

There is a mystery here of time and place. It was certainly February 1893 which Dodgson spent with Wilde and Bosie at Babbacombe, yet during that Hilary term Bosie brought out three numbers of *The Spirit Lamp* February 3 and 17 and March 10, to one of which Wilde contributed *The House of Judgment* which he later reprinted in *Poems in Prose* in *The Fortnightly*.

In *Oscar Wilde and Myself* Bosie says, in answer to accusations that he was 'sent down', that in fact he was 'sent down' for a term because he was ploughed in an examination. "I soon set this right by spending three weeks with a crammer". It must be assumed, then, that this was the term for which he was rusticated and that he edited *The Spirit Lamp* from Babbacombe, or that someone in Oxford edited it for him, or with him by correspondence.

He was certainly still with Wilde at Babbacombe in early March, for it was then that they had their first violent quarrel. They had now been together for nearly two years and no previous disagreement is recorded, even by Wilde in *De Profundis*.

What caused this quarrel neither of them afterwards said; it may have started with something quite trivial. Bosie had a habit, distressing to Oscar, of not taking him quite as seriously as he would have liked either as a King of Life or a Lord of Language, in fact of mischievously pulling his leg at times. For instance, Bosie had given him for his last birthday a turquoise set in diamonds which he wore in his shirt front. Bosie considered it rather ostentatious and since there was talk at the time of that famous blue stone, the Hope diamond, called it the Hope-Not, a crack which infuriated Oscar not by its feebleness but for its implications. Later Bosie was to rouse the same sort of anger by quoting an hotel *concierge* who had spoken to Bosie of Oscar as '*votre papa*'. And Bosie could never take the melodramatic parts of *The Picture of Dorian Gray* with the solemnity their author required and razzed Oscar by speaking of people who left rooms "in a marked manner". Oscar, whose wit was impeccable and very rarely malicious but who stumbled into bathos or over-writing when he wished to be serious, was not very good at having his leg pulled, even by Bosie. Moreover he was sometimes scared by Bosie's recklessness or hurt by the thoughtlessness of the younger and more carefree man.

At all events they quarrelled and after what Oscar described in *De Profundis* as a revolting scene, Bosie left the house. On his way back to town, however, he repented and stopped at Bristol to send Oscar one of the many telegrams with which their friendship was punctuated. Oscar hurried to join him and the two went on to London, where they took rooms in the Savoy Hotel. Bosie stayed a few days, and during that time almost certainly brought a boy to their connecting rooms. He then went down to his mother's house in Salisbury. He wrote to Oscar from there and received this reply, an astonishing document in view of Bosie's known carelessness with letters:

Savoy Hotel, London.

Dearest of all Boys,

Your letter was delightful, red and yellow wine to me; but I am sad and out of sorts. Bosie, you must not make scenes with me. They kill me, they wreck the loveliness of life. I cannot see you, so Greek and gracious, distorted with passion. I cannot listen to your curved lips saying hideous things to me. I would sooner (be blackmailed by every renter in London) than have you bitter, unjust, hating. I must see you soon. You are the divine thing I want, the thing of grace and beauty; but I don't know how to do it. Shall I come to Salisbury? My bill here is £49 for a week. I have also got a new sitting-room over the Thames. Why are you not here, my dear, my wonderful boy? I fear I must leave; no money, no credit, and a heart of lead.

Your Own Oscar.

13

Wilde did not leave the Savoy, however, and in the next few weeks while he remained there was guilty of some of his maddest indiscretions, for Taylor now introduced the brothers Parker who were to be the most effective witnesses against him in his trials.

Tree was rehearsing *A Woman of No Importance* at the Haymarket Theatre. It was produced on April 19 and repeated the success of *Lady Windermere's Fan*. Bosie who had been with Wilde at Babbacombe while he was writing it returned to London for the first night. "You enjoyed the brilliant success of my first nights and the brilliant banquets that followed them" Wilde wrote accusingly in *De Profundis*, and of course it was true. At twenty-two, as Bosie was now, the occasions must have seemed magnificent and his pride in Oscar swelled.

But two nights later, on April 21st, Cliburn came to the stage door. He had sent a copy of the 'Hyacinthus' letter to Beerbohm Tree and now admitted that he had the original. Tree had simply handed the copy to Wilde saying that it was open to misconstruction. Cliburn, Wilde said, made no attempt to blackmail him then but a few days later Allen appeared at Tite Street and said that he had been offered £60 for the letter. For what took place there is only Wilde's account, for neither Cliburn nor Allen gave evidence at the trials. Wilde said he treated Allen with contempt, refused to take the letter and sent him away with half a sovereign. A few minutes later Cliburn arrived and handing him the letter said that as they could not rent him and he had been kind to Allen, he could have it.

It is noteworthy that in the meantime Pierre Louÿs had turned the letter into a sonnet in French which Bosie published in *The Spirit Lamp*. Of this Carson was to say in defending Queensberry—

The turning of one of Wilde's letters to Lord Alfred Douglas into a sonnet was a very thinly veiled attempt to get rid of the character of that letter. A more thinly veiled attempt to cover its real nature has never been made in a Court of Justice.

A Woman of No Importance was playing to packed houses and Oscar designed, and had made at Henry Lewis's, a pair of "dainty sleeve-links—four heart-shaped moon-stones of silver mist girdled by alternate ruby and diamond for their setting" as a "special little present" to Bosie to celebrate its success.

CHAPTER FOUR

The Friendship: Third Year. Summer 1893–Summer 1894

I

BOSIE in his last term at Oxford was a spectacular figure. Since he had met Wilde and acquired *The Spirit Lamp* he had tended to abandon his hearty sport-loving friends and become an 'aesthete', but he still rode often and spent time on the river and he still went—as he did to the end of his life—to every race-meeting within reach. His freakishly youthful appearance and good looks, his impertinent sense of fun, his editorship and his friendship with Wilde gave him a mixed but notable reputation. He was popular but elusive, belonging to no clique but known to most of them—he wanted the best of all worlds. With allowances from both his father and mother and any extra money he needed from his doting Montgomery grandparents he had more to spend than most of his contemporaries even at a time when undergraduates were expected to be spendthrift.

He was accustomed to the devotion not only of other young men but of his elders and could not grow out of it; in later life and even after all his misfortunes he could never be anything but surprised at the sometimes jealous dislike shown to him. A spoilt child and a fatally attractive young man, he came to expect affection and to be hurt when he did not get it. Yet he was in no ordinary sense either conceited or vain, in spite of the flattery he was receiving.

John Addington Symonds, for example, made no secret of his admiration. Then sixty-three, Symonds had spent his life tormented by the doubts and fears of a consumptive and homosexual. He had written voluminously of the Italian Renaissance and Michelangelo and his *A Study in Greek Ethics*, of which only a hundred copies were printed, was treasured by the intellectual queers of the time. Though he rarely came to England, living in Switzerland and Italy for the sake of his health, Symonds had been elected a Fellow of Magdalen and had achieved an exalted position as an historian.

He had never admired Wilde and when *The Picture of Dorian Gray* was published he said somewhat enigmatically "if the public will stand this, they will stand anything". After he had met Bosie and in a repressed or sublimated way fallen in love with him, he was frankly jealous of Oscar. He had recently sent Bosie a contribution for *The Spirit Lamp* called *Beethoven Concerto in E Dur* and just three weeks before his death in Rome he wrote the following letter, which incidentally seems to indicate that after leaving Wilde at the Savoy in March and visiting his mother in Salisbury, Bosie went abroad.

Lencaspide,
Paraceto.
March 30th, 1893.

My dear Bosie,

As you do not care to be called Lord Alfred, I shall call you by what you say your friends call you.

Your letter from that awful place (it must be awful, if it is like its name) reached me today. I am staying here with an old friend Sir James Lacaita. It is a wonderful place, and the country is Magna Graecia untouched by all the centuries. The ground is called after a cavalry troop of noble Palatine youths, raised during the war with Pyrrhus, who are called the Lencaspides or White Shields. But the weather is awfully cold, and we had what my daughter calls 'a colony of cold English' in the house. Lord and Lady Wantage, Sir Arthur Gordon and his daughter, a Lady Gordon (*née* Herchel), all Coutts Lindsays and Aberdeens. They are very nice, of course, but they won't catch on to the people and the customs of this wild country. Such shepherds! Like young fauns.

I daresay it is rather dreadful for you at Klein Schmalkaden. But you'll shake down. You can't be always pampered in the Savoy. It was very pleasant for Oscar pampering you, I doubt not. I wish you would come and see how I can make you comfortable, and feed your soul on honey of sweet-bitter thoughts—in Italy—in Switzerland—it is all the same.

I wonder what you thought about Kains Jackson. He rather took me aback when I first met him. But he is a very good fellow, I think, and has a lot of enthusiasm. I wish all people who feel as deeply as he does, and had his courage and his brains, could be also attractive by their manners and appearance. This would help much.

We are going into Taranto tomorrow to see a Passion procession go by torchlight through the town and along the seashore. I mean to spend the night there with my daughter and my faithful friend and servant Angelo. We shall then part from the 'Old Glory' and make our way by Metapaitum to Paestum, and then Naples.

If you write, send to the address below, and believe me affectionately yours,

J. A. Symonds,
560 Zattere,
Venezia.

PS. If I see any nice photograph upon my way, I will send it you.

This letter has chanced to survive, but it is not unreasonable to guess that there were a good many other infatuated letters from scholarly old gentlemen with one foot in what they supposed was ancient Greece and the other in the St. James's bar. The cult of 'beautiful youth' based on an acquaintance with classic literature and art and on feverish but repressed passions was popular just then.

Bosie published Symonds's contribution in the May number of *The Spirit Lamp* and in the same wrote an obituary notice of the historian. Bosie had now enlarged the paper and made it a monthly; this and the June number were the last he was to edit, and as it turned out the last to be issued. He also published the sonnet Pierre Louÿs had written in French from the Hyacinthus letter and a short story by Robert Ross called *How We lost the Book of Jasher*. It was in the last issue of all, published on June 6, that he published Wilde's *The Disciple* and Beerbohm's *The Incomparable Beauty of Modern Dress*. He did very little work and though he read for the Honours school in a desultory way he had not much hope of taking a degree.

2

Wilde whose fortunes had risen with the success of *A Woman of No Importance* was growing more expansive in his tastes and appearance.

With money pouring in from his comedies, with invitations pouring in from the aristocracy, with the social and artistic world of London infected by the dialogue in his plays, with his name in everyone's mouth, Wilde had achieved his heart's desire,

writes Hesketh Pearson, and further:

'Two years of this kind of life produced a personality very different from the one his friends had known in the 'eighties. Now he surrounded himself with a crowd of parasitic young disciples, who followed him about everywhere, singing his praises, repeating his sayings, eating and drinking at his expense, and receiving cheques, cigarette-cases, tie-pins and what-not in return for their flattery and admiration. He took offence at criticism, and even resented honest advice. He displayed an abnormal arrogance, and his attitude to everyone who did not praise him or please him was lordly and disdainful. This was not the mere egoism of the artist, which, as Charles Ricketts acutely observed "is less profound than the covert vanity of the plain man, who has done nothing and feels secure in his borrowed opinions". It was the megalomania of a dictator, closely resembling the absurd vanity of a spoilt child. As he became more prosperous, he became more preposterous, and the hatred of him which blazed forth in the spring of '95 and pursued him for the rest of his life was in some measure the product of the three years between *Lady Windermere's Fan* and *The Importance of Being Earnest*, when Society fawned on him, while secretly envious of his success, annoyed by his assumption and condescension, and enraged by his insolent independence of thought and behaviour. . . . With the mental derangement or delusion from which Wilde suffered, there went a corresponding hardening and defiance of manner, while his physical appearance deteriorated, becoming coarse and bloated. He looked apoplectic, the veins stood out on his forehead, he breathed heavily, he seemed to exude good living, he was fat and unctuous. Worse still, he was bored. In 1894, though no new play of his had been produced that year, his income was £8,000 (between thirty and forty thousand in 1945 purchasing power), and as he went from place to place he disengaged himself from his hansom cab with difficulty.

He was careless of what was said of him and that summer took young Charles Parker about in public, on one occasion sitting alone with him in a box at the London Pavilion, making no attempt to disguise his relationship with him or with Atkins and Mavor whom he saw frequently.

Wilde wrote to Bosie that he really must be painted and have an ivory statue executed. He commissioned William Rothenstein to do some drawings of Bosie and one of them, at least, exists. Another was called "The Editor of *The Spirit Lamp* at work" and shows Bosie in profile lying back in an armchair.

3

When at the end of term Bosie came down from Oxford without a degree, Wilde delightedly pointed out that this was like Swinburne who had determined to remain an undergraduate all his life. Queensberry, however, did not see it so kindly and there was a sharp exchange of letters between father and son.

Wilde had taken a house on the river at Goring and Bosie joined him there. After a time Constance Wilde went away with the children and the two friends were left together. They engaged as a servant a boy called Walter Grainger who had been employed in Bosie's rooms in Oxford, a "peculiarly plain boy, unfortunately extremely ugly" as Wilde was to say tactlessly in evidence later. They shared the expenses

of the establishment and lived modestly for some months, having on
the river a Canadian canoe "curved like a flower" as Oscar said.

Harris has a story of this period supposed to be recounted to him by
Wilde a few months later. It may be true, partly true, or an invention
of Harris's, but most probably the last because if Wilde had really
recalled it he would either have dismissed it in a couple of sentences or
made something more of it than Harris's pedestrian version. As it
stands it reeks of Harris but in case there is a little truth here it is:

The summer was very warm and beautiful as you know [Wilde is supposed to
have said]. And I was up at Goring with Bosie. Often in the middle of the day
we were too hot to go on the river. One afternoon it was sultry-close, and
Bosie proposed that I should turn the hose pipe on him. He went in and threw
his things off and so did I. A few minutes later I was seated in a chair with a
bath towel round me and Bosie was lying on the grass about ten yards away,
when the vicar came to pay us a call. The servant told him that we were in the
garden, and he came and found us there. Frank, you have no idea the sort of
face he pulled. What could I say? 'I am the vicar of the parish,' he bowed
pompously. "I'm delighted to see you," I said, getting up and draping myself
carefully, "you have come just in time to enjoy a perfectly Greek scene. I
regret that I am scarcely fit to receive you, and Bosie there"—and I pointed to
Bosie lying on the grass. The vicar turned his head and saw Bosie's white limbs;
the sight was too much for him; he got very red, gave a gasp and fled from
the place. I simply sat down in my chair and shrieked with laughter.

It was while he was staying at The Cottage, Goring-on-Thames,
that Wilde first corresponded with an interesting woman whom he
called The Sphinx. Ada Esther Leverson was then thirty-one years old.
Her husband, Ernest David Leverson, was the son of a diamond mer-
chant and a man of some fortune. They were cultured and charming
Jews. The Sphinx was one of the few of Oscar's friends who was not
jealous of his friendship with Bosie and the only communication known
to be signed jointly 'Oscar and Bosie' was addressed to her. When
others were raging at Wilde's return to Bosie at Naples he could write
to her—"Bosie and I often talk over your delightful sayings." She
wrote wittily, but not too wittily for *Punch*, and published several
novels.

Oscar and Bosie had quarrels, and one which happened at Goring
was bitterly recalled later by Wilde in *De Profundis*. Bosie went off one
day after a violent scene with Oscar. Some of his Oxford friends had
stayed the week-end and when they had left the two stood 'on the
level croquet ground with the pretty lawn all round' them and argued

it out. The old, the perennial accusations between two lovers of the same sex trying to lead something like a married life were spoken angrily, they were ruining one another's lives, to part was the only remedy. After lunch Bosie 'sullenly' went up to London, to come back three days later when there was the usual delightful reconciliation.

Yet Bosie always remembered that summer at Goring without bitterness and spoke of the house and garden, and of Oscar on the river, and of their indolence and laughter. He wrote there two light-hearted lyrics, *Night Coming into a Garden* and *Night Coming out of a Garden* which are among the best of his early verses. Ornate and dated as they are, they show that the young man who wrote them did not have to go to his companion for poetic talent.

But neither of the friends wrote much that summer. Oscar was supposed to be writing *An Ideal Husband* but he got no farther than an outline. Bosie during the previous term had started translating Wilde's *Salomé* back into the English in which Oscar had originally drafted it before he wrote it in French with the assistance of Pierre Louÿs and André Gide. Bosie now finished it but this was not a difficult task for the dialogue was of pseudo-biblical simplicity. Oscar had probably asked Bosie to do it as a compliment to him as a writer and in order to have their names together on the title-page.

But it caused one of their fiercest quarrels when they were back in town. Robert Ross had become very friendly with Aubrey Beardsley and his mother and persuaded Wilde to let Beardsley do the illustrations. Wilde and Beardsley disliked one another but Wilde gave Ross his way and Beardsley responded by including unkind caricatures of Wilde in the *Salome* drawings which Wilde described as "cruel and evil and so like dear Aubrey who has a face like a silver hatchet with grass-green hair". It needed all Ross's gifts of mediation and diplomacy to smooth this over but when Wilde told him that he did not like Bosie's translation he audaciously suggested that Beardsley should do one in its stead, which would be in every way better. It was probably the first time Ross had heard Wilde make the smallest criticism of anything Bosie did and he wanted to take advantage of it. Then and thereafter Ross was always at hand when there was the hope of a quarrel between Oscar and Bosie, always hoping it was final and always disappointed by the inevitable reconciliation. This time he nearly succeeded and if Beardsley's translation had satisfied Oscar he would have had at least a temporary triumph.

But it did not. What Oscar wanted, of course, was his own original

F

version and Beardsley's was farther from this than Bosie's. Finally, Oscar compromised, using his own version with some of Bosie's. Instead of the title-page planned was one bearing the words "Translated from the French of Oscar Wilde: Pictured by Aubrey Beardsley" while the Dedication would read: "To My Friend Lord Alfred Bruce Douglas the Translator of My Play."

Ross's part in this is shown by the letter Beardsley wrote to him about it:

I suppose you've heard all about the *Salome* Row. I can tell you I had a warm time of it between Lane and Oscar and Co. For one week the numbers of telegraph and messenger boys who came to the door was simply scandalous. I really don't quite know how the matter really stands now. Anyhow Bozie's name is not to turn up on the Title.

Later in the same letter he wrote:

By the way Bozie is going to Egypt in what capacity I don't quite gather; something diplomatic I fancy. Have you heard from either him or Oscar? Both of them are really very dreadful people.

After their stay at Goring that summer Bosie went to stay with his uncle George Finch at Burley-on-the-Hill while Oscar went off to Dinard for a fortnight on his own. Though the words he used to describe this in *De Profundis* were, like most of that book, theatrical and exaggerated one can see what he meant:

To be perfectly frank with you, I could not under any circumstances have let you be with me. We had been together nearly twelve weeks. I required rest and freedom from the terrible strain of your companionship. It was necessary for me to be a little by myself.

But on his way back from France he called at Guernsey and on his return wrote to Bosie who was in Devonshire for the marriage of his brother Percy. A reference to 'proofs' in his letter showed that he still affected to think of *Salome* as translated by Bosie.

At the same time Bosie was vigorously defending Oscar against criticism from an Oxford friend, Charles Kains Jackson who had contributed to *The Spirit Lamp* and was now editing a paper with a homosexual slant called *The Artist*.

"With regard to Oscar [he wrote] I agree with you that to a certain extent he overdoes the "jewelled style" but I think with all that he has a very dainty fancy, a great felicity of expression, a sense of the phrase, and an *enormous* dramatic instinct. (I am not thinking of his plays, but of Dorian Gray and the

House of Pomegranates.) Of course his best things he has never written and I very much fear never will; some of his unwritten stories are quite astoundingly good, and convincing. Also I think the psychology in anything he writes will always bear the closest inspection which is a thing that can be said of very few people. Everything he writes grows out of an abstract psychological idea; whereas I think in most people that is just reversed. I can't explain what I mean on paper. Only I think the general philistine attacks him quite enough without any assistance from the elect. Perhaps nobody knows as I do what he has done for the "new culture", the people he has pulled out of the fire and "seen through" things not only with money, but by sticking to them when other people wouldn't speak to them. He is the most chivalrous friend in the world, he is the only man I know who would have the courage to put his arm on the shoulder of an ex-convict and walk down Piccadilly with him, and combine with that the wit and personality to carry it off so well that nobody would mind. I must be boring you horribly, but I feel very strongly on the subject.

4

Taylor, meanwhile, was being watched by the police. That August a plain-clothes man went to the house in Little College Street and on the pretext of being a friend of Taylor's, examined his rooms. Becoming aware of this, Taylor moved out during the following week-end without telling his landlady where he was going. He found rooms in Chelsea, at 3 Chapel Street and Charles Parker lodged at 50 Park Walk nearby.

It may have been this which decided Wilde to take Chambers of his own instead of staying with young men at the Albermarle Hotel. In fact the proprietor of this, a Swiss called Aloys Vogel, deposed later that many young men, who were at first thought to be from the theatre, called on Wilde and his suspicions were aroused.

Wilde found rooms—a bedroom and sitting room—on the ground floor at 10-11 St. James Place, which appears to have been a block of service flats, and occupied them till the following March. He took this 'set of chambers' he said in *De Profundis* "purely in order to work undisturbed". The statement does not bear scrutiny and the adverb was particularly ill-chosen as evidence in Court later showed, for Charles Parker, Sidney Mavor, a recent discovery of Taylor's named Ernest Scarfe, Fred Atkins, an 'actor' introduced by Atkins named Harry Barford, and Edward Shelley all visited him there on numerous occasions, sometimes staying the night.

Bosie came daily, and their programme was afterwards described by Oscar:

I arrived at St. James's Place every morning at 11.30 in order to have the opportunity of thinking and writing without the interruption inseparable from my own household, quiet and peaceful as that household was. But the attempt was vain. At 12 o'clock you drove up and stayed smoking cigarettes and chattering till 1.30, when I had to take you out to luncheon at the Café Royal or the Berkeley. Luncheon with its liqueurs lasted usually till 3.30. For an hour you retired to White's. At tea-time you appeared again and stayed till it was time to dress for dinner. You dined with me either at the Savoy or at Tite Street. We did not separate as a rule till after midnight, as supper at Willis's had to wind up the entrancing day. That was my life for those three months, every single day, except during the four days when you went abroad.

Though this was written with rancour in *De Profundis* in order to show how Bosie had wasted Oscar's time, the facts are probably accurate enough. To say 'I had to take you to luncheon' was, of course, a piece of cattiness on a par with much else in *De Profundis* for Wilde would have been furious if Bosie had not called every morning and could not at this time conceive of a day without a large and expensive lunch to break the hours of daylight. He was working spasmodically to finish *An Ideal Husband* and he had his own appointments with Taylor and his friends, but generally he and Bosie wasted the days of that autumn together.

What Bosie's appointments were will never be known for all evidence against him was carefully suppressed by Queensberry's solicitors in Court and Bosie himself made no more than a general confession in his *Autobiography*. But something happened that autumn to which there are two mysterious references in *De Profundis*. There is no other information and both these references are cryptic.

The first is partly in the passage just quoted—". . . every single day, except during the four days you went abroad." Wilde continues, "I then, of course, had to go over to Calais to fetch you back." The second comes later when Wilde is describing a letter he claimed to have written to Bosie's mother. Speaking of this time, the autumn of 1893, he says:

The reason of your going to Belgium you had placed to the fault of your companion in that journey, and your mother reproached me with having introduced you to him. I replaced the fault on the right shoulders, on yours."

Belgium or Calais? Or Belgium and down to Calais to await Oscar? Why did Oscar have to go to Calais to fetch Bosie back? Who was the 'companion'? Why did Lady Queensberry have to be informed? Whatever it was it did not reach the ears of Queensberry who would have made capital of it in his letters, as he did of the Oxford episode.

It may have been the cause of another shattering quarrel the two friends had that autumn. Once again this followed Bosie's appearance with friends and one cannot help wondering whether Oscar was not jealous of Bosie's contemporaries who treated Oscar as an older man. The scene was 'more than usually revolting'. This time it was Oscar who left in indignation, and while 'whirling up to Paris' thought

into what an impossible, terrible, utterly wrong state my life had got when I, a man of world-wide reputation, was actually forced to run away from England in order to try to get rid of a friendship that was entirely destructive of everything fine in me either from the intellectual or ethical point of view: the person from whom I was flying being no terrible creature sprung from sewer or mire into modern life with whom I had entangled my days, but you yourself, a young man of my own social rank and position, who had been at my own College at Oxford and was an incessant guest at my house.

Meanwhile Lady Queensberry, determined to separate her son from Wilde, had called on the assistance of her parents and produced the only kind of scheme which might have a chance of success, a scheme which would appeal to Bosie himself. One of her most intimate friends from childhood had been Ethel Errington, who was married to Sir Evelyn Baring 'Consul-General and Diplomatic Agent' in Egypt who had just been given a barony and become Lord Cromer (afterwards first Earl of Cromer). Lady Cromer, appealed to by Lady Queensberry, at once invited Bosie to come and stay at the Agency in Cairo for some months with the idea that after this private experience of the diplomatic service, he might be found an attaché's post somewhere else. Bosie welcomed the scheme, as his mother hoped he would, and it was arranged that he should leave for Cairo in December.

But Lady Queensberry was still a little apprehensive of a possible move by Wilde and wrote to him one of her most kind and tactful letters begging him not to 'meet Bosie abroad', by which she meant not to follow him to Cairo. She justified her letter by explaining that the friendship of such a distinguished man as Wilde was bad for Bosie's vanity, and association with Wilde and his friends had so educated the artistic side of Bosie's nature that he spoke of his elder brother as a philistine.

Wilde, with the kind of thick skin his vanity gave him, again read this as criticism of Bosie and percipient praise of himself and said he agreed with every word of it, adding grandly that he had not the slightest intention of meeting Bosie abroad.

During Bosie's last weeks in England the two friends came as near to parting as they ever did during their hectic friendship, not because of the violent quarrels of earlier in the year but because there was something like coldness, even a suggestion of boredom between them. That Wilde was occupied with his young roughs may be seen from this evidence at his trial:

Thomas Price, a waiter at a private hotel at 10 St. James's Place, said the prisoner Wilde had rooms there from October, 1893, to April, 1894. The rooms were on the ground floor, and consisted of a bedroom and a sitting-room comunicating. He recognized the prisoner Taylor, and he had seen him at St. James's Place on one occasion. Charles Parker came there five or six times. He used to ask for Mr. Wilde, and was shown into Mr. Wilde's rooms. He lunched there once. Witness knew Atkins by sight. He had called there twice. Scarfe called five or six times, and Barford about the same number of times. Mr. Wilde had a latchkey, but never slept there more than a dozen times.

It is not only young men of Taylor's circle he asked to his rooms in St. James's Place, but male writers of fan letters who promised to be interesting. "Will you come and see me? Your handwriting fascinates me, your praise charms me," he wrote to one, and to another:

Write to me about yourself; tell me your life and loves, and all that keeps you wondering. Who are you? (What a difficult question for any one of us to answer!) I, at any rate am your friend.

Bosie, excited by the prospect of going to Egypt, was a less regular caller than before, having preparations to make for his journey and his stay. There was, he said in his *Autobiography*, a 'slight coolness' between them perhaps because they both felt a little guilt for the year they had frittered away so pleasantly. Wilde had completed no play since the *Salome* débâcle and had published nothing; Bosie had come down from Oxford without a degree. Wilde had neglected his wife and Bosie had spent very little time with his mother. They had both lived beyond their means, Wilde ostentatiously and consciously, Bosie as a matter of course. In moments of recrimination, they blamed one another but at more honest and less emotional times each blamed himself. It was, as it became clear in the following years, a mere pause, a breathing-space in their extraordinary relationship which had not yet reached its culmination.

5

It speaks much for Bosie's charm as a guest that the Cromers kept him
in Cairo for three months and afterwards helped him to be appointed
an attaché in Constantinople. Lord Cromer had his difficulties at this
time, as he had throughout his long period of office in Egypt, and
Bosie, as a young irresponsible and pleasure-loving guest in the
Agency must have been something of an embarrassment, though he
said afterwards that he spent most of his time in the Chancery in
Cairo and was good friends with the secretaries and attachés. He
thoroughly enjoyed himself and looked back on his stay as 'a most
lively and cheerful time'. Cairo was a popular, even a smart, winter
resort for wealthy English visitors, with a British army of occupation—
something between Monte Carlo and Simla, with all the archaelogical
glories of Egypt as a side-show. This was novel and pleasing to Bosie
though he regarded the Egyptian monuments as ugly and unattractive.

Reggie Turner, as the guest of his rich half-brother Frank Lawson,
was living on a luxurious *dahabeeyah*. The very word, which in Arabic
means a 'gilded barge', must have appealed to a reader of *Antony and
Cleopatra* and Bosie frequently stayed on the boat. Reggie Turner
composed the only poem of his life to flatter his guest and it became a
joke between them—

> More fair than any flower is thy face
> Thy limbs from all comparison are free.

Then E. F. Benson and Robert Hichens, both intelligent young
queers, turned up in Luxor where Bosie was staying in a hotel, and
they, with Reggie and Bosie, made a vivacious and happy quartette.
Benson (who must have been at Marlborough with Taylor, incidentally) was three years older than Bosie and had just had a success with
his novel *Dodo*, a Nancy Mitford effort of the time. He was the third
son of the Archbishop of Canterbury and had come over from
Athens (where he was working for the British Archaelogical Society)
in search of more frivolous pleasures than digging. Robert Smythe
Hichens was the eldest of the four, being twenty-nine. He had published nothing of consequence but was perhaps the most ambitious as
his conduct showed. Although he had never met Oscar he had long
thought of writing a satirical novel about Aestheticism and Wilde, and
knowing Bosie's place in the *galère* he pumped him cleverly till he had
most of the material he wanted for his novel. Going back to London
with a letter of introduction from Bosie he met Wilde and completed

the picture on which he wrote *The Green Carnation*, published later in the year. It did considerable harm to both Wilde and Bosie and was, said Bosie in his *Autobiography* a 'piece of perfidy' for which he refrained from reproaching Hichens since he had publicly confessed his contrition.

Robert Hichens in his book *Yesterday* leaves his own account of the meeting and its sequel. He was at a race meeting in Cairo.

I was in the midst of the crowd near the stand when I heard someone say, "Here comes Cromer!" I pushed my way a little nearer to a place where I noticed that all heads were turning, and saw an open carriage drawn by a pair of fine horses drive slowly by. In it were two people. One was the great man wearing a white top-hat. By his side, on the left of the carriage, sat a young man, indeed almost a boy, fair, aristocratic, even poetic-looking I thought. I did not know who he was and no one told me. Later I learned that he was the Marquis of Queensberry's son, Lord Alfred Douglas, and that he was paying a visit to Lord and Lady Cromer.

He describes Bosie and Benson together—"the wit of the one seeming to call out and polish the wit of the other." Later in London when he had met Wilde and Beerbohm he wrote his skit which was read for libel by Sir George Lewis before Heinemann's would publish it, Hichens remaining anonymous.

On the day of publication there was an article about it in the *Daily Telegraph*, written, I believe, by Mr. Beatty Kingston, and the sales began at once. The journalists tried to find out who was the author and many names were put forward; among them the names of Oscar Wilde himself; of Marie Corelli—because she had written anonymously *The Silver Domino*; of Mr. Alfred Austin, afterwards the poet laureate; and of various others. Then an amusing thing happened. I received one morning, handed in together, two telegrams. One was signed "Oscar", the other was from Lord Alfred Douglas. I can't now remember the exact wording of them. But Oscar Wilde's told me that "all is discovered" and suggested instant flight on my part to escape his vengeance. And Lord Alfred's told me that I was unmasked and had better go into hiding. Both telegrams were burlesque and merely good jokes.

But in Egypt Hichens was only planning *The Green Carnation* and immensely enjoying himself with Bosie, Benson and Turner.

The four of them, Reggie, Bosie, Freddy and Bob, as they had become in conversation, decided to go up the Nile in a Post Boat, and the expedition was a huge success.

Bosie met Kitchener in Cairo and Queensberry and Colson made a senseless and irresponsible invention about this. It is now, I believe, an accepted fact that Kitchener was homosexual and the evidence for it, which is considerable, was known to Colson when he collaborated with Queensberry in the book *Oscar Wilde and the Black Douglas*. "He had, he told me, a romantic meeting with Lord Kitchener" must be taken, in the circumstances, to mean that Bosie actually boasted to one of the two authors, at a time when he was very far from boasting of any such thing, that he had made a conquest of the great soldier. In his *Autobiography* Bosie says that he had 'a slight personal acquaintance' (with Kitchener):

I had met him in Egypt when I was a boy staying with the Cromers, and again at lunch at Lady Henry Gordon-Lennox's, at Prince's Gate, when he had paid a lot of attention to me, and after lunch asked me to walk with him across the Park.

There is no reason to imagine anything more than this, and the phrase "he told me" is palpably untrue.

6

While he was in Egypt Bosie wrote three letters to his mother, two of which are immensely revealing of his character at the time, his attitude to Wilde and his mother and by implication of his mother's attitude to his friendship with Wilde, if not of her knowledge of its nature.

> British Agency
> Cairo.
> Sunday, Dec: 10th 1893.

My darling Damus,

I am enjoying this place very much. Yesterday I went over the bazaars, and today I am going to ride over to the pyramids with a chap called Rumbold who is one of the attachés, a very nice fellow. All the attachés are very nice. Today is the Khedive's birthday, and there is a great display of flags. I went to the opera the first night I was here, it is a beautiful house, and looks very smart with all the people, and the singers are really rather good, though they perform indifferent music.

What I really am writing about is the subject of our conversation on the night before I started. If I looked upon you as an ordinary mother or an ordinary woman, I should do what sons generally do when they disagree with their mothers on a vital point, shrug my shoulders, drop the subject and say to myself "what can one expect, they are all the same, unreasoning, illogical, it is no use talking". It is just because I do *not* think this about you, and because I know you to be different from ordinary women and vastly superior to them, and with little or none of the proverbial and undoubted lack of reasoning power which distinguishes the sex, that I write and reopen a subject on which perhaps you think everything has been said that can be said. And in doing this I have two objects in view, and I cannot say which is the most important, one is to defend my friend and to try and get you to treat him and think of him with ordinary fair play and common justice, the second is to try and remove *you* from a position which is unworthy of you, to get you to do yourself justice, in fact to show that you *are* different from other women.

Now in the first place you said to me the other night during the course of our conversation that even I had never tried to make you think that Oscar Wilde was a *good* man. In answer to that I say "have I ever tried to make you think that any of my friends were good, have I not all my life been consistent in my desire to protest against the dividing of people into good and bad?" Oscar Wilde says in his preface to Dorian Gray "There is no such thing as a moral or immoral book, a book is well written or badly written, that is all." Now transpose that principle a little and it is equally true of men, and it is my way of looking at men. "There is no such thing as a moral or immoral man, a man is well written or badly written, that is all." That is to say, either he has character or not, either he has style, distinction, individuality, possibilities, or he is lacking in these things either entirely or partly. I have never judged anyone by whether he was good or not, goodness means nothing or everything, it is absolutely vague; goodness in a man may be the result and companion of intellect, genius distinction and a thousand charming things, on the other hand it may be the direct result of crass stupidity and littleness of mind. Any man who makes it his business to study the souls of men will tell you the same thing. You know perfectly well yourself, that you do not judge people by whether they are good or bad, if you are frank you must admit that that is not your standard. Do not therefore expect me to do more than you do yourself or more than anybody does, except perhaps a dissenting minister. As you know perfectly well I admire good men just as much as you do yourself sometimes, I see that a good man may be a splendid creature, I can understand him, I can follow the course of the process of reasoning which leads him to be a good man, and I can sympathise with him, and can feel contempt for the idiot who thinks that a good man is necessarily a fool or a visionary.

Here I should like by the way to point out to you a curious thing. It was not *you* that taught me to see that a good man can be splendid, it was not the the pastors and masters of my youth, it was not Francis with his dissertations on Sociology, no it was simply Oscar Wilde who taught it me and no one else. And again who was it who taught me to believe if not absolutely in a God and the Christian religion, at least in the possibility of them, who taught me that it was ignorant and vulgar to scoff at mysteries which one did not understand, who animated for me the dry bones of the ugly dull religion I was brought up in, the religion which I had by the time I was eighteen flung aside with contempt and derision? Not you, not the good people who surrounded me, not even the good Ottley at Oxford for whom I had such a strong admiration, no, again simply Oscar Wilde. This is the man who according to you has ruined my soul. Why, I tell you I don't believe I had a soul before I met him. He has taught me everything that I know that is worth knowing, he has taught me to judge of things by their essential points, to know what is fine from what is low and vulgar, he has taught me to keep a clear head in my judgment of things, and not to be led away by ethical sympathies in matters of art, it is owing to him that I am able to admire Newman on the one hand, Milton on the other. The high priest of mystery and the propagandist of low church puritanism. These are the big things, now look at the smaller points. Why have I given up gambling and betting and going to race-meetings? Simply because Oscar Wilde told me that it was unworthy of me, that it was too ordinary, too silly. What have you got to accuse him of? You know perfectly well that he did not *teach* me to be extravagant.

Then to return to the subject of the goodness, on which you lay so much stress. When you wrote that letter to Fleming in which the unfortunate expression occurred that Oscar Wilde saw, I remember being both astonished, upset and very angry. I had no idea up till then of your feelings about him, or at least I did not think them really serious. I remember I sat down and wrote you an awful letter, full of bitter words, a letter that must have pained you very much. I refused to shew it to Oscar Wilde, for a long time, but finally he got it, read it and tore it up at once, he begged me not to write at all, I remember what he said exactly it was this "After all Bosie nobody has a right to be unkind to his mother". He was naturally very much hurt by what you had said, he feels now that you have been unjust, unkind and even uncivil to him. But I can hardly help thinking of what *you* said the other night about *him*, that you would almost like to "murder" him, I think on the whole you cannot deny that he has the best of it, even from the "good" point of view.

And now let me ask you, what you propose to give me in exchange for this man, where am I to go for my quickening? Who is going to "feed my soul with honey of sweet bitter thought"? Who is going to make me happy when I am sad depressed and ill at ease? Who is going to transport me out of this tedious world into a fairyland of fancy, conceit, paradox and beauty by the power of a golden speech? (A thing that you have never heard, for want of sympathy in a listener completely mars his conversation.) What do you propose to give me instead? That is what I ask. I am spoilt for society, I am a bohemian by nature, and must remain one. Why can't you leave me alone, why can't you help me to do what I must do? Be nice to my friend, be just and kind. Your present attitude towards him is so banal, so illogical, so shallow. Do try and look at the thing from another point of view. Remember for instance, that Oscar Wilde's mother exists as well as mine, that she loves her son just as much as you do yours, and that perhaps she has something to say on the subject which might put the thing in a different light. Believe me there is nothing so ludicrous, touching as it might be, as the one sided point of view of a mother, its always *her* son who is being led astray, other people are all brutes and blackguards. There is one more thing that I must say something about, that is that you cannot do anything against the power of my affection for Oscar Wilde and of his for me. I am passionately fond of him, and he of me. "There never was a better bargain driven" There is nothing I would not do for him, and if he dies before I do I shall not care to live any longer. The thought of such a thing makes everything black before my eyes. Surely there is nothing but what is fine and beautiful in such a love as that of two people for one another, the love of the disciple and the philosopher. I think when Oscar's life comes to be written, as the life of a man of genius and a man who has stamped his age, it will be remembered and written about as one of the most beautiful things in the world, as beautiful as the love of Shakespeare and the unknown Mr. W. H. or that of Plato and Socrates, and far more beautiful than the love of Alcibiades for Socrates.

There is no good in saying any more, except that while I perhaps have no right to say that Oscar Wilde is a good man, neither you nor anyone else has the right to say that he is a bad man. A really bad man I might admire intellectually but I could never love, and what is still more he could never love anyone faithfully, loyally, devotedly, unselfishly and purely as Oscar loves me.

I cannot say any more now, so goodby. Please try and like my friend who is so dear to me

With heaps of love
Ever your very loving son

Bosie

PS. This letter has cost me much time and trouble to write, please don't destroy it hastily.

British Agency
Cairo
Jan 6, 1894

Darling Damus,

I have just got your letter in answer to mine. I see at once that it is useless to try and bring you to look at the thing in a different light, you seem to me to have got a long way on the wings of your own imagination from the Truth.

However there are one or two points that I must say something about. You say "if Mr. W. has acted as I am convinced he has the part of a Lord H to you I could never feel differently towards him than I do, as the murderer of your soul". . . . My answer to that is that as for what OW has done for me, I have already told it you at considerable length in my last letter and if you call that acting the part of a Lord H then I suppose he *has* acted that part. I think however if you come to look into your own analogy you will find that it breaks down on very important and very essential points. Lord Henry's teaching to Dorian Gray is that he is to do everything he can, and realise and give form to every passion and every idea that can get into his head, to make life his art. He says to him in one place "I am so glad you haven't done anything else, but live, I am so glad you have never written a book or made a song, you have made life your art" or words to that effect. Lord H's intention was to make Dorian Gray a sort of experiment in a philosophy which was to consist in a triumph of the body over the soul; to bring this about he encouraged him to sink his intellect to the position of a pander to his vices, he tells him to *do everything*; he is not to write a book, he is to do nothing but live, live, live for pleasure, while Lord H looks on with a morbid and curious interest in the psychological study thus presented. I need hardly remind you of what happens, of the terrible ghastly moral that is to be found in the book. Now if you are so extraordinarily wrong-headed, so deliberately blind, and so monstrously unjust, as to seriously draw an analogy between the attitude of OW to me, and Lord H to Dorian Gray? I feel that anything I can say is utterly useless. There is not *one single* point of resemblance between the two. The whole thing exists entirely in your own imagination, and to me who knows the truth it is hardly possible to conceive how you can have got yourself in to such a state of mind. Only to a very superficial and shallow student of psychology is there any resemblance even between Lord H and OW, and the resemblance is so entirely on the surface and so obviously forced by the author that I wonder that it should deceive you, even with your studied and determined refusal to understand the real character of OW. The resemblance simply is that Lord H during the course of the book talks "Oscarisms", that is to say paradoxes full of humour and subtlety and often with a strong vein of real truth and real thought in them. There the resemblance begins and ends. There is not one real point in common after that between Lord Henry with his bitter cynicism, his cruelty, his heartlessness and his selfishness, and Oscar Wilde with his sunny nature, his buoyant "joie de vivre", his quick and splendid sense of humour, and his loyal kind and forgiving nature which make him altogether more like a grown up boy than the sort of cynical subtle and morbid creature which you want to make him out. Perhaps the truest and simplest way of putting it, is to say that Lord Henry is an artificial waxwork figure of what Oscar might be, without his enthusiasm, his humanness, his sympathy and his kind sweet nature.

The fact is that unless you can understand that Oscar is an Irishman through and through, you will never get an idea of what his real nature is. In many ways he is as simple and innocent as a child. He wouldn't hurt or wound any living creature, and your conception of him is a ridiculous and nonsensical unreality, which if you wish me to be frank, I should say springs from a certain morbidity of mind, which really exists in you though you are quite far from suspecting it. The fact is that no such person as Lord Henry Wotton ever existed. The whole book of Dorian Gray is a book of exaggerated types, it is all supernatural and unreal. Nobody wants to murder anyone else's soul, the whole idea and your whole attitude is really morbid and hysterical, you have created for yourself this imaginary tragedy that has no real existence at all. I verily believe that if Oscar had not written, or you had never read Dorian Gray, these ideas would never have occurred to you at all. It appears to me that the enormous power of the sort of uncanny half real half fantastic atmosphere of the book has got hold of your soul and made it a little mad.

Oscar has no desire to ruin my soul in order that he may have the pleasure of getting a morbid satisfaction from the contemplation of its ruin, he is merely a very brilliant and very irresponsible and very impulsive creature who is very fond of me, and who enjoys life thoroughly, and who wishes to be as happy as he can under the circumstances in which he finds himself placed. I am extraordinarily fond of him, and he is extraordinarily fond of me, and he wishes me to be successful and happy. He always encourages me as much as he possibly can to work and to do something, and so far from wishing to ruin my soul or ruin anything else, he doesn't think of such nonsense at all, and he and I can afford to laugh at all this hysterical twaddle and at the same time to regret that it is able to be a great annoyance a great hindrance and a great discomfort.

You talk very glibly about the murder and the ruin of my soul, but you must really excuse me if I venture to think that my soul so far from being murdered or ruined, is in a very healthy and very prosperous condition, and that I would not change it for anyone else's for anything in the world.

As for what you say about what you call "eccentricities and peculiar views of morality", I am so far from deceiving myself by thinking that they are a special characteristic of my own, that I know them to be shared and to have been shared by nearly all the great minds for whom I have special respect both in ancient and modern times, and I should also like to tell you once for all, that I did *not* imbibe those ideas from Oscar Wilde and that he did *not* put them into my head and encourage them. I had formed them in my own mind and I was quite certain of their truth *two years* before I had ever seen him or even heard of him. When I first met him, it was the finding someone with a really great mind and genius who agreed with me, that made me like him, and since then, although you will probably not believe it, it is nevertheless a fact that I have had more influence on him than he has had on me.

Now do try and get out of your head this absurd idea about the ruin of my soul and all that, and try and realise that both Oscar and myself are merely ordinary people who are very fond of one another and very anxious to live peacefully joyously and happily, and without scenes and tragedies and reproaches and all that sort of thing. I am so sick and tired of this sort of perpetual war that seems to go on whether I like it or not. Do let us for a change be a little more commonplace and a little less emotional. I am aware that in that respect I am as much to blame as anyone, I have in my blood the love of a scene and a tragedy, but I am convinced it is a mistake, and certainly in our family of all families somebody ought to make a determined stand against it. There is such a tendency to lift everything up on to the stilts of tragedy, we are such a theatrical family. Let us cease from this, and become a little bourgeois. I assure you my despatch box is very amusing reading. I get letters from Francis begging me to think of old times, letters from Percy in which he declares his willingness to lay down his life for me, letters from my father in which he talks about his miserable and lonely life, and yet all these three people are perfectly happy and contented and never lose their appetites. I am just as bad myself, there are times when my heart aches and my eyes fill with tears at the sense of the pitiableness of my position and the darkness of my future, and it is all really the result of a morbid imagination. I am perfectly happy really, and nobody enjoys life more thoroughly than I do. For you of course there is every possible excuse, for the rest of us there is absolutely none. Now I really must stop. Be assured of my love and admiration for you darling little Damus, and don't bother yourself too much about things.

Always etc.

7

Perhaps feeling it was expected of him, Bosie wrote a sonnet to the Sphinx and though it is a conventional piece it shows a more confident mastery of the form. He was at last beginning to grow up.

Whatever Bosie's mother may have thought about his letters, she was delighted with the success of her scheme. She went further and with the help of her father and Lord Cromer obtained for Bosie a post as honorary attaché to the Ambassador in Constantinople, at that time Lord Currie.

Lord Cromer gave Bosie the news but did not make it clear that he was expected to take up his appointment at once. Bosie was grateful but not impatient to reach Constantinople and live under discipline and when E. F. Benson, who had to return to his archaeological work in Athens, suggested that Bosie should come and stay with him for a week or two he accepted delightedly. Why not? It was April and he had never seen the Acropolis. Lord Currie could surely wait.

Benson had rooms in Athens and the young man who ended his life in Henry James's house in Rye, of which town he became Mayor, writing a series of chi-chi novels about Lucia and Miss Mapp, was an excellent host and cicerone.

Then—why not a week or two more? Why not telegraph to Oscar to meet him in Paris so that they could spend a few days together before Bosie took up his arduous work in Constantinople? He had already told Lord Cromer that he thought of running up to London, or at any rate Paris, before he reported for duty and Cromer had raised no objection. The wire was sent to Oscar and Bosie received

an eager reply. This became in poor Wilde's disordered recollections
in Reading Gaol a whole series of 'passionate telegrams' with which
Bosie was supposed to have pleaded for a reunion. To *De Profundis*,
too, we owe an account of the meeting in Paris which shows that
Wilde's sense of humour failed him in prison, for before or after
serving his sentence he would have been the first to find it comic.

When I arrived in Paris, your tears breaking out again and again all through
the evening, and falling over your cheeks like rain as we sat at dinner first at
Voisin's, at supper at Paillard's afterwards: the unfeigned joy you evinced at
seeing me, holding my hand whenever you could as though you were a gentle
and penitent child: your contrition, so simple and sincere at the moment:
made me consent to renew our friendship. Two days after we had returned to
London, your father saw you having luncheon with me at the Café Royal,
joined my table, drank of my wine, and that afternoon, through a letter
addressed to you, began his first attack on me.

Tears 'like rain' at Voisin's and Paillard's and Queensberry drinking
of his wine—how could Wilde, even under such a strain, have written
like this?

The Paris meeting was a great success so far as Oscar and Bosie were
concerned but unfortunately it was reported to Lord Currie who
immediately wrote to Bosie's mother expressing his indignation and
refusing in any circumstances to have Bosie as an honorary attaché.
At least, that is what must obviously have happened though Bosie
always believed that Lord Currie's anger was 'middle-class fussiness'
and caused only by Bosie's delay in taking up the appointment. He
devotes two pages of his *Autobiography* to justifying himself in this
long-forgotten matter and '*still* does not understand why Lord Currie
should have been angry'. He seems to have been unwilling to face the
fact, obvious enough now, that his friendship with Wilde had scotched
a promising career.

8

Queensberry was about to be divorced again. In 1893 he had married
a Miss Ethel Weedon who left him after a fortnight and would obtain
a decree of nullity in October of this year (1894).

Once again he chanced to enter the Café Royal when Oscar and
Bosie were lunching there and once again was persuaded to join them,
but the occasion was unlike that of two years previously. Queensberry
watched the two narrowly while he 'drank of' Oscar's wine, and they

From the original pastel by William Rothenstein, 1893.

Bosie, by A. de Belleroche.

must have been in a defiant, ostentatious or perhaps merely flippant mood, for Queensberry, primed by gossip from fellow clubmen, was horrified. "With my own eyes", he wrote to Bosie of this occasion, "I saw you both in the most loathsome and disgusting relationship as expressed by your manner and expression." He stumped away and very soon began writing savage letters. After an exchange or two he wrote from Carter's Hotel in Albemarle Street on Sunday, April 1st 1894

Alfred,

It is extremely painful for me to have to write to you in the strain I must; but please understand that I decline to receive any answers from you in writing in return. After your recent hysterical impertinent ones I refuse to be annoyed with such, and I decline to read any more letters. If you have anything to say, do come here and say it in person. Firstly, am I to understand that, having left Oxford as you did, with discredit to yourself, the reason of which were fully explained to me by your tutor, you now intend to loaf and loll about and do nothing? All the time you were wasting at Oxford I was put off with an assurance that you were eventually to go into the Civil Service or to the Foreign Office, and then I was put off with an assurance that you were going to the Bar. It appears to me that you intend to do nothing. I utterly decline, however, to just supply you with sufficient funds to enable you to loaf about. You are preparing a wretched future for yourself, and it would be most cruel and wrong for me to encourage you in this. Secondly, I come to the more painful part of this letter—your intimacy with this man Wilde. It must either cease or I will disown you and stop all money supplies. I am not going to try and analyse this intimacy, and I make no charge; but to my mind to pose as a thing is as bad as to be it. With my own eyes I saw you both in the most loathsome and disgusting relationship as expressed by your manner and expression. Never in my experience have I seen such a sight as that in your horrible features. No wonder people are talking as they are. Also I now hear on good authority, but this may be false, that his wife is petitioning to divorce him for sodomy and other crimes. Is this true or do you not know of it? If I thought the actual thing was true, and it became public property, I should be quite justified in shooting him at sight. These Christian English cowards and men, as they call themselves, want waking up.

Your disgusted so-called father,

Queensberry.

To this Bosie replied with a telegram which became mildly famous at the time of the trials but seems sadly facetious today. It would be interesting to know whether Wilde was amused by it or even knew that it was to be sent for somehow it suggests a silly joke shared between them. "What a funny little man you are," wired Bosie.

Queensberry rose to this:

You impertinent young jackanapes, [he wrote by return]. I request that you will not send such messages to me by telegraph. If you send me any more such telegrams, or come with any impertinence, I will give you the thrashing you deserve. Your only excuse is that you must be crazy. I hear from a man at Oxford that you were thought crazy there, and that accounts for a good deal that has happened. If I catch you again with that man I will make a public scandal in a way you little dream of; it is already a suppressed one. I prefer an open one, and at any rate I shall not be blamed for allowing such a state of things to go on. Unless this acquaintance ceases I shall carry out my threat and stop all supplies, and if you are not going to make any attempt to do something I shall certainly cut you down to a mere pittance, so you know what to expect.

In most of Queensberry's letters are to be found references to things he has heard or been told about his son and Wilde and one can guess that he was fed on a good deal of malicious gossip, no doubt by the kind of trouble-maker who enjoys watching a fight.

It was chiefly, however, a family affair. Queensberry's eldest son, who was killed in an accident in October of that year, took no part in it, but the second son, Lord Douglas of Hawick, then in Australia, was informed by Bosie of what was happening. Nothing that the brothers heard about their father surprised them and when they spoke to one another about him they referred to "that brute". On August 19th, at the time when he was sending an "utterly unreadable" postcard to his father, Bosie wrote to his brother Percy in Australia a letter in which he referred to his father as "that brute" and said that ever since he (Bosie) had returned from Egypt, he had been giving him a fearful time. He says that he (their father), first of all wrote and told him that,

unless I ceased to know or speak to my dearest friend, Oscar Wilde, he would cut off all my money, and also wrote me a most bitter and abusive letter, which enraged me so much that I wrote to him through a solicitor and told him that I would neither have any more money from him nor have any more to do with him.

Bosie could and did snap his fingers at his father even though his allowance was stopped but he could not defy his mother, and since the diplomatic career she had planned for him had been ended so sharply her concern had grown. Having spoiled him as a child and given him his own way as a young man she could not control him now but she wanted him to end his friendship with Wilde and pleaded with him in a way that influenced him more than all his father's threats.

In April (1894) she prevailed on him to go abroad for a time. Wilde was supposedly busy with his new play and would not, Lady Queensberry thought, follow her son to Florence which Bosie had always wanted to visit. She gave him a liberal allowance and in the middle of the month he left.

At first Wilde showed no sign of following, as two letters of his reveal. They were both written towards the end of April 1894, for there are references in them to the first number of *The Yellow Book*. Wilde had not produced a play for a year and it had been a time of witless extravagance. He was getting very hard up.

In the first he says how much he misses Bosie—'the gilt and gracious lad' having gone away, and he hates everyone else. He is in 'purple valleys' of despair and envies Bosie under Giotto's tower who must write poems like apple-blossoms. The second letter tells Bosie that he is always remembered at a barber's shop in Air Street where there are references to his gilt silk hair. Less exuberantly he says that he has had a telegram and call from Edward Shelley who is in trouble for money.

But soon afterwards Wilde wrote another letter which seemed to presage what happened a week after it was sent—Wilde's sudden flight to Florence to join Bosie. It is really absurd, he says. He cannot live without Bosie who is so dear, so wonderful. He thinks of him all day long and misses his grace, his boyish beauty, the bright sword-play of his wit, and above all Bosie himself. London is a desert without his 'dainty feet'. He has no words for how he loves him.

Bosie in the meantime writing to Kains Jackson from Palazzo Ferroni, Piazza Santa Trinita, says he finds Florence charming but feels homesick for Oxford now that the summer term is going on. He was spending time with Lord Henry Somerset, a song-writer who was forced to live out of England owing to his part in the Cleveland Street scandal. Oscar joined him before the end of May.

They remained together in Florence for about a month and Bosie says that Oscar wrote most of *A Florentine Tragedy* while they were there. From the fact that neither, in the bitter books which each was to write about the other in periods of stress and recrimination later, makes much reference to this stay it must be assumed to have been free from quarrels. Wilde, in *De Profundis*, does not say that in Florence

Bosie failed to bring him grapes when he was ill, and Bosie, in *Oscar Wilde and Myself*, does not call Wilde's Florentine conversation "preposterous and poisonous speciousness". So perhaps for a few weeks they enjoyed the beauties of the city and one another's company untouched by acrimony.

9

Queensberry until now had nothing to go on but hearsay and the fact that Wilde, to use another term current in this connection among homosexuals, was 'obvious'. It was not until a year later when Wilde had applied for a warrant against Queensberry that the agents of the Scarlet Marquis found Taylor and his circle. During 1894 he had no knowledge of the young men whom he later bribed and threatened into giving evidence, but had he employed a detective to watch them he would have made some interesting discoveries. His information was out of date and inaccurate when he decided to call on Wilde and threaten him. He had apparently heard two stories, both untrue. One was that Oscar had taken rooms for Bosie near Piccadilly, the other that Constance Wilde was threatening divorce. This interview at Tite Street has often been described but always from the account that Wilde gave of it and except for a passing reference to it by Queensberry in a letter to Alfred Montgomery, ("He plainly showed the white feather the other day when I tackled him") the other side of the story has never been heard.

Wilde's account of the interview was given in Court.

At the end of June, 1894, there was an interview between Lord Queensberry and myself in my house. He called upon me, not by appointment, about four o'clock in the afternoon, accompanied by a gentleman with whom I was not acquainted. The interview took place in my library. Lord Queensberry was standing by the window. I walked over to the fireplace, and he said to me, "Sit down." I said to him, "I do not allow any one to talk like that to me in my house or anywhere else. I suppose you have come to apologise for the statement you made about my wife and myself in letters you wrote to your son. I should have the right any day I chose to prosecute you for writing such a letter." He said, "The letter was privileged, as it was written to my son." I said, "How dare you say such things to me about your son and me?" He said, "You were both kicked out of the Savoy Hotel at a moment's notice for your disgusting conduct." I said, "That is a lie." He said, "You have taken furnished rooms for him in Piccadilly." I said, "Somebody has been telling you an absurd set of lies about your son and me. I have not done anything of the kind." He said, "I hear you were thoroughly well blackmailed for a disgusting letter you wrote to my son." I said, "The letter was a beautiful letter, and I never write except for publication." Then I asked: "Lord Queensberry, do you seriously accuse your son and me of improper conduct?" He said, "I do not say you are it, but you look it; and you pose as it, which is just as bad. If I catch you and my son together again in any public restaurant I will thrash you." I said, "I do not know what the Queensberry rules are, but the Oscar Wilde rule is to shoot at sight." I then told Lord Queensberry to leave my house. He said he would not do so. I told him that I would have him put out by the police. He said, "It is a disgusting scandal." I said, "If it be so, you are the author of the scandal, and no one else." I then went into the hall and pointed him out to my servant. I said, "This is the Marquis of Queensberry, the most infamous brute in London. You are never to allow him to enter my house again."

This has been accepted piecemeal by some writers on Wilde, including surprisingly Hesketh Pearson and Montgomery Hyde who have added—on what authority they do not state—that the 'gentleman with whom I was not acquainted' was a prize-fighter. They do not seem to find anything strange, not to say incredible, in the notion of Queensberry who had been an amateur boxing champion and was described by Harris as 'five foot nine or ten in height, combative and courageous', standing quietly to hear that he was the most infamous brute in London and meekly leaving the house at Wilde's bidding. Sherard says that Wilde did not 'show the white feather' "and even if he had shown some nervousness it would have been very unfair to charge him with cowardice". Harris says flatly that "the idea of Oscar 'standing up' to Queensberry or 'shooting at sight' was too absurd."

There is no reason to think that Wilde showed anything like cowardice in this little crisis for he never lacked physical courage and was a hefty fellow, but on the other hand the picture of Queensberry walking away with his tail between his legs is quite unconvincing. It would be interesting to know what Wilde's small servant Edward, known as 'Ginger', thought about it. He was then sixteen years old and terrified of the Scarlet Marquis. Probably Wilde's story, on which he was not cross-examined, was a witness-box version of what actually happened. Queensberry did call unannounced, he did expostulate with Wilde and he did leave without personal violence. The rest is guesswork.

Afterwards throughout July and August the correspondence between Queensberry and Bosie grew more hysterical, more silly and more full of vilification, and Queensberry wrote on the subject of

Wilde with as little control to Alfred Montgomery and to a firm of solicitors consulted by Wilde. Bosie retorted by saying that he always carried a loaded revolver and would not hesitate to use it if Queensberry tried to assault him.

The revolver was no piece of stage property. Bosie actually carried it.

All you could think of [wrote Wilde caustically in *De Profundis*] (besides, of course, writing to him insulting letters and telegrams) was to buy a ridiculous pistol that goes off in the Berkeley under circumstances that create a worse scandal than ever came to *your* ears.

But it was that explosion in the Berkeley—one of those droll moments of history which must tempt us all to the wish that we had been present—which kept Queensberry quiet for a few months. It was duly reported to him and there were no more blustering letters that year.

CHAPTER FIVE

The Friendship: Fourth Year. Summer 1894–Spring 1895

I

THROUGHOUT the first four years of their febrile friendship both Oscar and Bosie were wildly extravagant with money. Both spent everything they could lay their hands on, together, on each other and alone. Though Oscar had more to spend than Bosie there were times— like their stay in Florence—when they were both dependent on Bosie's allowance. But there was a difference between them in their prodigality for Bosie spent as to the manner born, with no care or conscience and without a thought of his obligations, while Oscar, to whom money had come recently and profusely, spent with a secret sense of sin in his thriftlessness which made it more perversely enjoyable. He spoke lightly of money, calling it 'gold coins dropping down from heaven to gladden me' or 'the gold the gryphon guards in Rude Armenia', but somewhere, perhaps in his subconscious mind, was that conscience-striken fear, common to all of us who have not inherited wealth from a long line of rich forbears, that it is 'wrong to waste money'. This would surface later when he came to write *De Profundis* in prison.

In August he sent his wife and children down to Worthing and intended to join them in order to write another play. He could not work in London for even when he took rooms away from his home, as he had done in St. James's Place, they soon became, in a particular sense a *garconnière*. But Worthing, he thought, would provide little distraction. He wrote despondently to Bosie begging him to follow him there and saying that he was in debt and could not stand it any longer. He hoped to work at Worthing but he would have no writing-room and the house was small. He also complained that Bosie's father was 'on the rampage' again. It might have been better, he thought, to have him bound over to keep the peace but that would have meant a scandal. Still, it was intolerable to be dogged by a maniac.

Everything would be done for Bosie when he came but Oscar feared he would find the meals, etc., tedious. He seems always to have under-rated Bosie's adaptability. Bosie when he came so much enjoyed this family holiday at the seaside with Wilde's wife and children that he returned twice.

How this strange family holiday at Worthing was passed may be gathered from one of the most characteristic of Wilde's letters to Bosie soon after Bosie's first visit. It starts with rather laboured and wordy praise for a poem Bosie had sent him making "the white feet of poetry dance among the flowers without crushing them". Wilde had been doing nothing but bathing and playwriting, for he was at work on what would eventually become *The Importance of Being Earnest*. But there is news of various youths. Percy, described as 'Hellenic', had left the day after Bosie, speaking much of him. Alphonso was still 'in favour', and with him and Stephen, Oscar had made a disastrous sailing venture. There was a letter for Bosie from 'dear Henry'. When Oscar and Bosie were out of tune all colour went from things, he said, "but we are never really out of tune". Oscar thought day and night of his 'honey-haired boy'.

Of the boys mentioned, Alphonse Conway was later discovered by Queensberry's agents and brought to London for the hearing though for some reason he was not put in the box. The Hellenic Percy was never identified and Stephen may have been a friend of Conway's. Under cross-examination about Conway Wilde said:

When Lord Alfred Douglas and I were at Worthing we were accustomed to go out in a boat. One day when the fishermen were launching a boat on the high beach, Conway with another lad assisted in getting the craft down to the water. I said to Lord Alfred Douglas, "Shall we ask them to come out for a sail?" He assented, and we took them. After that Alphonse and I became great friends, and it is true that I asked him to lunch with me.

Perhaps 'another lad' was Stephen.

The events of that warm and pleasant summer, the best-recorded of all periods the two friends spent together, were mercilessly dragged into evidence. They are so human and cheerful that now, seventy years later, they become vividly real from the few details given of them in Court, from Wilde's letters, and from a pathetic passage of *De Profundis*.

Although, as Wilde wrote to Bosie, 'children at meals are tedious' the cramped quarters in the apartment house—appropriately '5 Esplanade'—meant that Wilde and his wife ate with the two small boys, now aged ten and eight, and their 'horrid ugly Swiss governess', all of them, one supposes, red and sandy from the beach. The scene must be vivid to most of us of the middle classes old enough to remember such holidays, but a touch of the outré is added, not so much by the presence of Bosie, who was fond of Wilde's children and got on well with Constance Wilde, as by Oscar himself with his thick curled hair and flashy summer clothes and by the occasional presence of Alphonse Conway.

Wilde was writing and before his return to London had completed the gayest and incomparably the best of his plays, *The Importance of Being Earnest*. Agate called it 'the wittiest lightest comedy in the language' and said "Wilde's fame is sure in regard to this masterpiece as long as theatre audiences enjoy wit". Bosie said, "He wrote the whole of *The Importance of Being Earnest* at a house in Worthing where I stayed with him, and most of it while I was sitting in the same room with him." (Bosie never claimed, by written or spoken word, to have been Wilde's 'collaborator' as one of his detractors impudently states.) There may not have been a writing-room as Wilde complained in his letter, but he managed very well for he had so mastered the technique of playwriting that once he settled down to one of his comedies he could finish it in a few weeks.

When Oscar was not writing, he, Bosie, Alphonse, Oscar's two boys Cyril and Vyvyan, and the unknown Stephen and Percy of the letter, played in the sunshine and went on the sea in accord and contentment for six weeks. Oscar in many things had the nature of a boy, as Hesketh Pearson so perceptively shows, and between Bosie and Alphonse there were only six years and between Alphonse and Wilde's sons only eight. The weather was kind, Wilde had a new play coming on in January (*An Ideal Husband*) and was finishing another with which he was mightily pleased, Constance Wilde was (presumably) unsuspicious and well and happy as all of them were and Queensberry was quiescent. It was a delightful holiday.

2

When Bosie made his third visit to Worthing late in September, Constance Wilde and her small sons had left, and the two friends grew bored. Early in October they decided to have a few days in Brighton where Oscar was to revise his play. Here they quarrelled with the usual bitterness.

At first they had between them enough money for their customary extravagance and went to the Grand Hotel. After a week Bosie fell ill with influenza and with all the resources of a good hotel to call on, Oscar looked after him. "My friend is not allowed to go out today: I sit by his side and read him passages from his own life. They fill him with surprise", Wilde wrote to Ada Leverson and on the next day wired to her: "Much better, temperature gone down, is to be allowed chicken to the sound of flutes at 7.30. Many thanks for kind enquiries." In four days Bosie recovered and as their money had begun to run out they moved into inexpensive lodgings at 20 King's Road. Here Oscar had influenza, or believed he had, and care and attention were not so easily obtained or so necessary. Like most people who 'never have a day's illness' Wilde was a difficult invalid, petulant and exacting, and after a ferocious argument Bosie left him to his landlady and doctor. Wilde soon recovered and the quarrel was quickly ended by a letter from Bosie.

It was not the worst of their quarrels and both of them had (Bosie supposed) 'forgotten all about (it) a week after it happened,' but it took on monstrous proportions when Wilde came to write *De Profundis*.

The two friends did something that summer which had the gravest consequences for Wilde when he was on trial and for Bosie for twenty-five years afterwards. A handsome and homosexual undergraduate of Exeter College named John Francis Bloxam whom Bosie had known at Winchester and Oxford, asked Bosie for a contribution to a periodical he was starting, and hoped that Wilde might be persuaded to write something for it also.

The paper was to be called *The Chameleon* and to bear as its sub-title Stevenson's line—"A Bazaar of Dangerous and Smiling Chances." Bosie agreed to contribute two poems and Wilde had ready some *Phrases and Philosophies for the Use of the Young* which he had intended for *The Saturday Review* but preferred to give to the beautiful Mr. Bloxam. Only three numbers a year were to be issued of *The Chameleon* and each edition was to be limited to a hundred copies. The subscription was to be 15s. It was the sort of thing that appealed to Wilde whose obsession with Youth, in literature as in life, was growing.

The incident provided later an excellent example, if one more were needed, of Wilde's petty injustice to Bosie in *De Profundis*. At the time he enjoyed the thing in all its indiscretion. When *The Chameleon* was published Ada Leverson read a rather disgusting and blasphemous story in it called *The Priest and the Acolyte* which Bloxam had written himself, but published anonymously. Ada Leverson thought she recognized the style as that of John Gray (whom Oscar called 'Dorian') and wrote to tell Oscar this. " 'The Priest and the Acolyte' is not by Dorian," he wrote to her, "though you were right in discerning by internal evidence that the author has a profile. He is an undergraduate of strange beauty." This becomes in *De Profundis*:

One day you come to me and ask me, as a personal favour to you, to write something for an Oxford undergraduate magazine, about to be started by some friend of yours, whom I had never heard of in all my life, and knew nothing at all about. To please you—what did I not do always to please you?— I sent him a page of paradoxes destined originally for the *Saturday Review*. A few months later I find myself standing in the dock of the Old Bailey on account of the character of the magazine.

It is a reflection not without irony that Bloxam took his degree while Wilde was on trial and was ordained in the year Wilde came out of prison. He had a fine war record later and on the many occasions when his wretched short story was resuscitated in evidence against Bosie, held various London livings.

3

There was one very unpleasant event that August of which Wilde read in the newspaper while he was at Worthing. The police raided a queer party in Fitzroy Street and among others arrested were Taylor and Charles Parker.

Oscar must have discussed this uneasily with Bosie and perhaps it cast a momentary shadow across the Worthing sands, but he still felt himself invulnerable and regarded Queensberry and his threats as no more than an annoyance. He was relieved, too, when he heard that the arrest was such a sickener for Charles Parker that he joined the Army. In London earlier that August—perhaps on an occasion described in a letter to Bosie when he lunched with Alexander at the Garrick and got a little money from him—he had seen Parker in Trafalgar Square and (according to Parker) had stopped his cab to tell him that he was "looking pretty as ever". But he must have known from Taylor that Parker was with Allen and Wood and living by blackmail so the news that he had enlisted could not have been unwelcome.

4

Shortly after the exchange of letters which ended the Brighton quarrel, Bosie was called down to Somerset where, on October 18th, his eldest brother Francis (Viscount Drumlanrig) had been found dead in the grounds of Quantock Lodge where he was staying. Bosie attended the Inquest and heard the Coroner's jury find that Francis had died from the accidental explosion of his own gun. It was a great shock and a sorrow to him for the brothers had always been closely united and Francis, a handsome, gentle young man, a soldier and a sportsman with simple serious ideas about life, was deeply loved by his younger brother.

Bosie returned to London in time for the first night of *An Ideal Husband* which was on January 3rd. In the meantime *The Chameleon* had been published. At first both Oscar and Bosie were amused at the thing for it consisted chiefly of the writing of Bloxam whose story *The Priest and the Acolyte* was prominent. The whole publication reeked of self-conscious undergraduate homosexuality and Bosie's two peoms, including the one ending "I am the love that dare not speak its name", did little to save it from preciousness. Wilde's cynical and witty epigrams were wholly out of place. Jerome K. Jerome in his weekly *Today* pointed out the 'undesirable' characteristics of *The Chameleon*. Though in Court later Wilde claimed that when he realized the character of *The Chameleon* he urged the editor to withdraw it, he did not take so stern a view at the time, as his letter to Ada Leverson showed.

5

In those last months before the catastrophe, Oscar and Bosie must have been a singular pair as they drove about London. In one of several photographs of them together, taken at the same sitting, they are wearing, unfortunately, country attire, Oscar with butterfly collar severely starched, a cut-away tweed suit of pronounced pattern and a bowler hat, Bosie negligently lounging in white flannel trousers, a loose jacket and tie, with a boater on the back of his head. This was taken in 1894 probably at Brighton and in it, in spite of his Neronian haircut and dressiness, Wilde has a smooth young-looking face and looks a rather soft-cheeked easy-going man. But the caricaturist tells us more than the photographer and Beerbohm's famous drawing of the two together at a restaurant table shows Oscar with chins down to his chest and vast swollen outline with long curled hair and thick lips as he expatiates, facing and seeming about to swallow a shrimplike, unsmiling, eager and attentive Bosie whose profile is outthrust towards him.

They were, as a pair, unpopular, for no one likes to see two people satisfied with one another's company when they are individually liked.

There must have been many at that time to agree with Beardsley—'both of them are really very dreadful people'.

On January 3rd 1895 *An Ideal Husband* was produced at the Haymarket during Tree's absence in America. It repeated the huge success of the other comedies. The Prince of Wales was in a box and congratulated Wilde, telling him not to alter a line of the dialogue and even the press was more kindly disposed than after the previous productions. As soon as the play had commenced a successful run the two friends made true the prediction of "the Sybil of Mortimer Street (whom Mortals term Mrs. Robinson)". She had foretold that early in January they would go away together for a long voyage. They left for Algiers.

6

It is fortunate that we have a glimpse of them together in Algeria given us by a man of some insight. André Gide, a year older than Bosie, had met Wilde several times in Paris and now found himself at the same hotel at Blidah. He had published two books and was already drugged by the charms of North Africa which kept him in an elatedly narcotic condition for many years. He was homosexual but believed that Wilde was unaware of this. "Though Wilde had begun to reveal the secrets of his life to me, he knew nothing as yet of mine; I had taken care to give him no hint of them, either by deed or word."

Gide's account of events at Blidah and Algiers has been rigorously challenged by Sherard who 'proved conclusively'—at least to Hesketh Pearson's satisfaction—that the statements in his book *Si le grain ne meurt* are false, by Bosie himself who called them 'a mass of lies and misrepresentations', and by Reggie Turner who said "anything so preposterously untrue has never been written". Moreover Gide protests too much, speaking of 'Wilde's actual words which I transcribed with absolute fidelity'. And in his first account of his meeting with Wilde in Blidah he did not even mention that Bosie was there.

Yet much of what he writes has that mysterious quality, a ring of truth. One feels in reading it that no one, however skilled a narrator, could have invented it all. It has, in fact, just what is absent from Frank Harris's accounts of no less fantastic incidents. There may be exaggerations and small touches added either deliberately or because Gide, having long ago invented them, had come to believe them and made them a part of his memories. But the picture for the most part is vividly if unmercifully painted.

He begins by telling how he found Wilde's name on the hotel board beside his own and nearly rubbed his out to flee the embarrassment of the meeting, for 'Wilde's company had become compromising'. When they met he found Wilde changed, not in his appearance but in his behaviour.

Wilde began at once to sing Bosie's praises with extraordinary enthusiasm.

He called him *Bosy* so that I did not realize at first to whom these praises referred, especially as he seemed rather affectedly to make a point of praising nothing but Bosy's beauty. "You'll see him," he kept repeating, "and you'll tell me if it's possible to imagine a more charming divinity. I adore him; yes, I positively adore him." Wilde covered over his sincerest feelings with a cloak of affectation which many people found intolerable. He would never cease from acting—could not, no doubt; but the character he acted was his own; the role itself, which his everlasting demon kept prompting him, was a sincere one.

Wilde and Bosie dined in their sitting-room and when they came down to join Gide in a tour of the town

it was not sufficient for Wilde to tell the vile procurer who came to pilot us through the town that evening that he wanted to see some young Arabs, he added "as beautiful as bronze statues", and only saved the phrase from being ridiculous by a kind of poetical playfulness, and by the slight English or Irish accent which he took good care never to lose when speaking French.

One thing Gide remembered very well is that in the street Bosie took his arm and said—

"All these guides are idiotic: it's no good explaining—they will always take you to cafés which are full of women. I hope you are like me. I have a horror of women. I only like boys. As you are coming with us this evening, I think it's better to say so at once. . . ."

Gide hid his 'stupefaction at the brutality of this outspoken statement' which consisted, apparently, in Bosie's showing that he knew Gide was homosexual. "I could not think Bosy as beautiful as Wilde did; but though he had the despotic manners of a spoilt child, he combined them with so much grace that I soon began to understand why it was that Wilde always followed so submissively in his wake."

They went to an uninteresting café and the next day returned to Algiers. Gide found Wilde in a bar one afternoon reading his letters.

"I must tell you I have a friend in London who looks after my correspondence for me. He keeps back all the boring letters—business letters, tradesmen's bills and so on—and only forwards the serious letters—the love-letters. . . . Oh! this one is from a young . . . what do you call it? . . . acrobat? yes; acrobat; absolutely delicious."

There is a sharp picture of Bosie:

He [Wilde] was continuing to laugh and joke, when suddenly Douglas came into the bar, wrapped in a fur coat, with the collar turned up, so that nothing was to be seen of him but his nose and the glance of his eyes. He brushed past me as though he didn't recognize me, planted himself in front of Wilde and in a hissing, withering, savage voice, rapped out a few sentences, of which I understood not a single word, then turning on his heels, went out. Wilde had let the storm pass over him without a word; but had turned very pale and after Bosy had gone neither of us spoke for some time.

The fur coat was certainly apocryphal. Bosie never wore one in his life, least of all in Algeria.

Then Wilde told Gide of the 'scenes' Bosie made everywhere and as one is described when they were staying at the Savoy 'a little while ago' though they had not stayed at the Savoy since March 1893, these need not perhaps be taken too seriously.

Bosie, said Gide, had a personality "which seemed much stronger and much more marked than Wilde's; yes, Douglas's personality was overweening; a sort of fatality swept him along; at times he seemed almost irresponsible; and he never attempted to resist himself, he would not put up with anyone or anything resisting him either."

Add to all this [he says after reporting a quite incredible remark of Bosie's] a poetic gift of the rarest quality, which was apparent in the musical tone of his voice, in his gestures, his eyes and the expression of his features; there was apparent too in his whole person what physiologists call "a bad heredity".

The rest of Gide's account chiefly concerns Wilde for Bosie went next day to Blidah from which town he was going to take an Algerian boy to Biskra.

That he did in fact do so is proved by something more than Gide's account of it. Gide said:

Douglas returned to Blidah, where he was making arrangements to elope with a young *caouadji* he wanted to take with him to Biskra; for my descriptions of the oasis—where I intended to return myself—had captivated him. But to run away with an Arab is not such an easy thing as he had thought at first; he had to get the parents' consent, sign papers at the Arab office, at the police-station, etc; there was work enough to keep him at Blidah for several days.

Later, he says, Bosie left for Biskra. But years later Christopher Millard, a man of whom we shall hear more, gave to A. J. A. Symons, who became a friend of Bosie's in 1925, typescript copies of letters which Bosie wrote from Biskra to someone in England. One is immediately reminded of the typescript letters, also given by Millard to Symons, which were written by Frederick Rolfe ("Baron Corvo") to a similarly unnamed correspondent in England describing his corruption of young boys in Venice.★ It is true that Millard dealt in this kind of thing, but it is hard to see how he came to be in possession of Bosie's letters if they were not written to Ross (whose secretary he had been) or one of Ross's close associates—a probability in any case since Bosie was friendly with them all at that time and had few if any other homosexual friends to whom he would have written in those terms. The fact that the originals were not used against him in court, as his letters to Wilde were used by Ross, is accounted for by the fact that they would incriminate the person to whom they were written.

Not that Bosie wrote with the pornographic detail of Rolfe. He said no more than—"I am staying here with a marvellous boy. You would adore him." Nor can it be supposed by anyone who knows the Arab world that he 'corrupted' his companion. But he certainly took him to Biskra and certainly wrote enthusiastically about him.

7

Wilde had to hurry back to London for the first night of *The Importance of Being Ernest* on February 14th and left Bosie with his young *caouadji*. But very soon Bosie returned in response to a telegram from his brother Percy. A letter of explanation from Wilde awaited him in Paris. The Scarlet Marquis had made a plot to address the audience on the first night of the play. Algy Bourke had revealed it, and Queensberry was not allowed to enter. He arrived with a prize-fighter, but 'all Scotland Yard—twenty police' were guarding the theatre. He prowled about for three hours, then left 'chattering like a monstrous ape'.

This ridiculous incident did as much as anything, perhaps, to precipitate the case of Wilde *v.* Queensberry, for nothing infuriated the Scarlet Marquis more than being made to look foolish. That, and the success of *The Importance of Being Ernest*, reduced him to a state of insane frustration and four days after the performance, that is on

★ See *The Quest for Corvo*, by A. J. A. Symons (Cassell).

February 18, he called with a witness at Wilde's club, the Albemarle, and left his card. On the back of it, instead of a challenge to a duel, he had written what amounted to a challenge to litigation—"To Oscar Wilde posing as a somdomite". Fury had produced an extra 'm'. On this afternoon Bosie was still on his way back to London from Algiers.

Wilde was unaware of Queensberry's call. The club porter who appears not to have understood the card's significance but realized that as Queensberry himself had called it might be important, put it in an envelope and left it till Wilde should come to the club.

Wilde, in accordance with his custom, had engaged hotel rooms for the production of *The Importance of Being Earnest* but perhaps because he was no longer welcome at the Albemarle Hotel had chosen the Avondale in Piccadilly, from which he had written that letter to await Bosie in Paris. As soon as Bosie reached England he joined him there. It is significant to find from one of Wilde's answers under cross-examination that Ernest Scarfe, (another of Taylor's circle) visited him at the hotel at this time. Wilde had made another young friend in the last few days. He wrote to Ada Leverson that she had been kind enough to say he might bring someone to dinner that night so after carefully going over the list, he had selected a young man 'tall as a young palm tree'.

His Christian name is "Tom"—a very rare name in an age of Algies and Berties—and he is the son of Colonel Kennion, and lives at Oxford in the hopes of escaping the taint of modern education. I met him on Tuesday, so he is quite an old friend.

Kennion in after years ran an antique shop in Ebury Street with another queer called Courtenay Thorpe.

Bosie stayed a day or two then went down to stay with his mother. Oscar remained at the Avondale because he had not enough money to pay his bill and the manager, a Mr. Kinadete, would not release his luggage. He had just received £300 from Alexander but as he told him he was "already served with writs for £400". But he did not call at his club until February 28 when the porter handed him Queensberry's card.

Since he had been back in London and while Bosie was still in Algiers he had been seeing a good deal of Robert Ross who was at the first night of *The Importance of Being Earnest* in Bosie's absence. Ross had introduced him to his solicitors in the previous July and they had written their stern but ineffective letter to Queensberry, and it was to

Ross that he turned now. He went back to the Avondale and wrote two notes, one to Bosie asking him to call on him next morning and one to Ross who was in London asking him to come round that evening. The note to Ross reads as though Wilde was a little drunk when he wrote it.

He tells Ross about Queensberry's card and says that he sees nothing now but a criminal prosecution. He adds in his exalted way "the tower of ivory is assailed by the foul thing. On the sand is my life spilt." Will Ross call at 11.30 that night?

It is probable that Wilde had long been contemplating some action against Queensberry. It was suggested in a letter which the solicitors consulted by Wilde, C. O. Humphreys, Son and Kershaw sent to Queensberry and it was strongly suggested again in Wilde's letter to Bosie of a fortnight earlier. "Percy is on our side. I feel now that without your name being mentioned all will go well." The card gave him his opportunity. Instead of tearing it up and laughing over it with Bosie, as they had laughed over other antics of the Scarlet Marquis, he took it seriously and sent for the two young men in order to confer with them on his next move. This was his own most decisive step. Mr. Justice Wills said in the last trial that Queensberry's action in sending the card was 'one which no gentleman would have taken'. It was, in fact, the action of a guttersnipe or a madman and in either case Wilde should have ignored it.

In view of this, the question of whether Bosie egged him on or not is largely irrelevant. No very far-seeing wisdom or judiciousness was to be expected from Bosie, who was an irresponsible young man of twenty-four brought up by a mother and with three brothers who all had good reason to detest Queensberry or think him little more than a lunatic. The processes of the law, with which in after years Bosie was to become familiar, were mysteries to him and he probably thought it would be a simple matter for Oscar to get Queensberry sentenced to prison for criminal libel.

Bosie for some reason which neither he nor anyone else has explained did not come up to the Avondale that morning and Ross took Oscar to his own solicitor Humphreys. Bosie, when he heard about it on the next day, asked Wilde why on earth he had not gone to Lewis and Lewis. Sir George Lewis was a personal friend of Wilde's and had, it will be remembered, acted cleverly for Bosie at Oxford. But Wilde with a death-wishy-washy sense of doom preferred a lawyer who, believing him innocent, would advise action. (George Lewis almost certainly knew too much about him for that.) So it had to be Humphreys.

That, I believe, is the key to Wilde's actions from now on—he *wanted* to fight even if it meant his fall. He chose Humphreys as his lawyer because he could convince him of his innocence of Queensberry's charges and hence the strength of his position. If during the talk we must suppose he had with Ross on the evening of receiving the card Ross counselled caution—and it would be in keeping with Ross's character—Wilde overrode that caution.

This book is not the story of Wilde (except in so far as it affects Bosie) and rather than attempt an analysis of Wilde's motives I will quote the man who has probably understood them better than any other writer, Hesketh Pearson. In a passage from his book (*The Life of Oscar Wilde*) as clear as it is credible he shows his insight into Wilde's dilemma.

The question why he ever embarked on such a course, and why he maintained it after recognising the danger, has troubled many people, and no satisfying answer has yet been given. The explanation is to be found in his nature. We have already seen how from his earliest days he had dramatised himself and his career, his histrionic capacity being a part of that emotional life which never reached maturity. Gradually the performance had become so much a part of his being that he was convinced of its reality, seeing himself at first, as a symbolic figure climbing slowly to the heights of success, and at last, when he had tasted the fruits of victory, as a symbolic figure plunging suddenly to the depths of failure. The story of Jesus intensified the make-believe, and he saw himself in the role of Christ, the shouts of his first-night audiences being his hosannas, with Calvary to come. Now if it had been put to him exactly as here written, his intelligence would have ridiculed the picture; but unfortunately whenever called upon to act either in reality or in the imagination, his intelligence became an uncertain quantity, and the actor was left in possession of the stage. Further, he had been corrupted by applause and success; he was suffering from swelled head; and in his action against Queensberry we seem to see two conflicting characters: the one hurrying towards an inescapable destiny, the other marching with assurance towards a victory that would crown his previous triumphs. A third element entered into the drama: he was embroiled in the family quarrel of an historic house: he stood between a lord and a marquis in the eternal conflict of youth with age. Had his friend's name been Smith, whose father was a "mister", things would not have come to this pass, and he might have been deprived of his downfall. For, primarily, the motive that drove him onward, consciously or unconsciously, was the feeling that his life would not be complete without disaster and tragedy, and that he must plumb the depths as he had scaled the heights. "It is what we fear that happens to us," he once said, and his admission after the event—"I admit I lost my head. I was bewildered, incapable of judgment"—is proof that he was acting through-out almost automatically, the slave of his own imagination, playing the part that had become second-nature to him.

So 'on that fatal Friday' as Wilde called it, he went to Ross's solicitor Humphreys accompanied by Ross who was probably noncommittal in his attitude. Humphreys asked Wilde whether there was any truth in the accusation and on Wilde's denial agreed to act. Then Wilde went to the police court with Humphreys and applied for a warrant. Queensberry was arrested next day, March 2nd, and was remanded for a week.

On March 9th Wilde drove to the Court in a carriage-and-pair with Bosie and his brother Percy (Lord Douglas of Hawick) who was now Queensberry's heir. The Magistrate ordered Bosie to leave the Court at once. From the evidence given it was clear that Queensberry had as yet nothing with which to justify his action except two letters Wilde had written to Bosie and a lawyer's interpretation of some of Wilde's writing. Relieved, perhaps, to think that Queensberry had been bluffing, Wilde and Douglas went off to Monte Carlo while Queensberry was released on bail. How Wilde raised the money to pay for this was revealed, like so many other things, by Mr. Rupert Hart-Davis's publication of his letters. He had just borrowed £500 from Ernest Leverson and Bosie had scraped together £360, all he could raise from his family, for the costs of the action.

Perhaps of all their follies this rush to Monte Carlo was the greatest. The money they had raised should have been spent in suborning witnesses as unscrupulously as Queensberry was about to do. As it was, they left the field clear and with an ex-police inspector and perhaps some voluntary helpers Queensberry soon had all the evidence he wanted.

They returned before the end of March and with only a few days left before the trial of Queensberry, they spent a day at the office of Wilde's solicitor studying the plea of justification which Queensberry had put in.

From this document they should have seen that Queensberry's agents had secured such evidence that it was wholly impossible for Wilde to get a verdict. There was *The Chameleon* and *Dorian Gray* but these constituted only the 'literary side of the case' on which Wilde was quite prepared to be cross-examined, though even on these the issue might be doubtful. There were also mentioned Alfred Wood, Edward Shelley, Alphonse Conway, Sidney Mavor, Fred Atkins, Maurice Schwabe, Charles Parker, Ernest Scarfe, Walter Grainger, even a Savoy page-boy Tankard.

To anyone but a man deliberately walking to his own doom, these names would have been sufficient. There was only one thing for Wilde to do—drop his action and go abroad. Frank Harris told him this with brutal frankness and sincerity at an interview at the Café Royal at which Bosie and Shaw were present. "It was no use", said Shaw afterwards. "Wilde was in a curious double temper. He made no pretence either of innocence or of questioning the folly of his proceedings against Queensberry. But he had an infatuate haughtiness as to the impossibility of his retreating." He was, in other words 'acting almost automatically, the slave of his own imagination'.

To suggest, as many writers have done, and as Wilde himself did in *De Profundis*, that Bosie was responsible for the actions of a man in this condition is either to misunderstand or deliberately to distort the truth. Bosie was capable of realizing neither the impossibility of victory nor the consequences of defeat. He certainly encouraged Wilde to fight, he certainly wanted to see his father punished, but Wilde needed nothing of this for he was already mesmerized by the bright eyes of danger. Bosie believed afterwards that he had screwed Oscar up to the 'sticking place' because of his own faith in Oscar's victory which was to be brought about through Bosie being put in the box to give revelations of his father's behaviour and character. This was sheer delusion. Wilde needed no screwing up for he was already walking blindfold to the scaffold and Bosie's evidence might easily have been disallowed and was in any case not very relevant to the main issue. Certainly if it had depended on Bosie whether Wilde should fight or not (even after seeing Queensberry's plea of justification) Bosie would have urged him to fight. But it did not depend on Bosie. From the moment Wilde failed to laugh at Queensberry's card he walked in a straight line to destruction. Or, some may think, to destruction and immortality.

CHAPTER VI

The Friendship: During Wilde's Trials and Imprisonment

I

BOSIE was in Court throughout the trial of his father for libel which has come to be considered the first of three trials of Oscar Wilde. He saw his father enter the Court alone and stand in the dock where he muttered angrily at the proceedings. He heard Oscar, who looked dressy and debonair, give his evidence with what must have seemed to the jury an affected and contemptuous air. He heard the smart repartee of his friend, the retorts which have been so often quoted with delight but which did Wilde's case so much damage. At the end of the first day, (Wednesday, April 3rd 1895) during which nothing had been touched on but *The Chameleon*, *Dorian Gray* and the letters, with some not very damning references to Shelley and Alphonse Conway, the two friends did not actually congratulate themselves, but could still hold to the extraordinary illusion that Wilde would in some mysterious way be victorious. They had consulted 'the Sibyl of Mortimer Street' who had predicted complete triumph. They were able to wire jointly to Ada Leverson that evening that everything was very satisfactory.

But on the following morning Sir Edward Carson, who had been briefed by Queensberry's solicitors, began to cross-examine Wilde about Taylor and his rooms in Little College Street, about Sidney Mavor and Fred Atkins. By the time he came to the Fitzroy Street raid and Wilde's meeting with the Parkers there could not be the slightest hope. The visit to Paris with Atkins, Ernest Scarfe and Walter Grainger followed. (It was in connection with this last that Wilde let fall the gaffe about not kissing him 'a peculiarly plain' boy, of which Carson made great capital.) Incidents at the Savoy Hotel, Alfred Wood again, a number of cigarette-cases—Carson never missed a trick. On the third day when it became known that Carson had his blackmailers and male prostitutes handy and would put them in the witness-box, Sir Edward Clarke (for Wilde) hurriedly withdrew the prosecution and Queensberry was acquitted.

Oscar and Bosie went to the Old Bailey that morning till Sir Edward Clarke made him his withdrawal but did not wait to hear the cheering in Court for Queensberry, which was quite unchecked. They drove at Bosie's suggestion to the office of Lewis and Lewis to see what could be done. Sir George Lewis said, "What's the use of coming to me now? I am powerless to do anything. If you had had the sense to bring Lord Queensberry's card to me in the first place I would have torn it up and thrown it in the fire, and told you not to make a fool of yourself."

They went on to the Holborn Viaduct Restaurant for lunch in a private room and were joined by Lord Douglas of Hawick and Robert Ross. From here Wilde dictated to Ross, signed and dispatched a letter to the *Evening News and Post* which was published that afternoon:

It would have been impossible for me to have proved my case without putting Lord Alfred Douglas in the witness-box against his father. Lord Alfred Douglas was extremely anxious to go into the box, but I would not let him do so. Rather than put him into so painful a position, I determined to retire from the case, and to bear on my own shoulders whatever ignominy and shame might result from my prosecuting Lord Queensberry.

It could now only be a question of hours before Wilde would be arrested and charged under 'Section 2' of the Criminal Law Amendment Act of 1885. He had not been in Court that morning when Carson continued his speech for the defence and it was generally assumed that he had left for abroad. But no. Oscar—as Augustus John said—'chose to sit tight (in every sense) and await the police, rather than face freedom in the company of Frank Harris'.

After lunch the four of them went to Bosie's rooms at the Cadogan Hotel in Sloane Street. Here they all tried to persuade Wilde to leave but he sat drinking and putting them off with feeble excuses. "It's too late now." "The train has gone." Again to quote Hesketh Pearson—

Having little sense of reality, he could not imagine what was in store for him, and, if partially paralysed by the shock, he was half-hypnotized by the picture of himself as one predestined to suffer.

Bosie decided on action. His cousin George Wyndham had been a Member of Parliament for six years and had many friends in the Government and Bosie hurried down to the House of Commons, where Wyndham was to be found, hoping to learn whether Wilde was to be prosecuted, hoping perhaps—for he had a childlike belief in the power of his family to 'arrange' things—that it might be prevented. Whether he saw George Wyndham or not, or what he was told if he did so, is not recorded, but when he got back to the Cadogan Hotel it was to hear that Wilde had been arrested and taken, chatting tipsily, to Bow Street. Wilde had left a note for him:

My dear Bosie, I will be at Bow Street Police Station tonight—no bail possible I am told. Will you ask Percy, and George Alexander, and Waller, at the Haymarket, to attend to give bail. Would you also wire Humphreys to appear at Bow Street for me. Wire to 41 Norfolk Square, W. Also, come to see me. Ever yours, Oscar."

Bosie followed Wilde to Bow Street. He was, he said, in 'a frightful state of despair and consternation' but he never thought of leaving the country. Ross, Reggie Turner, Maurice Schwabe and a good many others were on the boat train that night and remained abroad till nearly a year after Wilde had been convicted and the scare had died down. Frank Harris, roaring merrily with exaggeration, gives a fabulous description of the exodus:

Every train to Dover was crowded; every steamer to Calais thronged with members of the aristocratic and leisured classes, who seemed to prefer Paris, or even Nice out of the season, to a city like London, where the police might act with such unexpected vigour. . . . Never was Paris so crowded with members of the English governing classes; here was to be seen a famous ex-Minister; there the fine face of the president of a Royal society; at one table in the Café de la Paix, a millionaire recently ennobled, and celebrated for his exquisite taste in art, opposite to him a famous general.

Bosie was in far greater danger than any of them and at Wilde's second trial the foreman actually asked the Judge if a warrant had ever been issued for his arrest. Whether or not he had been hot-headed and indiscreet in encouraging Wilde to attack Queensberry, his behaviour after the collapse of the case shows the highest courage and loyalty and is in stark contrast with that of Wilde's other friends. It must be remembered that the public was howling for his blood, his mother was prostrate with despair and anxiety for him, his family and his family friends who had pressed him for years to drop Wilde were now saying that they 'had told him so' and begging him to 'cut clean away from the whole horrible business' as one put it; he was quite penniless and except for his brother Hawick he was entirely alone. On the other side Lady Wilde and Oscar's brother and wife held him scarcely less to blame than his father. He knew that the witnesses who would appear against Wilde were no longer in the pay of his father but were acting under the orders of the police and could and would give their evidence as readily against him as against Wilde. For most young men of twenty-four the decision to stay would have been a difficult one; for Bosie there was no decision. "I never for a moment thought of 'clearing out'", he wrote afterwards with simple truth. Believers in heredity will see that with 'the fatal Douglas temperament', as Wilde called it, went other inherited qualities and instincts. In fact as a desperate little letter to Kains Jackson shows he was, as might be expected of him, thinking only of Oscar.

Dear Kains Jackson,

Can you do anything or suggest anything at this terrible moment? I have lived through what seems like countless aeons of anguish since Friday. Can *nothing* be done? Do you know no strong fearless man who will stand up? Do try to help me if only with sympathy. I am staying with my brother at Chalcott House, Long Ditton. But I am in London all day and call here two or three times a day for letters. I should like to see you.

Yours in misery,

Alfred Douglas.

April 8th, 1895, Cadogan Hotel.

He hurried that evening to Bow Street and tried, in vain of course, to bail Wilde out. Ross had already tried, equally in vain, to bring some clothes for Wilde and had found the police station surrounded by a mob who knew that Wilde was inside and were 'shouting indecencies'. Bosie was not allowed to see Wilde or bring him anything, and returned to the Cadogan Hotel, after hearing that he might be allowed a short visit after Wilde had been before a Magistrate on the following day.

2

Bosie had one friend and loyal supporter at this time, his brother Percy (Lord Douglas of Hawick, afterwards the ninth Marquess of Queensberry). Summoned home from Australia after the death of his elder brother, he had reached England on January 1st of that year and almost immediately Queensberry had started to blackguard him for standing by Bosie in what was already a feud.

On the morning after Wilde's arrest, Percy went to the Cadogan Hotel where Bosie was staying and brought him £250, knowing that all his money had gone to Wilde's solicitors. He assured Bosie he would 'stick to him through thick and thin', and by going bail for Wilde later and in many other ways he proved this.

Bosie went round to Bow Street where Wilde was to be brought before a Magistrate that day, Saturday, April 6th. The police were friendly and during the intervals of Wilde's appearance in Court Bosie spent several hours with him in a comfortable room upstairs and was allowed to bring in whisky and cigarettes. It was on this day that he saw Sidney Mavor outside the Court, with the result already described. Mavor was called and it must have been a shock to the prosecution when one of their well-drilled witnesses, asked what had taken place when he stayed with Wilde at the Albemarle, said "Nothing." Had he not made a statement to Lord Queensberry's solicitors? "No." It was a courageous little action.

Even more courageous was that of Alfred Taylor. He had been promised immunity—in the way of such prosecutions, which are often little better than conspiracies—if he would give evidence against Wilde. He refused to do so and was now arrested and put in the dock with Wilde.

But there was no lack of evidence. Charles Parker answered according to instructions; so did his brother and Alfred Wood. The case was adjourned for a week, Sir John Bridge, the Magistrate, refusing bail. Wilde and Taylor were taken to Holloway prison.

Every day until the adjourned proceedings on April 11th and from then till the eve of the trial on April 26th, Bosie visited Oscar at Holloway. Oscar was on remand, and by the ancient and farcical formula, believed innocent until he was proved guilty. Yet the conditions (which have scarcely changed today) were such that Bosie said "nothing more revolting and cruel and deliberately malignant could be devised by human ingenuity". Bosie went into a box 'rather like the box in a pawnshop'. There was a whole row of these each occupied by a visitor, and opposite, facing each visitor, was the prisoner he was visiting. The two lines were separated by a corridor about a yard wide and a warder paced up and down between them, (this, at least, is no longer a rule.) Visitors and prisoners had to shout to make their voices heard and the din became ear-splitting. Oscar was rather deaf and could not hear Bosie much of the time. He looked at Bosie with tears running down his cheeks and Bosie looked back during the quarter of an hour they were allowed together.

But Oscar was allowed to write letters and as soon as Bosie had left he wrote to him each day and told him that his visits, such as they were, were all that made life bearable for him and he looked forward to each as the one bright spot in his day.

He felt himself deserted by all his friends except Bosie, the Leversons and Sherard, and it was in those weeks that he was forced to realize that whatever the result of his trial the *beau rôle* he had watched himself play was over. His prison sentence when it came with its monasticism and the scope it gave him to see himself in a wholly tragic part, was almost a relief after this squalid period on remand during which he tried to think there was still hope.

What Bosie's visits meant to him may be gathered from his letters to the Leversons and those to Bosie himself. "Not that I am really alone", he wrote to the Leversons, "A slim thing, gold-haired like an angel, stands always at my side. His presence overshadows me. He moves in the gloom like a white flower." "Today Bosie comes to see me early. I don't know where to turn. I care less when I think he is thinking of me. I think of nothing else." He wrote to More Adey and Ross, apparently supposing that Ross was still in London—"Bosie is wonderful. I think of nothing else. I saw him yesterday." To Sherard: "Nothing but Alfred Douglas's daily visits quicken me into life."

When Bosie had been prevailed upon to go abroad by the combined entreaties of Wilde himself, Humphreys the solicitor and Wilde's Counsel, Sir Edward Clarke, who told him that his presence in London would compromise Wilde's chances, Wilde wrote to Ada Leverson— "Now that he is away I have no one who brings me books. I have had no letter as yet today from Fleur-de-Lys. I wait with strange hunger for it." On the next day—"I had two letters from Jonquil today to make up." On the next:

I had not had a line from Fleur-de-Lys. I suppose he is at Rouen. I am so wretched when I don't hear from him. . . . Letter from Bosie, at Rouen, just arrived. Please wire my thanks to him. He has cured me of sorrow today.

To Bosie himself he wrote a number of significant letters, some while he was still in Holloway, others while he was on bail. These letters were, Bosie maintained, of paramount importance to an understanding of Wilde. They

show Oscar in a light which has never been revealed to anyone except myself and the few people to whom, at various times, I showed the letters. At the time he wrote them the anguish of his mind, coupled with what shone out at that time unmistakably as his real love for me, lifted him into realms of altruistic beauty and pathos which he never reached at any other time of his life or in any of his published works. I have never known anyone who could read these letters without genuine emotion. I have shown them to persons who hated and despised Oscar Wilde, and they have read them and shed tears over them. They showed him to be, at that time, one who had forgotten self in his love for someone else. They were a million miles removed from the artificial, slightly repellent epistles which were produced against him at the Old Bailey by my father as specimens of his attitude to me, with their Hylases and Hyacinthuses, "slim gilt souls", "flower-like lips", and all the other bag of tricks. These letters had the ring of genuine feeling, tragic emotion, sub-limated passion. For once in his life, and for a period extending over many weeks, facing, as he was, a world which was one vast nightmare of unknown terror and hostile glares, he thought more about someone else than of himself. His letters were really noble and really fine. The alchemy of passionate sin-cerity transmuted his thoughts into pure gold. One of them contained an *apologia* for his whole attitude towards me, and what I meant to him, which would have gone far to disarm the criticism of his worst enemies. I do not believe that my father himself could have read them without a feeling that here was something which he did not understand and which could not be spat upon without terrible risk to the spitter. I defy anyone who retains the least spark of honour to spit upon the real, essential love of one human being for another. And when I say love, I mean love, and not physical passion or desire or anything else.

He adds that he bitterly regrets that years afterwards, at a time when he was 'fool enough to be ashamed of having received such letters from a man', he burnt most of them on the advice of a friend who was 'also a friend of Robert Ross and that the advice he gave (Bosie) to destroy these letters was tendered only a few months before the trial of the Ransome action'.

To anyone who does not know what havoc prison life may make of a man's loyalties and reason, his recollections of those he loves and of his own character, it will seem incredible that these letters should have been written to Bosie less than two years before *De Profundis*, and that during those two years Wilde had no logical cause to change his attitude towards his friend and lover. Bosie had wanted to write a defence of Wilde in the *Mercure de France*, quoting from these and other letters, and this had become in the scorched mind of Wilde a malicious betrayal. Also Bosie had continued to live, in freedom and abroad, and Ross, who had stayed with him in Capri, had made the most of this in his reports to Oscar. But the letters Wilde wrote in prison and on bail before his sentence reveal, with a desperate sincerity, his true feelings and show the malice of *De Profundis* to have been the result of the mental tortures of prison.

Three of them have been almost miraculously preserved. Rupert

Hart-Davis tells the story (on page 393 of his *Letters of Oscar Wilde*) of how he obtained their text, and they may be read in that book in all their pathos, the only true love-letters Wilde ever wrote.

3

Bosie still believed he should be called to give evidence. To the end of his life he never doubted that if he had gone into the witness-box he would have saved Wilde. But Clarke knew better. It was possible that in the state of public feeling, as exemplified by the foreman of the jury later when he asked whether a warrant had been issued for Bosie's arrest, the Public Prosecutor would have had him charged, if only to answer those who talked of one law for the rich and one for the poor. That, needless to say, was not put to Bosie who was told simply that his presence might be prejudicial to Wilde. He left on the morning of April 24th. On that day, under the pretext of an execution order from Wilde's creditors, a mock auction was held at the house in Tite Street and a 'rabble of thieves and sensation-mongers crowded the house, broke into rooms, burst open drawers, stole manuscripts and anything else they could get away with; and at last the disorder and rowdiness became so great that the police were called in'.

Before leaving England, Bosie gave £50 to Arthur Newton, Taylor's solicitor, for that unfortunate young man's defence. He scarcely knew Taylor but was grateful and deeply impressed, as Oscar was, by his self-sacrifice and loyalty.

To his lasting credit [Bosie wrote afterwards] Taylor refused to give evidence against Oscar Wilde, and preferred to go, as he did, to two years' hard labour rather than, by betraying his friend, to sully his honour, which to my mind remains, from this very fact, far brighter than that of many of those who helped to hound Oscar Wilde to his doom.

After his imprisonment Taylor emigrated to America and lived there and in Canada but no details are known of his after-life. He deserved happiness.

During Wilde's trial Bosie stayed in Calais at the Terminus Hotel of the Gare Maritime. The English newspapers came over daily on the packet boat and gave him, twenty-four hours late, the more blood-curdling details of the proceedings.

Wilde as a witness in his own defence was better than when he had been prosecuting. In answer to Charles Gill's question, "What is the

love that dare not speak its name?"—a question he must have anticipated—he made a remarkable speech which has often been quoted,
and at no time did he try to be funny. He was cross-examined not only
about the suborned witnesses already produced but about others,
presumably less docile, who did not appear, like Alphonse Conway
and the page-boy, Tankard. But on the whole he bore up well. On
the fifth day the jury retired and failed to reach agreement. Two days
later Oscar was at last given bail while awaiting his second trial.

Bail was fixed at £5,000. Wilde himself was responsible for half
this, while Lord Douglas of Hawick and the Reverend Stewart
Headlam, the Christian-Socialist founder of the Guild of St. Matthew
already mentioned as a frequenter of the Crown in Charing Cross
Road, were responsible for the other half. Though Headlam's kind
action brought him into conflict with friends and fellow-workers, he
ran no financial risk, for his share of it was covered by Hawick and
Ernest Leverson.

Every day Wilde wrote to Bosie and every day Bosie wrote from
France. In his letters Bosie continued to beg to be called as a witness
in the case when it came on again. During the recent hearing he had
telegraphed to Sir Edward Clarke, giving him certain information
which he implored him to use, though it was compromising to himself,
and again offering himself for the witness-box. The precise nature of
this information is unknown but Bosie once said that it concerned an
incident at the Savoy Hotel. Wilde in *De Profundis* seems to refer to it.
"The sins of another", he says, unwilling to commit to the scrutiny of
the prison authority a fact which might even then bring trouble to his
friend, but intending that it should be understood that 'another' was
Bosie, "The sins of another were being placed to my account. Had I so
chosen, I could on either trial have saved myself at his expense, not
from shame indeed, but from imprisonment." It is extremely unlikely
that even if Bosie had announced himself to blame for one of the
incidents of the case it would have affected the outcome. Indeed, it
would have told against Wilde who would have been held to have
'corrupted' Bosie as he was originally accused of 'corrupting' the other
young men. But it is good to know that when this arose Bosie tried to
persuade Wilde's Counsel to call him.

The theme of all his letters was his loyalty. Again and again
he offered any sacrifice he could make to help Wilde and when
assured that there was nothing he could do he gave his most solemn
promise that for the rest of their lives he would 'stick to him through

thick and thin, and that neither bribes nor threats would move me an inch from my determination that when he came out of prison he should find me exactly the same as I was when he last saw me a few weeks before his conviction'.

While Wilde was on bail, Bosie moved to Paris and wrote to his brother Percy begging him to tell Oscar to leave England while he could. Percy wrote that he sincerely hoped Wilde would go and that he was quite prepared to "stand the racket" for the whole of his bail. Frank Harris joined his entreaties to theirs and, (at least as he claimed afterwards) had a yacht 'with steam up' waiting in the Thames to take him. Bosie wrote from Paris one of the few of his letters to Oscar which survives.

It seems dreadful to be here without you [he said] but I hope you will join me next week. Do keep up your spirits, my dearest darling. I continue to think of you day and night, and send you all my love. I am always your own loving and devoted boy. Bosie.

Oscar wrote to Bosie to explain why he would not leave. It was, Bosie said, a very touching letter and made him weep at the time. Even thirty years later he could not bear to think about it. Oscar said he could not 'run away' and 'hide' and 'let down' those who had gone bail for him. "A dishonoured name, a hunted life, are not for me to whom you have been revealed on that high hill where beautiful things are transfigured." He also thought he had a good chance of being acquitted at the second trial. So Bosie stayed on in Paris and Oscar, accompanied by More Adey, the only one of his homosexual friends who remained in England, drove to the Court to surrender to his bail.

4

The case went as by this time everyone except Wilde knew it must go. Taylor was tried first and found guilty, on which Queensberry sent the following telegram to his daughter-in-law: "Must congratulate on verdict cannot on Percy's appearance looks like dug up corpse fear too much madness of kissing Taylor guilty Wilde's turn tomorrow. Queensberry." As he was coming away from the St. James's Street post office from which he had dispatched this he ran into his son Percy who asked him whether he intended to stop writing filthy letters to his wife. A scuffle ensued and the police, having failed to separate the two, took them both into custody. They were brought before a magistrate in the morning and bound over to keep the peace. So Queensberry arrived late at the Old Bailey for the first day of Wilde's last trial, and, being unable to get a seat, remained standing at the back of the Court sucking the rim of his hat and staring at Wilde.

Wilde was found guilty, told by the Judge that it was the worst case he had ever tried and that he had no shame and had been 'the centre of a circle of extensive corruption of the most hideous kind'. Both Wilde and Taylor were sentenced to two years' hard labour.

Frank Harris described the scene outside the Court 'as obscene and soul-defiling as anything witnessed in the madness of the French Revolution'. He caught a glimpse of Wood and the Parkers getting into a cab, 'laughing and leering'.

More relevant to the story of Bosie are the references to him in the Judge's summing-up. "In dealing with the case of Wood", said Justice Wills,

it is impossible for me to avoid dealing also with that of Lord Alfred Douglas. Now Lord Alfred is not present and is not a party to these proceedings, and it must be remembered in his favour that, if neither side called him, he could not volunteer himself as a witness. Anything, therefore, which I shall have to say to Lord Alfred Douglas's prejudice arises simply out of the facts which have transpired in the course of the evidence you have heard. I am anxious, too, to say nothing in the case of a young man like this, who is just on the threshold of life, which might to a great extent blast his career. I do not desire to comment more than I can help either about Lord Alfred Douglas or the Marquess of Queensberry, but I must say that the whole of this lamentable inquiry has arisen through the defendant's association with Lord Alfred Douglas. It is true that Lord Alfred's family seems to be a house divided against itself. But even if there were nothing but hatred between father and son, what father would not try to save his own son from the associations suggested by the two letters which you have seen from the prisoner to Lord Alfred Douglas? I will avoid saying whether these letters seem to point to actual criminal conduct or not. But they must be considered in relation to the other evidence in the case, and it is for you to say whether their contents lend any colour to Wood's story.

So Bosie's name was not spared and the Press took full advantage of this. Queensberry, who was in Court, must have realized at last what he had done to his son and to his house.

Caricature by Max Beerbohm.

Wilde and Douglas, 1894 and 189
lunching in Naples.

5

Wilde served the first six months of his sentence at Wandsworth (after a short time at Pentonville) and the remaining eighteen months at Reading. It is noteworthy that his sentence allowed no margin for remission. He served the full twenty-four months and knew that he would not be released until May 1897.

Bosie meanwhile went to stay in Rouen, and on the day after the verdict was given wrote to Sir Edward Clarke:

> Hotel de la Poste,
> Rouen.
> Sunday, 26th March 1895.

Dear Sir Edward,

You will forgive me I am sure for writing to you now to thank you from the bottom of my heart for your noble generous and superb efforts on behalf of my friend.

It seems almost an impertinence from one so miserable as myself, so broken in heart [and] in spirit, so defamed and ruined to offer you my poor gratitude, but believe me I shall never cease to think of you but with the profoundest gratitude and admiration. That you were unable to get a verdict seems to me, a layman, a piece of monstrous injustice, and the sentence was worse than I would have thought possible after the first disagreement.

Forgive this intrusion from one who is lying in the lowest hell of misery, and believe me to be

> Yours ever gratefully and sincerely,
> Alfred Douglas.

He was joined for a time by Ross with whom, it seems likely, he had also been at Calais. The two were exiles for the same reason and temporarily united by fellow-feeling over Oscar. In Bosie's frank, impulsive, volatile mind there was no perception at all of Ross's dormant jealousy.

Meanwhile Bosie's mother, one of the most tragic figures behind the scenes of the trial, was in distress and anxiety about the son for whose wilfulness she blamed herself and her indulgence to Bosie in his childhood. Though not a Catholic, she turned now to a Catholic priest, an old friend of hers at the Oratory, Father Sebastian Bowden. She asked him to get 'some steady and trustworthy friend' to look after Bosie, warning the priest that Bosie would grievously resent the notion of being looked after. Father Bowden immediately suggested More Adey, a Catholic of thirty-eight years, a friend of Bosie and Ross and

I

a homosexual of what, among his fellows was, and is, called the 'discreet' kind. Father Bowden's letters to Adey survive. He spoke of this as a work of charity. He was to look after Bosie to prevent him, as far as possible, from running into wild courses "through a mistaken sense of standing by one who is down", and "generally draw him into a good and sensible mode of life". If Adey, who was already in Rouen on a short visit to Bosie and Ross, would prolong his stay there and do his best to "calm and quiet the youth aright", Lady Queensberry would gladly defray his hotel expenses for a month or two if he could manage to stay so long. Father Bowden had told her that these would not exceed £3 a week as he knew Adey was a careful man. Lady Queensberry would also be very grateful for 'any reassuring intelligence' he could send her. Bosie's brother Percy had been over to see him in the previous week, so perhaps he and Adey had 'hit upon some common' plan.

Adey, who had returned to London, replied that he would accept the task as soon as he felt himself secure about Robert Ross who had the prior claim on him. Father Bowden was very glad that Adey was "able to rescue others from evil". He feared that Bosie was at present so self-willed and so blinded as to be humanly speaking past Redemption. Father Bowden thought he had better tell Lady Queensberry that Ross's family had forbidden him to stay with Bosie, also about a crazy plan of Bosie's to go to Florence to see Lord Henry Somerset. This was another exile, a talented man, a song-writer, some of whose ballads are still remembered, who had left England after a homosexual scandal some years before. This proposed visit would be, Father Bowden thought understandably, 'a great mistake'.

Ross left Bosie about June 20th for Dieppe, and Bosie wrote to Adey to say it was depressing to be alone and hoped Adey would join him. Adey eventually did so at the end of June and seems to have stayed some weeks, but he reached Rouen too late to prevent one of Bosie's wildest gestures of loyalty to Oscar.

Bosie was in frustration and despair but felt increasing indignation on behalf of his friend. He waited for chances to defend him, openly taking up his position beside Wilde. Away from the moderating influence of his mother, he wrote furious letters in defence of Wilde and of homosexuality, damning the hypocrisy which had put his friend in prison and in a hot-headed way trying to take some of the onus on his shoulders. He was doing himself harm for his family and the friends of his family wanted to forget that he had been publicly associated with Wilde, but with a boyish stubbornness and perhaps a guilty feeling that Oscar was suffering for the two of them, he persisted in writing to politicians, editors, friends and relations letters which must have been both disturbing and embarrassing to them.

How far away from publishing them were their recipients may be guessed from the following, which was addressed to W. T. Stead, the editor of *The Review of Reviews*. It was posted on the day of Adey's arrival in Rouen.

Hotel de la Poste,
Rouen,
28th June 1895.

Sir,

I have just read your comments on the Oscar Wilde case in the *Review of Reviews*. I believe you to be a man with a conscience and one who, if he thought a terrible wrong had been done, would not sit with his hands folded and do nothing. Now, sir, you admit that the common cant about "unnatural" offences is not worth anything, you have sufficient philosophy to understand and sufficient boldness to say that to call a thing unnatural is not only not necessarily to condemn it but is even to a certain extent to commend it. Everything that diverges from the normal may to a certain extent be called unnatural, genius and beauty among them. But while you admit broadly all this, you uphold the horrible and barbarous law which condemns a man who is guilty of these so called "offences" to a sentence which you calmly describe as "probably capital", and you give surely the flimsiest and feeblest reason for this. Your argument apparently is that if these laws did not exist a taint or suspicion might be thrown on friendships between people of the same sex which at present does not exist. Now, sir, you are probably aware that such laws as ours do not exist in France, and that these "offences" are there ignored by the law just as fornication is ignored in England, and yet you will hardly venture to say that this taint or suspicion exists in connexion with friendships between people of the same sex in France. Why then do you anticipate that a similar absence of laws in England would produce the result you dread? My opinion is that no such taint would attach to friendships between those of the same sex unless the suspicion was justified by facts. Thus in England there are no laws against "Lesbianism" or intercourse of an erotic character between women, and yet there are several women in London whose friendship with other women does carry a taint and a suspicion simply because these women are obviously "sapphic" in their loves. On the other hand a great friendship may exist between two ordinary women and nobody would think of imputing to them "improper" motives. I hope you follow my argument and observe the analogy.

Perhaps you are not aware that "Lesbianism" exists to any extent in London, but I can assure you that it does, and though of course I cannot mention names, I could point out to you half a dozen women in society or among actresses who would be considered as "dangerous" to young girls as Oscar Wilde will I suppose henceforth be considered to boys. Why on earth in the name of liberty and common sense a man cannot be allowed to love a boy, rather than a woman when his nature and his instinct tell him to do so, and when he has before him the example of such a number of noble and gifted men who have had similar tastes (such as Shakespeare, Marlowe, Michael Angelo, Frederick the Great, and a host of others), is another question and one to which I should like to hear a satisfactory answer. Certain it is that persecution will no more kill this instinct in a man who has it, than it killed the faith of the Christian martyrs. I am not pleading for prostitution, but I think if a man who affects female prostitutes is unmolested it is disgraceful that a man who prefers male prostitutes should be thus barbarously punished. The only difference is that the man who brings bastards into the world, who seduces girls or commits adultery does an immense amount of harm, as you have yourself pointed out, wheras the paederast does absolutely no harm to anyone.

While on the point, sir, may I ask you if it ever occurred to you to consider the relative deserts of Mr. Oscar Wilde and the man who ruined him, my father, Lord Queensberry? Mr. Oscar Wilde seduced no one, he did no one any harm, he was a kind, generous and astoundingly gifted man, utterly incapable of meanness or cruelty. Lord Queensberry was divorced from my mother after, for twelve years, she had silently endured the most horrible suffering at his hands.

He broke her heart, ruined her health and took away all joy from her life, and after his divorce till the present day he has not ceased to persecute her with every fiendish ingenuity of cruelty and meanness that a man could devise. Hardly a week passes without her receiving some letter from him containing some horrible insult, he has been to beat on the door of her house when she was nearly dying upstairs, and he has taken away from her every penny of money that as an honourable man he should have given her, and left her only that which he is forced to give by the Scotch law which is so hard on a woman who divorces her husband. In the meanwhile he flaunts about with prostitutes and kept women and spends on them the money which he should give to his children, for he has cut off all money supplies from my brother, myself and my sister.

Last year he induced a girl of seventeen to marry him in a registry office against the wish of her people.

On the following day he deserted her, and has since been divorced for a second time. Not content with practising fornication and adultery, he has written pamphlets and given lectures advocating what he calls a "sort of polygamy" which is neither more nor less than free love. This is the man who has been made into a hero by the English people and the *press*, who is cheered in the streets by the mob, and who has crowned his career by dishonouring and driving out of England his son who now writes to you.

I am, sir, your obedient servant,

Alfred Douglas.

Bosie also wrote in the same month to Henry Labouchère, not as the mover of the Amendment to the Act of 1885 under which Wilde had been prosecuted but as the editor of *Truth*. Labouchère had called Bosie 'an exceptional young scoundrel' and Bosie retorted. Labouchère published only the following extract from Bosie's letter, with his own editorial comment on it.

I stayed for three weeks after Mr. Wilde's arrest, and visited him every day, and I did everything my mind could devise to help him, and I left on the day before his trial at his own most urgent request, and at the equally urgent request of his legal advisers, who assured me that my presence in the country could only do him harm, and that if I were called as a witness I should infallibly destroy what small chance he had of acquittal. Mr. Wilde's own counsel absolutely declined to call me as a witness, fearing the harm I might do him in cross-examination, so that had I been called as a witness at all, it would have only been under a subpoena from the prosecution. Now, sir, you must give the devil his due, and granting, for the sake of argument, that I am an exceptional young scoundrel, you have no right to call me a coward. Perhaps you will pause to consider whether or not it is consistent with cowardice to do what I did—remain for three weeks in London with the daily and momentary expectation of being arrested and consigned to a fate like Mr. Wilde's, receiving every day letters of warning, implored by all my friends and relations to go and save myself, and held up to execration of every catchpenny rag in England.

Labouchère added:

Certainly this exceptional moralist has the courage of his opinions but, these opinions being what they are, it is to be regretted that he is not afforded an opportunity to meditate on them in the seclusion of Pentonville.

The rest of Bosie's letter was filed and produced against him several times in after years.

He may also have written to his father, he certainly received a letter from him in which Queensberry offered to supply him with money and an allowance if he would renounce Wilde, suggesting that Bosie should go to the South Sea Islands for a time, since there he would find 'plenty of beautiful girls'.

Bosie would certainly have been a nasty little cad if he had dropped

Oscar at this point, or at any time, or for almost any reason, during the remaining years of Wilde's life, but not dropping him and publicly proclaiming himself one with him in opinion and practice were two very different things. Bosie would have been more helpful if he had been more discreet.

When various French writers refused to sign a petition for Wilde's release, Bosie wrote an unequal but scathing sonnet which he sent to André Gide:

> Sonnet, dedicated to those French men of letters
> (Messrs. Zola, Coppée, Sardou and others)
> Who refused to compromise their spotless reputations
> or imperil their literary exclusiveness
> By signing a merciful petition in favour of Oscar Wilde.

> Not all the singers of a thousand years
> Can open English prisons. No. Though hell
> Opened for Thracian Orpheus, now the spell
> Of Song and art is powerless as the tears
> That love has shed. You that were full of fears
> And mean self-love, shall live to know full well
> That you yourselves, not he, were pitiable
> When you met mercy's voice with frowns or jeers.

> And did you ask who signed the plea with you?
> Fools! It was signed already with the sign
> Of great dead men, of God-like Socrates,
> Shakespeare and Plato and the Florentine
> Who conquered form. And all your petty crew
> Once, and once only, might have stood with these!

At the end of July he went to stay at Havre, where More left him in rooms overlooking the sea. He bought a small sailing-ship, something between a yacht and a fishing-smack. That he was almost one of the Ross, Adey, Turner circle at this time, with their private jokes and small homosexual intrigues, is shown by a line in one of his letters to Adey—"Am surprised at not hearing from Bobbie to whom I sent a gourmet of great personal beauty".

He is dull since More left but his yacht is now ready and he goes out in that. "I must thank you, dear More, for being so kind and nice to me."

But soon he was made to suffer some of the consequences of his friendship with Wilde. He had engaged two young sailors for his boat and had not been to sea with them more than three or four times

when the local paper, *Journal de Havre*, accused him of corrupting the
youth of the town. He replied with his usual spirit and this time his
letter was published (August 1st, 1895):

*C'est déjà trop evident que le monde a le droit de m'insulter et de me injurier parce
que je suis l'ami d'Oscar Wilde. Voilà mon crime, non pas que j'étais son ami, mais
que je serai jusqu'à la mort (et même après di Dieu le veut).*

Bosie left France and went to Naples, where his grandmother, Mrs.
Alfred Montgomery, lived. She, it will be remembered, had been
separated from her husband and children when she became a Catholic.
(She was converted by Cardinal Manning, whom she had known
while he was still an Anglican and Rector of Pulborough, which was
close to Petworth, the house of her father, the first Lord Leconfield.)

He then took a small villa at Sorrento, the Villa Tarnasse, and on
August 25th wrote to Adey—

I cannot think why neither you or Bobbie ever write to me, especially Bobbie,
it is so unlike him not to write, and he certainly owes me a letter. Your telegram about Pomatti was so belated that my answer may have been somewhat
snappish. The fact is Pomatti turned out a complete fraud and the subject is a
sore one. Also I told Percy all about this weeks ago, and surely you will not
endeavour to do anything about the bankruptcy without consulting him. He
told me he was going to find the money for it, but he also told me to mention
it to no one, so this is strictly entre nous. I only tell you to prevent useless
efforts on your part. Dear More, if you could only come out here a little I
can't tell you what it would be to me. I am utterly wretched for want of a
kindred spirit. Gatty is awfully nice and very enthusiastic about the scenery
and the ruins and what not. *But but* there is not an atom of real sympathy between us and I am lonely and deserted to a degree. I can't stand him alone much
longer. He understands nothing of our dear familiar clichés and he has never
read Oscar's books. Do come and see me, you or Bobbie, or I shall really go
mad. We have here 2 sitting-rooms, one of which could be turned into a
bedroom, 2 bedrooms and a kitchen, price 112 francs a month! Food at the
hotel very good indeed, French cook and complete run of the most lovely
hotel for 6½ francs (a special favour: the other guests pay 11!) a day. I mention
this fact in case expense is a consideration, you would pay nothing for lodging
and 6½ francs a day for board. Do come and save from despair. I need
hardly say the place is supremely lovely, and the weather perfect. Yrs always,
Bosie.

From Sorrento Bosie crossed to Capri and rented a villa for some
months, (Villa Caso) spending most of the time in the water. Here he
wrote some of the best of his earlier poetry, including *The Legend of*

Spinello of Arezzo and the exquisite little *Vae Victis*, which is wholly free from the lush verbiage and pretty figures of speech which he had inherited from Swinburne and Rossetti and others of the time. He also wrote *The Image of Death* and a sonnet in memory of his brother Drumlanrig, who had died a year earlier:

> God is very wise
> All that this year had in its womb He knew,
> And, loving you, He sent His Son like Death
> To put his hand over your kind grey eyes.

6

Late in November Robert Ross arrived to stay with him and brought him the news, which he in turn had heard from Adey, of Oscar's sudden half-insane hostility towards him. This had been set off by an unfortunate series of events.

While still at Le Harve Bosie had written excitedly to Adey—

Get the *Mercure de France* of this month, August, a splendid article in defence of Oscar. Do buy several copies and distribute them. Send one to Frank Harris.

He had been given at last the opportunity for which he had longed of writing an apologia for Wilde, and of identifying himself publicly with all that had brought Wilde to prison. He had been asked by the editor of the *Mercure de France*, whose publishing company intended in any case to publish a book of Bosie's poems in French and English, to write an article which would appear in the review before his poems would be issued as a book. The *Mercure* at that period was a progressive literary monthly of considerable popularity and status, a splendid platform from which to shout all the things that Stead and Labouchère had refused to hear.

Bosie seized the opportunity. Oscar himself in his letters from Holloway had asked Bosie to try, as far as he was able, to set him a little right with some small portion of the world (as he afterwards admitted in *De Profundis*), and here, as it seemed to the very sanguine young Bosie, was a chance to set Wilde *wholly* right with the *entire* civilized world. Since his rebuffs from *Truth* and *The Review of Reviews* he had almost lost hope of publishing anything which would vindicate his friend, and he grabbed the chance. He wrote an article, illustrated by extracts from Wilde's letters from Holloway, in which he thoroughly incriminated himself, maintaining that it was no incrimination, and openly defended Wilde and all that in the public mind he stood for. At the same time, unable to communicate with Oscar himself, who was allowed to receive only one letter a month and was trying to avoid being divorced by Constance Wilde, he wrote to the Governor of Wandsworth asking him to obtain Wilde's permission for the publication of the letters.

Then poor bungling Robert Sherard, who had always the best intentions but was continually baffled by the strange twists of temperament of the homosexuals among whom he incredulously found himself, complicated the situation. He was granted a second visit to Wilde that November.

[He] tells me [wrote Wilde], that in that ridiculous *Mercure de France*, with its absurd affectation of being the true centre of literary corruption, you are about to publish an article on me with specimens of my letters. He asks me if it really was by my wish. I was greatly taken aback, and much annoyed and gave orders that the thing was to be stopped at once.

Six weeks later, for things move slowly among prison officials, Bosie's request reached Wilde.

I am called out of the hospital ward, where I was lying wretchedly ill, to receive a special message from you through the Governor of the Prison. He reads me out a letter you had addressed to him in which you stated that you proposed to publish an article "on the case of Mr. Oscar Wilde" in the *Mercure de France* (a "Magazine", you added for some extraordinary reason, "corresponding to the English *Fortnightly Review*") and were anxious to obtain permission to publish extracts and selections from . . . what letters? The letters I had written you from Holloway Prison: the letters that should have been to you things sacred and secret beyond anything in the whole world! These actually were the letters you proposed to publish for the jaded *decadent* to wonder at, for the greedy *feuilletoniste* to chronicle, for the little lions of the *Quartier Latin* to gape and mouth at.

The article was at once withdrawn and now Ross came to tell him, not perhaps without secret pleasure, of the effect of this incident on Oscar. Bosie at once wrote to Adey a letter which, for all its nearness to hysteria, crudely reveals Bosie's state of mind:

My dear More,
    The arrival of Bobbie has cheered me up a great deal, we are doing well and the weather is very nice.
    I hear you are going to see Oscar soon. Of course I *know everything* and I know from what I have heard from Bobbie that my instinct was right and

that Oscar has changed about me. I am writing to you now, dear More, unknown to Bobbie, to beg you to do what you can for me with Oscar. If only you could make him understand that though he is in prison he is still the court the jury the judge of my life and that I am waiting and hoping for some sign that I am to go on living. There is nobody to play my cards in England, nobody to say anything for me, and Oscar depends *entirely* on what is said to him, and they seem all my enemies. I can't put my case to you, because you know what it is, I can't tell you what to say to Oscar because you know. I won't argue, I will only say one thing and I beg you to believe it, that I shall kill myself if Oscar throws me over. I don't want to be melodramatic and absurd and it is so difficult to avoid it and to make people understand what is such a commonplace truth to me, namely that my life really and not metaphysically hangs on Oscar. I am inordinately conceited and have a great opinion of myself as a poet, I think myself a very great poet, or rather I think I *was* a great poet. If I thought I could go on writing splendid works of art I would live for *that*, but the fact is that I *know* that the power has left me, and that being so I have nothing on earth to live for except Oscar. And if he does not want me and is going to leave me there is not only no pleasure but no use for me to live for.

I am not in prison but I think I suffer as much as Oscar in fact more, just as I am sure that he would have suffered more if he had been free and I in prison. Please tell him that. Can't you tell him this and tell him to send me some message. If you could only shew him a photograph for a minute I think it might give him back his soul again. Do try and do this, there is the little photograph of me in cap and gown at Oxford that Bobbie had. How can he expect anything from his wife, what did she do for him when he was in trouble and how can he have changed so? The only thing that could make his life bearable is to think that he is suffering for me because he loved me, and if he doesn't love me I can't live and it is so utterly easy to die. Do work for me, More, and even if you cut him to the heart and make him unhappy you will really be doing him good if you can only make him love me again and know that he is being martyred for my sake. It is such a joy for me to suffer anything for him. Tell him I know that I have ruined his life, that everything is my fault, if that pleases him. I don't care. Doesn't he think that my life is just as much ruined as his and so much sooner? I am drivelling now, so goodbye and do something for me.

Ever yours affect[y]

Bosie.

Adey's reply was conciliatory. He was able to do little, he said, to be comforting though he would do all he could. He had seen Oscar just before receiving Bosie's letter. He understood what Oscar's change must mean to Bosie, but from the first he had never believed it was more than a passing delirium of gaol moral fever. No man like Oscar, subjected to such conditions as Adey had seen, could be considered capable of exercising his ordinary mental or moral faculties, and what he was saying no more represented his feelings than the ravings of someone in delirium. In former interviews he had spoken of Bosie as a lunatic speaks of those he loves best, but now he only complained of some letter which Bosie had written. Adey had told him he was certain Bosie would write no more.

Adey ended his letter with a few words of sincere advice: "You must try to show the love which I know you have for him by the most difficult of all ways—*waiting*."

This advice Bosie attempted to follow, and since it apparently distressed Oscar, made no more attempts to communicate with him. During the previous August he had managed to convey a greeting through a clerk who interviewed Wilde in connection with his bankruptcy proceedings, but he made no more moves of that kind.

7

Robert Ross stayed abroad until April 1896, when he returned to England. In May he went with Sherard to Reading to see Wilde who at this period of his imprisonment was allowed two visitors together once every eight weeks. On this journey Sherard repeated to Ross the story of the *Mercure de France*. Ross also knew of this from More Adey but he remembered other differences and disputes between Oscar and Bosie which had quickly passed and it seems he decided to wait and see how matters stood before committing himself to one side or other in the quarrel. He had remained on outwardly friendly terms with Bosie, and until there was a chance of a permanent rift he would not risk being in the position of one who takes sides during a quarrel which is to be repaired and then finds himself at odds with both parties.

But when Ross brought up Bosie's name during his first visit, saying that Bosie's poems were to be published, and dedicated to Wilde he must have been delighted to observe Wilde's response. "When I told him", wrote Ross to More Adey afterwards, "that Bosie's poems were coming out and that I had message in letter which I showed through the bars, he said *I would rather not hear about that just now*."

What more Ross told Wilde during that interview can only be guessed but almost certainly he described Bosie's life in the villa on

Capri and afterwards in Rome and Monte Carlo with a gloating vividness which aroused Wilde's jealousy. He was rewarded by receiving from Wilde the letter he had awaited for six years, though he may have been subtle and intelligent enough to see that even in his resentment all Oscar's thoughts were of Bosie while he, Ross, was being used as a mere messenger of ill-will.

Ross had told Wilde that Bosie intended to dedicate his book of poems, shortly to be issued in Paris, to his friend Oscar Wilde. This proposal, Wilde said, was revolting and grotesque. Bosie was to hand to Ross all the letters Wilde had written him, together with things Wilde had given him, books and jewellery. Wilde wished to be certain that Bosie had nothing in his possession given him by Wilde. Wilde spoke—a foretaste of *De Profundis*—of the way Bosie had thrust him into ruin and disgrace "to gratify his hatred of his father and other ignoble passions". He had ruined Oscar's life, and that should content him. Ross was to write immediately he had obtained possession of these articles.

Ross carried out Wilde's instructions and received a sharp retort from Bosie, who said in effect . . . "I don't care what you say, it may be true that Oscar has turned against me, but that is probably only because he is half mad as a result of his sufferings in prison, and in any case, whether he has turned against me or not I have not turned against him. I promised him on my most sacred word that I would stick to him, and I shall go on doing it. When he comes out of prison, if he chooses to say he does not want my friendship, and that he wants his letters back, he can do so with his own mouth:" But Bosie withdrew the Dedication as Oscar required.

By the time Ross went down to Reading again Wilde had so far created a grievance out of Bosie's actions that Ross felt safe in fanning the flames. As Hesketh Pearson says:

Ross had known Wilde several years longer than Douglas, and was intensely jealous when Douglas supplanted him in Wilde's affection. The enforced separation of the two gave him an opportunity to re-establish himself as Wilde's most intimate friend, and he made the best of it. He probably told Wilde that Douglas was enjoying himself in Italy, that he was showing Wilde's letters to everybody, and that he had completely forgotten the man for whose ruin he had been primarily responsible. In the state of remorse and despair to which Wilde had been reduced, it is easy to see how galled he must have been at every mention of Douglas's light-heartedness, how the least hint must have magnified the contrast between Douglas's freedom and his own bondage.

Ross, we may be sure, missed no opportunity and he had excellent material to work with. A man in prison is perpetually seeking objects for his resentment, is desperately trying to pass his own bitterness to others, to implicate others in his disaster. The smallest incident of his past or present may become exaggerated into an affront, a wound, a contemptuous and heartless attack or a cruel humiliation. Some trivial story from the world in which he has no part may be enough to reduce him to impotent fury or grinding despair. Wilde, already in a state of tearful self-pity and remorse, needed only an apparently casual reference to Bosie, who was the one human being he loved, to sink into hatred and malice.

Bosie remained abroad and with every attempt to prove his loyalty angered Oscar more. Bumbling Sherard was soon converted to the view that Bosie had 'ruined' the friend Sherard had once revered, and Constance Wilde, when Sherard and Ross had talked to her, began to feel the same. "There is evidence", says Mr. Hesketh Pearson, "to show that he [Ross] was partly responsible for the arrangement whereby Oscar's income from his wife would be stopped if he joined Douglas after the release."

Ross was also the only go-between for Oscar and Bosie. There seems no doubt that he made play of this. Wilde in *De Profundis* speaks bitterly of letters from Bosie for which he had waited in vain. Bosie explains this:

I decided to go to England and to visit Wilde in prison. I wrote informing Robert Ross of my intention and, in reply he told me that he had just come from Wilde and that, as his correspondence and visitors were strictly limited, he desired that I should neither write to him nor visit him. . . . I was very much upset on receiving this news, and I had some thought of trying to obtain an interview with Wilde through influence which I possessed; but I was told that it would be bad for Wilde if I did so, and I accordingly determined to follow out his wishes and to wait until he could write or send to me.

His poems appeared in English with a clever French translation by Eugene Tardieu, a man on the staff of the *Echo de Paris*. There were two limited and signed editions of 50 and 25 copies respectively and an ordinary edition of 1,000.

In June of that year (1896) Bosie at last got his views into print— not in the *Mercure de France* but in an *avant-garde* little weekly review which had already published some poems of his, the *Revue Blanche*. The article did Wilde no harm, but it was damaging to Bosie and was used against him later. It seems possible that it was based on the original article for the *Mercure de France*, since it was entitled "*Une Introduction a mes poemes avec quelques considerations sur l'affaire Wilde*".

H. Montgomery Hyde in an Appendix to his *Trials of Oscar Wilde* gives an account of it, from which it appears that it was largely a repetition of the letter to W. T. Stead with a suggestion added that the trial of Wilde had been a political frame-up. It ended:

There is nothing more to say. Oscar Wilde is in jail and will remain there till the expiration of his sentence. A national crime has been committed, a crime from which no element of morbid intrigue, sensuality, cruelty and hypocrisy is wanting.

Fortunately, the *Revue Blanche* had an extremely small circulation and the article came to the notice of no one connected with Wilde. If Ross had seen it and taken it to Reading on his next visit, Oscar in his state of mind at the time might have had a stroke. Sherard in one of his books speaks of his efforts to stop it, but he is confusing it with the original article for the *Mercure de France*, in the withdrawal of which he had a hand. He was writing soon after the *Revue Blanche* article had been used against Bosie in the Ransome case.

8

Though Wilde did not see the *Revue Blanche* article, he had now persuaded himself into an extraordinary state of mind in which Bosie figured as his chief betrayer, yet was perpetually in his thoughts. He wrote to More Adey

[Sherard] saved my letters from being published. I know there was nothing in them but expressions of foolish, misplaced, ill-requited, affection for one of crude and callous nature, of coarse greed, and common appetites, but that is why their publication would have been so shameful.

But for all this abuse, there was perceptible, as there is in *De Profundis* itself, Wilde's persistent love for the man he believed he hated. From Adey's silence he gathered that Bosie still refused to return his presents and letters. "It is horrible he should still have the power to wound me", he wrote. Then in a letter to Ross, after similar tearful maledictions, he added pathetically—"In your letter tell me how he lives, what his occupations are, his mode of life."

Fed by Ross with accounts of Bosie's doings abroad, Wilde pictured the contrast between Bosie's present circumstances and his own. "Rome, Naples, Paris, Venice, some beautiful city on sea or river, I have no doubt, holds you", he was to write in *De Profundis*. "You are surrounded, if not with all the useless luxury you had with me, at any rate with everything that is pleasurable to eye, ear and taste. Life is quite lovely to you." He remembered that his own disaster had been brought about by his action against Bosie's father and that if Queensberry's solicitors had not skilfully suppressed the evidence against Bosie during the hearing of that action, Bosie might well have been with him in prison. He had been told by Ross that Bosie was deliberately neglecting him. ("I waited month after month to hear from you.") At last he began to write a letter to Bosie which would, he said, explain everything. He was not prepared to sit 'in the grotesque gallery' they put him into for all time.

It seems that at first he intended actually to send this letter of some 40,000 words to Bosie. There are, towards the end of it, instructions on how to answer it and practical suggestions about their re-meeting which argue this. When it was finished he decided to send it to Ross. "If you are my literary executor you must be in possession of the only document that gives any explanation of my extraordinary behaviour." But he was not allowed to send it out at all. It was to be kept with his possessions and handed to him on release.

There have been many attempts by Wilde's defenders to excuse it, including the suggestion that the strain of prison life had unbalanced his mind. This is gross exaggeration. Wilde was as sane as he ever was when he wrote *De Profundis* but his sanity was always one of highflown logic based on monstrous assumptions, the logic of the paranoiac.

During his last ten months in prison he was given privileges and comforts which no convicted man today could dream of, so that although his time at Wandsworth and his first months at Reading (during Isaacson's governorship) were far worse than anything the modern prisoner has to endure, with broad-arrow clothes, shaven head, perpetual silence and filthy food, his last ten months were more bearable. His friends had not only been able to arrange for his transfer to Reading but had secured the removal of Isaacson and the appointment as Governor of a charming and humane man, Major J. O. Nelson. Wilde did only very light work, as schoolmaster's orderly, and was allowed to have sent in all the books he wanted. He wrote and dispatched what letters he pleased, received a great many visits, writing to his friends of his 'next At Home day', and a light was left on in his cell to whatever time he pleased. He was called 'Sir' by the screws who brought a daily newspaper, hot beef-tea and biscuits to his cell and carried his notes to other prisoners. He was able to talk to them and within limits to his fellow convicts.

In these circumstances his nature began to expand again after the stricken numbness of his first fourteen months. But with that returned his megalomaniac concern with his place in the world and his place in history. He was not broken by his tragedy, but in his mind it had to be a great tragedy and his fall a fall of the mighty. He was not wholly oppressed by squalor and humiliation so long as they could be extreme and devastating. It was for the silliness and pettiness of his actions that he had to find a scapegoat. He did not want someone to share his disaster but he wanted to blame someone for his own discreditable invoking of the law he despised to protect him. It all had to be larger than life in order to give him back his self-adulation. In high-sounding phrases he wrote of his art, his place as an artist, his tragedy, and by doing so he could regain not his former pedestal but a new and more interesting one.

He did it persuasively. Though much of the prose of *De Profundis* seems highfalutin and many of the statements were deliberate and conscious lies, though the agile arguments sometimes ran away with him and led him to bathos, he was fighting to restore his vanity and he achieved it. Small wonder that he did not care what happened to the manuscript after he was released. It had fulfilled its purpose. In it he left all his rancour and much of his regret. When he came out of prison he surprised everyone by not being the broken, scarcely sane, feebly acrimonious man they had known during earlier visits, but a gay and genial, though outwardly aged Oscar. All that had nearly made him mad he had put into *De Profundis*. In this he wanted to force Bosie to share his humiliations and sufferings by assuring him that he was to blame for them.

But chiefly *De Profundis* is remarkable for those pieces of braggadocio, those grandiloquent estimates of the writer's former greatness and the high drama of his fall, which reveal its unconscious purpose. Perhaps the most significant sentence in it is: "In the lowest mire of Malebolge I sit between Gilles de Retz and the Marquis de Sade."

This figure of speech, which he repeated later in the letter, and which he had already used in a letter to Ross, must have been supremely satisfying to Wilde. It was thus that he wanted to see himself. It was a novel kind of self-aggrandizement that he was enjoying, through which he groped his way to his old self again. He pursued it with words to both heights and depths, scarcely knowing which he preferred so long as they were towering peaks or black hell-pits. He went from it to such bitter boasting as that fantastic estimate of himself which opens with the claim "The Gods had given me almost everything." There is much more in this vein of high tension but only one passage which seems to epitomize it all, a passage in which he remembers the closing speech of prosecuting counsel at his last trial: "Lockwood's appalling denunciation of me—like a thing out of Tacitus, like a passage in Dante, like one of Savonarola's indictments of the Popes of Rome." A man who could write that of the vigorous platitudes of a sound lawyer because they were spoken of *him*, must have been in a state of self-exaltation only just within the frontiers of sanity.

Such was his desperately regained megolomania. The passages in which he attacks Bosie are no less interesting and for sheer bitchiness have never been surpassed. But the whole letter should be read in *The Letters of Oscar Wilde*, in which, for the first time, it is printed accurately and in full.

Between the railings of the first part of the letter and the petulant falsity at the end are some passages as sincere as anything Wilde was capable of writing, and though the philosophy of humility and suffering he expounds need not be taken too seriously in view of his life after prison, the prose here is at times very fine, unaffected and telling. He was a maker of comedy and always fell into melodrama when he tried to write seriously, as may be seen from *Dorian Gray*. But at moments here he achieved the forceful expression of his moods in words both moving and rhythmical. It was chiefly this portion which appeared originally as *De Profundis* before it was known that it was part of a larger more ignoble work.

I have used the word bitchiness, for it is irresistible. Another manifestation of it—since the letter was presumably written to be sent to Bosie on its completion—was the frequent dragging in of Ross's name, always lit with approval. It seems likely that Wilde now realized Ross's jealous longing to appropriate him as a friend and was perhaps naïf enough to suppose that Bosie might feel some envy for Ross, or that Bosie had the secret animosity towards the little man that Ross had for him. Bosie at this time regarded Ross as kind, pleasant and useful, an honest if somewhat officious go-between and a fellow friend of Wilde's. Even if Bosie had received the letter it would not have changed this opinion. "In the early days I was very fond of Ross", wrote Bosie, and to the end of his life he never could see that even 'in the early days' Ross was not very fond of him, or why this should be. He thought that some mysterious change came over him.

I cannot recall another instance of such a complete change of character as that which took place in this nervous, affectionate, sentimental and emotional little man, between the time when I first met him and the last twelve years of his life.

It was, in fact, a simple matter. From the time Ross first met Wilde he had no other serious interest. Wilde, in triumph or prison, alive or dead, was Ross's life. The green fires of jealousy which blazed up or burned down were inevitable in one who had nothing else to warm his nature but a little rancid promiscuity and a dilettante interest in art and letters. Ross did not 'in the early days' hate Bosie as a person but as an impediment. While Wilde was in prison he thought that impediment could be forever removed.

When Wilde had finished the letter to Bosie which was afterwards called *De Profundis*, Major Nelson, the obliging governor of Reading Gaol, asked the Prison Commissioners at Wilde's request if he might send it to Ross to be forwarded to Bosie. Had they agreed, the course of history—as they say—would have been considerably changed, for Ross would not have dared to disobey instructions and if Bosie had received it at that time, while he was still waiting for Wilde's release, the document would not have ruined several lives and been a bone of contention still gnawed over at the present time. But the Commissioners refused. Wilde might take it out with him. (He would not be allowed to do so today, dealing as it does with his own case and the circumstances of his conviction.) But it must not be sent from the prison.

While Wilde was awaiting permission to send it, never doubting that Nelson would obtain this, he wrote a letter to Ross which was of great significance later. It is a very long letter and all of it is of great interest to the student of Wilde. So far as it affects Bosie, its chief importance is in the instructions it gave about the manuscript of *De Profundis*. This was to be copied carefully. Since Wilde wanted Ross to be his literary executor in case of his death, Ross must be in possession of the only document to explain his extraordinary conduct. Wilde was not content to sit in the 'grotesque pillory' into which he had been put, for he had inherited from his father and mother a name of "high distinction". He thinks the letter should be typewritten. "The copy done and verified the original should be sent to A.D. by More."

There was no need to tell Bosie a copy had been taken, unless he should write and complain of injustice or misrepresentation. It would be the first time anyone had told Bosie the truth about himself and Wilde hoped it would do him good.

But there follow some sentences which hint at the truth—that Wilde had unburdened himself of an immense weight of resentment. Of the many things for which he was grateful to the prison governor, he said, none was more important than his permission to write fully to Bosie. For nearly two years he had within him a growing weight of bitterness, much of which he had now got rid of.

Three things are noteworthy in this letter which appears in full on pp. 512-517 of Mr. Hart-Davis's *Letters of Oscar Wilde*. Firstly, the opening paragraphs gave Ross the only authority he had at the time of Wilde's death nearly four years later to assume his literary executorship, and a great deal, including Wilde's reconciliation with Bosie, had happened in the meantime. Secondly, the instructions were explicit that the manuscript was to be sent to Bosie when the copies had been typed. It is possible, indeed likely, that Wilde cancelled these instructions when he handed over the manuscript or later. But on them Bosie based a not unreasonable claim to the possession of the manuscript. If this letter, he argued, had sufficient authority to make Ross literary executor it also had authority to give him possession of the letter addressed to him. Thirdly, Wilde realized that its value to himself as a cathartic was its chief importance, and by the time he had finished *De Profundis* had almost lost interest in its effect on Bosie. So that when he came out of prison he did not even want it delivered to him.

That was understandable for another reason. Within a few weeks of Wilde's release he was writing to Bosie as 'My own darling boy' and saying that his only chance of 'doing beautiful work in art' was to be with him. His letter, *Epistola In Carcere et Vinculis* as he facetiously called it in imitation of an Encyclical, (*De Profundis* was Ross's title,) had achieved its object and he was a happier, more spleen-free man for having written it. It is probable that he never made up his mind, during the remaining years of his life, what should be done with it and that he died without giving further instructions. There is a rather cryptic reference to it in a letter to Ross just a month after his release: "You never told me anything about the typewriter and my letter; pray let there be no further conspiracies." A month later there are some instructions to have the letter typed by Mrs. Marshall. After that,

silence. It is likely that Wilde pushed the thing to the back of his
mind and let Ross take his own course of action.

Even while still in prison he soon had more urgent things to occupy
him and during his last six weeks there attacked his other friends with
almost as much venom (which was always prison venom; never
natural to him) as he had shown towards Bosie.

Money was his chief concern, security, some kind of future, all
familiar preoccupations of prisoners nearing release and fearful of the
world to which they must return. He had lost confidence in himself
and it made him write mordantly and reproachfully to his friends.
The difference between his letters to them and his letter to Bosie was
that they received theirs and could conceal or destroy them while
Bosie's was kept by Ross for twelve years, to be fired at him in court.

Most of Wilde's anger was caused by a great deal of dreary wrang-
ling over his life-interest in his marriage settlement and his wife's
divorce, also the loan from Leverson. He wrote to More Adey that he
and Ross had both assured him by letter and personally that enough
money had been subscribed for him to enable him to live in comfort
for 'eighteen months or two years'. He believed this. He now understood that there was no such sum at all, that there was no more than
£50, from which Hansell's and Holman's charges had to be deducted,
so that nothing of any import would be left. It was extremely wrong
of Adey and Ross to have made such a statement to him. It was wrong,
unkind, and injudicious.

What advantage was gained by deceiving me and my wife? Why did you do
it? Had the thing been done by others I would say it was a heartless, stupid
and offensive hoax. . . . For Leverson to come now and claim alone of all my
creditors to be paid 100 per cent and have his pound of flesh is simple fraud
and dishonesty. . . . I detest fraud, when united to gross sentimentality, and
wordy, vulgar expressions of devotion.

There was a great deal more abuse of Adey who was 'utterly incompetent', who had nearly repeated down to the smallest detail the whole
of the Queensberry episode, and so on. To Ross he wrote that he had
caused him the greatest pain and disappointment by foolishly telling
him a complete untruth. Ross's attempt to arrange matters with his
wife was 'stupid and ill-advised'. Ross and his other friends had so
little imagination, so little sympathy. But Wilde had a harsher rod
in pickle for Ross. He was sorry he had asked if Bosie was directing
these operations for this was unjust to Bosie. Later he asked how Ross
would have compared himself to Bosie if his (Ross's) scheme had had

the results Wilde feared. "I can only tell you he would have shown up very well beside you." When Wilde reflected on Ross's conduct and More Adey's he felt he had been unjust to 'that unfortunate young man' (Bosie).

If *De Profundis* in its entirety had been published with these letters as an appendix to show Wilde's state of mind at the time, there would have been no injustice. But it was neither published nor delivered to its addressee. It was looted for the uncompromising passages, then presented to the British Museum to be published after the death of everyone concerned, then brought out under subpoena as evidence against Bosie in a civil action for libel on which his life, and no one else's, depended.

9

During the second year of Wilde's imprisonment Bosie's family, and particularly his mother, tried to disentangle his life from Wilde's. While he was writing letters to newspapers and behaving with quixotic idiocy, as they saw it, he was kept short of money but after Wilde, through Ross and Sherard, had snubbed his efforts the Queensberry family found him more tractable. They wisely did not try to persuade him then to make any promise for the future but his mother, who had continued to send cheques to Adey for 'looking after' Bosie, in 1896 increased Bosie's allowance and spent some months with him in Rome. By tacit agreement they did not discuss Oscar and Lady Queensberry may have thought that Bosie was forgetting him.

It was while he was in Rome that he met Harry de Windt who remained his friend for the rest of his, de Windt's life and was on the 'Lord Kitchener and Jutland Publicity Committee' through which Bosie was convicted of criminal libel in 1923. With some justice he could give himself that name, a glamorous one at the time but now dated, an 'explorer'. He had already published four books about his travels—*On the Equator* (1882), *From Pekin to Paris by Land* (1887), *A Ride to India* (1890), *Siberia as It is* (1892). He was a tough interesting man who wrote his adventures rather than boring his friends with endless anecdotes.

De Windt, who had once been a friend of Queensberry and of other members of the family, met Bosie in the bar of the Grand Hotel and at once went up and spoke to him. Bosie who had been treated very distantly by the English abroad since the Wilde case, was pleased at this and the two became fast friends, eventually parting at three o'clock in the morning after having accompanied one another to their homes a number of times. Somewhere that evening there was a drunken 'gentleman from the Colonies' who carried a revolver and threatened to shoot de Windt in the intervals of buying him drinks and considering him the finest fellow in the world.

Bosie went to Monte Carlo with his mother then back to Paris where he remained till Wilde came out of prison.

10

In Paris, in the autumn of 1896, he was made to realize the full gravity of Oscar's artificial enmity. He wrote to More Adey on September 20, apparently in answer to a letter repeating Oscar's request for a return of his letters:

In the meantime I say nothing except that I utterly decline to entertain for a moment any proposition relating to the giving up to him of anything which belongs to me, and I prefer that you should tell him so quite frankly if you see him. Of my undying (I use the word in its real sense, not that in which he so often used it to me) love and devotion to him he may rest assured.

A week later, in answer to another letter from Adey he wrote:

I know quite well that you are not a traitor to my interests, and have never had such a thought about you. At the same time I think that you as well as most other of Oscar's and my friends in London have quite *forgotten* all the old traditions and conditions of my friendship with Oscar and you all are very different from yourselves and more like the rest of the world (and if I may say so without offence) more English than you used to be. Now you want me to do a thing which will for ever put me in the wrong. I have never quarrelled with Oscar although you talk about "reconciliation". The last time I saw him he kissed the end of my finger through an iron grating at Newgate, and he begged me to let nothing in the world alter my attitude and my conduct towards him. He wrote to me in the same strain many many times and he warned me that all sorts of influences would be brought to bear upon me to make me change, but I have not changed, from first to last I have been absolutely consistent, and absolutely the same. I shall not change now. I decline to listen to anything that he says while he is in prison. If he really means what he says and if he is really not mad, he is not the same person that I knew and he is not Oscar, the Oscar to whom I shall always be faithful, and who belongs to me quite absolutely. When lovers quarrel, they return to each other their letters and presents. I and Oscar were lovers, but we have not quarrelled, and as I have not asked for a return to my letters and my presents he cannot ask for his. If Oscar really meant what he says now, I should despise him utterly, for no meanness could be lower, and I should be obliged to think that what many people have over and over again told me about him is true. But I do not believe that he means what he says, and I regard what he says as non-existent, I ignore the cruel insults and the unmerited reproaches which I am told his lips have uttered against me, I attribute them simply to an evil and lying spirit which at present inhabits Oscar's body, a spirit born in an English prison, out of English "prison discipline" and which I hope in spite of everybody and everything to ultimately cast out of him. But even if I shall never cast it out, even if Oscar's body is always to be inhabited by this thing, even if the last time I saw Oscar I really said goodbye to him for ever and ever (at least in this world), I should still love and be faithful to my own Oscar the real one, and I should always refuse to take any notice of English prison spirits. I daresay you think I am talking nonsense, but I mean every word I say, and this is enough on this subject.

'Newgate' was evidently a mistake for 'Holloway'. He adds "Love to Bobbie" to his letter, but in February 1897 he speaks of the "extraordinary change of front" of both Ross and Adey. One of them has told him that Wilde is writing him a letter—the letter, (though Bosie had no idea of this,) which was to become *De Profundis*—and of this he says:

I wonder he writes. What he can have to say to me, unless one thing, I cannot understand, and if he is going to abuse me I would rather not see it. In all his life he has never written me a letter that was unkind or at least unloving and to see anything terrible in his writing written directly to me would almost kill me. However he must do as he pleases, and I will write again only what I think will be agreeable to him. Please let me know if possible by return

> (1) when exactly may I expect his letter?
> (2) when exactly will Oscar be released?

I suppose you will let me know any other necessary directions about writing the letter. I suppose it would be inadvisable to put more than *My dear Oscar* at the beginning, or might I put dearest? Forgive what seems harsh or disagreeable in this letter. My nerves are much unstrung by this incident and you know I am truly fond of you, dear More, and appreciate your kindness, though your ways are not my ways and I can't see with your eyes.

Bosie's attitude, as revealed in these letters to Adey, was exactly what he always claimed it to be, one of constancy in his love for Oscar, in spite of Wilde's prison bitterness towards him, in spite of his own interests and the appeals of his mother and family, in spite of his own disaster, in spite of the whole world. Misguided, indiscreet, headstrong, and socially suicidal it was called by everyone about him, and by mundane standards it was all of these. Yet there was an adolescent heroism in it.

CHAPTER VII

The Friendship: Berneval and Naples

I

WHEN Wilde was released from prison on May 19th 1897 he became at once a centre of intrigue which involved nearly all his acquaintances, his wife and her family, as well as Bosie and his family. This intrigue continued with intensity for a year or more and its machinations and cross-currents can be deduced from the letters of Wilde and others involved. Its reverberations have never quite died out.

Wilde as the centre of stratagem was by no means a passive figure, in fact as will be seen, he showed in his genial way as much cunning as most of the others. But he was conditioned by penury, which he made no serious attempt to relieve by writing. Ross had powerful weapons, the control of nearly all Wilde's financial resources, the ear of Wilde's wife, the assistance of More Adey and his own industry and perseverance. Bosie had one great advantage, Wilde's helpless love for him, but he was restrained by his family, by his blind failure to realize that he had determined and crafty enemies and by the fact that he was not prepared to dedicate his whole life to this warfare.

At first Ross was in undisputed possession. Wilde's letters during his last months in prison had been largely concerned with money,* and Ross held a sum which has been variously calculated, but was probably about £200, for his immediate needs. Wilde had signed an agreement with his wife by which she had control of his children but would give him an income of £150 a year so long as he did not associate with 'disreputable persons', and this was paid through Ross.

The terms of this agreement and its corollary considerations are clearly shown in a letter written to More Adey by his own solicitor nine days before Wilde's release. It is rather confusing that the three solicitors concerned in Wilde's affairs had somewhat similar names, Holman who acted for Adey, Hansell who was supposed to act for

---

* Indeed, as Cyril Conolly points out in reviewing the *Letters*, "of the thousand letters here printed I should say that two thirds were about money".

Wilde, and Constance Wilde's solicitor Hargrove. Holman's letter had repercussions which later affected Bosie as well as Wilde.

My dear Mr. Adey,

You will be glad to hear that Mr. Hansell and I had a very satisfactory interview with Messrs. Hargrove & Co. on Saturday. Mr. Adrian Hope was present as guardian for the children, & we finally settled the Deed of Arrangement.

As I told you in my former letter, it is arranged that after Mrs. Wilde's death the £150 is to be paid to me for Mr. Wilde for his life *unconditionally*: during her life Mrs. Wilde will pay the same amount to me quarterly subject to Mr. Wilde doing nothing 'which would entitle his wife to a divorce or a decree for judical separation, or be guilty of any moral misconduct, or notoriously consort with evil or disreputable companions'.

We obtained the insertion of the two words "moral" and "notoriously", which we think meets the case. In point of fact, the arrangement will be that Mrs. Wilde's bankers will have orders to pay till further notice the allowance to me every three months, and I shall at once forward it to Mr. Hansell to be applied for Mr. Wilde's benefit.

Mr. Hope stated that he practically was now the sole advisor of Mrs. Wilde, both in her own interests and in those of her children; that it was immaterial to him what kind of life Mr. Wilde led, provided he did not molest his wife or children, and *provided he kept out of the newspapers*, but he also said that in case of there being any *public* scandal in which Mr. Wilde was mixed up he would at once put the matter before Mr. Hansell, and ask his authority to stop the allowance. These terms are, I think, all that we can ask, and the deed will therefore be engrossed in triplicate on these lines. Mr. Wilde has approved it, and he has been made a party to it (though this is not necessary) in order that he may never in the future be able to accuse you or his other friends, or Mr. Hansell, or myself of entering into any arrangement with which he was not fully conversant.

I have no doubt that you or Mr. Ross or some other one of his friends will be seeing him before his release on the 19th, and I do hope you will impress upon him, as Mr. Hansell has already done, how absolutely fatal to him any further intercourse with Lord Alfred Douglas will be; apart from the fact that Lord Alfred is a 'notoriously disreputable companion' Lord Queensberry has made arrangements for being informed if his son joins Mr. Wilde and has expressed his intention of shooting one or both. A threat of this kind from most people could be more or less disregarded, but there is no doubt that Lord Queensberry, as he has shown before, will carry out any threat that he makes to the best of his ability.

Yours sincerely,
H. Martin Holman.

Cornhill, May 10 1897.

It was therefore known to Adey and Ross, though perhaps not realized by Wilde himself, that by this little conspiracy he would be likely to lose his allowance if he rejoined Bosie. Moreover Ross could, and did, name Queensberry as a bogyman who was supposed to keep detectives in Dieppe and might come over at any minute if Wilde were seen with Bosie. To Wilde the Scarlet Marquis was no longer a joke but a very real threat to his peace—and to his allowance.

2

Wilde crossed the Channel with More Adey on the day of his release and travelling on the night boat reached Dieppe where Ross and Reggie Turner awaited him. The four went to the Hotel Sandwich but during the first week Reggie Turner returned to London and More Adey went to Paris where he met Bosie and gave him the news of Wilde. Ross stayed with Wilde for another week, settled him at a small hotel in Berneval, a village three miles from Dieppe, then he too returned to London. He had every reason, including a sight of the *De Profundis* letter, to think that Wilde would never wish to see Bosie again.

Bosie was not well prepared for what followed. He was in Paris at this time and as soon as he heard from More Adey of Wilde's whereabouts he wrote to him and Wilde replied. By June 2nd, that is within a fortnight of Wilde's release, Wilde was writing to 'My dear boy' and two days later had become, 'ever, dear boy, with fondest love'. At first he tried to reassure Ross about Bosie—he was never going to see him again. But during June, when Wilde and Bosie were planning to meet, all mention of Bosie ceased in Wilde's almost daily letters to Ross.

Thus on May 28, the day following Ross's departure from Berneval, Wilde wrote to him of Bosie's 'revolting' letter and said he had a real terror of 'that unfortunate ungrateful young man with his unimaginative selfishness'. To be with him again, he assured Ross, would be to return to the hell from which he had been released. Wilde felt Bosie as 'an evil influence'.

Next day he reverted to this *De Profundis* attitude in a shorter letter to Ross. He is terrified about Bosie who can almost ruin him. Bosie's letters to him are 'infamous'.

But three days later, on June 2, he wrote a long, affectionate though not yet loving letter to Bosie whom he addressed as 'my dear boy' signing himself 'ever affectionately yours'. On the same day he told Ross that Bosie had written, 'for him nicely'.

Next morning he wrote to Bosie again having seen in *Le Jour* an interview about him which Bosie was supposed to have given. It was quite harmless, he said, and he was sorry Bosie had taken any notice of it. On the same day he wrote to Ross mildly ridiculing Bosie for threatening to fight a duel over the interview.

On June 4, that is barely two months after the completion of *De Profundis*, Wilde wrote to Bosie: "Don't think I don't love you. I love you more than anyone else." But their lives are severed so far as meeting goes. He is 'ever dear boy with fondest love'. On the next day he wrote to Ross, perhaps in answer to a query, that Bosie telegraphs every day. "This is an exaggeration but I made him wire about the duel." The duel never took place.

On June 6 Wilde wrote to Bosie that he (Wilde) must give up the *absurd* habit of writing to him every day. It comes from the strange joy of talking to Bosie daily. He is glad Bosie went to bed at seven. Modern life is terrible to vibrating delicate frames like Bosie's.

Wilde was visited by Rothenstein and others and for some days had little time for letter-writing. But by June 15 he was arranging for Bosie, 'dear honey-sweet boy', to visit him under the name of Jonquil de Vallon. On the following day he wrote again, underlining "I have asked you to come here on Saturday." He has a bathing-costume for Bosie but wants him to bring lots of cigarettes and books. The weather is very hot so Bosie will want a straw hat and flannels. Wilde hopes to be in his chalet by Saturday so Bosie will stay with him there.

This proposed meeting was reported to Ross who immediately went to Wilde's solicitor, and Wilde was warned that if Bosie came down to see him Queensberry would cross to Boulogne and make a scene. This reduced poor Oscar to a condition of panic. He wired to Bosie to put him off and on 17 June he wrote to Bosie that he had had to send his friends away because he was so 'distressed in nerve' by his solicitor's letter. It was impossible for them to meet. "I think of you always and love you always, but chasms of moonless night divide us."

Bosie for the first time seems to have realized something of what was happening and on the same day wrote to Adey:

Dear More,
    As you are probably aware the fact that I am going to meet Oscar has resulted in a protest and a threat on the part of the solicitor who has been appointed by you and others, as the arbiter of his conduct. As you are responsible for the agreement under which Oscar has been placed in the ridiculous and ignominious position involved by these facts, and as you on a certain recent

occasion *positively assured me*, that you had stipulated that the mere fact of his meeting and being on good terms with me, would not constitute "bad conduct" on his part, I should like to have some explanation from you as to what your views are and what steps you propose to take to free Oscar (and myself) from the ridiculously transparent Jewish trap which has been laid for him by the admirable George Lewis, and into which you have guided him.

Yours ever,

Bosie.

Three days later he wrote to Ross.

As long as Oscar was a captive in prison and I was morally bound hand and foot, you and More could make your own arrangements, but now your interference is simply an impertinence and the fact that your interference between two perfectly free people is conducted by intrigue and backstairs wire-pulling only makes it more intolerable. . . . I may point out that I never suggested that you were responsible in any degree for the silly and old-womanish attempt to separate me and Oscar but you have in your letter today deliberately claimed the responsibility and as you seem to be rather proud of it I have no hesitation in giving you the full credit of it.

Ross replied with a sarcastic letter in which the triumph was not concealed. Bosie was welcome, he said, to all the verbal scores and ebullition of bad taste on which he prided himself. Bosie was much better off than any of them—why did not *he* provide the £150 a year which Oscar would lose through associating with him? "With your £150 he will have the added pleasure of your perpetual society and inspiring temper."

Ross had received a letter from Wilde "A.D. is not here, nor is he to come," and another sent on the following day, June 19, saying: "I have now put off Bosie indefinitely. I have been so harrassed, and indeed frightened, at the thought of a possible scandal or trouble." Ross was therefore feeling cock-a-hoop. But Wilde continued to write to Bosie as 'my own darling boy' while he told Ross of a long indictment of him which Bosie had sent. "You can understand in what tone I shall answer him."

Whether or not Bosie received this reproof he wrote to Adey on June 30 saying that he had been overwhelmed by letters of abuse and insult from Ross, one being of fourteen pages.

I have written to Bobbie to say that I cannot receive any more letters from him, and indeed that I cannot continue my friendship with him. I am very sorry, it is a great distress, but he has really left me no choice at all. He has said things to me which are quite unforgiveable and which would make it positively dishonorable for me to continue my friendship for him. It is a dreadful blow for me, but I do not think it is a thing that can possibly be adjusted, or referred to as a misunderstanding. It seems to me that he is possessed by an extraordinary spirit of animosity and vindictive hatred towards me which is entirely inexplicable to me but which makes the situation utterly impossible and incapable of adjustment.

Adey once again tried to smooth things over and Bosie replying from Nogent-sur-Marne is glad that Adey does not associate himself with Ross's insults and violent abuse.

Please remember that I have been through a terrible trial, that more than two years ago I was parted from the person I love best in the world and that ever since I have waited and hoped and longed to see him again. That after all this time and when at first it seemed that he had turned against me and ceased to love me, and that the first terrible involuntary separation was to be followed by a still more terrible voluntary one, at last the light broke, I knew that my friend still loved and wished to see me. He wrote to me to say, come on Saturday and I thought to myself "all the misery is now over and everything is going to be right at last after so long waiting and so much sorrow". Then 16 hours before I was to start to see him, I get a telegram to say that a sudden terrible difficulty had arisen, a letter following to say it is the solicitor who has intervened, I write to you, remembering the assurance you had given me, and then I get this cool letter from Bobbie in which he seems to go out of his way to let me know that he is responsible for what has happened, and in the letter I read behind the words his own satisfaction that after all I have been baffled of my long hope and long expectation. I say remember all this, and I do not think you will find it very hard to forgive my sudden irritation, my rudeness, my bad taste (call it what you like), and remember that as soon as I knew that I had wronged any one I was ready to make ample amends.

Wilde then assured Ross (6 July) that he had pointed out to Bosie how grotesque, ridiculous and vulgar it was to consider himself a grand seigneur in comparison with a 'dear, sweet, wonderful friend' like Ross, and on the following day (7 July) wrote to Bosie as 'My darling boy' ending his letter 'with my love, dearest boy, ever your Oscar'.

On August 28 Wilde went to Rouen to meet Bosie. They stayed at the Hotel de la Poste from which Bosie had written his letters to Clarke and W. T. Stead two years earlier. This made it impossible for Bosie to use an assumed name which disappointed Wilde who loved such things and spoke of himself as "that strange purple shadow who is known as Sebastian Melmoth."

Wilde went by train.

The meeting was a great success [wrote Bosie in his *Autobiography*]. I have often thought since that if he or I had died directly after that, our friendship would have ended in a beautiful and romantic way. Poor Oscar cried when I met him at the station. We walked about all day arm in arm, or hand in hand, and were perfectly happy. Next day he went back to Berneval and I returned to Paris, but we had settled that when I went to Naples about six weeks later he was to join me there.

This left both of them with some difficult explanations to make. Wilde had to break the news to Ross who was, says Hesketh Pearson, "extremely angry", as well he might be. Bosie wrote to his mother whose reply was to hurry over to France and take him to Aix-les-Bains for some weeks in the hope of persuading him not to see more of Wilde.

After Wilde's return to Berneval the three-cornered correspondence continued. On August 31 Wilde sent to Bosie what was perhaps the most sincere and significant letter he had written since he came out of prison. Addressing him as 'My own Darling Boy' he assured him that his only hope of doing beautiful work in art was being with him, for Bosie could really recreate in him that energy and sense of joyous power on which art depended. Everyone, he said, was furious with him for going back to Bosie but they did not understand. "Do remake my ruined life for me", he wrote, and wished that when they met at Rouen they had not parted at all.

Finally he closed this episode of attempted equilibrium between himself Bosie and Ross by a letter to Ross which must have curdled in its recipient's mind. "Yes, I saw Bosie", he said, "and of course I love him as I always did."

3

The letters in which Wilde and Bosie planned their flight together to Naples have not come to light. Wilde wrote to a number of people to say that he was going to Italy or to Naples but gave no hint of who his companion would be. As the date planned for his departure approached Wilde wrote to Bosie to say his money was exhausted and Bosie sent him his fare. It was, unfortunately, characteristic of the post-prison Wilde that on his way through Paris he lunched with Vincent O'Sullivan and said he would start for Naples tonight if he had the money. O'Sullivan drew sufficient from his bank and gave it to him, afterwards reflecting, "It is one of the few things I look back on with satisfaction. It is not every day that one has the chance of relieving the anxiety of a genius and a hero."

Bosie came straight from Aix-les-Bains and they met on the train between Paris and Italy. They had scarcely any money between them so, being Oscar and Bosie, they went straight to the Hotel Royal in Naples and in two weeks ran up a bill of £60, at that time a vast amount to spend in a Neapolitan hotel. This bill remained unpaid until Bosie obtained the money from his mother several months later. He wrote about this in his *Autobiography*:

I must explain that the proprietor, or manager, of the Hotel Royal, being of course under the usual impression that obtains, or used to obtain, on the Continent, that an "English Lord" is invariably a millionaire, seemed quite undisturbed by my request that he should let the bill stand over. He expressed himself enchanted to oblige me, and beyond sending in the bill again after two months he made no kind of demonstration. I would not have the cheek to do a thing like that nowadays, but in the year 1897 I still lived under the pleasing illusion that life more or less belonged to me, and that money was not a thing to take seriously.

Their staying together in Naples had at first the added delight of being clandestine. Bosie had not told his mother at Aix-les-Bains what he intended to do. Wilde had not told his wife or her solicitors, or, so far as is known, Robert Ross. But very soon their flight and whereabouts were known to everyone, to Ross and his friends, to Constance Wilde and her family, to Bosie's mother and brother. All hell, as they say, broke loose.

Wilde's first letter of explanation was to Ross, (Sep 21): "My going back to Bosie was psychologically inevitable." He went on to explain in conciliatory terms that he could not live without an atmosphere of Love and though he could have lived his whole life with Ross, Ross had other claims on him and could only give him a week of companionship. He begged Ross that when people spoke against him for going back to Bosie, Ross would explain that Bosie offered him love and that after three months struggle with a hideous Philistine world, he had turned naturally to him.

To Reggie Turner he wrote in less pompous terms. He loved Bosie and had always loved him. Bosie was the first of all the young poets of England. "So stick up for us, Reggie, and be nice."

Ross's expostulations must have been violent, judging from Wilde's reply on October 1. "I have not answered your letters, because they distressed me and angered me."

To Leonard Smithers, the publisher who was issuing his *Ballad of Reading Gaol*, Wilde wrote even more irritably on the same day: "How *can* you keep on asking is Lord Alfred Douglas in Naples? You know quite well he is—we are together. He understands me and my art, and loves both. I hope never to be separated from him."

After this there was comparative peace from outside for exactly six weeks during which the two friends tried to create a way of living together.

In appearance both had changed greatly since their first meeting six years earlier. Wilde had come out of prison with short hair and he never again attempted the elaborate Neronian hair-do of his London days, for he was growing somewhat bald. His features were not marked by suffering in the way one might have expected, his expression was not tragic but almost commonplace. Contemporary photographs show him looking like a Dublin businessman on holiday. His height and weight and his rich speaking voice gave him some distinction but the arrogant and dressy figure of Tite Street was no more. His teeth which had given him much concern when he took great trouble over his appearance were now badly decayed. He was also increasingly deaf.

Bosie at twenty-seven had lost his peach-bloom complexion, though he still looked freakishly young. He had suffered no physical inconvenience but the last two years had given his face a peaked and serious expression and his laugh, which was quick and ready always, had not quite the whole-heartedness of before. But the two were delighted with one another and with their defiance of all discretion and all advice in coming together. Both were dependent on allowances, Wilde's from his wife's family, Bosie's from his mother. These might be stopped and each could feel he was risking all to be with the other.

They found a villa at Posilippo and moved into it at once. "We have a lovely villa over the sea", wrote Oscar, "and a nice piano." Servants were cheap and they had a cook called Carmine, a maid Maria and two boys who waited on them Peppino and Michele. The villa had a terrace and marble steps leading down to the sea but as they discovered at once it was overrun with rats. Bosie had a horror of rats and mice and to Oscar's amusement took a bedroom in the house opposite till their own was cleared. His description of this trivial incident seems to carry the memory of cordial humour between the

two friends, for one of the very foundations of their friendship was
that they laughed together and at one another.

After a time, however, we got rid of the rats, partly by means of a professional
and orthodox rat-catcher, but also (and chiefly, according to Oscar's opinion)
owing to the ministrations, hired for a small fee, of a potent witch who was
recommended as infallible by Michele, and who came and "burned odours"
and muttered incantations, which she assured us no rats could resist. She also
told both our fortunes, and Oscar professed to regard her as a wonderful and
powerful sorceress. In appearance she was quite the witch of literature and
drama. She had a distinct beard and "with age and envy was grown into a
hoop". Anyhow the rats disappeared.

Bosie's allowance was about £8 a week and Oscar's £3 and in
view of the cheapness of Naples this should have kept them in comfort. Though he did not mention it in his letters to Ross, Wilde also
received £100 from Dal Young for a libretto he was to write. (It
never got further than a few lyrics.) This did not prevent him from
obtaining £9 from Ross's own pocket, and writing to him to say
that if he could not obtain £300 through the agent Pinker 'we will
not be able to get food'—'Bosie is penniless as usual.'

Bosie was working himself and at the Villa Giudice wrote the four
sonnets called *The City of the Soul*, his *Sonnet on the Sonnet* and *A Triad
of the Moon*. Both the friends were busy and for the most part happy
though their life together for more than three months produced its
quarrels and nerve strains. They went over to Capri together and
lunched with Axel Munthe at San Michele, "a great connoisseur of
Greek things. He is a wonderful personality."

In his novel *L'Exile de Capri* Roger Peyrefitte gives a picture of them
at the Hotel Quisisana where an Englishman he says, threatened to
leave if they were served. But as he portrays Wilde with 'long grey
hair' and his fingers 'loaded with rings' and says that Bosie had again
rented the Villa Federico which he had occupied two years earlier, the
whole scene must be taken for what it was—a piece of fiction. (They
stayed only a day or two in Capri and Bosie's home on his previous
visit was the Villa Caso.) But I like the description of Bosie who
'carried himself insolently' and when refused service tapped the *maître
d'hôtel* on the shoulder with his cane saying, "In England's name, friend,
my congratulations."

They both regarded their life together in Naples as permanent.
They had no thought of parting or giving up the villa—they meant
to write, and to collaborate in the libretto of *Daphnis and Chloe* for

Dal Young and do other work in order to establish themselves in their home. They let this be known to their friends and Ross threatened to leave for Canada.

4

But those determined to separate them were busy. Oscar and Bosie were first made to realize this by a visit from one of the *attachés* from the British Embassy whom Bosie had met in the previous year when he had been in Rome with his mother. This was Beauchamp Denis Browne, an acquaintance of Reggie Turner's. He came ostensibly to make a friendly call and was 'very witty and talkative'. However he told Bosie privately that the *ménage* at the Villa Giudice was *mal vu* at the Embassy and a cause of great embarrassment to them all.

The intrigue between the various parties determined to part the friends then grew intense. At least five principals were directly involved in this and several more played minor parts, adding their advice or criticism or threats as occasion demanded. First of all was Ross, who was outraged at Wilde's return to the man he regarded as his rival. Next Constance Wilde who had been pumped full of anti-Bosie propaganda by Ross and others and had begun to talk of 'that *beast* A.D.' and to threaten to cut off Wilde's small allowance. The two solicitors, Hargrove who acted for Constance Wilde and Hansell who was supposed to be protecting Wilde's interests, agreed in their determination to break up the friendship, though Queensberry, inexplicably, seems to have taken no part in the affair. More Adey supported Ross, Robert Sherard added his indiscretions and Leonard Smithers his advice. It was a full-scale conspiracy.

Oscar at first did not realize the scope of it and thought he had no one but Constance to contend with. He even wrote to Ross for sympathy and support, asking him how Constance could really imagine she could influence or control his life. He supposed she would now try to deprive him of his 'wretched £3 a week'. Women were so petty and Constance had no imagination. If for revenge she managed to bring Wilde to trial again she would be able to claim that for the first time in her life she had influenced him. Things were dark with storm.

Then Oscar heard that Sherard had been abusing him in the Authors' Club for returning to Bosie, abusing him so loudly that Oscar could hear him from Naples. Sherard received a stiff letter from Wilde and dropped out of the running for a time.

Ross now had a major success. Wilde heard from his solicitor that he was to be deprived of his allowance since he was living with Bosie, who was, Hansell agreed with Hargrove, a 'disreputable person'. Wilde had caused a 'public scandal' by returning to him.

Still Wilde failed to see Ross's hand in this and wrote in fairly dignified distress to Ross to tell him what had happened, not to worry him about the prejudged matter but "because I tell you everything". It was unfair to say that he had created a 'public scandal' by returning to Bosie—his very existence was a scandal but he did not think he should be blamed for continuing to live. He could not live alone and Bosie was the only one of his friends who was able or willing to give him his companionship.

"If I were living with a Naples renter", he said bitterly, "I suppose I would be all right."

A few days later he wrote to Ross again and said he was writing to More Adey and Adrian Hope about "this monstrous attempt to leave me to starve because I live with the only human being—amongst gentlemen—who will live with me." His solicitor had apparently told him that he held 'any member of the Queensberry family' as being in the category of 'a disreputable person'. He had always distrusted Hansell but had not thought he would strain the meaning of a legal document to ruin his own client.

He was still under the impression that Ross, though he might resent his return to Bosie, would not join Wilde's enemies to gain his ends. But the letter he received from More Adey disillusioned him and revealed the whole mean little conspiracy, for Adey, a franker man than Ross, admitted that when he and Ross had been asked whether Bosie was a 'disreputable person' they had felt bound to answer yes, and had agreed that Constance was 'strictly within her rights' in cutting off Wilde's allowances.

This roused all the anger of which Wilde was capable and it seems probable that if it had not been for Ross's hold on his resources his quarrel with both Adey and Ross might have been permanent. In what way, he thundered, was Bosie more disreputable than they were? Constance herself had expressed her horror when she heard that Adey had been to see him in prison and had required that he would have nothing more to do with such 'infamous companions'. This had been on information about Adey and Ross supplied to her by George Lewis. She knew what Ross's life was and had been. Wilde simply did not know how to describe his feelings of utter amazement and indignation.

He wrote to Reggie Turner, not wanting, as he said, to mix him up in the matter but to say that Ross and Adey had done a most unjust and illegal thing. What they had done was 'unfair, stupid and utterly unjust'.

Constance Wilde, in a letter to her brother, confirmed that the betrayal had taken place. Wilde's 'legal friends' in London made no defence and no opposition to her stopping Wilde's allowance. She, poor woman, was in a difficult position, being pressed by members of her own family. Harris was later to publish the fact that her father, Horatio Lloyd, Q.C., had himself been in trouble for a sexual offence and in his Notes to Harris's book Ross was to say that the charge against Horatio Lloyd was of a 'normal' kind. "It was for exposing himself to nursemaids in the gardens of the Temple." With her father and husband both involved in scandals and with two small sons to look after while she herself was in failing health, she relied on others to advise her.

But Oscar could not afford to maintain this attitude of indignation towards those on whom he depended for a livelihood and by November 23 was writing to Ross miserably to know whether, if he agreed not to *live* with Bosie, in the same house, it would be regarded as a concession. To say that he would not speak to him again would be childish and out of the question, but he was quite ready, as Bosie was, to agree that they would not live under the same roof. He wrote with this suggestion to Adey, but the poor little olive branch was ignored.

Ross carried his frustration and anger to greater lengths of malice, writing to Smithers (who was to publish *The Ballad of Reading Gaol*) that he did not think Wilde's work had any market value and opposing the sale of serial rights in the poem for which Wilde had received an offer. "I hope", he wrote to Smithers, "you will refuse to publish Oscar Wilde's poem if he insists on publishing first in a newspaper." Finally, on November 25, he wrote haughtily to Smithers that he regretted to inform him that he had ceased to be on intimate terms with Oscar Wilde or to enjoy his confidence.

Meanwhile Lady Queensberry joined her efforts to the others' and and got in touch with Adrian Hope and perhaps with Constance Wilde. She was as anxious as everyone else that the 'scandalous Naples menage' should be broken up. On November 13 she wrote to More Adey:

I found that Mr. Hope had only just been informed and had already written to have a meeting with the two solicitors to settle about withdrawing the allowance as (at) Mrs. W.'s request. It is a pity this was not done sooner. What view does Mr. Leverson take, do you know? he appears to be about the only rich supporter Mr. W. has. Will you think of what you can do: it would be a great help if you could write to warn him that the people who have been providing him with money are disgusted at this and will not send any more, otherwise the allowance being so small he may think he can do without it and count on his friends. Do you know the name and address of the priest at Dieppe who influenced Mr. W. very much? he might be a good emissary if he could be persuaded to go. Mr. Hope quite sees the advantage of sending an emissary who would prevail of (on) him to leave with him and stay till the matter was settled, if we could only find the right man. [Four days later she wrote]: I regret to find the allowance cannot be stopped conditionally, that is not in the terms of the agreement. Please let me know if you have any further news. I would of course provide necessary money (without my name appearing) to faciliate his getting away, etc.

More was also bombarded with letters from Bosie:

Both Oscar and I were astounded to hear that you had quietly acquiesced in the monstrous proposal to take away his money and leave him penniless because he was living with me. You have apparently completely forgotten the assurance you gave me on that point when I wrote about it from Nogent. You assured me that our being together would not constitute a breach of the contract. You are a wonderful person, and I give up the problem of trying to solve the mysteries of your motives and of your character.

The terms of Oscar's agreement are that he should forfeit his allowance if he lived with disreputable people in such a way as to cause a public scandal. I am not a disreputable person and there has not been the smallest vestige of a scandal. And yet you and the wretched Bobbie who are supposed to be trying to represent Oscar's interest quietly acquiesce in and approve of the proposal to deprive him of all his money which is as much his own by right and equity as the clothes I wear on my back are mine.

Then you talk to me as if I was living with Oscar in order to annoy other people or to prove that I always get my own way. But as a matter of fact the other people are completely indifferent to me; if there really are people who are sufficiently idiotic to mind whether we live together or not I don't know their names and they don't interest me. Putting aside Bobbie who objects from obstinacy and jealousy, and who has forfeited any right to my consideration, and my mother whose objection is founded on a complete ignorance of the real facts of the case, I know nobody who really could possibly object, except on the same principle that they might object to my not going to church on Sunday. And as I shouldn't think of going to church every Sunday to please those sort of people, so I shouldn't dream of leaving Oscar against his will to please ridiculous asses and meddling busybodies. The reason I went to live in

Naples with Oscar was not to prove that I always got my own way but firstly that he asked me to do so, and secondly that I naturally wanted to go, that is all.

Of course if Oscar and I are to be starved to Death for living together, it does make a reason for not doing so, but it is odd to find you and Bobbie quietly acquiescing in this system of abominable tyranny. And as we are far from being starved yet we can and shall certainly wait till that catastrophe is more imminent before surrendering the plain right of any two single human beings to hold intercourse with each other. In the meantime I wish I could feel certain that you and Bobbie (at any rate the latter) will not think it your 'duty' to try and assist the starvation process by advising its adoption, or by throwing obstacles in the way of Oscar's gaining money by his literary work. I think Bobbie is perfectly capable of it. When Oscar wanted to try and get a little money by publishing his poem in an English paper Bobbie wrote to Smithers that "he hoped Smithers would *refuse* to *publish Oscar's poem* if it appeared in a newspaper before it appeared in book form". This I suppose is the sort of thing that he imagines is justified by the fact that he thinks he is acting for Oscar's "own good" as the cant phrase says. I have very different opinion of it. However enough of this.

All through November and early December the acrimonious correspondence continued. Then a heavier blow fell. Lady Queensberry wrote to Bosie saying categorically that if he did not leave Wilde his own allowance would be stopped.

Both friends recognized this as final. Bosie wrote to his mother saying in effect that if she would send him enough money to settle up matters in Naples, pay a quarter's rent on the villa in advance so that Wilde could remain there, and give Wilde £200 for his immediate living expenses, Bosie would agree not to live with Wilde again. His mother accepted these terms readily. She sent Bosie what he required in Naples and paid the £200 in two instalments to More Adey for Wilde. As these arrangements were denied later, it is fortunate that letters still exist from Adey to Wilde saying, (December 9) "I enclose a cheque for £100, the amount I have just received from Lady Queensberry", and (January 6) "Your second £100 has been paid in to me and awaits your disposal at my bank". Fortunate, that is, for the ultimate establishment of truth. Bosie lost a vital libel action on a letter which Wilde wrote to Ross saying that Bosie had abandoned him in Naples and Adey seems to have refused to give the unequivocal evidence necessary to disprove this.

When Lady Queensberry heard from Bosie she immediately wrote to Adey (Dec 1):

I have good news at last, I was beginning to despair. Can I see you very soon.

I want your advice to clinch the matter as quick as possible. If you do not like to act for me you can advise me who should.

On the next day she told him that it was "all as we wish" and Bosie was leaving for Rome. But four days later she is anxious:

I have been expecting to hear from you and am beginning to feel anxious at having no news of Bosie since the telegram the beginning of last week saying he was going to Rome the next day, have you heard? please let me know and also what you decide I had best do about the £200 I have agreed to pay.

She received a telegram from Bosie in Rome saying that the pledge (not to live with Wilde) was in the post, and asking that the money should be sent to Wilde at once. She asked Adey to send £100 that night. She was disturbed at not having a similar pledge from Wilde, but on December 18 she received this, 'just what Bosie gave me, not to live together'. She thinks Constance Wilde will renew the allowance "but I hope the question of frequent association will be raised and will you do what you can in advice to prevent it, without naming me".

5

With his first £100, Wilde went to Sicily with someone referred to by Adey as "the Russian Elder" and made the acquaintance of an amusing and notorious old homosexual called the Baron von Gloeden who, according to Rupert Hart-Davis, "acquired some reputation for his photographs of Sicilian youths posed 'noble and nude and antique' in the guise of Theocritan goatherds or shepherds".

Bosie, meanwhile, wrote to his mother from Rome a letter which shows better than any other contemporary document what kind of young man he was:

Darling Damus,

I am glad, O so glad! to have got away. I am so afraid that you will not believe me, and I am so afraid of appearing to pose as anything but what I am, but I am not a hypocrite and you must believe me. I wanted to go back to him, I longed for it and for him, because I love him and admire him and think him great and almost good, but when I had done it and when I got back, I hated it. I was miserable, I wanted to go away. But I couldn't. I was tied by honour.

If he had wanted me to stay I would never have left him, but when I found out that he really didn't want me to stay and that I might leave him without causing him pain and without a breach of loyalty, then I was glad to go. Even then I hid it from myself, I struggled not to let my inward thought get the better of me, and it is only since I have been here two days that I have completely realized and admitted how glad I am to be away. Even when I got here I persuaded myself that I was miserable and that I wanted to go back and I wrote to you in that sense. But now I know what a relief it is to have escaped *honourably* from a sort of prison.

I still think it was right to go to him when he asked and at that time I longed to go to him. I felt I must clear up the matter. And as long as I was there, I was bound to fight in his interests and I did it even to the last bitter point. The knowledge that I didn't really want to stay with him only made me more determined not to show the least disloyalty. I was prepared to carry it to the very end. If he had proposed joint suicide I would have accepted.

Don't think that I have changed about him or that I think him bad or that I have changed my views about morals. I still love and admire him and I think he has been infamously treated by ignorant and cruel brutes. I look on him as a martyr to progress. I associate myself with him in everything. I long to hear of his success and artistic rehabilitation in the post which is his by right at the very summit of English literature, nor do I intend to cease corresponding with him or not to see him from time to time in Paris and elsewhere. I give up nothing and admit no point against him or myself separately or jointly. Do not think either that he has been unkind to me or shown himself to me in an unfavourable light. On the contrary he has been sweet and gentle and will always remain to me as the type of what a gentleman and a friend should be. Only this, I am tired of the struggle and tired of being ill-treated by the World, and I had lost that supreme desire for his society which I had before, and which made a sort of aching void when he was not with me. That has gone and I think and hope for ever.

Up to this, however, I had no excuse to leave him. I simply couldn't do it. If he had been disagreeable to me or if he had turned out different from what I thought, if he had ever behaved in any way differently from how a man of honour and humanity should behave I would have seized the chance. But he didn't. He has always behaved *perfectly* to me. The only thing that happened was that I felt and saw that he really didn't wish me to stay and that it would really be a relief to him if I went away. So at last I was able to get away with a clear conscience.

And it is no use wishing I hadn't ever gone with him to Naples. It was the most lucky thing that ever happened. If I hadn't rejoined him and lived with him for two months, I should *never* have got over the longing for him. It was spoiling my life and spoiling my art and spoiling everything. Now I am free.

CHAPTER VIII

The Friendship: The Last Years

I

THE last three years of the friendship were in many ways the best. There were no more quarrels or recriminations, no more attempts to live and work together, no more passionate letters or accusations.

Wilde in those years showed himself the courageous, humorous and enchanting man that he could be when he was not involved in the intrigues of his friends. He abandoned all attempt or pretence at writing and with a prodigality that was magnanimous put his genius and imagination into his talk, which had never been better. He led a pleasant rather aimless life in Paris, with one or two journeys to Rome and Switzerland, and achieved a kind of realism in his human relationships which had never been his before. No longer a King of Life or a Lord of Language he met and talked to people not from his pedestal, as Bosie had once called it, but from the café seat beside his friends'. He had got rid of that passing and uncharacteristic bitterness which, in prison, had made him write *De Profundis* and other letters and could abandon himself to the things and the people he liked. Sexual experience was no longer heightened by a sense of sin or drama but was simple and down-to-earth.

In the last book he wrote, *Oscar Wilde—a Summing-up*, Bosie recalls this period:

Oscar Wilde's last days in Paris were by no means all dismal and gloomy. He had, as Shaw truly says, an unconquerable gaiety of soul which ever sustained him, and, while he had lost the faculty of writing, he retained to the last his inimitable supremacy as a talker. I retain glowing memories of dinners at *cafés* and subsequent amazing 'talks' when he held his audience spell-bound as he discoursed in his exquisite voice of all things in heaven and earth, now making his hearers rock with laughter and now bringing tears into their eyes. Such talk as Oscar's now no longer exists, as far as my experience goes. I have never known anyone to come anywhere near him. . . . I can bear witness to the fact that in his last days after the 'bitter ruin' that came on him, his talk was just as wonderful. He talked better, if possible, after his downfall than he did before. As Shaw rightly points out, after he could no longer write but could still talk as no other man ever did, he was entitled to all the money he could get. If he could have "sent the hat round" every time he entertained a company of friends (or enemies or the indifferent) he would have been a richer man in Paris than he was when he was drawing royalties on the gross receipts of his plays in London.

Wilde reached Paris from Naples in January 1898. He did not at once meet Bosie but did not want him or the Naples experiment criticized. "It is very unfair of people being horrid to me about Bosie and Naples," he wrote to Ross from the Hôtel de Nice, at which he stayed for his first few weeks in Paris, and in another letter to Ross a few weeks later asks: "Who are the people who object to my having been with Bosie at Naples and spent my days with Heliogabalus and my nights with Antinous? I mean are they people who were *ever* my friends?" But Ross seems to have persisted in his questions about Naples. He evidently wanted some sign of repentance for that return to Bosie. Wilde wrote telling Ross to write to his wife asking for his allowance to be renewed now that he and Bosie were "irrevocably parted". But this was not enough for Ross who was working for this object and we may charitably suppose that it was in answer to a request for something to show Constance Wilde which would convince her that the association was over that Wilde finally wrote a most fateful letter. It has an exasperated air about it, as though Wilde were sick of Ross's nagging questions and had decided to give him what he evidently required. The facts, he said, were bald and brief. Bosie, for four months, by endless letters, offered him a 'home', love, affection, and care, and promised that he should never want for anything. After four months he accepted his offer, but when they met at Aix on their way to Naples he found that Bosie had no money, no plans, and had forgotten all his promises. His one idea was that Wilde should raise money for them both. Wilde did so, to the extent of £120, and on this Bosie lived, quite happy. When it came to his having, of course, to repay his own *share*, he became terrible, unkind, mean, and penurious, except where his own pleasures were concerned, and when Wilde's allowance ceased, he left.

This gave Ross all he required. He knew from More Adey that it was untrue, and that Bosie had got his mother to send Wilde £200, but the words must have delighted him.

The tone of the letter, says Mr. Hesketh Pearson,

was due partly to a desire to propitiate Ross, but chiefly to a desire to see himself as one doomed to betrayal, the central figure in a drama of woe. In this letter he portrays Douglas for the second time as Judas. Having enticed him from Berneval with promises of a home and a carefree life, he says, Douglas deserted him the moment there was a money-shortage. "It is the most bitter experience of a bitter life", he sums up. He probably believed every word of this at the moment of writing, because his solitude at the Villa after Douglas's departure depressed him, and he was in a state of mind when reproaches came more easily from the pen than praises. But the letter must be regarded solely as a scene in the epic of Oscar, not as a record of fact, and his decision never to see Douglas again was reversed from the moment he saw Douglas again.

It was this letter, carefully kept, which enabled Ross fifteen years later to let Ransome suggest in his book on Wilde that Bosie had abandoned Oscar. When Bosie sued Ransome for libel on this and other statements the letter was produced as justification, while Bosie could produce no unequivocal evidence that the £200 had been paid at his behest and had been a condition made to his mother of his leaving Wilde.

We do not know what Ross said to Constance Wilde but we can gather its gist from the fact that she described Bosie in letters to her brother as an 'inhuman brute' and spoke of him 'in terms of indescribable loathing', as her son admitted to me in a letter sixty-four years later.

By March Wilde and Bosie were seeing one another again but their friendship was now on such light and easygoing terms that they could laugh at one another in letters to friends. While the memory of Naples still rankled with Ross, Wilde could appease it by retailing mildly malicious stories about Bosie but he soon ceased even to do this and with one exception he never again found it necessary to pacify Ross by abusing Bosie. On the contrary he wrote to Ross and the others as though they were all one happy family with Bosie the prodigal son. His references to Bosie in letters to Ross are frequent and not unfriendly.

Bosie was anxious to return to London for the publication of his book of poems, *The City of the Soul*. But he still thought it might be dangerous to return. In a letter to Wilde of September 20, 1898, from Aix-les-Bains, only fragments of which survive, he wrote:

. . . I can't make it out. George Wyndham wrote as if it was practically settled, but a month has elapsed and I have heard nothing more. A letter was received from Asquith saying that no steps had ever been taken against me by the

Treasury and that as it was impossible for anything fresh to have occurred since I left England it was obvious that there was nothing to prevent my return. The letter began—"I have communicated privately with the director of public prosecutions and I learn etc. etc." so that it is quite official information. However on the top of this Cuffe the public prosecutor has written to my uncle George Finch (his cousin) saying that he hears that I think of coming back and that he thinks it would be *very inadvisable*. So it is rather contradictory. It was all settled that I was to go to Clouds, a party had been got up there to meet me, and now it is all off. My mother is going to see Cuffe personally and ascertain whether there. . . .

It seems that matters were satisfactorily cleared up, however, for in November Bosie left for London.

Wilde was anxious to know how he was received and wrote to Ross on November 25: "Do let me know about Bosie. I suppose London takes no notice at all: that is the supreme punishment." Wilde also asked Turner about Bosie in London. Was he happy to be back? Were people kind to him? How was he behaving?

Early in 1899 Bosie's book of poems, *The City of the Soul*, was published by Grant Richards and when Bosie returned to Paris, he and Oscar celebrated its first review, in *The Outlook*, in the Horse-Shoe bar. They drank to the Great Unknown, for Bosie's book was published anonymously.

During that year, while Bosie had a small flat in the Avenue Kleber, he wrote several poems, among them a sad little *Ennui*—"The pearls are numbered on youth's rosary, I have outlived the days desirable", and an even more desolate *Ode to Autumn*. He translated, with a humble fidelity to the original of which one would not have thought him capable at this time, two poems of Baudelaire, *Harmonie du Soir* and *Le Balcon*. He had very little money that year but he spent what he could on Oscar who frequently came to the flat in Avenue Kleber. When he could afford it there was nothing he liked better than to invite Oscar to dine at Paillard's, Maire's or the Café de la Paix. And well he might for an evening with Oscar was a joy which he was by no means alone in seeking. Their friendship had lost its intensity and was pleasant and mature.

Bosie had got over his dislike of Frank Harris who came frequently to Paris. In 1898 Harris sold *The Saturday Review*, then a valuable property, to Lord Hardwicke and either invited Wilde to the South of France or met him and entertained him there. Bosie at this time was 'on terms of great friendship' with Harris.

I liked and admired him, and the way he went on sticking up for Oscar and making a point of entertaining him at Durand's, which at that time was a favourite resort of the British Embassy people, greatly appealed to me.

Bosie believed he was also now on amicable terms with Ross, More Adey and the rest of Wilde's circle, for they were particularly civil to him now that Wilde no longer regarded him as the pivot of his life and Bosie was no more than fond of Oscar, as they all were. Wilde's allowance and almost everything else continued to be paid through Ross, who then and thereafter behaved discreetly in the matter of money, controlling Wilde's extravagance as best he could. Bosie was pleased that there was someone to undertake all this with such ability and devotion. "Ross was a person whom Wilde and I found useful because he was always willing to attend to occasional matters of business for us which we were too indolent to attend to ourselves", he admitted frankly.

Indeed at this time the jealous warfare which would follow Wilde's death, with mortal enmities and much side-taking between Ross, Adey, Sherard, Harris and Bosie, seemed a long way off and though there may have been some secret invidiousness they all did their best to make Wilde's life a happy one, while he, responding amiably to their efforts, treated them with unquenchable high spirits and the glorious generosity of his talk. Whether either Wilde or Ross had any sense of guilt about *De Profundis*, which was lying among Ross's papers, or whether they ever discussed it, will never be known. The most reasonable deduction is that Wilde forgot it or put it out of his mind while Ross kept it, not as a secret weapon, but merely as a piece of literary property which could not yet be used. Now that his often-proclaimed love for Bosie was no longer an obsession with Wilde but had become a more everyday comradeship which did not exclude Ross from his share in ministration, the little man was relieved of his burning envy and could be the companionable and often amusing person who endeared himself to several generations of writers and artists. He was occupied at this time with the affairs of Aubrey Beardsley who died on March 16th, 1898. He wrote an 'Eulogy' of Beardsley for an edition of Ben Jonson's *Volpone* which contained Beardsley's drawings.

2

Bosie's book, *The City of the Soul*, was reviewed with rather pompous caution but on the whole favourably. Edmund Gosse wrote to Robert Ross about it and his letter was typical of the critics' reaction:

You asked me if I had read *The City of the Soul*. I had it in the house, but had not glanced at it. I have now read it, and thank you for calling my attention to it. The writer has a good deal of the poetic art in him,—a little imitative and a little languorous, but often very charming. Some of the ballads are very striking, and I like the last three or four pieces in the book particularly. What he seems to want most is not fancy, or purity of style, but variety of interests. Don't you think so?

That Bosie was not finding it easy to live down the notoriety which had come to him at the time of Wilde's trials may be adduced from the behaviour of the President of his College, Dr. Warren, a social weather-vane if ever there was one. Bosie sent him his book and Warren, who had written so fulsomely about Bosie's early verses, sent it back by return of post with a letter saying, "I regret I cannot accept this book from you", an action which Bosie called 'rather a brutal and unnecessarily unkind thing to do'.

Other friends of Winchester and Oxford days, and of his family, were more courteous, and he was pleased to find how many of these seemed to have forgotten the calamity of four years previously and the association which had preceded it, though it was typical of the hypocrisy of the age—perhaps of every age—that Bosie was blamed far more for living with Wilde in Naples, for remaining loyal to him, than for the original scandal.

3

There emerges from *The Letters of Oscar Wilde* a good deal of rather startling confirmation for Harris's stories of Wilde's affairs with the raffish boys of the *boulevards* but it shows that Bosie, Ross, Turner and others were no less promiscuous. There is no more nonsense about 'strange sins' and 'feasting with panthers'; these associations were earthy and realistic and discussed with humour. Wilde's allusions to the subject might be the remarks overheard in any homosexual bar or club from London to Beirut today. A young man called Maurice Gilbert walks gaily across the Parisian stage, the lover in turn of Wilde himself, Bosie, Reggie Turner, Ross, I. D. W. 'Sir John' Ashton and Rowland Strong. There are also mentioned and usually laughed over Edmond, (known as Edmond de Goncourt,) Eugene, Giorgio, Joseph, Alphonse, Eolo, le petit Georges, André, Pietro, Didaco, Henri, Casquette, Maetchak, Arnaldo, Omero, le Boucher, and Bosie's little friend known as the Florifer because "in the scanty intervals he can snatch from an arduous criminal profession he sells bunches of purple violets in front of the Café de la Paix".

4

In autumn 1899 Bosie was in London again, staying with his mother in Cadogan Square, probably for the wedding of his sister Edith to St. George William Lane Fox-Pitt. In the previous year Edward Arnold had published a book of his nonsense verse called *Tails with a Twist* and now he arranged with Leonard Smithers to publish a long absurd rhyme called *The Duke of Berwick*. An illustrator was needed for it and this illustrator, Captain Anthony Ludovici, who afterwards had a distinguished career as private secretary to Rodin, then as a writer and translator, sends me the following delightful portrait of Bosie at the time:

I learnt with great pleasure that you are on the point of completing a biography of Lord Alfred Douglas, for it enables me to hope that justice may at last be done to a man whose character recent widely publicized slanders have done much to misrepresent and even to blacken. I remember very vividly my first encounter with him; for his was a personality no one at the impressionable age of 17 would be likely to forget. I also recall the circumstances which led to our first meeting. At the beginning of autumn in the year 1899, I received a letter from Lord Alfred sent by hand to our house in N.W. London, asking me to call at 18 Cadogan Place that afternoon at five o'clock.

Lord Alfred Douglas must then have been on the threshold of thirty, and I was instantly struck by his handsome features, charming manner and his still youthful and distinguished appearance. Tall and slim, he was dressed in the elegant négligé style of an artist and as he introduced me to Smithers and motioned me to a chair, he at once made me feel wholly at ease. I was enchanted and faintly bewildered by the simple cordiality of his welcome and without a trace of the embarrassed awe I had expected to come over me, I fell to examining the details of my surroundings.

In a few moments, a footman brought in tea and we settled down to the business of discussing the publication of *The Duke of Berwick*, the nonsense rhyme I was expected to illustrate. There were to be twelve full-page illustrations, including the designs for the cover and the title-page, and Smithers seemed not at all shocked when with some trepidation I suggested two guineas as the price for each drawing. Although the charge seemed to me exorbitant, it was in fact what my father had advised me to ask, and Lord Alfred Douglas anticipated Smithers in fully approving of it.

After tea, Lord Alfred Douglas read *The Duke of Berwick* to us, and I listened enraptured and immensely amused whilst in his melodious light baritone voice

he half-read and half-recited from memory his delightful skit on his father—
or at least that is what at the time I understood the verse to be.

Smithers explained that he could not run to multi-coloured illustrations
like those I had done for Mary Kernahan's book and it was therefore agreed
that I should limit myself to black and red. Both he and Lord Alfred Douglas
then asked me to be so good as to start on the work at once and to bring two
or three specimen illustrations to No. 5 Old Bond Street for their inspection
as soon as I conveniently could.

The production of the twelve illustrations and my various calls at Old Bond
Street to get them passed, led to many more meetings with the charming author
of the book and made this brief period in my life one of the happiest I can
remember. Both Smithers and Lord Alfred Douglas thoroughly approved of
my work, and I remember particularly one afternoon in November when the
latter, taking me aside and giving me a playful dig in the ribs, asked me in a
whisper what on earth had induced me to caricature Smithers' poor typist and
secretary in the drawing I had made of "Mademoiselle de la Ponghera" (the
eighth in the book).

Utterly horrified, I then perceived for the first time the ridiculous likeness
and protested vehemently that it was all wholly accidental and unintended. I
offered to take the drawing back in order to alter it; but he would not hear
of it, and merely advised me earnestly to keep out of reach of the lady in
question.

These few precious interviews I had with the author of *The Duke of Berwick*
in Smithers' bookshop during the last few weeks of the year 1899 would have
been for me an ample reward for the time and labour spent on my illustrations,
and I deeply deplored the inevitable result of submitting my last drawing.

Although in those early days I had not yet formed any settled philosophical
views about the nature of Man and the relation of Body and Soul, I have since
reached many strong convictions on these matters, and among these I hold
none more firmly than that, contrary to the Socratic belief, Bodily form and
appearance are intimately and inseparably related with character and disposi-
tion, and that therefore no one who possessed Lord Alfred Douglas's com-
pelling comeliness and charm could possibly be capable of the infamies which
his enemies have ascribed to him.

5

Queensberry died in January 1900.

Under the hatred between Queensberry and Bosie there had never
ceased to be a buried bond of fellow-feeling, for they had much in
common. As a boy Bosie had adored the father he so rarely saw who
was in his mind a paragon of sportsmanship. At a public school in
Bosie's time a boy was prouder of his father's athletic and sporting

distinctions than of any other honour he might have gained and it was as a one-time stroke in the Oxford boat that a prime minister or bishop would be admired by his offspring. Queensberry as author of the rules of boxing and as a famous steeple-chaser gave Bosie plenty of scope for hero-worship and in spite of the telegrams and anger, in spite of the fact that Queensberry had ruined both Wilde and Bosie himself, he never quite lost this. His mercurial temperament, and perhaps a subconscious feeling, which he would have furiously and sincerely denied, that his allowance should be renewed, caused him to seek a reconciliation.

Queensberry had gone downhill in those four years. If people could have seen his persecution of Wilde as an honest action by a fond father with moral force behind it, they might, though with some embarrassment, have forgiven him. But Queensberry's own life and character contradicted such a notion and after their brief cheers for his mean little victory people had come to despise him and he found himself ostracized almost as completely as Wilde. His atheism, his disgraceful divorce, the scenes he was for ever making in public culminating in his big scene at the Old Bailey had brought him an unpopularity in Victorian society which even his ancient name, his money, his achievements in sport and his marquisate could not repair. Many who did not much care what happened to 'Queensberry's boy' after his life was wrecked wanted nothing to do with the man who had brought it about. Bosie's godfather, Lord Robert Bruce, who had been in the Navy with Queensberry and had been his friend since then, after the Wilde case never spoke to him again and Queensberry was estranged from his son and heir and his grandchildren.

He led a forlorn and sordid life, staying in London hotels, drinking too much and having as his associates a curious miscellany of people from many walks of life who spent almost every day at race-courses.

While in Paris, Bosie had enquired about his father from his (Bosie's) cousin Algie Bourke. On hearing of his father's condition Bosie asked Bourke to go to Queensberry and find out whether he wanted to see his son. Bosie made it clear that he could not undertake not to see Wilde but said his relations with him were entirely harmless and "only dictated by my feeling that I cannot abandon him now that he is poor and broken after being his friend when he was rich and flourishing". He also said that he had given his word of honour to his mother that he would never live in the same house or sleep under the same roof with Wilde again.

Algie Bourke was a popular and highly entertaining man-about-town of the period who knew everyone and heard everything. It was he who gave warning of Queensberry's plan to make a public scandal on the first night of *The Importance of Being Earnest* in a letter to Lady Queensberry. He had remained on speaking terms with Queensberry and, kindest and most untiringly good-natured of men, he now approached the Scarlet Marquis and showed him Bosie's letter. Queensberry said he would be delighted to see Bosie and spoke in the most affectionate way about him.

The meeting took place in the unlikely surroundings of the smoking-room of Bailey's Hotel. Queensberry formally forgave Bosie and embraced him with tears, calling him his poor darling boy and promising him his allowance back. He actually wrote to Arthur Douglas, who managed his affairs, telling him to arrange this.

But a week later when Bosie was in bed with influenza at his mother's house in Cadogan Place he received an abusive letter from his father saying that he did not intend to give him a penny till he knew what Bosie's relations were with "that beast Wilde." Bosie wrote one of his letters and there the matter ended.

Bosie saw him only once more, from a cab window, and was struck with compunction by his appearance for he looked ill and wild and haggard. Queensberry was suffering from delusions and told his son-in-law St. George Fox-Pitt that Bosie hated him and he was being 'persecuted by Oscar Wilders' who had driven him out of various hotels and disturbed him at night by shouting abusive epithets at him. He had always been a suspicious man, tortured by persecution mania and now, it seemed, he had lost all sense of reality. There may have been some cause for his delusion about 'Oscar Wilders' for London homosexuals, driven underground by the Wilde scandal, may have found a means of harassing the man who had caused it, but there is no doubt that Queensberry was mentally ill.

Bosie wrote to Fox-Pitt a reassuring letter to show Queensberry in which he said he did not hate his father and this seems to have calmed him. But he was a dying man.

His last days were characteristic of one whose life was hectic and contradictory from childhood. Bosie's mother, who had divorced him twenty years earlier, went to see him on his death-bed and he told her that she was the only woman he had ever loved. Bosie's cousin, a Catholic priest, (Very Reverend Canon Lord Archibald Douglas) said that Queensberry renounced his atheism and professed his love for and faith in Jesus Christ to whom, he said, "I have confessed all my sins." But when Percy, his heir, went to his bedside he sat up and spat at him. He died in January 1900 just ten months before Wilde.

Percy now became the ninth Marquess and Bosie inherited from the remains of the family estate some £15,000 of which £8,000 was paid to him at once. He immediately returned to Paris and Percy accompanied him. "Bosie is over here with his brother", Wilde wrote to an American friend. "They are in deep mourning and the highest spirits. The English are like that."

6

Looking back wisely after events gives us a squint-eyed view of them. We know that 1900 was Wilde's last year of life but to Bosie it was the ninth of their friendship of which there would be, as far as he thought, many to come. He accepted his obligations to Wilde quite cheerfully and enjoyed his company as he had always done, but he was making a life of his own in which Oscar had no interest. Though Wilde remained a friend and a magnificent café companion and also a responsibility, his influence had weakened.

As soon as Bosie received his inheritance in London he sent Wilde £100 and during that year gave him in all, in cash and cheques, about £1,000. He told no one of this and only in after years and in answer to accusations that he had abandoned Wilde did he make any claim to have behaved generously. When he came to write his *Autobiography* thirty years after Wilde's death he was able to include in an appendix a statement from his bank, the National and Provincial in Piccadilly, which showed that between February 12 and November 15, 1900, ten cheques were paid to Wilde for sums varying from £10 to £125. Quite properly, he apologized for producing this evidence. He was forced to do so in answer to his 'traducers'. He did not mean it to reflect on Wilde.

He was twenty-nine years old now and by contemporary standards, and for a brief while, a rich young man. But not as rich as he imagined when he decided, within a month of his father's death, to do what he had long dreamed of doing—set up a racing stable of his own at Chantilly.

He had already bought two horses when he heard news of the death at Spion Kop of his boyhood friend, Wellington Stapleton-Cotton. He immediately went to London to enlist. It is doubtful whether the South African War fever would have touched him otherwise.

He offered himself as a trooper in Paget's Horse, but Colonel Paget advised him to join The Duke of Cambridge Corps, which was being recruited entirely from gentlemen prepared to pay for their own equipment, a gambit typical of the time. He went to the depot of the corps and joined it after passing the riding, shooting and medical tests, leaving a cheque for £250 to pay for his horse and equipment.

But 'Queensberry's boy' who had been an associate of Oscar Wilde was not welcome and for the second time in six months Bosie was made to realize that he could not easily live down the past. His cheque was returned to him with a letter saying that his services were not required. This was a stinging blow. He wrote, in terms which may be imagined, to Lord Arthur Hill who was raising the corps and told him what he thought of him and the Duke of Cambridge. Then, his feelings somewhat relieved, he returned to France and bought another horse.

For the next two years, until he had lost a great part of his inheritance, he kept the stables at Chantilly and they gave him, he said, the happiest time of his life. During his friendship with Wilde he had not been encouraged in his love of horses ("Bosie's ridiculous horses," Oscar called them,) or his love of exercise. His life in London, Naples and Paris was unhealthy and he had scarcely ridden or fired a gun or played a strenuous game of any kind for six years.

The wholesome atmosphere of his sporting little racing stable enchanted him and he would get up two hours before breakfast to ride gallops in the splendid morning air, recovering his health and the youthfulness of his appearance. Like his father, he could ride anything. Friends from England who were first-class men to hounds and who came out at exercise at his stables found that when they rode in a gallop the horses got away with them, for as Bosie maintained, there is a difference between riding a well-schooled hunter and a thoroughbred horse in full training. He could ride a hard-pulling horse in a string and keep him in place, an unexpected quality in a man whose poems were thought decadent, a man who would be sitting next evening in the Café de la Paix fascinated by the conversation of Oscar Wilde.

Bosie's inheritance was much discussed and before long Wilde made a foolish and uncharacteristic attempt to share it rather more fully than he was already doing.

The suggestion came from Ross. It would be illuminating to read the letter in which he egged Wilde on to approach Bosie, no doubt giving his reasons that Bosie now had *plenty* of money, that he *ought* to provide for Wilde, and perhaps also that Wilde would do well to get something settled before Bosie's inheritance had been dissolved at Chantilly. What he suggested was that Wilde should ask Bosie for an annuity which would cost about £2,000 and, supplementing Wilde's £150 a year, would mean that Wilde would be amply provided for. The whole scheme was contrary to the nature of Wilde who never wanted anything but 'gold', as he always called it, ready to spend and in lavish quantities. It would, moreover, have been an extremely poor investment, for Wilde died six months later. It is probable, moreover, that when Ross suggested it he knew nothing would come of the request but looked forward to the effect on Oscar of Bosie's predictable refusal.

Both Wilde and Bosie have left accounts of Wilde's attempt to obtain this money, but Wilde's is in a letter to Ross and shows Ross to have been the initiator of the plan, while Bosie's was written thirty years later.

"I asked Bosie what you suggested—without naming any sum at all —after dinner." Bosie had just won £400 at the races, and £800 a few days before, so he was in high spirits. Wilde told Ross that when he made his suggestion Bosie "went into paroxysms of rage, followed by satirical laughter", and refused. Wilde then told Frank Harris about it, and he was greatly surprised, but made the wise observation, 'One should never ask for anything: it is always a mistake.' He thought Wilde should have got someone to sound Bosie on his behalf. The affair occurred in the Café de la Paix, so Wilde made no scene, but said that if Bosie did not recognize the claim there was nothing more to be said.

"He had bluntly told me," wrote Bosie, "that it was my bounden duty to give him a large sum, several thousand pounds, or at any rate a couple of thousand." However it seems that Oscar brought this out without much conviction and soon let the matter drop. Wilde was no more grasping than Bosie about money but he was now living on his wife and friends. While he probably thought as he made his suggestion that it was justified he did not take the matter too seriously. Nor did Bosie. He said he would see that Oscar wanted nothing so long as he himself had money but would not hand over a large sum because Oscar would certainly get rid of it in a few months, giving a good deal away. As to buying an annuity—a dribble of money was useless to either of them. Oscar sadly and humorously recognized the truth of this and settled for another gift of ready money.

Since, however, Frank Harris was also in Paris, Wilde approached him* and told him what Bosie had said and according to Harris who must never be trusted when he quotes Wilde, grumbled about Bosie's refusal in terms very similar to those of his letter to Ross above quoted. This is typical Harris chicanery. He had read the letter to Ross when he wrote his account of the scene. But it suggested something to Harris who went to Chantilly a few nights later to see Bosie.

The sequel is almost comic, for of course it was Harris who got the £2,000. He agreed at once that it was preposterous of Oscar to ask for it, since he would probably spend it 'in riotous living' in a few months. But if Bosie would like to be in on the ground floor of a scheme which he, Harris, was just then floating it would bring Bosie £2,000 a year for life:

"This will put you in a position to treat Oscar in the most handsome way and still have plenty for yourself."

Bosie seems to have accepted this estimate and given the good news to Wilde who wrote to Ross that Frank Harris had spoken to Bosie, who now seemed to have more sense of the situation. He suggested that if Ross wrote to Bosie it would be better to say how pleased he was to hear from Wilde that Bosie was going to arrange some scheme for him.

It must be remembered that Harris at this time was known as the former proprietor and editor of *The Saturday Review* and not as the impostor and pornographer that he became. His love of literature and particularly of Shakespeare was perfectly genuine and impressed everyone who knew him. Of this particular confidence trick Bosie said he 'did it very cleverly' but from the account he gives of Harris's scheme it is clear that no one but a young man with no experience of finance, and a young man who had just inherited a fortune, would have been fooled by it.

"Do not decide anything about it now", Harris said—and where have we heard those words before?

But come and stay with me as my guest in my hotel at Monte Carlo. I am running an "hotel for millionaries", and I have put in Cesari (the celebrated *maître d'hôtel*) to manage it for me. This hotel will shortly be paying fifty per cent. on the capital, and if you like, I will let you into the company; but I have

* "Frank Harris has sent me nothing—I think of writing to him", Wilde had written to Ross.

another much bigger thing on, a real gold mine. I prefer to say nothing about it now, but come to Monte Carlo any time you like within the next four weeks and I will show you everything. Then, if you are convinced that it is a good thing, you can be right in on the rock bottom and get a hundred per cent. for your money. Meanwhile do not mention a word of this to Oscar or to anyone else.

Bosie went to Monte Carlo and saw the first part of Harris's scheme in action, a scheme which has since been used by others with remarkable success and profit. He had a small hotel which he called Cesari's which consisted entirely of ultra-expensive beautifully furnished suites, each of which had its own bathroom at a time when many French hotels had no usable bathroom at all. He had a splendid cook and his purpose was to attract only American, South African and other millionaires.

But that was not all. Next day Bosie was taken in Harris's motor-car —Harris was an early motorist—and shown the Restaurant de la Reserve at Eze. Here they had an excellent lunch on a terrace overlooking the sea while a Hungarian band played. Bosie was impressed but Harris clutched his arm excitedly.

"My dear man," he said, "this is nothing. The real gold mine is not yet revealed to you; but listen to this. I have a concession from the French Government allowing roulette and *trente-et-quarante* to be played here!"

Bosie fell for that. A hopeless gambler himself, the idea of a casino won him and he wrote out a cheque for £500, paying the balance of £1,500 in the following week. For this he received two thousand shares in 'The Cesari Reserve Syndicate'.

Within twelve months he knew the truth. The restaurant was mortgaged and the gambling concession was an invention of Harris's. No such concession had been promised nor had the French Government granted such a thing for fifty years, for roulette was illegal except in Monaco. Bosie recovered nothing but in money matters he was a good loser. He did not squeal to Harris and, a little ashamed of being a mug, told very few people about it. Twenty years later, when he read in Harris's *The Life and Confessions of Oscar Wilde* a fantastic version of the interview at Chantilly, complete with Bosie's 'strained white face', he told the full story in his paper.

7

Things began well with his stable. George Woodhouse was his trainer, 'one of the best and loyalest natures I have ever come across'. They started with a horse called Hardi which Bosie bought out of a selling race for £250. He was a six-year-old chestnut gelding which had never won a race and had belonged to Edmond Blanc, the owner of the Casino at Monte Carlo. Hardi had been leading Blanc's horses in their work at Chantilly. He was put in a race at Lille which was run while Bosie was in Monte Carlo with Frank Harris. Bosie left Woodhouse £40 with which to back Hardi, and in those days in the French provinces a bet of this size meant that the horse was pretty sure to start favourite. Hardi won at 6-4.

This was Bosie's first win and though the race was worth only about £120 it gave him enormous pleasure. He next entered Hardi for the opening race of the French Derby at Chantilly and backed him for £240. Hardi won at 6-1. His career went on triumphantly. Against Woodhouse's advice, Bosie entered him for a five-furlong race at Maisons-Lafitte. (There were not many races in France for which geldings were qualified.) Woodhouse said Hardi had no chance over any distance less than a mile but Bosie wanted to see his colours and Hardi started at 50-1. Bosie, watching the race through his glasses, saw his horse in the ruck halfway from home with apparently no chance but in the last two hundred yards Hardi came with a rush and made a dead heat. Bosie's each-way bet netted him over a thousand pounds.

Bosie used to ride Hardi at exercise and had a great affection for him. At the end of the season he entered him for another race at Maisons-Lafitte but did not go to see him run as he was taking a French girl to lunch in Paris. He did not intend to back Hardi but at the last minute gave Woodhouse what change he had, about £4, to put on each way in the Pari Mutuel. He was sitting outside the American Bar near the Gare du Nord waiting for a train to Chantilly when a boy selling papers said, "*Achetez-moi un journal, mon beau petit prince,*" an appeal which Bosie could neither ignore nor forget. He saw that Hardi had won and that the Pari-Mutuel was paying 68-1. "If I had been on the course I would certainly have had at least 25 louis each way on him."

Inevitably luck turned. Hardi was entered for the Oos Handicap at Baden-Baden, a race worth nearly £1,000, and was beaten by a short head "entirely owing to a jockey hitting him with his whip when he had been warned that if he touched the horse with a whip he would stop". While this was happening Bosie went to Deauville with two other horses of his which went wrong "owing to the neglect of a man engaged by Woodhouse", who had gone off on a drunken bust. Bosie instead backed a horse called Fourire for the Deauville Cup.

It won by two lengths at 5-1 but was disqualified, the Stewards' decision causing a riot.

He had several losers and a run of bad luck but worst of all was the loss of Hardi. He bolted on a frost-bound road, chucked off the boy who was riding him and ran away for about five miles. When he was caught he was broken down badly all round and eventually had to be shot because as a gelding he would have ended up in a cab if he had been sold with the other horses when Bosie gave up his stable.

Bosie never regretted his two years as an owner. He won a lot of money and lost much more, but it was a bracing and invigorating experience which took him out of the hot-house influence of Wilde. A quarter of a century later, after all his grubby experiences in the English courts of law, I spent a racing season with him at Ostend and saw the same transformation, the 'other side' of his nature triumphant. "If I had my life to live over again," he said, "I might even go in more for sport and less for literature. Even now I am not sure that I would not rather have ridden the winner of the Grand National than have done anything else."

He certainly treated the English law courts much as he had treated the race-courses of France.

8

As the racing season came towards an end that year (1900) Bosie joined with his brother Percy, now the ninth Marquess of Queensberry, in taking a shooting-box at Strathpeffer in Ross and Cromarty. Before leaving Paris early in August he asked Oscar to dinner at the Grand Café in the Boulevard des Capucines and found him in high spirits. It was one of the happiest of their several hundred meals together and it was also the last.

Just before they separated Oscar grew suddenly and briefly depressed as he had a way of being in his last years. He told Bosie he had a presentiment that he would not live long and when Bosie tried to pass this off as a gloomy nothing he said he did not think he would see the new century. "If another century began and I was still alive, it would really be more than the English could stand."

They parted quite cheerfully, however, Oscar amused at Bosie's haste to reach Scotland in time for August 12th. Bosie promised to send him a cheque from Scotland and kept his word, as an entry of £15 on August 16th shows.

Ross was due to reach Paris in October and hastened his visit when he received a telegram from Wilde saying that he had undergone an operation—this was on his ear. He found Wilde worried about his debts and complaining that Harris had let him down again over the play, *Mr. and Mrs. Daventry*.* When the doctor told Ross that worry about money was retarding Wilde's progress, Ross wrote to Harris and Bosie. Bosie sent another ten pounds at once and promised more.† Harris did not reply.

Wilde was now seriously ill and was being given morphia at night but, according to Ross, he drank too much champagne during the day. When 'a very nice letter from Alfred Douglas' arrived 'enclosing a cheque' Oscar wept a little. Ross then left for the South of France.

Bosie blamed Ross bitterly for not telling him of the gravity of Oscar's illness but this one at least of his complaints against Ross seems unjustified. Ross did not yet realize himself how serious was Wilde's condition or he would not have left him.

Reggie Turner remained in Paris and saw Wilde every day. His devotion to the sick man was beyond all praise. On November 28 he telegraphed to Ross, "Almost hopeless", and Ross came back to Paris. Wilde was unconscious and died two days later, on November 30.

It was only on the following day, December 1st, that Bosie received a telegram telling him that Wilde was dead. His complaint seems to have been that he was not given a chance of seeing Wilde while he was still conscious. In a letter to Ross, Reggie Turner explained that he wanted to wire Bosie but had not his address; Ross was already on his way to Paris when this letter was dispatched, however, and it is easy to understand how in the stress and uncertainty of those last days this could occur.

Reggie Turner [wrote Ross] had the worst time of all in many ways—he experienced all the horrible uncertainty and the appalling responsibility of which he did not know the extent. It will always be a source of satisfaction to those who were fond of Oscar, that he had someone like Reggie near him during his last days while he was articulate and sensible of kindness and attention.

On the other hand, Bosie's feelings about this were natural enough: "If I had had any inkling of the seriousness of his state of health I would

---

* The complicated story of this play of which Wilde wrote the scenario and on which Harris made several thousand pounds forms no part of this book but may be found in any biography of Wilde.

† It is noteworthy that this cheque which reached Wilde on November 1 was dated, according to Bosie's passbook, November 15. The fact that he sent a post-dated cheque suggests that he was, as usual, short of ready money.

have rushed over to Paris at once." When he reached Paris (on December 2) Oscar had been dead two days and was already in his nailed-up coffin.

9

"Reggie was a perfect wreck", wrote Ross, but he (Ross) kept his head remarkably well. He handled the complicated business of a death certificate (Oscar had registered as Melmoth) with ability and tact, managing to avoid 'the final touch of horror' of Oscar's body being taken to the Morgue, with which he was threatened. When Bosie arrived on the Sunday morning, Ross was ready for him. He was resolved from the first to obtain the executorship and from one point of view it was a good thing he did so for no one could have handled Wilde's posthumous affairs with more determination. But since he had the manuscript of *De Profundis* in his possession together with countless letters written to Wilde in the last few years, including all Bosie's, the executorship would put him in a position of extraordinary power in the jealous struggle against Bosie for possession—there is no other word —of all that would henceforth be Oscar Wilde.

Bosie was wholly unconscious of this. They had had their disagreements but he did not distrust Ross in such matters and respected his fidelity to Oscar. He never gave a thought to the question of literary executorship, and if he had done would probably have wanted Ross to handle it, as he had busily handled other things for Wilde. Bosie arrived in Paris after a long and difficult journey tired and heartbroken and was distressed to hear that he would not be able to see Oscar's body. Ross depended on this and on Bosie's dislike of documentary details and fuss. Not yet strong enough for a show-down, he received Bosie affectionately and gave him all the details of Oscar's illness and death and paid particular tribute to Reggie Turner. Bosie, said Ross, must be chief mourner at the funeral tomorrow. To this Bosie responded by agreeing to pay the funeral expenses.

Then Ross very casually mentioned that he had been through Oscar's papers and found 'nothing of the slightest importance'. What did Bosie want done about them? Bosie accepting this enquiry as his natural right but not feeling in the least like doing anything about Oscar's papers, told Ross to do what he thought best. He did not remember the matter till several years later when he was made to realize what that casual enquiry had portended. From that moment Ross called himself Wilde's literary executor and in 1906 was legally confirmed in the post with the agreement of Mrs. Wilde's family and the Official Receiver.

Wilde had been received into the Catholic Church on his deathbed and a requiem Mass was arranged in the fine old church of St. Germain des Prés, to which a small party walked behind the hearse—Bosie, Ross, Turner, Dupoirier the hotel proprietor and Jules, his waiter, the male nurse, Dr. Hennion and Maurice Gilbert. There were fifty-six people present at Mass, though Ross had wisely sent out no official notices to attract the merely curious. Only four carriages followed the hearse to Bagneaux Cemetery; in the first rode Father Cuthbert Dunn, an English Passionist who had Received Wilde and given him the Last Sacraments, with his acolyte. In the second were Bosie, Ross, Turner and Dupoirier. A veiled woman was present who afterwards revealed herself to Bosie as a friend of his Catholic grandmother, Mrs. Alfred Montgomery.

In his *Autobiography* Bosie gives no account of his feelings at the time, and it was nearly a year before he expressed them in one of the loveliest of all his sonnets—*The Dead Poet*. Two years later he wrote another sonnet which he preferred, perhaps because *The Dead Poet* had been so much anthologized. It was called *Forgetfulness*. In his last book, published during the Second World War, he says of Wilde's death: "It certainly seemed to me then, and for many a long day afterwards, that the sun had gone down."

10

There were no storms or estrangements between the two friends during that last year of Wilde's life, but a calm and cheerful affection which they both enjoyed after the passionate, the prosperous, the tragic and the quarrelsome stages through which their friendship had passed.

Wilde was out of Paris for some months in the spring, at Gland in Switzerland, and afterwards in Italy, and Bosie was in Scotland after early August, but in the summer they met often and with a new whole-hearted delight in one another's company. No one tried to prevent these meetings, for Queensberry and Constance Wilde were dead, Lady Queensberry had Bosie's promise that they would not live together, Harris had just taken £2,000 from Bosie, Sherard was rarely in Paris, (and in any case wrote, "I saw nothing whatever wrong in their association. They seemed to admire each other very much. Oscar pontified and Douglas listened with a certain amount of humorous criticism in his remarks"), while Ross was shrewd enough to perceive that the post-Neapolitan relationship did not exclude him, as the former one had done.

"The sun had gone down", said Bosie and it had sunk in a bright serene sunset after a tempestuous day.

II

After Bosie had returned to Scotland he wrote two letters to Adey which make a rather curious epitaph for Wilde from one who was to become a devout Catholic eleven years later. But, written by the only human being whom Oscar loved, and perhaps the only one who truly loved him, they have the ring of honest mourning:

I am miserable and wretched about darling Oscar. It seems so beastly that I couldn't have seen him before he died, and nobody told me a word about his illness till the day before his death when it was too late. It seems to get worse every day. I try to think that perhaps it is better than when he was in prison, but then one had the hope of seeing him again and now I don't believe I ever shall. I suppose Bobbie is consoled by the R. Catholic tomfoolery, though why he should be I don't know, for he knows perfectly well that Oscar was never really received at all (he being quite unconscious when Bobbie got the ceremony performed) and even if he was according to your Church he is certainly damned. I suppose Bobbie is sustained by the thought of meeting him in "Hell". Please don't mind my talk. I know it won't offend you as it would Bobbie and it is a vent to my feelings which I have had to bottle up. I did so loathe the whole idea of his 'being received' on his death-bed à la Aubrey Beardsley. It was so utterly unlike him. My dear More what is to be done with one's life? I simply don't know. I am utterly sick of the whole business.

In the second letter he says:

As regards Oscar and Catholicism. I dislike the untruth of it, the pretending that he died a Catholic when he didn't and *never* under any circumstances would have. His unconscious body was consigned by Bobbie to the Catholic Church entirely without consulting him or any of his friends, and it was publicly stated that he had become a Catholic a few days before his death which of course is absolutely untrue. Still I suppose it doesn't make much difference. It is only a matter of sentiment. I shall feel exactly the same if somebody (with the best intentions) published an exhaustive work whereby he proved that Oscar was entirely guiltless of the charges brought against him, and that he was really a confirmed and secret mulierast. I love Oscar's faults and vices just as much as his virtues and splendours, because they are all part of him and part of his intellectual attitude towards life. He was as a matter of fact the most complete sceptic imaginable, and would never have bowed his intellect to any dogma or any form of religious belief however fine. He was never in his life self-convicted of *sin*, which is the touchstone of religious belief. He was proud of the so-called sin or crime for which he was persecuted, and he was in fact a martyr to a new Humanism of which Christianity in any form is the deadliest and most powerful enemy. Christianity with its Judaic origin and therefore indirectly Roman Catholicism is responsible for the fact that Oscar, the greatest intellect of his age, was condemned as a felon to two years hard labour. The moment he becomes a christian and professes Christianity, he admits that he was wrong, and that the morality whose Vicar on earth is, say Mr. Justice Wills, is justified.

CHAPTER IX

Radiant Beginning

I

IT was a sad if not an altogether broken young man who came to live in London after Wilde's death. He could not yet realize that people, and particularly people in what was still called Society, had an uneasy conscience about their treatment of his friend and would fasten on him as a convenient scapegoat. *We* did not kill the man's genius, they said in effect, *we* did not encourage a conspiracy to imprison him by means of a preposterous law, *we* are not to blame for his barren last years and early death; it was all the fault of this young man who bewitched him into a disastrous attack on his father, who is still free, rich, handsome, as we are not.

Bosie was the only one of Wilde's friends on whom this fell. Socially he was alone among them in having anything to lose. Ross and the rest, with their acquaintance solely among artists and writers, lost nothing and Ross, after a while, gained a kind of kudos till eventually the reparation the world owed to Wilde was made to him, so that he wrote prefaces and went to first nights and generally deputized for the dead man whose name he did much to re-establish. But Bosie who had been brought up and made his early friends among the powerful, sport-loving, generally rather stupid peerage of the late Victorian era was cold-shouldered by the only people he knew. Not until his last years was he able to come to terms with the bourgeois or the bohemian worlds and, partially excluded from his own, he was at a loss.

He has described some of the snubs he received in those years, but there must have been countless other small humiliations of which we cannot know, countless mean little slights and hypocritical turnings away which, by accumulative slow degrees, wore down his natural amiability and that trust in the general friendliness of the world which had characterized his youth. At first, not realizing the role that was being forced on him, he behaved as he had always done and expected his friends to do the same. Meeting hostility and occasional discourtesy, he was reduced to a condition of raw sensitiveness. He adopted an attitude which he maintained to the end of his life, of avoiding an appearance of making advances to other people, in friendship, love or mere acquaintance. He formed a habit of not even speaking to old friends who did not address him first. He was so sensitive to slights that he learned to make it difficult or impossible for slights to be offered to him. From this developed after a time his aggressiveness, his fierce counters to often imagined attacks, his ferocious sensitivity which for some years turned him into a victim of persecution mania and an habitual litigant.

He should have appreciated immediately after Wilde's conviction that sentence had been passed on him too, and perhaps partially he did so, though not in those terms. He regarded the situation as a challenge and only when he came to live in London in January 1901 did he learn what slow cruelties the forces of hypocrisy and public self-esteem had in store for him. His reactions were at first those of any spirited young man and if his courage degenerated later into malice at times and his satire into invective, it is not altogether surprising. He had neither sagacity nor patience enough and within a few years he had run amok.

2

But not at first. The money inherited on his father's death had greatly diminished during his first year as a racehorse owner but his brother Percy had come into about £300,000, and though much of this had been due to creditors there was still wealth in the family. Bosie found rooms in Duke Street and spent much time with his brother at a place Percy had taken called Smedmore, where the shooting was good.

Bosie discovered that among his former friends were some who cut him but many good fellows who were glad to see him and spend time with him. If he could have been a little more tolerant and understanding of the problem he posed to young peers and the sons of peers with whom he had formerly associated he would soon have been generally accepted but in his own words he consigned to the Devil those who behaved coldly towards him and—a very Douglas note—found that the Devil took him at his word in many cases.

But one friend welcomed him and his company: this was young George Montagu, "Jidge", of whom Bosie had been fond at Winchester and for whom he had always "made a bee-line" when he returned to the school from Oxford.

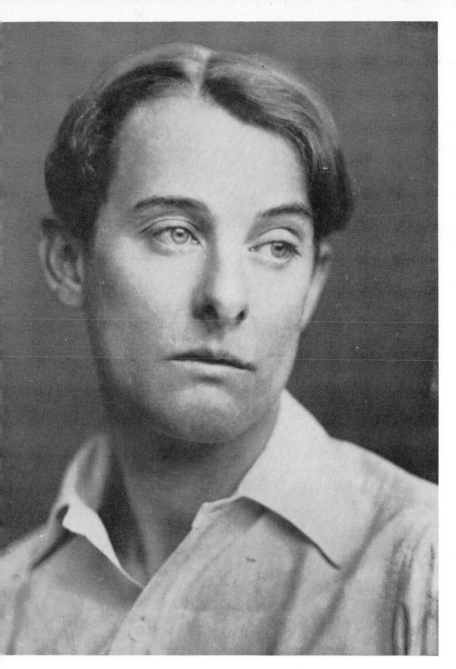

In 1903.

*Olive Douglas in yachting cap, in
1937 and in 1903, soon after her
marriage.*

In his *Autobiography* Bosie tells a story of his friendship with this young man which seems to be an excellent example of his proneness to imagine slights and his entirely reasonable conviction that he suffered these as a result of his friendship with Oscar Wilde.

George Montagu, he says, was as friendly and pleasant to him as he had always been and just before Bosie went to America, that was in October 1901, for a period of two or three months they were inseparable. George Montagu was kept short of money and was in the habit of lunching and dining with Bosie almost every day and using his rooms as if they were his own. Then his family arranged for him to stand for Parliament and hearing that he was constantly in Bosie's company told him the acquaintance must be ended as a preliminary to an election campaign. Bosie was dropped without compunction. He wrote one of his letters and later a sonnet called *The Traitor*—"I shall know his soul Lies in the bosom of Iscariot".

Now there is no doubt that when Bosie wrote his account of the incident thirty years later he truly believed this was how it happened. Yet a glance at *Who's Who* would have told him, as it has told me, that George Montagu, (later the ninth Earl of Sandwich) to whom he was referring had already been Assistant Private Secretary to the President of the Board of Agriculture for two years and had been elected Conservative M.P. for South Huntingdonshire the year before (1900) when Bosie was still at Chantilly or in Scotland with his brother. Bosie in other words may have been dropped for one reason or another but that it was to give his friend a better chance in an election is simply not true. It is, however, interesting evidence of Bosie's state of mind at the time and though he admitted that it was absurd to write as he did, we owe to it a fine furious sonnet which loses nothing by having been so trivially inspired.

Bosie's loyalest friend, now as six years previously at the time of the Wilde crisis, was his brother Percy. This most well-beloved of the Queensberry family had led a wandering life before he inherited the title. He left the Navy at nineteen and worked on a ranch in the Western States from which he went to Ceylon as a tea-planter. With another Scottish 'younger son', he made for the Australian goldfields. His companion was David Carnegie, the youngest son of Lord Southesk. They staked out claims and Percy returned to London to sell them and was lucky enough to run into the West Australian gold-mining boom. He sold at a profit for him and his partner of £20,000 each, but this turned his head, and during the five years between the death of his older brother and that of his father he speculated with money which he raised on his expectation of his inheritance. His ranching and gold-digging days had made him a hard drinker and his innate optimism and generosity did the rest. Bosie said he had a flair for good things and at one time owned the Bruce Mines copper-mine which became a part of the Mond empire, but Percy was a poor manager of his own affairs, recklessly spendthrift and trusting. On one occasion he handed out nearly a thousand pounds in notes to the down-and-outs on the Embankment. He died in 1920 and at his funeral hundreds of people unknown to his family appeared, for he was popular in many unsuspected ways. But he had by then dissipated his large inheritance.

At this period Bosie spent much time with him at Smedmore, for Bosie was never by nature a townsman. One of the most curious of the misrepresentations by his nephew Queensberry in his book, *Oscar Wilde and the Black Douglas*, was that "the beauties of nature meant nothing to him—he hated the country".

3

In the spring of that year (1901) that is within six months of the death of Wilde, Bosie's poetry brought him a fan letter from a girl called Olive Custance who was a fellow-contributor to a literary weekly, *The Academy*. John Lane had published a collection of her poems under the title of *Opals* in the previous year.

Bosie, as we have seen, was not unaccustomed to receiving such letters from men but was delighted at one from a young woman who was a fellow-poet. He sent what he calls—without the sinister implication of the words when applied to most of his letters—'a suitable reply' and before long the two agreed to meet.

This, however, was not quite the simple matter it would be today. Bosie says they met 'in a romantic way' and certainly they both thought that to become acquainted surreptitiously, but with every propriety, was romantic, even if it was in a museum. Olive was the only daughter and heiress of a distinguished soldier and a rich man, Colonel Custance, formerly of the Grenadier Guards, who had just returned from the South African War. It was intended that she should make a brilliant marriage and her parents would have been horrified to hear that she was secretly meeting Bosie, whose name they probably knew as that of 'Queensberry's son who got in such a mess over the unspeakable Oscar Wilde'.

Bosie and Olive made an appointment by letter to meet at the South

Kensington Museum and Olive set out 'chaperoned by her maid', but they had not been sufficiently specific about their meeting-point and in that huge mausoleum missed one another. Bosie went 'to the wrong door or the wrong room' and after waiting in vain returned to his rooms in Duke Street. Olive, who was a determined young woman, decided when Bosie did not appear to go to the address from which he had written and, still chaperoned by her maid, arrived in Duke Street shortly after his return.

It was—what else could it be between two resolutely romantic poets? —love at first sight. They were both shy, but both thrilled by the idea of what from the first was to be a 'hopeless passion'. Fervid Shake-speareans with the early plays in their minds, they saw one another as Romeo and Juliet.

They met several times in London, their rendezvous being an up-stairs room at the little picture gallery called the Carfax in Ryder Street of which Robert Ross had become one of the proprietors. Ross, who had already started his long campaign for the recognition of Wilde, was delighted to be of assistance to the two young lovers, enjoying the intrigue and sentimentality of the thing.

More boldly, Olive took Bosie to meet her mother who was staying at a hotel in Dover Street. Mrs. Custance seems to have been neatly hoodwinked, for she was aware of no danger in the situation. They were all amused to discover in the conversation that Bosie, in an Eton jacket, and Olive, a ten-year-old bridesmaid, had been together at the wedding of one of Bosie's innumerable cousins.

Then Olive went to Dinard to stay with her cousin, Lady Anglesey, a famous beauty who afterwards became Mrs. John Gilliat. She too joined the intrigue and took Olive to Paris, where Olive and Bosie could meet as often as they wished. Bosie hurried over and put up at the Hôtel Rastadt in the Rue Danou, and for the next ten days the two were together daily. Bosie still had his stable at Chantilly and took Olive to see his horses and afterwards to walk in the forest hand-in-hand. At Lady Anglesey's hotel there was a separate table for 'the children' and they went together to restaurants for lunch and dinner.

But much of the enchantment of their relationship was in its secrecy and hopelessness. They were to love one another for ever while the stern demands of Olive's duty to her parents and Bosie's need to marry money would separate them in body but not in spirit. The whole romance has a literary and dated air as one reads of it today. Olive's

letters, addressed to her 'Prince' by his 'Page' would be embarrassing
and perhaps a little silly written by a modern girl but they were sincere
enough in 1901: "Beautiful Prince," she wrote soon after they had met,

I must send a few words to you by the early post . . . just to thank you for your
sweetness to me. . . . It was so lovely to look into your clear brave eyes and
talk to you . . . and hear your voice and your laugh. . . . It was so lovely that
I can hardly believe it was not all a dream. . . . When shall I get another letter
from you . . . and tell me are you pleased with your little Princess? No! I am
not your Princess. . . . *She* will be very beautiful . . . but meanwhile love me a
little please, kind and beautiful Prince. Opal.

Another letter stresses the nature of their relationship and talks of the
'beautiful rich princess' whom Bosie is to find and marry.

My own Prince,—The little heart is sweet . . . [this was a locket Bosie sent her
with a lock of his hair] and I shall always . . . always wear it . . . even when
you have forgotten me and married the beautiful rich princess who will give
you all those lovely things you ought to have. . . . I miss you more than I can
say . . . for I love you beyond everything in the world . . . and I think we shall
never be happy together again. . . . Write to me soon . . . soon and tell me
you love your little Page and that one day you will come back to 'him' . . .
my Prince, my Prince . . . I found Mummy rather unhappy as "Tannie"
[Tanie, Olive's governess] had told her we met that time in London . . .
wasn't it horrible of her? However, Mummy has forgiven us and all will be
well if she doesn't find out about Paris. . . . She would never forgive any of us
then, I am afraid! Good-bye my darling . . . may all your dreams come true.
I cannot write more. . . . Goodbye. . . . Olive.

Marriage between them in that first year of their meeting was
considered quite out of the question. Olive's father was a Victorian of
stern principles and narrow prejudices who had fixed ideas about
Olive's future. In one of her letters to Bosie she writes: "A dreadful
thing happened to your last wire! It was opened by Daddy! However
'Bosie' conveyed nothing to him . . . so I said it was from Nathalie."
Bosie, on the other hand, had long since decided that there was only
one solution for the problem of his diminishing means, the conventional
one of an American heiress. He had planned before meeting Olive to
leave for the States later in the year, and this was accepted by both of
them as inevitable. It gave an extra tenderness to their love, a delicious
sadness to their highly emotional hours together, and any number of
literary precedents for their behaviour.

4

Bosie has been blamed for that trip to the States as he has been blamed for many things which in other men would have been taken for granted. It was—and to some extent still is—an everyday occurrence for the holder of any European title to barter it for a rich bride, as a glance at a *Debrett* of the time will show. It was a perfectly equitable arrangement and at its best it meant a better chance of a more successful love-match. If Bosie had gone through with it and returned with a smart, handsome and rich young woman, no one would have thought twice about it; it was precisely because he could not go through with it that he was criticized, perhaps as a failure. He said afterwards that he had less compunction in mentioning 'these sordid ideas' because they never got beyond the region of ideas. He thought it exceedingly unlikely that he would ever have married any girl, however many millions she had, if he had not loved her, and this was probably true enough, for what it is worth. Love *and* a million dollars is obviously a more attractive proposition than love without it, especially to a young man whose only skills were sonneteering and riding, who had been brought up to the idea of wealth and who had just run through most of his inheritance. A young man, moreover, who believed as Bosie did that with plenty of money behind him he would have no difficulty in breaking down the barriers which Society had erected against him for his concern in a very nasty scandal. His judgement in this was almost certainly sound and it is pleasant to think that nowadays there would be no barriers to break down, perhaps because there is no Society to erect them.

At all events, his resolve was made and with £800 as his capital for the venture he sailed in October 1901 for New York, after a tearful leavetaking with 'the only girl he would ever really love', however cruelly 'the world' might force their separation. It was a situation so much of other centuries that it is startling to remember that Bosie and Olive were still alive less than twenty years ago.

He spent a month or six weeks in New York* and a fortnight in Boston and, as he says that he had an agreeable time among pleasant people, it may be supposed that he ran up against none of the slights or embarrassments which he had learned to fear in England. There would have been no difficulty about the 'heiress'—indeed, he was given to understand in writing that he would not be rejected by any one of

* He met George Sylvester Viereck, another stormy petrel, then a schoolboy of sixteen, and they corresponded for the rest of Bosie's life.

three, one of whom had 'quite £20,000 a year'. Perhaps the Americans in these cities were more tolerant than his own people or had another sense of humour or shorter memories. They certainly welcomed the handsome young man with the courtesy title of Lord, whose father had created the rules under which they boxed.

That matters went no further was, according to Bosie, due to himself. He was receiving love-letters from Olive and these made the heiresses less attractive and the thought of 'the Prince's Page' a disturbing one.

Then he made the mistake of going to Washington, where Percy Wyndham, another nephew of Bosie's beloved Uncle Percy, was Second Secretary in the Embassy.

The Ambassador then was Lord Pauncefote, a man of seventy-three who had held the office for twelve years. (He died five months after Bosie left Washington.) He was a diplomat of some ability and had already dealt with several difficult problems including the negotiation of a treaty on the subject of the Panama Canal which was known as the Hay-Pauncefote Treaty. He felt no apprehension about the reception which would be given in Washington to his Second Secretary's cousin and left a card at Bosie's hotel.

A day or two after arrival Bosie moved into his cousin's rooms and for about three weeks had a most 'cheerful and lively' time, meeting a number of charming people. Percy Wyndham made him an honorary member of the Metropolitan, which was the most exclusive club in Washington.

Then there was a highly unpleasant incident. To assess its importance to Bosie, one must remember the period and the place and the state of smarting sensitivity in which he was. He went into the club one day, totally unconscious that his membership as one 'connected with a disgraceful scandal' had been questioned, and from a group beside him at the bar heard a man make an offensive remark about Oscar Wilde in a voice intended for Bosie to hear. He drank up, as we say, and walked out, making straight for his cousin's rooms.

Percy Wyndham told him then that he had received a letter from the club committee asking for an explanation of his introduction of Bosie as a member. Wyndham replied sharply that no explanation was necessary. Bosie was his cousin, on intimate terms with the British Ambassador and Lady Pauncefote and—a nice touch—a member of White's. He would, Percy Wyndham said, be most unlikely to wish to enter the club again, in view of the committee's attitude. But the harm was done, and in all the circumstances it was brutal.

Everyone at the Embassy behaved splendidly. Pauncefote sent for Bosie and told him the Metropolitan Club was a pot-house, and that members of it never missed a chance of insulting anyone on friendly terms with the Embassy or himself. Bosie was to consider the whole thing beneath his dignity. Lady Pauncefote asked him to take her to a concert that afternoon and to dine next day. The Naval Attaché asked him to lunch and the whole staff showed themselves with him. But the *New York Herald* spread the story in headlines and Bosie, bitterly hurt, felt he was an embarrassment to his friends in Washington and decided to return to New York.

This was probably the wisest and certainly the most chivalrous thing he could do but it shows that he was not yet the hardened fighter, armed against insult, who appeared later, but still a very easily wounded young man who found it hard to believe in the hostility of others. If he had stayed it would have made things difficult for his host and for the Pauncefotes, but the Americans would probably have liked him for it. Already there were many who regretted that a visitor should have been insulted, for it outraged one of their national principles, that of hospitality. Senator Cabot Lodge, a man already of high prestige who had been Chairman of the Republican National Convention in the previous year, at once invited him to dine. But Bosie received the invitation forwarded to New York, where he had gone two days after the incident.

In New York he was well received and invited to give his version of the affair to the *New York Herald*, which had published an account of it. This he did in a long letter which was prominently published. The University Club retorted to the Metropolitan by making him an honorary member. But he had received a wound which took many years to heal and, trivial though the incident may seem today, it was one of the things which helped to make him later an angry, self-justifying litigant.

He left for England a fortnight after returning to New York, having written 'at the request of Nathalie Barnes' a sonnet from the French of Baudelaire's *La Beauté*.

5

Reaching Liverpool in January, he went straight to the Hebridean island of Colonsay, which his brother Percy had taken for a year. The island was beautiful, some twelve to fourteen thousand acres in area, with a charming house and—a rarity in those often treeless islands— plenty of coverts for pheasants.

Bosie and his brother spent their time shooting. The bag was an all-round one, for there was a grouse-moor of a kind, partridges, woodcock, duck and snipe. There was a hard frost on the mainland that year which did not reach the islands and sent in swarms of woodcock. In five days, Bosie remembered proudly, he and an Argyllshire laird called Graham shot 147 woodcock.

While on Colonsay he received a letter from Olive which told him that she was engaged to be married. Though it was understood between them that one day this must happen, and though Bosie had himself just returned from his study of the American marriage market, this news amazed and stung him. But what made it harder to bear was that Olive's fiancé was that very George Montagu to whom Bosie had written and dispatched his sonnet, *The Traitor*, the man who, he believed, had betrayed him for a political career, whose soul in fact lay 'in the bosom of Iscariot'.

What had recommended George Montagu to Olive's parents was obvious—he was heir to an earldom and a fortune and, apart from this, a charming young man with a bright political future. What had recommended him to Olive was the fact that he had been a friend of Bosie's and did clever impersonations of Olive's 'prince'. Olive explained that she loved Bosie but said that he did not want to marry her and finally, to the great relief of her mother who by now knew of her meetings with Bosie, became engaged to Montagu. Colonel Custance, who had not been informed of those meetings, was delighted, especially when his wife received a letter from the King congratulating her on her daughter's engagement to Montagu.

Bosie learned all this later, but the letter he received on Colonsay sent him into action. In words which suggest the truth, that he never ceased to regard his life as a piece of Border minstrelsy, he wrote years later 'the blood of a hundred Douglas ancestors surged up' and he said in his heart, "No, you dont"!

He hurried down to London and asked Olive to dine with him. She agreed, and their meeting took place—rather curiously in view of the past—at Kettner's restuarant. Bosie has left an account of what passed between them but the imagination is a safer guide here than the autobiographer's memory. They were certainly in love and both wanted to forget the false steps they had been trying to take. Olive told Bosie she had only agreed to marry George Montagu because she thought Bosie did not want to marry her; Bosie said he had never cared for any other girl and had given up all idea of the American heiress. These two statements of his were true enough, but when he went on to say, as he naïvely claims he did, that he had come back to England simply because he could not live without Olive, he was guilty of a little rhetorical exaggeration. He warned her, however, that he had no money at all and would in future be dependent on his mother. In the end they decided to run away together. This, they knew, was the only way to avoid being 'separated for ever', but to each of them the idea of an elopement made its appeal, and both sincerely believed that the world was well lost. They probably talked about poverty, even perhaps—a favourite contemporary figure of speech—love in a cottage.

Their promises made, they discussed no practicalities that evening but agreed to meet some days later in Robert Ross's picture gallery. This time they worked out the details. Olive was to go that week-end to Hinchingbrooke, Lord Sandwich's place in Huntingdonshire, to meet the family. During her absence Bosie would obtain a special licence. Neither seems to have been much troubled by the thought of Olive's appearing with her fiancé at his uncle's home and spending two days there as the bride-to-be, though Bosie admitted afterwards that he did not feel perfectly certain she would turn up at the appointed time.

He obtained the special licence but before the wedding, which was to be at St. George's, Hanover Square, at nine o'clock on the following Tuesday morning, he took several people into his confidence. First, Robert Ross. In after years he said that he only did this because he and Olive used to meet in Ross's gallery. He also said that Ross 'for some extraordinary reason' always seemed to resent his marriage, though he admitted that he 'subsequently discovered' that Ross was at the church 'in the background'. What seems more likely is that Ross, who no longer felt Bosie to be a rival, was perfectly well-disposed to the marriage and pleased at being treated, as he was by so many people and in so many circumstances, as a confidant. He may have been no more of a snob than most young men of his type and time but a girl jilting the heir to an earl to marry the penniless younger son of a marquess in itself must have intrigued him. It was his life's policy to cultivate people of talent, of birth and of position, and he sincerely liked being liked. He had rarely shown Bosie any open hostility and up to this time it had only been when Bosie monopolized Wilde that he had felt his jealous little hatred for him, and if Bosie had continued to welcome him in the years ahead he would probably never have revealed it. He was certainly pleased to feel he had aided the run-away marriage.

Then Bosie told his friend Cecil Hayes, a young barrister who was private secretary to Lord Denbigh. Hayes later appeared as Bosie's Counsel in his two most disastrous appearances in Court, but he was a loyal friend to Bosie to the end of his life.

Bosie also confided in his sister Edith, another staunch supporter in his future struggles. She agreed to come to the church with Bosie, and, a conventional detail even in a secret marriage at the time, they would drive there in her carriage-and-pair.

Then, at the last minute, Bosie told his mother. She gave him her fondest blessing, a diamond ring for Olive and, of more practical importance in the circumstances, £200 and the promise of an allowance.

Olive was staying with her mother in the hotel in Dover Street to which she had taken Bosie nearly a year earlier. She took her maid into her confidence and a single portmanteau, all that could safely be smuggled out, was packed overnight to be taken by the maid in the morning to Victoria Station where she would await the married couple. On the morning of Tuesday, March 4, 1902, Olive told her mother that she was going to spend the day with Tanie, her former governess who lived in the suburbs, and left the hotel unnoticed. She arrived punctually at St. George's and the two were married.

Before they left Victoria Station Olive sent a telegram to her mother saying what she had done and giving their address as the Hotel Rastadt, Paris.

6

The Custance family had been settled at Westons Longeville in Norfolk since 1726. James Woodforde, who wrote *The Diary of a Country Parson*, was appointed to the living of Weston Longeville in 1776 and remained there till his death in 1803. He recalls the Custance family moving into the house which John Custance, whom he calls 'my Squire', had built in 1781. He refers to this as the New House or the New Hall, but by the time Olive Custance was born and brought up there it had become Weston Old Hall. The property remained very large even by Norfolk standards and the family, since Parson Woodforde's day, had never left it.

Olive's father was Colonel Frederic Hambledon Custance. The son of Sir Hambledon Custance, K.C.B., he was now fifty-seven years old and more than six foot tall. He had been in the Grenadier Guards and had commanded the 3rd Battalion of the Norfolk Regiment in the Boer War, being made C.B. in 1900.

He was a Victorian to the core, a sound unimaginative soldier, an autocrat and at times a tyrant to his family, an upright man who could do a dishonorable thing only when he had persuaded himself that it was justified. His very consciously held status was of a country squire with a foot in Court. He was exactly the kind of man, with family pride and a reverence for convention as his twin stars, to be most outraged by what had happened, to be horror-stricken when he learned that one connected with the Wilde case should have become a connection of his own. Moreover, it meant that his daughter had lost one of the most eligible bachelors alive. Nothing like this had happened to him since his only sister had married, and become, a Catholic.

He raised every kind of hell and King Edward the Peacemaker, who only a week or two earlier had written to Mrs. Custance to congratulate her, supported him with an expression of his great displeasure. Custance, with the notion common to his class and period that there were only about a dozen homosexuals in the country and all of them known to the police, rushed round to Scotland Yard and demanded to see Bosie's 'record'. Hearing that he had not one and that the marriage had been performed in a perfectly regular manner with Bosie's sister present, he retired to think things over for a week or two. Had he been able to play his part of outraged parent to the full and cut off his daughter with a shilling he would certainly have done so but unfortunately this was impossible, for the property was entailed on Olive.

There was only one thing to be done and with as good a grace as possible he wrote to the couple and, saying he had forgiven them, invited them down to Weston Old Hall for a fortnight. So after a very happy Parisian honeymoon, Bosie and Olive were received into her family. What, if anything, Mrs. Custance was allowed to think or do about it is unknown. Custance had married her when he was twenty-five and she had not produced an heir for him. She was a granddaughter of the first Lord Hylton and appears to have been a kind and colourless woman. It seems she had failed to warn her husband of what had been going on and possibly, in the way of Victorian fathers, he blamed her for the disaster. Bosie liked her and got on well with her but says nothing of her attitude towards the run-away marriage. She died a year or two later.

Custance for a time was friendly and the marriage promised to be a happy one. Many years later Olive wrote in a letter: "Alas, our marriage ended in misery for both of us, whatever Bosie may say. But, at least, it did have a radiant beginning."

7

There followed a long period of calm and happiness. Having once made up his mind to accept his son-in-law, Colonel Custance behaved impeccably and during the next few years the young couple made several long visits to Weston Old Hall.

Custance, who was a masterly fisherman and had a splendid trout stream, taught Bosie to fish. Up to the time of his marriage Bosie had never fished and now began to love it as much as shooting. After the death of Mrs. Custance the Colonel lived alone and on more than one occasion Bosie went without Olive to stay with him and the two got on exceedingly well. They shot and fished together and their relations were 'almost affectionate'. It is a pleasant but in view of all that happened later a rather curious picture one gets of the tall, stiff, reserved soldier and the talkative, excitable poet following the only thing they had in common, their love of field sports.

Bosie took Olive abroad several times in the first few years of their marriage, to the South of France and to Corsica. In 1903 they were together at Ostend where Bosie played a system at roulette and starting with £50 ended by winning £350. The strain was so great, however, that he decided never to do this again.

A son was born in 1902 at a house in Chelsea and christened Raymond. This delighted Custance who had wanted a son himself. From the first he took a rather more than grand-fatherly interest in the baby who would be, in a sense, his heir. But no alarm was felt about this at the time.

One of Bosie's innumerable cousins, Pamela Wyndham, was married to Edward Tennant who was afterwards to become Lord Glenconner. She and Bosie had been friends since childhood and when Bosie went down to stay with the Tennants at Wilsford in Wiltshire she showed him a beautiful old farmhouse on the Amesbury to Salisbury road only a hundred yards from the River Avon, one of the best trout streams in the country. It was called Lake Farm and belonged to an old gentleman named Lovibond who lived at Lake House, an Elizabethan mansion not far away. Bosie was enchanted with the house, the setting and the prospect of fishing, for this was after his father-in-law had passed on his own keenness. Bosie took the house and he and Olive and the baby moved to it in 1904, spending the next three years there. It was the happiest time of their married life.

Hypotheses in a life like Bosie's are absurd but it is difficult to resist one here. If he could have been satisfied with the life he had at Lake, which gave him everything that people of his background most coveted, in a few years the past would have been forgotten and he himself reclaimed by the associates of his youth. He would have become a country gentleman with a taste for writing poetry, teaching his son to ride and shoot, on correct terms with his wife, devoted to his dogs and horses, entertaining and being entertained by people of the narrow, closed society in which he was born. His friendship with Wilde would have been forgotten, not by him but by those who would have felt it unsportsmanlike to remember it against this husband and father who was so obviously one of themselves. He might even have lived to a period of broader views when he would have been chaffed about it or interviewed by the press in a friendly manner after Wilde's rehabilitation. He might have died without learning of the 'unpublished parts' of *De Profundis*. He would not have lacked money either during the lifetime of Custance or after it. It is fortunate for his biographer that after a few years of Wiltshire Bosie was back in London for the controversies and lawsuits, the violence and hatreds of his middle period, but it was fortunate for no one else, least of all for him.

Meanwhile his neighbours made much of Bosie and Olive. The Tennants at Wilsford who had been responsible for their introduction to the neighbourhood were delighted with them but their most intimate friends were a couple called Antrobus, Sir Edmund, known as 'Strobus', and his eccentric wife, familiarly called 'Wavie', who lived at Amesbury Abbey. This magnificent Palladian house was built by Bosie's ancestor, the third Duke of Queensberry, cousin and predecessor of 'Old Q', who married that lovable and extraordinary creature 'Kitty', a famous beauty and friend of Swift, Walpole and Gay. Gay wrote *The Beggar's Opera* at Amesbury Abbey.

Bosie used to talk warmly of Strobus and Wavie in after years, for they were extremely kind to him and his wife. Their only son who was in the Grenadier Guards was killed in the 1914-18 War and it will surprise no one who remembers that sort of family at that time that he was known as 'Toots'. 'Strobus' himself had commanded the 3rd Battalion of the Grenadier Guards and seen service in the Sudan. He owned about 8,000 acres of Wiltshire, including Stonehenge.

For fishing Bosie had the run not only of Mr. Lovibond's water but several miles belonging to Sir Edmund Antrobus. He also had leave to fish in the water of a Mr. Devenish farther down the river and sometimes in that of Mr. Louis Greville, so one way or another he had miles of the finest trout fishing for nothing and became very skilful. He recalls with the kind of pride which puts stuffed fish in glass cases that in one day he caught the second largest basket of trout ever known on the Amesbury Abbey water, one fish of three pounds, eleven over two and eighteen over a pound and a half, putting back, according to the rule of the river, over a dozen just under a pound and a half.

8

During these years a great deal of poetry of a kind came from that corner of Wiltshire for Pamela Tennant, Olive Douglas and Bosie were all contributing to a literary weekly called *The Academy*, edited by a Mr. Harold Child.

Bosie does not say in what years his sequence of sonnets *To Olive* was written—it was first published in *The Academy* in 1907. It contains some of his finest work. The two sonnets commencing "I have been profligate of happiness" and "When we were Pleasure's minions, you and I" show Bosie at his best and most characteristic, the lines have a bite and are never woolly or precious, the emotion is deep and well communicated, the metaphors not far-fetched, as in earlier sonnets they were apt to be. He wrote *To a Silent Poet* and *Palmistry* in 1905 and 1906, while in the following year came *Silence* and *Green River*.

He was also writing and publishing during these years some light verse and nonsense rhymes. The first of these, *Tails with a Twist* by "Belgian Hare" had been published in oblong folio by Edward Arnold in 1898 and Wilde had read it for he describes a criticism of it in the *Evening News* as 'rather silly'. The illustrations were by E. T. Reed and Bosie never liked them. In my copy he wrote in 1936 "I dislike intensely the drawings by E. T. Reed. In fact they completely spoil the book." They certainly distract attention from the verses. This, as we have seen, was followed in 1899 by *The Duke of Berwick*.

There is a little preface to *Tails with a Twist* in which "Belgian Hare" says that these rhymes were suggested to him when a lady at a country house-party quoted to him some verses on the leopard which Wilfrid Scawen Blunt had written for children in India. He promptly wrote *The Lion* which, he says, is the first animal rhyme proper to see the light. Blunt's Leopard made sense, "Belgian Hare" has attempted to write pure and unadulterated nonsense. His rhymes mean nothing and are intended to mean nothing.

It is noteworthy that both 'the lady' (Pamela Tennant) and Wilfrid Blunt were Bosie's cousins and some lines in the book, he says in a Note to the Preface, are due to the collaboration of 'the lady'.

But such was Bosie's fate that he could not even bring out a book of nonsense rhymes without controversy. It was not until after the publication of his *Tails with a Twist* that he first became aware of Hilaire Belloc's *Bad Child's Book of Beasts*, a far more polished if less truly nonsensical production. No one suspected him of plagiarism though he found to his dismay that Belloc's book had been published two years before his own. But it was not enough for Bosie to recognize this as the unfortunate coincidence it certainly was. In a preface to a later collection, *The Pongo Papers*, he carried the war into the other camp. His book of pure nonsense *Tails with a Twist*, he says, achieved great successes, among them the flattering one of being 'very closely imitated' by Mr. Hilaire Belloc in a book called *The Bad Child's Book of Beasts*. He goes on to state calmly that this actually appeared *before* his book but most of his own rhymes had been written at least two years before Mr. Belloc's and were widely known and quoted at Oxford where Mr. Belloc was his contemporary.

I have no grievance against Mr. Belloc—as I have already said, his imitation of my rhymes was flattering, and legitimate—but as I have been constantly accused of plagiarising Mr. Belloc's rhymes, I take this opportunity of stating the exact facts.

It shows Bosie for the dangerous man he was that he actually believed this when he wrote it.

While he was at Lake he wrote the verses for two more collections, *The Placid Pug* (1906) and *The Pongo Papers* (1907), in both of which he printed his own name under his pseudonym. In these the humour is wearing a trifle thin.

Some of these nonsense rhymes were published in a weekly called *The English Review*, in no way connected with the monthly which Austin Harrison edited later. The original *English Review* lasted only four months and was one of the countless unsuccessful periodicals started by T. W. H. Crosland.

Bosie and Crosland differed later about everything—even the manner of their first meeting. Bosie said they were introduced at a music-hall by a man named Hannaford Bennett, Crosland recalls their first introduction being made by Frank Harris (in a fur coat) outside the office of his paper *The Candid Friend* in 1905. He describes Bosie as 'a young-looking, clean-shaven man attired in a black-fitting overcoat and a bowler hat, and on whose face there was a gentle smile'.

Wherever the meeting took place it was a fatal one for Bosie, though for the moment it led to nothing but his contributing to *The English Review* almost weekly. It was here that *The Dead Poet* made its first appearance in print though Bosie had written it four years earlier. Olive also sent poetry to Crosland who after insisting on a contract by which Bosie would receive £5 for each of his poems was of course able to pay nothing at all.

Meanwhile Bosie continued to contribute to *The Academy* for the first six years of the century until in the seventh year it became his own. There is a curious discrepancy to be found in Margery Ross's *Robert Ross: Friend of Friends* in connection with this. A letter is printed from Vincent O'Sullivan to Ross which, while making one of the many claims that its author had helped Wilde with money in his last years, complains very bitterly about the *Academy* and Bosie, and answers what seems to have been a suggestion from Ross that he should bring an action against them.

Since I have written for the *Academy* Douglas has written me friendly notes now and then dealing with the business of the paper, so that the dash of brutal impudence I sent you had the additional piquancy of surprise.

This letter is dated (in Miss Ross's book) 26 February 1905 and a footnote explains that Lord Alfred Douglas had become proprietor and editor of the *Academy*. Now the *Academy* was not bought for Bosie till the summer of 1907. There are two possible explanations. It may have been that Bosie had reviewed unkindly something of O'Sullivan's in 1905 and O'Sullivan confused him with the editor, but the tone of the letter and its mention of Douglas dealing with the business of the paper does not suggest this. Or it may be that the letter was written after Bosie had taken over *Academy* and the date on the letter in Miss Ross's book is an inaccurate one. It is a small point but Miss Ross in printing an attack of this kind on the man her uncle so greatly wronged should at least have avoided an erroneous footnote.

9

Ross himself, in those years, had been working assiduously and with considerable success to revive interest in Wilde's writings. In January

1902 he explained to Adela Schuster some of the difficulties he was encountering with the Official Receiver over Wilde's copyrights though he was now on satisfactory terms with Mrs. Wilde's cousin Adrian Hope. In 1906 he was appointed Wilde's literary executor by the English courts.

It is not known exactly when he realized the potentialities of *De Profundis*, the manuscript of which he still secretly held. It could not of course be published as it was, first because of its libels on Bosie and secondly because it would defeat the object for which Ross was quite conscientiously working, the rehabilitation of Wilde. But there was a mass of material in the body of the letter which, if skillfully pieced together, would make a strange and interesting book, very different in purport from the letter as a whole. In this Wilde would appear if not repentant at least concerned with ideas of repentance and remorse, a man in agony but with hope and faith in himself.

With E. V. Lucas, a clever and amiable essayist and a director of Methuen's, Ross went to work and from the letter which Wilde had entitled *Epistola: in Carcere et Vinculis* produced what he (Ross) called *De Profundis*. All reference to Bosie was entirely obliterated and by saying the signed introduction was written by 'my friend' Ross left the impression that it had been addressed to himself. Holbrooke Jackson, in fact, in *The Eighteen-nineties* wrote "during his imprisonment he [Wilde] wrote 'De Profundis' in the form of a long letter to his friend Robert Ross."

Bosie accepted it as this. Nearly ten years later when Ross was rash enough to bring a libel action against him, he stated on oath what had happened at this time. He read an announcement that a manuscript by Wilde was to be brought out by Ross. He was on quite friendly terms with Ross and was surprised that he had been told nothing about it and tackled Ross on the subject.

Ross explained that it was a long letter which Wilde had written in prison to him, Ross, and contained a lot of abuse of Bosie and other people which Ross was cutting out. "It will make," he said, "a very interesting book on Wilde and his character."

Bosie was furious, particularly when Ross refused to show him the MS. He abused Ross who said: "If you talk to me like that I'll publish the manuscript as it stands and that will finish you off."

There were further exchanges in which Ross reminded Bosie of letters of his—presumably to Ross—which he had, and Bosie said he was no better than a blackmailer.

o

Peace this time was restored, however, and three days later Ross apologized for talking about the letters, and "spoke very nicely".

That this account was substantially true is strongly suggested by two facts. Bosie wrote for Frank Harris's paper *The Candid Friend* a review of *De Profundis* which praised it heartily and showed that he believed it had nothing to do with him, and Bosie and Ross remained friends for another three years, Ross writing for the paper which Bosie came to edit.

De Profundis, published in 1905, had considerable success. Unlike *The Ballad of Reading Gaol* little more than five years earlier it was widely and on the whole kindly reviewed. It ran through several editions and cleared away the last burden of debt. Ross was universally congratulated, as he deserved to be, and it should be noticed in fairness to him that Hamilton Fyfe said

Robbie's main motive in publishing *De P.* was, I am sure, to put O.W. in a more favourable light and to do it as soon as possible. In this he was successful and I doubt whether he really thought whether the whole thing would ever be printed.

But he still kept the unpublished portions and he still kept the compromising letters from Bosie to Wilde which he had found among Wilde's papers after his death.

The publication of *De Profundis* in that form did nothing to change Bosie's attitude either to Ross or to the memory of Wilde. He was still frankly a pagan and regarded his past without a shadow of repentance. He was no longer 'actively homosexual' but felt no coldness towards those who were and he had long since accepted Ross as Wilde's literary executor. He remained on the best of terms, too, with More Adey, Arthur Clifton, Max Beerbohm and Reggie Turner all of whom he met from time to time in London, and though he did not meet Robert Sherard at this time he read his *The Story of an Unhappy Friendship* without dismay when it appeared in 1902.

What he called the other side of his nature had asserted itself and so long as he remained at Lake and had plenty of field sports to occupy him and there were no recurrences of those slights which had disturbed him in London and Washington, he was pleased to leave the arduous work of editing Wilde's writings to Ross. If he did not think that Ross was better equipped to handle it than he was, at least he must have known that Ross would take more pains and give more time to it.

CHAPTER X

The Academy

I

THIS unprecedented period of serenity in Bosie's life was broken by a well-meaning act of Pamela Tennant's. As we have seen, she was, like Bosie and Olive, a contributor to *The Academy* and was aware that the editor had been given a job on *The Times*. *The Academy* if not actually in the market was no particular favourite with the group that owned it and could be bought quite cheaply. She suggested in a bright breakfast-table way that her husband should buy it, appoint Bosie editor and keep the whole thing in the family.

Edward Tennant, an extremely rich man with an eye on a peerage, (which he was given four years later), saw no objection to this whim of his wife's. He had never taken Bosie's politics seriously and in any case the paper was more literary than political. When he found he could buy *The Academy* for £2,000 he did so.

Tennant was a brother of that remarkable woman Margot Asquith and consequently brother-in-law to the Chancellor of the Exchequer, H. H. Asquith. (Asquith became Prime Minister on Campbell-Bannerman's death in the following year.) Tennant was M.P. for Salisbury, his ticket being that anomalous thing 'Liberal Imperialism'. Bosie was a Tory of a romantic, die-hard kind, not so much jingoist as 'patriotic'; what views he had expressed at Wilsford seemed too captious or academic to be taken seriously and Tennant, concerned with grim practical politics, Tariff Reform and the struggle with the House of Lords which was coming to a head in those years, foresaw no danger to himself or his own prospects in giving his wife's young cousin his head.

Bosie was to have a salary of £300 a year and an office for purely editorial purposes, the printing, advertising and circulation were cared for by a wholesale newsagent. It would be, everyone thought, a delightful hobby for the young man, and any sparks that flew would be literary. Olive and Pamela Tennant would remain among his contributors and he would doubtless find others innocuously poetical, so that the standard of the paper, which was a high one, would be maintained. It was a time of sixpenny weeklies which espoused unpopular causes or voiced the prejudices of their editors. Bosie in the editorial chair of one would be picturesque and interesting. Any political views he might express would be, as they had been at Wilsford, a joke.

But Bosie remembered *The Pentagram* and *The Spirit Lamp* and took his new position seriously. His first step, necessary in the circumstances, was to move to London and establish his small family in a charming Queen Anne house, 26 Church Row, Hampstead, where his landlords were the Provost and Fellows of Eton College. He went, regularly at first, to his office in Lincoln's Inn Fields, where he had a secretary and office boy.

This editorial secretary had been with *The Academy* when it was among the Country Life group of periodicals and had a distinguished career after her somewhat hectic *Academy* days. She was Miss Alice Head who became in 1909 editor of *Woman at Home* and in 1924 of *Good Housekeeping*, returning in 1942 to a directorship of Country Life Ltd. which she had left thirty-five years earlier to follow Bosie when he took over *The Academy*. To one of those who have written most disparagingly about Bosie she gave recollections of him which must have baffled him. To her Bosie was always charming and her friendship with him and Olive continued for many years. She remembers—like others—Bosie's 'exceptional beauty' for though he was now thirty-seven years old he had 'blue eyes, perfect teeth, a schoolgirl complexion and a smile of infinite charm'. Bosie gave her 'a taste for good literature' and she was 'everlastingly grateful for his many kindnesses'. To hear this from a woman who has spent her life in the disillusioning atmosphere of journalism and held positions which call for coolness and shrewd judgement is only surprising to those who accept the caricature of Bosie which emerges, largely it must be owned from his own writings.

2

He started bravely and well and almost immediately made a discovery. He was invited to a pub meal by a number of unsuccessful writers who called themselves the New Bohemians. There was Arthur Machen, a militant High Churchman, who had already some reputation, a fine writer who missed the highest achievement by a hair's breadth. Novelist, ghost-story writer, essayist, critic, translator and scholar he worked for a long life-time with brilliance and a scrupulous respect for his trade and died in poverty without more than an echo of the recognition which was his due. There were also Randal Charlton, Louis McQuilland and T. Michael (Tommy) Pope.*

Among the New Bohemians was also a shy, bearded young man who had published nothing to speak of and said very little but was invited to *The Academy* offices a few days later. This was Richard Middleton, a near-genius who as soon as Bosie gave him the encouragement of an editor who liked his work began to pour out lyrics, essays and short stories of a peculiar, highly personal, somewhat fantastic beauty which then and since have found a few devoted readers. Of his most famous short story *The Ghost Ship* Arthur Machen wrote after poor Middleton had killed himself:

I declare I would not exchange this short, crazy, enchanting fantasy for a whole wilderness of seemly novels, proclaiming in decorous accents the undoubted truth that there are milestones on the Portsmouth Road.

Middleton was a misfit, resigned and wistful rather than rebellious. He had left a suburban family and a safe position as an insurance clerk to live in a room in Blackfriars and make a name by writing. Bosie realized at once that he had found someone exceptional and for all the time he kept *The Academy* he continued to use Middleton's work and sent him with a note to Frank Harris who published his longer stories in *Vanity Fair*. He also gave Middleton some reviewing and Middleton wrote to Henry Savage: "Oh, but reviewing is great fun and the man Douglas is a peach with a stone in it to let me do it."

Bosie had other remarkable contributors, some of whom he inherited with the paper, others he found for himself. Bernard Shaw wrote for him so did James Elroy Flecker, then a young schoolmaster whose first book of poems, *The Bridge of Fire* was published in that year. Bosie also published work from Robert Ross and More Adey who were living in Kensington.

Towards the end of 1907 when Bosie had been running the *Academy* for some months Crosland wrote an article in *The Future*, one of his

---

* Tommy Pope was still in Fleet Street when I reached it in the 1920's and a lively, talkative witty old boy he seemed to me. I should like to rescue from oblivion one quatrain of his, written after a fire in Gloucestershire—

> A fire has destroyed the Chameleon at Strood
> Whereat I'm exceedingly glad,
> For the waitresses there were disgustingly rude
> And the food was incredibly bad.

many short-lived broad-sheets. The article which appeared on November 23, 1907, was called 'Distinguished Journalism'. It spoke disparagingly of *The Academy*:

The Academy, under Lord Alfred Douglas's editorship, has exhibited a distinct tendency to deteriorate into a feeble organ of the feebler and lesser cults, and at the present moment it is of no more use to the serious principles it might have served than the proverbial headache.

It went on to mention *The Academy*'s "pseudo Roman Catholic contributors." This reference was a highly pertinent one for Arthur Machen had converted to High Anglicanism not only *The Academy* but its editor.

Bosie was one among many thousands of people in the last hundred and twenty years for whom High Anglicanism has been an intermediate stage of their journey from Protestantism or mere unthinking categorization as 'C of E', to Catholicism, and among them could be named a score of writers. I can only think of two of any achievement who never made the final step, and one of them was Machen. But as Protestantism itself has been considered by many a religion of antithesis as its name suggests, so Machen's faith, at least as expressed in his writing, was more Anti-Protestant than anything else. He wrote, and Bosie published in an article which was quoted in court some years later, these sentiments about the religion of which his father was a minister—"I cursed the Protestant religion with all my heart and soul, and still do. I curse it and hate it and detest it with all its works and all its abominable operations, internal and external. I loathe it and abhor it as a most hideous blasphemy, the gravest woe, the most monstrous horror which has fallen upon the hopeless race of mortals since the foundation of the world."

Bosie, consciously or not, was looking for unpopular causes to defend in *The Academy* and there was much to appeal to him in this one. Kensit was still raging and by disgraceful tactics working to deprive High Church incumbents of their livings and the mass of church-going English people looked upon High Anglicanism as a danger more subtle and more treacherous than Popery itself. Anything detested by the 'mass of church-going English people' recommended itself to the man who believed that he and his great friend had suffered from their hypocrisy. He became, almost overnight it would seem, a convinced and rancorous High Churchman and gave Machen the freedom of his columns 'at full rates on the highest scale for contributors'. He serialized Machen's *Views and Opinions of the Revd Dr. Stiggins* and himself wrote from a similar standpoint.

His politics, after he became editor, began to grow more coherent and less the harmlessly over-stated prejudices he had used to voice at Wilsford. Asquith he held in contempt and Lloyd George's very name was repugnant to him. He began to regard his little office in Lincoln's Inn Fields as a bomb shop and, not without gaiety or a sense of humour but in the most violent phraseology, he attacked Liberalism, Lords Reform, anything that he opposed, with a fluency that increased with each number. What was a weekly paper for, he seemed to ask, if it was not a medium of attack?

'Some member of his family', he recalled (and one guesses it may have been the amiable Algie Bourke) pointed out to Bosie that it was 'rather rough on Eddie Tennant' that Bosie was using the periodical Tennant had bought for him as a means of attacking Tennant's party and brother-in-law. Bosie saw the point of this and wrote to Tennant offering to make *The Academy* entirely literary if he objected to its politics. Tennant, a tolerant man, replied that he did not mind in the least; the paper was very lively and he found a great deal in it to agree with.

But Tennant's wife, who had first proposed the arrangement was less amenable. With what is sometimes called feminine logic she complained at the outcome of her well-meant plan and between her and Bosie there was 'constant friction and trouble.'

This must have been exacerbated when a few months after Crosland's unkind article on 'Distinguished Journalism' its author joined Bosie's staff first as an occasional contributor and then as a sub-editor.

3

Thomas William Hodgson Crosland whose part in Bosie's troubled life was almost as large as Wilde's and no less unfortunate, was then (1908) forty-three years old, a diabetic, a dyspeptic and an alcoholic. He was a product of the vigorous philistine Non-Conformity of provincial England in the last century, his father being a preacher in that very sect with which General Booth quarrelled on a point of doctrine before starting his Salvation Army.

Brought up in the grim suburbs of Leeds he wrote verse which was published in the local papers and in his early twenties while editor of *The Hunslet and Holbeck News* began the practice of scurrilous vituperation which he called bluntness, and which he continued till his death. With this as his chief talent he went to London at the age of twenty-five to 'become a writer'. He nearly starved before he engaged himself to a Brighton firm which sent him about the country to write descriptive articles on wealthy men and their families and homes which were reproduced with photographs in a fake society periodical. They paid Crosland at the rate of half-a-crown a thousand words and the barest and most closely calculated expenses. He continued this for five years, writing, his biographer says, three and a half million words for less than £450. On this wage he married and while he was still living on it a son was born.

Courageously he moved to London and fought his way to a living from writing parodies, verses, odd articles and book reviews. Fleet Street at the beginning of the century was the home of countless little journals, political and literary weeklies, papers devoted to strange causes or tiny sections of the community, kept alive by pride or hate or fanaticism. A periodical could exist on a circulation of two thousand and grow fat on three, and the 'sixpenny weeklies', of which there were dozens, opinionative, clever, idealistic, seemed firmly established. Small publishers issuing small books abounded, though most of them vanished after a season or two, and pamphlets and tracts poured from the presses.

There was a population of 'literary men' distinguished from the journalists of the day by their shiftlessness and sometimes by their egotism or their optimism. All news was presented anonymously and 'writers' were only required for other sections of the paper so that from pub to pub and among the editorial offices moved a talkative, boastful, individualistic mob of professional hacks, some of them talented and all of them penurious.

Into this came Crosland with his aggressiveness, his cross-grained disputatious 'bluntness', his poverty and unkempt appearance and his determination to get his own back on something or someone, a wronged and bitter man with a passionate love of words and a wide unacademic knowledge of letters. He looked, it was said, like an inspired bus-conductor, he talked with bearish assertiveness and after those three-and-a-half million obsequious words about wealthy tradesmen he was prepared to write anything for anyone who would pay him a guinea or so to believe in what he wrote.

He got a job as sub-editor of *The Outlook* which was then a weekly of considerable prestige. Henley, Arthur Symons, Francis Thompson, Lionel Johnson, Conrad and William Archer were contributors and

Crosland wrote weekly prose odes and book reviews. But though this kept him and his wife and (now three) children, it did not give him scope for the bludgeoning invective which was his natural medium and he determined to write a book in which he need pull no punches. He chose the Scots as his enemies—why is not known. It has been said that he was snubbed by some Scotsmen during his early days in Fleet Street, and he himself said it was to 'get even' with one or two Scottish journalists whom he particularly disliked. It is far more likely that he chose almost at random. He wrote, in a week or two, a book called *The Unspeakable Scot* which had an instantaneous success, running through several editions in the next year. It is almost unreadable now though it is possible to see why it was thought witty at the time. There is a ham-fisted humour in it and a brutish satire which appealed to the Edwardians. The Scot

is the one species of human animal that is taken by all the world to be fifty per cent. cleverer and pluckier and honester than the facts warrant. He is the daw with a peacock's tail of his own painting. He is the ass who has been at pains to cultivate the convincing roar of a lion. He is the fine gentleman whose father toils with a muck-fork. And, to have done with parable, he is the bandy-legged lout from Tullietudlescleuch, who after twelve months at "the college" on moneys wrung from the diet of his family, drops his threadbare kilt and comes south in a slop suit to instruct the English in the arts of civilisation and in the English language.

This book was published by Grant Richards for whom Crosland was reading at the time and for whom he made an anthology of songs and ballads, edited a children's annual and wrote a children's book called *The Coronation Dumpy Book*. At the same time he started the first of his short-lived periodicals *The Tiger* "Andrew Carnegie ... the bloated disseminator of public libraries"—that sort of thing. Then, seeing the success of *The Unspeakable Scot* he anonymously wrote *The Unspeakable Crosland* as a Scot's reply, a *tour-de-force* which kept interest going in the first book. To cap both he wrote *The Egregious English* by "Angus McNeill".

But he never repeated the success of *The Unspeakable Scot* though for years he tried to apply the same technique to other subjects. He wrote *Lovely Women*, *The Abounding American*, *The Beautiful Teetotaller*, *The Suburbans*, *The Wild Irishman* and, towards the end of his life, *The Fine Old Hebrew Gentleman* as well as projecting though never finishing *Taffy was a Welshman*. None of them was more than a feeble repeat performance and in spite of his phenomenal output he was pursued by poverty as well as ill-health to his death. Grant Richards went bankrupt and Crosland was told by the Judge to whom he applied that he was in the position of an unsecured creditor so he lost even his later benefit from *The Unspeakable Scot*. *The Tiger* ceased publication and was followed at different times during Crosland's life by *The English Review* (a weekly, which lasted six months) *The New Review* (three months), *The Future* (three issues), *Public Interest* (one issue), *The Antidote* (four issues) *The Last Word* (one issue) *The Flying Horse* (four issues).

When Bosie met him, Crosland had already dabbled in litigation, losing an action for libel against a newspaper whose review of one of his books he considered defamatory. Costs had been given against him but, since he never paid them, he was not deterred by that. He would have letters from his solicitors sent on the slightest provocation and the only reason why he had not been sued for libel himself was that he had no money and a libel in one of his periodicals was usually not worth noticing. This would change when he wrote for *The Academy* which was a weekly of high standing and considerable popularity.

He was a tall but pot-bellied man, with a high forehead, heavy jaws and a hostile, scowling face. He had left behind both the beard with which he first faced Fleet Street and the shaggy moustache which followed it. He wore clothes which made the worst of him, shabby ill-fitting morning coats and battered toppers. He affected a gruff and assertive manner of speech, but he was kind-hearted and brave. He was wholly inconsistent in his prejudices and loyalties but could talk or write himself into a passionate if passing sincerity. He was disgruntled and argumentative, always in debt, often in liquor and usually in bad health. He had a weak heart which would get him admission at any time to hospital and in periods of stress he would retire to Charing Cross or Gray's Inn Road Hospital or occasionally to the Royal Free Hospital in which he would write enough to get himself out of pawn. But he was not a swashbuckler or a conscious hypocrite and in achieving the enormous volume of his written work he had forged an energetic style entirely without grace or elegance or good taste, but with a hammer-stroke quality which made him formidable. Like most of his shiftless kind who considered themselves grossly underpaid he was throughout his life proud but unscrupulous in money matters.

No more incongruous friend, and no more disastrous influence could have been found for the mercurial Bosie. Miss Alice Head states that Crosland influenced Bosie most unwisely and led him into all sorts of difficulty. That can only be called an under-statement.

4

Bosie and Crosland quarrelled, briefly while they had *The Academy*, irrevocably thereafter. Yet when Bosie came to look back on their turbulent friendship five years after Crosland's death it was with warmth and gratitude. Crosland carried his thriftless eagerness for money almost to the point of blackmail in after years and Bosie suffered from this, yet all he can find to say about it in his *Autobiography* is that Crosland's idea of finance was based on the assumption that Bosie's family would provide him with what Crosland called "stacks of boodle", and that his vision of the future for the *Academy* was golden and rosy. In a time of depression in the editorial office he said "In about another couple of years this paper will be making at least £10,000 a year. You will hear people in the street whispering: 'Who is that fair youth?' And the reply will be: 'That is the wealthy Lord Alfred Douglas, who owns *The Academy*.' Then they will ask: 'And who is that dazzling object by his side?' 'That's Crosland', will be the reply." Bosie says the idea of Crosland as a 'dazzling object' was irresistibly funny because he was a strange and uncouth-looking person who always conveyed the impression that he had slept in his clothes.

It is as friends rather than fellow-editors or fellow-litigants that it is most pleasant to recall the two. Bosie took Crosland about with him at night and Augustus John recalls seeing Bosie 'with his ponderous friend Crosland' in the Café Royal. For such evenings he would have to force Crosland into evening dress and do his tie and hair for him. He was 'a delightful companion when he was in good form', says Bosie, and throughout their association of seven or eight years he always took delight in the gloomy humour and cantankerous verbosity of the Yorkshireman.

Bosie had the greatest trust in Crosland as a writer and he never lost it. Crosland taught him, Bosie says, almost all he knew about journalism and editing a paper, and was nearly always right in the long run about people and things. He lifted Bosie out of the cheap cynicism, log-rolling and determination to be smart of the literary amateur. Crosland's articles were 'models of the literary journalist's art'. This is high praise from Bosie who, at the time he wrote it, felt little enthusiasm about most of his past associates. It is also bad judgement.

Crosland as a 'literary journalist' was a pamphleteer who lunged blindly at any adversary in sight, a hollow tautologist and a self-convinced time-server. If, as Bosie says, the success of *The Academy* was due more to Crosland than to him it was a *succes de scandale* for Crosland used the paper for his private battles and small personal controversies.

Bosie was delighted to leave the spadework of the paper to Crosland while he went racing. Crosland with an adequate regular salary for the first time in his life was ready to do it. (He was a perfect cormorant for money, Bosie said. He was supposed to be paid £7 a week but always managed to obtain £10 and sometimes more. His lunch every day was on Bosie.) Crosland had to do some pretty violent mental gymnastics over religion, for though not a religious man he had always pronounced himself, as part of his 'bluntness', a Methodist. "I was born a Methodist and shall die a Methodist" was a defiant catch-phrase of his. The religious bias of *The Academy*, established by Arthur Machen before the arrival of Crosland, being High Anglicanism, Crosland had somehow to become adapted to this. But his long training in convincing himself by writing of the moral correctness of what was expedient helped him here. He was soon thundering with the rest of them.

From Crosland's first employment on *The Academy* it lost the last of its character as a staid and serious literary journal with sedate comments on politics, a character it had kept for forty years. It became noisily partisan and started to 'go for' people and causes as Crosland had one 'gone for' the Scots. Bosie reflected later that some of the people they 'went for' he would 'go for' any time but others were comparatively harmless and might well have been left alone. Crosland saw himself and Bosie as a couple of lonely fighters, standing shoulder-to-shoulder against the onslaughts of all other editors, most politicians, countless writers, everyone who had ever annoyed either of them, any firm which failed to advertise, most authors of books for review, nearly all dramatists, the 'Carmelite Wolf', Bernard Shaw, Clement Shorter, Suffragettes, 'Pulpit Politicians', and a score of other enemies.

Bosie did nothing to check Crosland's iconoclastic zeal, indeed he delighted in it. Staying up at Weston Old Hall with Custance he wrote to Crosland that his articles were 'corkers'.

There is a close and interesting parallel between the two most significant friendships in Bosie's life and the characters of the two older men who most influenced him. Just as to Wilde homosexuality was a dark, infinitely alluring, mysteriously compulsive thing and himself an inspired adventurer among its mysteries while to Bosie it was a simple desire simply satisfied, so now to Crosland controversy and vilification were his life's breath, his way of getting his own back on fate which had made him a penurious, sick, unrecognized genius while to Bosie they were an entertainment, almost a field sport. Wilde had once blamed him for laughing on various occasions at warnings they had received; he was perhaps more to blame now for laughing at Crosland's psychopathically conceived enmities and the portentous expression he gave to them. Crosland's view of the two of them may be seen in a sonnet he wrote after they had appeared as defendants in a libel action against them which was dismissed:

> *We spoke the truth and bared their shame, and so*
> *They bring the gag, the thumbscrews, and the knout,*
> *And hired mouths to spit their venom out,*
> *And marshal all their bullies in a row;*
> *Whereat—mark well their sick chagrin—we go*
> *To give them thump for thump and shout for shout,*
> *And shake the bowel of their leading lout*
> *Who would have killed our honours for a show.*
>
> *Chiefly to you this victory, by God's grace,*
> *Most "disagreeable Witness" with the thrust*
> *That withers liars in their obscene place—*
> *The honour in which kings have put their trust,*
> *The name that was a name at Chevy Chase,*
> *Shine on, serene above the smirch and dust.*

Bosie, flattered by the rôle given him by the more experienced Crosland, by the support of cranks and disgruntled people who wrote to congratulate him on the truth of what he published, and by the opinions of men like Sorley Brown* who thought that *The Academy*'s standard of fearless and independent criticism was maintained in a manner which has not been surpassed, if equalled, in the history of English literary papers, began to feel that he really was fighting for the purity of English letters and the highest ideals of morality. What had been light-hearted word-play began to take hold of a nature more simple and sincere than Crosland's, a dangerous and fateful development.

* The editor of *The Border Standard* and a loyal supporter of Bosie all his life.

5

The Academy was by no means negligible, in fact its circulation under Bosie and Crosland greatly increased. If it lost prestige it gained the kind of unpopularity that made it read and sometimes feared. To the contributors he had already secured Bosie added Andrew Lang with whom Crosland had crossed swords in his *Tiger* days, Cardinal Gasquet, Siegfried Sassoon, Rupert Brooke, "Baron Corvo", Colonel Repington, who was to raise hell in Whitehall some years later, Douglas Goldring, Professor Skeat and a good many others, most of whom had very little sympathy with its highly personal editorial policy.

Crosland brought the paper into conflict with *Punch* which parodied *The Academy*'s pontifical *Life and Letters* series of notes. You can tell a man by the company he keeps, Crosland replied, and a paper by its advertisements. That being so, the readers of *Punch* must be a queer crowd.

Apparently they are suffering from bad legs, indigestion, nits, fleas, bugs, and other troubles. They must be bald or nearly bald to a man, and those who are not bald must have superfluous hair or skin disease. Further, they must be panting for alcohol in the form of beer, whisky, brandy, gin, and other beverages.

Then *The Spectator* was unlucky enough to print an article which had recently appeared in *The Academy*. This was accidental and came about through the writer having submitted his work to several editors at the same time. Bosie wrote to J. St. Loe Strachey, the editor, for an explanation and was given none, whereupon legal proceedings were threatened. Strachey countered by sending a cheque for £5 for the use of the article but to Crosland's annoyance, expressed in several issues, gave neither explanation nor apology. The £5 was disdainfully sent to the Royal Literary Fund.

Crosland then fought *The English Review* over its title. The words *The English Review* were printed under *The Academy* because Crosland had once had a weekly of that name, and Hueffer's monthly was indiscreet enough to call this a breach of copyright.

But there were more personal quarrels than these. Soon after Crosland joined the paper Bosie wrote a 'strongly-worded attack' on Asquith whom he blamed for the suppression, at the last minute, of a religious procession which was planned to celebrate the Catholic Eucharistic Congress. For Bosie's 'strongly worded' it is safe to read 'personal' and Tennant was at last incensed into writing to Bosie. His article, Tennant said, was in 'the worst possible taste' and he, Tennant, had decided to sell *The Academy* and cut his connection with it. This was not a surprising reaction from a man who was expecting Asquith to give him a peerage, but it made Bosie highly indignant.

Crosland, however, saw an occasion for 'bluntness'. He persuaded Bosie that this was not to be taken lying down. Bosie was not dependent on 'the whim of a *nouveau riche* millionaire' but was the editor of a powerful paper installed in a position from which he could not easily be removed. Let *him*, Crosland, handle this and they would soon see that Tennant could not treat Bosie in this way. Bosie agreed and Crosland, adopting a 'bullying and aggressive tone' got his own way with Tennant who did not want trouble of any kind. Bosie was given the paper as a gift together with £500 to keep it afloat, but this jeopardized his friendship with Tennant and his cousin Pamela.

Crosland wrote an article on 'The Monopoly and the Muzzle' in which he attacked the wholesale newsagents in such a way that Messrs. W. H. Smith and Sons 'as a matter of public duty' withdrew *The Academy* from their bookstalls. His naïve faith in the 'stacks of boodle' behind Bosie seems to have blinded him to the impolitic nature of his attack.

6

Then Crosland helped to involve Bosie in another quarrel, with Robert Ross, which, though it seemed trivial at the time, had far graver consequences than any of these. It would probably have come sooner or later for Bosie since his marriage and above all since Machen's influence had brought him to High Anglicanism had conceived a distaste (which later, and for a number of years, became a loathing) for his own homosexual past and those associated with it. In his last years he regretted this as much as the thing itself and realized that he was guilty of uncharitableness in criticizing others for what he had ceased to practice; that is, he continued to condemn homosexuality as a sin of the flesh, but blamed himself for having being 'righteous' about it.

The beginning of that righteousness in 1909 did not change his affection for the memory of Wilde or his appreciation of his work—that came later when he learned of the existence of the 'unpublished portions' of *De Profundis*. It did not yet make him detest Ross—that too would come when he learned how Ross had kept *De Profundis* and Bosie's letters to Wilde and how he eventually used them. At the moment it was no more than a rather priggish disapproval of Ross and other queers who continued to associate with youths of the kind who had betrayed Wilde.

There was no immediate quarrel which is a pity for if it had come early it might have led to reconciliation and saved both of them from the tragic and very horrible events ahead. What happened was that Crosland heavily blue-pencilled an article sent in by Ross who—together with More Adey and Reggie Turner—was a fairly frequent contributor to *The Academy*. Crosland with his loathing for everything he thought savoured of 'decadence' and his blank incomprehension of homosexuality, disapproved of Ross as a contributor. He had heard, he told Bosie, that Ross was 'an unsavoury person' and 'not the kind of man who ought to be writing for us'. Pamela Tennant shared this view and told Bosie so. Bosie's reply was that if Ross sent in anything of which Crosland honestly disapproved he could cut it out, but he had known Ross for nearly twenty years and they had gone through much together and he did not want him banned from the paper. Crosland interpreted this as he wished and made several changes in one of Ross's articles. Ross complained to Bosie who told him why Crosland disapproved of him. This, of course, led to a scene which Crosland describes in somewhat melodramatic terms. Ross, a Catholic, was scornful of Bosie's High Church conversion and may have said so and Bosie probably expressed some kind of disapproval of Ross's morals. It was all rather petty and stinging but it ended without door-slamming or unforgivable insults.

Bosie was then under fire from three quarters. Crosland, who had joined Bosie in his praise of Wilde as a writer but had sheered away from any discussion of Bosie's personal relations with Wilde, wanted him to make the gesture of a complete rupture with Ross. Bosie's own increasing acceptance of Christian morality demanded, or seemed to Bosie to demand, the same thing, and Olive, who had always detested and distrusted Ross, added her influence. Bosie decided simply to avoid the issue. He gave instructions at his house that he and Olive were 'not at home' when Ross called and hoped it would be left at that. "I did not want any open quarrel with Ross", he said, "but I wanted to drop him."

This was not so easy as he thought. Ross as Wilde's literary executor was "getting on". He was no longer the rather insignificant little man of Wilde's lifetime but with the return to popularity of Wilde's works, to which he wrote prefaces, he had become a quite considerable figure. He valued *The Academy*'s championship of Wilde as a writer

Robert Ross, by Sir William Rothenstein, 1900.

Frank Harris, by Sir William Rothenstein, 1896.

Frank Harris in the custody of the Tipstaff on his way to Brixton Prison, 1914.

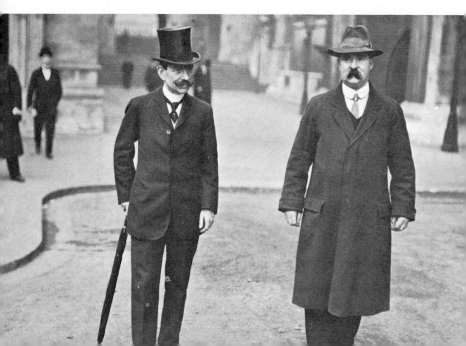

and he valued his association with Bosie and Olive who during Bosie's editorship of *The Academy* were notable figures in the world he had entered. He called a number of times in Church Row without success then very foolishly wrote to Olive demanding an explanation. Olive handed the letter to Bosie who detected in it "an undercurrent of insolence and menace."

Bosie, of course, wrote one of his letters, and because he was Bosie used furious and unforgivable terms. As Ross insisted on his telling him why he did not wish to keep up any acquaintance with him he would tell him. "I no longer care to associate with persons like yourself who are engaged in the active performance and propaganda of every kind of wickedness, from Socialism to Sodomy."

Ross made no reply but Bosie heard, perhaps not without satisfaction, that "his rage was extreme." This seems probable. Hell knows no fury like a woman scorned except, perhaps, a queen who has been 'sent up'. Like many of his kind Ross had a ready wit but not a great sense of humour. He could not see that this piece of inept alliteration from the man who had telegraphed to an enraged father "What a funny little man you are !" was meant to be 'smart' and should have been ignored or laughed over. "Bosie again," Ross might have sighed as he showed the letter to Reggie Turner, More Adey and the rest of them. Instead of that it was a furious—"And from Bosie, of all people !", and a flush of resentment which showed that Ross was deeply hurt and viciously angry, not perhaps so much at the terms of Bosie's letter but at being barred the house. It is noteworthy that it was at this time (1909) that Ross persuaded the librarians of the British Museum to take charge of the whole manuscript of *De Profundis* which was to be kept sealed until 1960.

Bosie having dispatched his letter thought no more about it. He was blithely unaware of the other's secret weapons.

7

He and Crosland had other fish to fry, small and large. Their first essays at libel actions were made late in 1909 when apparently by a coincidence, the undergraduate weeklies of both Oxford and Cambridge printed articles which referred to Bosie's association with Wilde in terms which, legally at least, were defamatory. Crosland who claimed to know all about libel, writted them both and secured apologies and fifty guineas from each "in consideration of discontinuance of legal proceedings." In one case, (we are unfortunately not told which,) Crosland journeyed to the university to tackle "the Dons" who he maintained, tried to make the damages pounds instead of guineas by a promise to dismiss the editor.

Then a far more serious situation arose and Crosland found himself making his first appearance in the dock of the Old Bailey, charged with having written and published a 'false scandalous and defamatory libel' about the Honourable Frederick Manners-Sutton.

This was one of the most unfortunate of Bosie's cases and for a curious reason—it was won by Crosland largely on Bosie's evidence and this gave Bosie such an inflated notion of himself as a witness that he became litigiously-minded. It was his first appearance in the witness-box which he had wanted to enter fifteen years earlier and he was cross-examined by Marshall Hall, an advocate with a reputation far above his merits. Bosie was loquacious but successful and he left the Court to hear that a novelist of the time (F. C. Philips) had said, "Douglas simply ate him, he *ate* him; there's no other word for it." This went to his head and Crosland's victory was directly responsible for the greatest mistake in Bosie's life, his action for libel against Arthur Ransome three years later.

The Manners-Sutton case against Crosland made a considerable stir at the time. Manners-Sutton was heir to Lord Canterbury, a friend of Olive's who had become an intimate friend of Bosie's. The action was brought because what Bosie called Manners-Sutton's "feline sarcasm and banter" had maddened Crosland into writing him a violently offensive letter, and Manners-Sutton was "ill-advised" enough to go with his solicitor and apply for a summons.

A great deal of very dirty linen was washed for the entertainment of a packed Court. Crosland pleaded justification and each side, Marshall Hall for Manners-Sutton and a brilliant junior named Valetta for Crosland, depended on blackening the other. Crosland was cross-examined on his bankruptcy, on his attempt to get Manners-Sutton to invest in *The Academy*, on the letters he had written to Manners-Sutton's solicitors including the statement that Manners-Sutton was "a person whom it would be difficult for reasonable people to libel". "Your solicitor tells me that you are a difficult man to handle," said Marshall Hall. "I am, and *you* can't handle me," shouted Crosland.

Manners-Sutton was reminded of a visit to a brothel in Buckingham Gate five years earlier, of a girl called Maggie Dupont whom he was alleged to be concealing, of two publishing firms in which he had invested, one issuing 'spicy' or 'naughty' books the other religious literature, of a great deal in his past and present which was supposed to be discreditable.

But when Bosie was in the box and Marshall Hall asked him if there had ever been anything to be ashamed of in his relationship with Wilde, it was felt that this question, put to a witness and not a principal in the case, was carrying the business of backbiting too far and sympathy went to Bosie and Crosland. Bosie answered "No" which was the right answer by any standard, but it would not have mattered if he had said "yes" for the case was won. Crosland was acquitted and returned to *The Academy* office to write of Marshall Hall:

He may learn from this unfortunate affair that the Buzfuz method, while no doubt excellent when you are dealing with unintelligent policemen or frightened widows, is apt to get you into serious trouble when persons of average pluck and intelligence happen to come along. Both for the present writer and for Lord Alfred Douglas Mr. Marshall Hall prepared what Bunyan called "the grievous crabtree cudgel". To this own great surprise and consternation he got cudgels in return. The spectacle of the most relentless cross-examiner at the bar appealing to the Common Serjeant for protection against a couple of simple literary persons such as ourselves and Lord Alfred Douglas is one which is long likely to be remembered in the humorous annals of the Old Bailey.

Bosie felt in after years that Crosland's letting him in for this quarrel with Manners-Sutton, which caused him "an enormous amount of unpleasantness, grief, and regret" was the worst turn his bellicose sub-editor did him. There was a reconciliation some seven years later after Manners-Sutton, by then Lord Canterbury, had admitted that the responsibility was not Bosie's and that his attempt to send Crosland to prison for criminal libel made Bosie's support for Crosland a matter of honour. For the last two years of Canterbury's life they were friends and Bosie was staying with him just before he died.

8

Encouraged, perhaps, by this Crosland and Bosie decided, six months later, to bring an action for libel against a Nonconformist writer named R. F. Horton and the *Daily News*. Horton had written a letter to this paper saying that *The Academy* had passed into 'Roman hands' and was to be read, though the public did not know it, with *The Tablet*, *The Month* and *The Universe*.

The action was a piece of sheer litigiousness for apart from the fact that to be called Roman Catholic, even in 1910, was scarcely to be

libelled, the defendants had published an apology. Moreover they
secured Sir Edward Carson and this, considering what Bosie had seen
of him in 1895, should have given the plaintiff second thoughts. But no.
He had 'eaten' Marshall Hall and had the scent of battle in his nostrils.

He did not do badly in the witness-box. Asked if he was 'strongly
against the Reformation' he denied this but was 'against the way the
Reformation has been distorted'. Asked if he objected to calling himself
a Protestant he said he did not *protest* against anything. Surely he could
be a loyal member of the Church of England without hating and
detesting the Church of Rome?

There was some much-needed laughter in Court when Crosland,
asked what was his religion, assumed his most ferocious stance and
stressing his Yorkshire intonation said—"Ah'm a Methodist."

The jury could not agree, tried again and then brought in a verdict
for the defendants, adding a rider that Horton should have verified
his facts.

Counting the Oxford and Cambridge victories the score was now
3-1 to Bosie, but because this action was brought by the *Academy*
Company on a libel against the paper not against himself Bosie never
counted it among his failures and maintained that among all the
actions for libel brought by him or against him he only lost two, his
own against Arthur Ransome and Winston Churchill's action against
him. Nothing could have been more reckless than this gleeful kind of
reckoning, this suggestion that the Old Bailey was the Oval and the
Law a sport. But it took many more appearances, including his final
most disastrous one in 1923, to convince Bosie of this, and Crosland
never learned.

9

After *The Academy* had been for two years in his ownership and three
under his editorship, Bosie decided to sell it. To keep it going he had
raised money on a reversionary interest in his mother's property and
although he had doubled the price and trebled the circulation it was
still running at a loss. This was not altogether surprising for neither
Bosie nor Crosland had any business sense and both believed they were
far-sighted and shrewd. Bosie, moreover, spent much of his time at
race-meetings or staying in country houses leaving the paper to Crosland who worked with a brandy bottle at his elbow.

Through another of his cousins, George Wyndham, Pamela Tennant's brother, he sold the paper to Lord Fitzwilliam and Lord Howard

de Walden for £2,000 but calculated that on balance *The Academy* cost him £2,000 of his own money. However he gave Crosland £250 out of the purchase price.

When the paper changed hands in July 1910 it appeared with "Edited by Cecil Cowper Esqre., J.P. Barrister-at-Law". This was the gentleman of whom Bosie wrote later that he was utterly without experience in journalism or letters. Bosie "believed he was by profession a land agent". He wrote to Crosland—

The Academy of last week is too appalling for words. The 'Esqre., J.P. Barrister-at-Law' business has produced howls of laughter in the town. It is all very sickening, and I think we have good cause of complaint against H. de W. and Fitzwilliam. When we sold them the paper we hardly supposed that it was going to be made the laughing-stock of London. We really would have done better to have sold it to Harmsworth or Alfred Mond at once! Fitzwilliam, of course, knows no better, and he is a decent chap. Nevertheless, I have told him fairly straightly what I think of it all.

Cowper's assistant editor, Bosie told Sorley Brown, was Ashmead Bartlett, "a conceited self-advertising ass."

The Academy declined and a few years later was offered to Bosie for £25. When he refused the offer it expired after a life of more than half a century.

CHAPTER XI

The Night of the Long Knives

I

BOSIE was now forty years old, still youthful in appearance and flagrantly youthful in character. His parenthetic remark in his *Autobiography*, "When you go to heaven you can be what you like and I intend to be a child", was the key to much in his character. He resisted maturity until his late middle age and still expected from the world the indulgence—he called it justice—which he had been given in childhood. Even when he came to write about the events of his life and enemies and disasters it was with the confidence of a child in his readers' sympathy.

The Academy had made him many enemies, but it had given him status in his own right. At this time, before the Ransome case, his association with Wilde was far less often remembered than his recent editorship. He was slowly emerging from the shadow of an immense scandal and though it could never have been wholly left behind it would have grown lighter with the years if he had not himself brought it back.

Some ten months after selling *The Academy* Bosie became a Catholic. It was an unusual conversion as he describes it briefly in his *Autobiography*, and doubly so for him. He maintains that it came to him entirely through the intellect. In the *Academy* office he received for review a translation into English of Pope Pius X's *Encyclical Against Modernism* and this "stately and magnificent piece of argument" had the effect of convincing him that the Catholic Church in communion with the See of St. Peter is the only true Church. History showed him that the High Anglican position "however attractive it may be does not hold water".

The theory that the Church of England is a 'branch of the Catholic Church', and that the continuity was never broken at the Reformation, seems to me to be demonstrably false. I held it for a long time, and abandoned it, reluctantly, only because the evidence was too strong for me.

But what he rather quaintly calls "the emotional side of Catholicism" did not reach him until some time after he had been a Catholic and what he refers to as the years of persecution had begun. At the time of his conversion, he would have us believe, he felt no emotion about it. On the contrary he thought that to become a Catholic was a tiresome necessity which he would have avoided if he could.

I find it hard to accept this tidy account of what must have been a most complicated tangle of thoughts, emotions, and actions. Bosie was not the man for coldly intellectual conversion—or coldly intellectual anything. But doubtless he made himself believe that he had come unwillingly by a straight road of hard logic to the Church and only in adversity later found the comfort of his religion. Most attempts, even by more articulate writers than Bosie, to explain "Why I Became a Catholic" are failures, just as attempts to explain miracles are failures.

What can be said about Bosie's conversion was that in the following years it saved his sanity if not his life. The grossest sceptic will accept that or the meanest psychologist. The Church gave him no encouragement to think of himself as a persecuted martyr but seeing his obsessed belief that he was hated of all men and imprisoned for bearing witness to the truth, his religion gave him the only consolation there was.

2

Bosie's view of his 'persecution' was Dantesque, and self-inflicted or not his sufferings were infernal. The fact that he threw himself into the flames by indiscretion, pride and obstinacy is irrelevant to an understanding of his agonies. The fact that he saw himself as a modern Job is irrelevant, too. He sincerely believed that he was the victim of deep laid plots, of satanically wicked men, of supernatural forces of evil.

The authors of this persecution in his mind were two, and though they were linked only by having the same solicitor and probably never spoke to one another, Bosie saw them and the solicitor as the three prongs of a diabolic trident with which he was being driven towards the pit.

There is nothing in fact to support this melodramatic view. There is no reason to think that Ross was anything worse than a vindictive little queen who had long-fingered habits with other people's letters. Custance was certainly unscrupulous but only in the way of a man who believes himself right and above scruples. He behaved in some respects like a blackguard but nothing would have convinced him of that. On the contrary, he was a high-minded Christian gentleman in his own view and in the view of most who knew him. He could afford to be a cad because he believed it impossible for him. As for the third, the solicitor, Sir George Lewis, the son of Sir George Lewis of Wilde's time, it is difficult to avoid the impression that he was impelled by some particular malice. He acted not only for Custance and Ross but for Ransome, and for *The Evening News* when Bosie sued that paper, producing compromising letters and details kept from the first two cases to serve his clients in the later ones. It may have been that defendants or plaintiffs in cases against Bosie went to Lewis because they knew he had valuable material, but one feels that to crush Bosie had become something of a personal ambition with Sir George. It is certainly more than coincidence that he prepared instructions for almost all Bosie's opponents over a period of more than twenty years.

But none of these three could with justice or sanity be called villains, still less the monsters of evil and malevolence which they became in Bosie's eyes. Nor can Bosie himself, with Crosland at his elbow, be seen as the parfit gentil knight he truly believed himself. He certainly had cleaner hands than his opponents but his hands were not immaculate. He did nothing dishonourable, as both Ross and Custance did, but for some years he was fanatical, vengeful and self-righteous to a degree that almost amounted to dishonour—though he could never see it.

3

Frederic Custance, like many outwardly bluff and conventional men, had an obsession. Neither he nor his cousin Admiral Sir Reginald Custance had a son. He had wanted one beyond everything else and had, in the manner of a lonely man, peopled his remote and beautiful home with the ghosts of sons he would never teach to ride and fish and shoot and be like himself. Olive was a disappointment because she was a girl. After her marriage Custance had tried in a baffled way to find in Bosie some outlet for his baulked paternalism. When Custance lost his wife he remained entirely alone.

The birth of a son to Bosie and Olive was a great event for him, since at last he had an heir. From the first he was pathetically possessive with the child and his stiff soldierly letters begging the young couple to bring the little boy Raymond to Weston were very moving. When Raymond was old enough to go to school Custance offered to pay his school fees and asked more and more insistently that the boy should be allowed to spend some part of his holidays with him. All this was at first accepted quite gladly by Bosie and Olive and Raymond grew up very largely in his grandfather's house.

Custance, in the impatient don't-want-to-know manner of the time, disliked and distrusted Catholicism and "those priests". His only sister had been converted when she married a Catholic and Custance had never spoken to her or her husband again. When Bosie became a Catholic and made Raymond one it caused one of the disputes which had become frequent between Custance and his son-in-law with Olive bewildered and torn between them. Eventually Custance agreed not to interfere with the boy's religion, but some time later threatened to cut Raymond out of his will if he did not renounce Catholicism, on which Bosie, of course, wrote one of his letters.

After that Custance determined to get full possession of the boy. Doubtless he persuaded himself that he was justified and brooded on all the things that made Bosie in his mind an unsuitable father, from his friendship with Wilde to his Popishness, from his splenetic editing to his penchant for litigation. But while the boy's mother remained with Bosie he was powerless to intervene.

If at this distance and with nothing but a few yellowing letters and Bosie's prejudices to guide me I am right about Custance, he did not deliberately plan to break up Bosie's marriage in order to get possession of his grandson but what he did had that effect. That is to say he did not formulate the matter thus: "No Court of law will separate a child from his mother except in the most exceptional circumstances. Therefore, since I cannot separate Raymond from Olive I must separate Olive from Bosie, then *her* possession of the little boy will become *mine*. Now Olive is my heir by entail, the property tied up on her by her grandfather and I cannot dispossess her. But I can persuade her to agree to a re-settlement and so get control of her money. As Bosie has only a small allowance from his mother, I shall then say that I will continue Olive's allowance only if I have Raymond, and they will have to give in."

That is how Bosie believed Custance plotted, and in a way it cannot be denied. The distinction is that Custance never knew he was plotting at all. He was doing what he thought right. He was keeping Raymond away from "those priests" and away from his unstable father. It was for the boy's good and he, Custance, was justified, a fine and honest Englishman dealing with an unpleasant situation by resolute means.

That he carried this out is not in dispute. The resettlement was made in 1911. Custance asked his daughter down to Weston Old Hall at a time when Bosie could not be there and breezily told her that he wanted to settle his property on his grandson. In consideration of her agreeing to this re-settlement he would pay her an income of £600 a year during his lifetime and a life-interest of the whole property on his death with the remainder to her son. If £600 seems a small amount we must remember that it was equivalent to nearly £2,000 today and in any case was more than Olive was receiving at the time.

This meant that Olive would voluntarily surrender her rights and allow the entail to be cut. She decided to talk it over with Bosie before agreeing and he immediately pointed out both to her and to her solicitors the risks of what she was doing and said she should insist on a binding legal agreement for the £600 a year. But on her next visit to her father all the documents had been prepared and when she asked about her income Colonel Custance haughtily said that his "word was good enough". She signed, and lost all control.

Custance was too impatient to allow even a discreet month or two to pass after this. He asked for the boy and very soon added a threat that he would discontinue Olive's 'allowance' unless Raymond was handed to his care.

Bosie decided to take Raymond from the school Custance had chosen for him. He kept for years the damning letter Custance sent his daughter when he heard of Bosie's intention. "The moment he takes the boy away all payments to you will cease", Custance wrote.

I wrote to him [says Bosie inevitably] pointing out that to stop payment of the income which was the 'consideration' which had induced my wife to abandon her rights as heir in tail of the property was neither more nor less than fraudulent, and that if he carried out his threat he would in fact be committing a fraudulent, as well as a disgraceful and dishonourable action.

All through 1911 and 1912 the struggle continued. Custance used his only weapon and cut off Olive's allowance, Bosie replied with a barrage first of letters but when Custance refused to open these, of telegrams and postcards. These dealt in detail with the settlement, told Custance he was a despicable scoundrel and threatened to give the same information to his clubs, his bank, his relations and his tenants. Again and again Bosie challenged him to bring an action for libel against him.

It was one of those irreconcilable sad and bitter family quarrels in which both sides have utterly convinced themselves that they are in the right. Custance saw Bosie as both a bad and a fanatical man from whom Raymond must be separated at all costs. He justified his behaviour over the settlement by asking himself why Bosie should be supported by Custance money while he was defying his father-in-law over Raymond. Bosie was prepared to make no allowance. He saw Custance's conduct as dishonourable and that was that. He was not interested in trying to understand the unhappy man and his motives and illusions. He knew only one way of fighting it out—by a lawsuit. Publicity had no terrors for him now, indeed he would welcome it. Let the whole world see what he had to contend with to keep custody of his own son. Let Custance's shady behaviour to his daughter be known to everyone.

But he could only get Custance in Court as plaintiff in an action for libel, and for a long time the Colonel resisted this. He was the last man to want litigation, not because he was in any way ashamed of his conduct but because the idea of a lawsuit with its publicity was repugnant to him. It was only when Bosie threatened to write to his club and his tenants that he succumbed. When he did so at last he acted swiftly and effectively by consulting George Lewis who advised criminal proceedings. A writ was issued. This was dated for February 26, 1913.

4

So much, for the moment, for Custance. Ross in the meantime had been given the opportunity he needed. For nearly two years he had smarted under Bosie's insulting way of dropping him and for twenty-two years, since Wilde had fallen in love with Bosie, he had suffered a humiliating jealousy, which he had usually found it wise to conceal, of the man who, he believed, had supplanted him.

He was securely entrenched in his position as literary executor and faithful friend to a re-established Wilde. On December 1st 1908 a public dinner had been given in his honour at the Ritz at which nearly two hundred guests celebrated the emergence of the Wilde estate from bankruptcy and the publication of the first Collected Edition of Wilde's works. Sir William Conway was in the Chair, H. G. Wells and William Rothenstein toasted Ross with appreciative speeches and he replied with wit and grace. Both Wilde's sons were present—so incidentally was Somerset Maugham. Ross was a popular man and his industry on behalf of the Wilde estate was rightly respected.

But it was time now, he believed, for his long-awaited reckoning with the man he had hated so patiently and so long. He had the ammunition and the skill to use it.

A writer named Arthur Ransome was introduced to him. Ransome was the son of a Professor of Literature at Leeds University and had already published two books, one of them on Edgar Allan Poe. He wanted to write a book about Wilde and his work, indeed had already a commission to do so from Martin Secker.

Martin Secker's account of this as given to Douglas has been endorsed by the fact that Martin Secker published it:

> I must say that Ransome was perfectly innocent in the matter. He came to me and suggested a book on Wilde, and, after hearing what his idea of the book was, I commissioned him to write it. He then said that it would be a tremendous help to him in writing the book if he could get an introduction to Robert Ross. He subsequently met Ross, who was very friendly and seemed inclined to give him every assistance. Ross told Ransome that if he would be guided by him and do the book on certain lines he would give him access to all sorts of documents and sources of information which had not been available to anyone else. Naturally, Ransome gratefully agreed to all that Ross proposed, and after that it was easy for Ross to get in the attack on you which the book contained and which in itself was only a matter of a few words.

But the 'few words' were very telling. Without mentioning Bosie by name Ransome implied that Wilde attributed his downfall to Bosie who had afterwards abandoned him. No one interested could fail to identify Bosie and Ross had material with which to justify both charges—the unpublished portions of *De Profundis* for the first and Wilde's letter, mentioned on page 170, for the second. He also had the letters from Bosie to Wilde which he had appropriated from Wilde's room after his death. Though Ransome himself may not have realized it, the trap was therefore very cunningly laid and Bosie, predictably, walked straight into it.

Not without opposition, however. Olive begged him to ignore the matter and his mother and many friends saw no purpose in a public revival of all they wanted to forget in Bosie's past. On the other hand there was Crosland. His account of it is brightly illuminating:

> After I had become editor of the *Penny Illustrated Paper* Douglas wrote to me saying that he had something important to communicate and would I meet him. I arranged to meet him, and he told me that a man named Arthur Ransome had written a book about Oscar Wilde, and that this book was dedicated to Ross and evidently inspired by him, and that it contained passages which were libels on Douglas. I read the passages and the book and I said that Douglas ought not to let them pass unchallenged. We had previously had similar things to deal with, and in each case proceedings had been taken and the people concerned withdrew and apologized.

So Bosie made the greatest mistake in a life of mistakes. He issued a writ for libel on Arthur Ransome.

He would never afterwards admit it was a mistake. If he had ignored the libel, he said, it would simply have been repeated more boldly and more openly as time went on, and added with his usual weakness for over-statement that if he had not sued Ransome for libel he might as well have committed suicide, "as far as any prospects in this world are concerned". This is nonsense. Ross would probably have been satisfied by his shot from cover and might not have had the means of repeating it. And if the libel had been repeated more boldly and openly it would have been time to bring an action with far greater chances of success. Moreover, Secker at once agreed to withdraw the book so that Bosie might well have considered honour satisfied.

The truth unhappily lies in the last sentence of Crosland's statement. Both he and Bosie thought it would be a walk-over. With Bosie twelve years married and secure from any possible imputation of immorality in that time and Ross—to whom the book was dedicated and by whom it was demonstrably inspired*—a 'notorious homosexual', they probably did not suppose the case would come into Court at all.

But they under-rated Ross and were ignorant of the strength of his hand. Ransome pleaded justification.

5

So at the beginning of 1913 Bosie was involved in two libel actions, plaintiff in one, defendant in the other. All trials are trials for one's life, said Wilde, and it was true of these, at least in the figurative sense in which it was written. Both Custance and Ross were as implacable as Bosie and neither had his dangerous over-confidence. Both had a great deal of money and support behind them and Bosie was almost penniless. Both were popular and Bosie was unpopular. Both stood for things that would appeal to jurymen and Bosie stood for himself.

Before either case came to Court Olive left him and went to her father which enabled Custance through Lewis and Lewis to commence proceedings in the Chancery Court to get Raymond away from Bosie. It also made it difficult for Bosie to plead justification for his libels on Custance.

* Martin Secker announced it as a book "in which Mr. Robert Ross has rendered the author invaluable assistance".

On January 14th he was made bankrupt. Then, just before Custance's action was heard in the Magistrate's Court he received Ransome's Particulars of Justification and for the first time read the unpublished portions of *De Profundis*.

6

This was his darkest time. Olive's leaving him was carried out in a—perhaps not deliberately—unkind manner. Bosie had been staying with his mother and sister at a house called Hinton St. Mary and Raymond, now a boy of twelve, had been with him. He returned to Church Row to find that Olive had gone and taken her property for the house was 'half dismantled'.

Her state of mind had been one of distress for a long time and this can be seen from some letters she wrote later in the year to Bosie's mother:

Bosie was cruel to me before I went to Weston, and I have often been very unhappy with him, but I love him above everything, and would never have left him if he had not taken away Raymond. Everybody I know takes my father's part, and, God help me, I don't know where to turn to for advice and comfort. My father is angry all the time because I love Bosie still—and I am utterly miserable. But would it do Bosie any good if I am turned out to starve? I am utterly helpless since I made those settlements. Perhaps it would be better for Bosie to divorce me for desertion? I only wish I had courage enough to kill myself!

In another letter, also to Lady Queensberry, she said:

I have told Daddy that you spoke to me, and that I am so much happier. . . . He will be angry, perhaps, but he knows I shall always love Bosie, though I am afraid to live with him again at present. I don't think Bosie loves me any more. I trust you. I have done all this for Raymond's sake, though you know I love Bosie.

It was not simply a matter of choosing between her father and her husband. Her father had quite ruthlessly cut off her income and left her virtually no choice. Moreover she probably did not realize that in leaving Bosie and going to Custance she was hopelessly prejudicing Bosie's chances in a plea of justification, or that justification was the only possible defence for the libels he had uttered, or that through her action there was a very real risk of Bosie being committed to prison for criminal libel. If he could not prove the facts of Custance's behaviour over the entail and Olive's income he could not hope to justify the libels with which he had stung Custance to action. Olive saw only her powerful, rich and righteous father on the one hand and her volatile, penniless, bellicose husband on the other. She did not intend to betray Bosie, but her going to her father at that juncture seemed to him the most crass and treacherous betrayal.

This was intensified when Custance commenced his Chancery Court action for Raymond. Such an action would have had no chance of success while the boy's father and mother were united, but when the grandfather and the mother joined against the father they were almost certain to win and Bosie believed he would lose his son entirely.

Then his bankruptcy. Like his elder brother, he had frequently had recourse to money-lenders and had always been given time to pay. But at this moment with so much chancy litigation pending he was not considered a good risk and on a money-lender's petition a receiving order was made against him. Among other unpleasant consequences of this Bosie ceased automatically to be a member of White's. It was twenty years since he had been elected and nothing that had happened to him so far had affected this. Wilde used to complain of Bosie's leaving him in the afternoon to visit White's and in De Profundis voiced the complaint in another way. White's, the oldest club in London had been for many years the personal property of Bosie's cousin Algy Bourke. His loss of membership was a blow, and though he would have been re-admitted without a ballot if he had shown the committee that there was no disgrace in his bankruptcy he never applied for re-admission. A man's club in 1913 was still an important part of his life and status, even if he rarely visited it, and to Bosie it must have seemed that he was being sent farther into the desert.

But to Bosie the greatest betrayal seemed that by a man more than twelve years dead. The thought of Bosie sitting alone in his half-empty house reading the 'unpublished portions' of De Profundis is a blood-curdling one. That Wilde had written the thing under the brutal stresses of imprisonment, that within a month or two of writing it he was hand-in-hand with his "own dearest boy" in Rouen, that Wilde's credulity and tendency to resentment had been skilfully exploited by Ross while he was in prison—all this could mean nothing to Bosie, and he was unaware of letters no less malicious, which Wilde had written to others at the same time.

The complete De Profundis is a catalogue of petty recriminations such as any homosexual could list (if not in the same lordly language) against his partner in the artificial relations of a two-male love-affair.

This may be evident now but could not for a moment be glimpsed by Bosie then. Much of it was flatly untrue, some of it, more painfully, had an element of cruel truth, but all of it was written to wound a young friend whom the writer believed to be amusing himself while he suffered. That it should have come at last into the hands of a man in his forties engaged in a life-and-death struggle was a refinement of torture which would have sickened Wilde at his most bitter.

Wilde, as we have seen, soon put the thing out of his mind and spent the last years of his life in broken but for the most part sunny amity with Bosie. He had wanted to hurt the youth he loved, as may be seen from the whole tone of the thing, or perhaps only to hurt Bosie's vanity, but after they were re-united he no longer wanted to hurt anyone. He was the least malicious of beings and it had taken the crushing blows to his conceit which trial and imprisonment had inflicted to draw these turgid lamentations from him. The book was more than half addressed to himself, to his own folly and lazy sensuality.

But how could Bosie see any of that? It was all treachery to him, black devilish treachery by the man he had loved and for whom he had been suffering for nearly twenty years. Until the very hour of reading it he had kept Wilde's image bright, had remained loyal to his memory, had written and spoken of him with all his wordy might, and even since becoming a Christian he had refused to renounce him or criticize him. Now as part of the Particulars of Justification of a man he was suing for libel he was handed this brilliantly presented mass of falsity and spite, and it struck him down.

It took him many years to recover from it. For the next decade or more he lived in loathing of Wilde and it was only with time and as the unquenchable sweetness of his nature re-asserted itself that he first forgave him and finally held his memory in the old affection.

7

The unpublished portions of *De Profundis* were read by Crosland, too. His reactions, as may be imagined, were violent. He had no ancient loyalty to consider and no happy recollections of a charming friend to live down. He, Crosland, had always hated everything to do with Wilde and felt impatience with Bosie's obstinate loyalty to the man and his work. Now he let himself go and in December 1912 published a ferocious diatribe in free verse called *The First Stone*. As an exercise in hysterical obloquy it is not without interest but as verse, or prose, it s very, very bad and it is hard to accept the statement by Crosland's biographer that on its publication "the rage of the members of the Wilde cult knew no bounds".

The usefulness of *De Profundis* to the Defence was another matter which Bosie and his advisers had to consider. He could counter much of it by documentary proof and the production of his passbook. He could also effectively answer Wilde's letter to Ross after Naples by testimony that through his mother he had sent Wilde £200 and paid a quarter's rent of the villa. But he did not realize that he was caught in an ingenious trap so far as evidence was concerned. The more he disproved one accusation against him the more he proved the other. If he showed that so far from abandoning Wilde in the last years he had been devoted to him and given him money it would be taken by the jury to imply that he had lived with Wilde in sin and so would make him guilty of the charge of having 'ruined' Wilde. If he denied that there had been anything immoral in his relations with Wilde in the early days it would make it easy to believe he had 'abandoned' him at the end. At all events the forensic skill of a remarkable collection of lawyers ranged against him would make it appear so.

But there was no withdrawing now, and no thought of withdrawal. That the unpublished portions of *De Profundis* were being produced on *subpoena* showed Bosie plainly enough whom he was really fighting. He even supposed that Ross would enter the witness-box. Though without his customary relish, though in perturbation of mind and disillusionment, he prepared for battle.

The chronology of that year is important if we want to understand Bosie's conduct in the three cases, Custance's action against him, his action against Ransome, and the Chancery Court proceedings. Bosie was brought up in a Magistrate's Court (Marylebone) to answer a charge of criminal libel against Custance on February 26. He was committed to be tried on March 6 but asked for an adjournment to give his Counsel time to put in a plea of justification. The case was heard on April 24.

His action against Ransome came up on April 18 and lasted four days so that he had to answer Custance's charges within a week of losing his action against Ransome. And before he had a chance to breathe after this the Chancery Court action was heard in May. Perhaps it would be best to recall the Ransome case first.

8

Contemporary newspaper accounts are never very reliable as sources of information on long ago lawsuits for they were sometimes prejudiced and through limitations of space or for reasons which may have been strong at the time they often misplaced the emphasis.

I have before me four recently-written accounts of the Ransome case from which entirely different conclusions are to be drawn though all four are based on old newspaper stories. One is a silly piece of sensation-mongering which appeared in an evening paper, the others are more detailed but no less partial.

All agree on the discomfiture Bosie suffered in listening to large portions of *De Profundis* read aloud, and all share a glee, which they seek to communicate to their readers, at the result of the action. None of them expresses the smallest disgust at the production of Bosie's stolen letters and the unpublished portions of *De Profundis*, and none of them calls attention to the vicious bias of the judge. Yet one of them attributes Bosie's defeat solely to *De Profundis*, another to Bosie's absence from the witness-box for a time while it was being read. In fact it was fore-ordained and only a miracle could have gained him a verdict.

He had against him J. H. Campbell, afterwards Sir James Campbell, and Mr. McCardie, afterwards Mr. Justice McCardie, for Ransome, and F. E. Smith, afterwards Lord Birkenhead, for a lending library which had refused to withdraw the book. He also had Mr. Justice Darling who disliked the case from the beginning and disliked it more as it went on, and showed his prejudice against the plaintiff who had caused him to hear it. His attitude may be guessed from the fact that he asked the Press to make their reports on that part of the cross-examination which dealt with Wilde "as disguised as possible". Every one of his interventions was directed against Bosie and his interventions were frequent and crushing.

Bosie was in a cleft stick. His letter to Labouchère (see page 133) and his article in the *Revue Blanche* (see page 141) were produced and he was asked if he repudiated them. If he said "No" he was admitting himself to hold homosexual views and so to have been the "ruin" of Wilde; if he said "Yes" he showed that he had now "abandoned" Wilde and had probably done so in his lifetime. He was asked about his father; if he had been reconciled with the man who ruined Wilde he had "abandoned" his friend, if he still hated Queensberry he was an unnatural son and likely to have been the "ruin" of Wilde. And so on.

The Defence by brilliant if unscrupulous legal strategy which had every support from Darling, never for a moment let the issue be the clear one of whether or not Ransome had libelled Bosie, but concentrated on so discrediting Bosie that the jury would lose all sympathy with him. Although as Cecil Hayes, Bosie's Counsel, pointed out, they had delivered sixty-three pages of justification the defendant Ransome had not gone into the witness-box to justify any of them. Darling intervened to tell Hayes that his object in trying to get Ransome into the box was not to prove these particulars but to enable him to ask questions which he did not wish to put to his own witnesses. He did not point out that the Defence had very firmly kept Ransome out of the box since he would have been asked the source of his information and laid Ross open to cross-examination.

The unkindest cut was the production of Bosie's letters to Wilde which, though natural and sincere at the time, were now highly compromising if not damning. Since these were not in Ransome's possession there was no mention of them in his affidavit of documents and when they were read in Court it was the first Bosie knew of their existence. That Ross had appropriated these when Wilde died and before Ross had any standing as Wilde's executor, had kept them secretly for years instead of returning them to Bosie as anyone with the smallest pretence of honour would have done when he saw the nature of them, seemed to Bosie to be infamous. Even across the years and after Shaw's plea, "Let Ross alone: the world has had enough of that squabble", this action by Ross is still quite indefensible. Moreover these letters had no direct bearing on the case and were read, with deadly effect, to create prejudice.

It is an old and a lamentable matter. Poor Ross paid for it in tears later, and like so much else in the story of Wilde's friends after his death it would be best forgotten. But since it explains Bosie's relentless behaviour afterwards it must be set down here with all its implications.

Bosie should never have brought this action. As F. E. Smith said, tautologically but truthfully—"With regard to Oscar Wilde, years have passed since his fall, and men are beginning to think of the artist rather than the man's life. Now this legacy of infamy has been resurrected—unnecessarily resurrected—again." Bosie was wrongheaded and litigious. But it must be realized that he believed he lost this action, and with it his good name, because Ross had stolen his letters and used them against him. Whatever the truth about *De Profundis*, and there are several theories which have their adherents, on this matter of the letters there can be no doubt and it explains the shocking and deplorable events which followed.

The jury was out for nearly two hours. Bosie's action was dismissed with costs.

A lamentable part was played by More Adey. His letters to Wilde already quoted on page 166 showed clearly that he had been paid £200 for Wilde in Naples by Bosie's mother on Bosie's behalf. If he had admitted this unequivocably, Ransome's plea of justification—at least so far as this part of the alleged libel was concerned—would have collapsed, for it would have shown that Bosie did *not* leave Wilde in Naples until he had secured this sum for him. But Adey admitted only that he had received money from Lady Queensberry leaving it to appear that this had been sent in shame for Bosie's abandonment of Wilde.

Bosie at once wrote to him and sent a copy of his letter to Justice Darling:

Mr. More Adey,
    I see that yesterday, when you were recalled by the Judge to give evidence, you, too, played the Judas Iscariot to me, your old friend. You deliberately misled the jury.
    You know perfectly well, for I have discussed the matter with you a dozen times, and you discussed it with my solicitor, that the £200 was sent to Wilde in November, 1897, within a week of my leaving him at Naples, and you also know perfectly well that this £200 formed no part of any debt of honour. I wish you joy of what you have done, knowing as you do that I have for years led a clean, straight life, and have struggled hard to be a good Christian and a good Catholic, and knowing that Ross, who put up Ransome to write the book, is a filthy beast. . . .
    Our friendship is at an end. I shall never speak to you again. It is no business of mine to seek for revenge on you or on Ross, but the reckoning will surely come sooner or later.
                                                                Alfred Douglas.

Darling called F. E. Smith and Cecil Hayes on the day after the verdict and handed them this and the covering letter from Douglas to him. These were, he said, undoubtedly libellous and left Adey and Ross to take proceedings if they wished. They did not.

Bosie decided to appeal against the verdict and did so immediately. But on the other side's serving him with a notice of motion to furnish security for the costs of the appeal he was forced by lack of funds to withdraw it. That was as well, for he would never have had a chance.

Opinion on the case was not quite so unanimous at the time as modern commentators would have us believe. This is shown in an interesting letter sent to Crosland by Randal Charlton then editor of *The Daily Graphic* on April 22, 1913.

> The Daily Graphic,
> Tallis House,
> Whitefriars, E.C.

My dear Mr. Crosland,

I feel I must write you a line about the abominable verdict in the Douglas case. I have felt for some time that Darling had made up his mind to act as a sort of pimp for a dead villain in Wilde and a living one in Ross. But I thought I would wait until the verdict was declared before writing you. The case has been a staggering experience for anybody who has an ounce of friendship for Lord Alfred Douglas or the smallest sense of abstract justice. The spectacle of Wilde spitting filth at Lord Alfred from the grave while Ross plays with stolen letters, Campbell bullies, and a pinchbeck Judge "nobbles" the whole case, is about as unholy a thing as I have ever seen or read about. In the face of Ross and Wilde, Judas begins to look a very old-fashioned person indeed.

I believe you know by now what faith I have in you, and I feel certain that matters are not going to rest where they now stand. Surely Ross and company are not going to escape Scot free! I am not a violent person, but I cannot conceive of any measures too strong which may bring some sense of retribution to Ross and his companions. I am sure you agree with me that anything that can be done to bring these people to their proper state of shame must be done. Why Lord Alfred should be afflicted by such injustice is a question quite beyond me unless God in His wisdom purposes to turn him into a little saint through an earthly martyrdom! I should like to see you very much indeed.

> Believe me,
> Yours ever sincerely,
> Randal Charlton.

Mr. Martin Secker also remembers:

While the case was pending I formed the opinion that Ross, who was providing at his own suggestion the finance for defending, was doing so solely to accomplish his own ends, and that A.D. was being unfairly treated. I wrote to A.D. to the effect that I would prefer not to defend and had cancelled by mutual agreement my contract with the author. That was how I came to be dismissed from the case. Ross's original plan was that all four defendants should be represented by his own solicitors (Lewis & Lewis) but Brendons (the printers) would not agree and made their own separate settlement. In spite of the jury's verdict that the statements specifically complained of were true, it is significant

that when Methuens subsequently re-issued the book these statements wer
omitted. After the case A.D. called to see me (our first meeting) and w
remained on friendly terms for the rest of his life.

9

Five days after the verdict, Bosie had to come before the Recorder on
Custance's charge against him of criminal libel.

When he had deliberately provoked Custance to charge him, seeking
to bring into the light Custance's treatment of his daughter, things had
been very different. He had not foreseen Olive's defection, he had not
lost an action on which he had gambled his reputation and he had not
been bankrupt. It was one thing to call Custance a dishonourable man
who had defrauded his daughter when that daughter was beside him to
prove it, it was quite another to justify the words when Olive had left
him and gone to her father and he himself had heard read in open
Court an article by Labouchère of *Truth* which called him, Bosie, an
"exceptional young scoundrel". Admittedly this had been published
eighteen years earlier but only a week ago the press had quoted it from
F. E. Smith's speech in the Ransome case.

When he attacked his father-in-law he believed that Custance's
letter, "the moment he takes the boy away all payments to you will
cease", was justification enough, legally and ethically, and though he
was now persuaded not to plead justification he never lost that belief.
Whether accurately or not he quotes Comyns Carr as telling him years
later that he had overwhelming justification for his libel on Custance
and that the letter alone would have been sufficient to settle the case in
his favour.

But at the time he listened to more cautious and perhaps wiser advice.
He pleaded in mitigation of his libels that they had been written under
great stress and tendered an apology, withdrawing his accusations.

In spite of a strong plea by Sir Richard Muir for Custance that Bosie
should be given "the most severe sentence possible", he was bound
over on his own recognizances of £500. He had, as he called it, thrown
in the sponge, at least for the time being.

The Chancery Court a few weeks later decided that Raymond
should spend three-fifths of his holiday time with Custance and the
remaining two-fifths with Bosie and that Bosie should pay his school
fees.

CHAPTER XII

The Night of the Long Knives (concluded)

I

BOSIE, deserted by his wife, deprived of his son, his home broken up, a bankrupt and almost an outcast, became a man with a single idea: "I recognized that the author of all this havoc was Robert Ross."

Ross on the other hand, urbanely pleased with the result of the case, smiling under the congratulations of his many friends, probably unconscious that he had acted at all dishonourably, went off to Moscow at the invitation of the Moscow Art Theatre to see the first Russian production of *Salome*. He had been in Court throughout the Ransome case and had watched with satisfaction the discomfiture and defeat of Bosie and felt perhaps that his enemy had been given a lesson. Telling his servants he was not at home to Ross! Writing him that letter! This would teach him. The little man was no longer 'kittenish' but a plump bald neat person with a reputation for 'knowing about pictures', an indefatigable correspondent with a great variety of literary and artistic friends young and old, popular, even loved. He could afford to be amused at the humiliated bankrupt Bosie, and probably thought he had seen the last of him. Yes, Bosie had got his deserts. Everyone agreed about that.

But everyone did not know Bosie. Ross was, he decided,

the High Priest of all the sodomites in London, and it was he who was held up to the world as the faithful friend of Wilde (out of the exploitation of whose cult he had made a fortune), the noble disinterested friend, the pure, the holy person, in contrast to the wicked and depraved Alfred Douglas who had "ruined" Oscar Wilde and "deserted" him. Flesh and blood couldn't stand it, and I swore the day after the Ransome trial that I would never rest till I had publicly exposed Ross in his true colours.

An unworthy object to be sought by unworthy means but to be sought with all the violent energy, all the terrible intelligence, all the

fury and all the malevolence of which Bosie was capable. With Crosland as his too-eager henchman and the gentle influence of his wife
extinguished, with hate in his heart masquerading as righteousness, he
opened his attack.

He could never wholly convince himself that his cause was good
though he believed it just. One of the things he most regretted in his
life, he wrote in his last book, was that in the Ransome case he was
cowardly enough to take up the moral attitude he did. Though there
was nothing half-hearted, alas, in the way he 'went for' Ross, his abuse
of Wilde as a man and a writer, which continued for at least ten years,
was wholly unconvincing. He whipped up his moral indignation
because only with this could he nerve himself for the long desperate
struggle in which at the last he was, in a sorry fashion, victorious. But
his whole faith was never behind it and he had to perform mental
contortions to reconcile it with his religion.

What he wanted, whether he knew it or not, was revenge, both on
Ross and Custance. They had wronged him, the one treacherously, the
other selfishly and by the power of his money and position. They had
in that spring and summer of 1913 reduced him to the depths, a lonely
desperate abandoned man, without money and almost without
friends. He fought back with the only weapons he had. Custance he
assaulted by writing another letter which, though it did not repeat the
accusations on which he had given his recognizances, only varied
them. Ross he attacked by altogether more malignant means. He
exposed him as a homosexual.

There was nothing heroic in all this. It is a wretched story which
leaves little credit to anyone concerned, Bosie, Ross, Crosland, Custance
or the supporters of any of them. To Bosie it may be granted that he
had courage to rise from the ground to which he had been beaten
down and fight back. But the manner of his fighting cannot be
condoned nor his victory, such as it was, applauded. For Ross and
Custance it must be said that neither realized the meanness of what he
did, Ross because he was that sort of man, and Custance because he
was not. To Ross it was natural to appropriate and keep Bosie's letters
against a rainy day and behave as he did over *De Profundis*. To Custance
it was so very unnatural and against all his principles and breeding to
blackmail his daughter that he never realized he was doing it. Nor do
the lawyers come very well out of the mêlée. Nor those who simply
cried havoc and encouraged the combatants. It is a chapter which for
all its dramatic possibilities I would like not to write.

2

Bosie had no scruples about his harassing of Ross but as I say he was never very whole-hearted in his hostile attitude to the memory of Wilde, even in these dark days just after he had read the whole of *De Profundis*. Crosland, with his puritanical upbringing, his facility for writing to order and his gift for convincing himself conveniently of the rightness of what he was doing, had no scruples of any kind in blackguarding either the dead man or the living one. To him the 'Wilde cult' and its 'arch-priest' were one. He worked himself up to a state in which he was an avenging angel, destined to expose an abomination. All his truculent nature and his better qualities of loyalty to Bosie, whom he saw as a man greatly wronged, were in his campaign. He wrote to Sorley Brown, the Scots journalist who supported him and Bosie—"We have got a bit of the light on the Wilde foulness as it is. In due time we shall get more. I hope you will continue to stick up for Douglas no matter what happens. He is a sound, clean man, besides being the poet you have made him out to be, and he will win in the long run."

Unfortunately Crosland carried Bosie with him. In his state of mind in 1913 Bosie was only too ready to see himself ranged with Crosland in a fight against "the Wilde foulness". And very soon they were given an opportunity to go forward. Douglas was approached by an enterprising publisher named John Long who saw in his friendship with Wilde and the recent publicity given to it by the Ransome case an opportunity for a lively book. But it had to be written and published quickly before the echoes of the Ransome case had died down. Could it be ready by July?

Bosie was quite incapable, in that year, of the sustained effort of writing a book of eighty thousand words. Writing was never easy for him and his ideas on the subject were not well ordered or considered. But Long offered an advance of £500 which was a large sum for a book in those days, and there was Crosland who had recently ceased to be editor of *The Penny Illustrated Paper* and was eager to do the actual writing of the book for half the proceeds.

Crosland began work at once and in about a couple of months produced one of the most unpleasant books of the last hundred years. Bosie, though he later repudiated much of it, never sought to shift the responsibility for it from his own shoulders.

I am, of course, myself responsible for this mistake, because I asked Crosland to write this part of the book, feeling at the time so shaken and unnerved by the experiences I had been through at the Ransome trial that I felt I could not bring myself to write about it. Crosland wrote the story and I read and passed it.

And later he wrote in the *Autobiography*:

What happened when I began to write that book was that Crosland, with whom I was then in close association (arising out of the fact that he had been my assistant editor on *The Academy* for more than two years), said to me: "You will never write this book as it ought to be written. Even now, after all that has happened, and after you have got the complete proof of what an unspeakable swine Wilde was, you are still too soft about him to put it right across him as you ought to do. Let me do that part of the book. In fact you had much better let me write the book altogether, you of course giving me the facts and revising it after I have put them into shape." In the end, after much discussion, I agreed to let Crosland collaborate.

It is evident from the prose of the book, if from nothing else, that it was written by Crosland as he himself proudly claimed. If anyone troubles to examine the particular kind of journalistic bombast, pseudo-Johnsonian, laden with clichés and laboured jeers, which Crosland had been employing for twenty years he will see that *Oscar Wilde and Myself* is written in exactly this manner and the bad taste, the presumptuous folly of the arguments, the snobbishness that apes bluffness, are all pure Crosland. But that in no way exculpates Bosie and the hypocrisy with which the book is rank is his.

"In Paris", wrote André Gide in his journal a few years later,

I read (in part) Douglas's abominable book, *Oscar Wilde and Myself*. Hypocrisy can go no further, nor falsehood be more impudent. It is a monstrous travesty of the truth, which filled me with disgust. Merely from the tone of his writing it seems to me that I should be aware he is lying, even if I had not been the direct witness of the acts of his life against which he protests and which he claims to whitewash. But even this is not enough for him. He claims that he was ignorant of Wilde's habits! and that he upheld him at first only because he thought him innocent! Whom will he convince?

Whom *did* he convince? Certainly not Crosland who was perfectly aware of the truth and shows it by the over-emphasis of the denials. If I were writing an all-out defence of Bosie there would be nothing in his life I would find harder to excuse than *Oscar Wilde and Myself*.

The manuscript was ready in July but the joint authors had yet to reckon with Ross. They had quoted portions of *De Profundis* in order to answer them and also certain letters of Wilde which were then under copyright. Ross obtained an injunction against this, also by a swift and clever move he made the whole of *De Profundis* copyright in America.*

It was not for another year that *Oscar Wilde and Myself*, purged of libel and breach of copyright, could be issued and it came out on the day war was declared.

But if Bosie and Crosland could not make their attacks between the covers of a book to be issued by a publishing firm with a healthy fear of injunctions and damages, they were not to be daunted. All through that summer and autumn of 1913 they continued their vendetta, but until 1914 it did not come to a head.

3

At first there were only three supporters in Bosie's camp and one of these, Crosland, was so to speak a mercenary. Bosie's mother never failed him and his cousin George Wyndham rallied to him in adversity. He had been in Parliament since 1889 and had more than once shown his friendship for his cousin, for it was he who sold *The Academy* for Bosie three years earlier. It was not the smallest of Bosie's disasters in that year that he lost the support of this powerful ally when, two months after writing a letter in support of Bosie George Wyndham died in Paris.

But he had one other companion in disaster. On the day before he was due to appear at the Old Bailey to answer Custance's charge of criminal libel, a young American girl arrived at his half-dismantled home in Church Row. In his *Autobiography* Bosie does not say whether he had met her previously, or whether, as it would be pleasant to think, she acted wholly on a quixotic and romantic impulse. She brought her jewels including a pearl necklace and implored Bosie to raise money on them for his defence and immediate needs. The offer he refused but he was "inexpressibly touched and grateful" and after he had found her waiting outside the Court next day she became his constant companion.

He told the story of this friendship with naïvety which was almost childlike and has laid it open to the smirks and giggles of one at least of those who have described it from Bosie's own words. Only the fact that he was trying in his *Autobiography* to do that impossible thing

---

*For this purpose, sixteen copies were printed by Paul Reynolds in New York. Ross distributed some of these in England as a letter from Edmund Gosse (October 25, 1913) indicates. By so doing he laid himself open to a more serious libel action than the Ransome case if Bosie had known of it.

for any writer, tell the whole truth about himself, induced him to mention it.

She was, he says, beautiful. She was also, if one remembers the period, a highly independent young woman with a flat of her own. For a month they went about together every day and she helped to revive Bosie's drooping spirits. In the disgust with Wilde which he had felt since reading *De Profundis* he did what none of his previous acute necessities had caused him to do, sold Wilde's books and letters. This gave him the money to take his American friend about London in the most conspicuous way.

For the first month this was, he says, "innocent". "I explained to her that being a Catholic, I could not consent to lead an immoral life. In the end, however, I succumbed."

Bosie admitted frankly that this association was partly a gesture of defiance. He knew that Custance was having his movements watched by private detectives and he and his friend used to laugh at the sight of them in Church Row or outside her flat. He never expected to see Olive again and felt a natural if somewhat petulant desire to show 'them all' that he did not give a damn for them.

But less than four months after Olive had left him she telephoned and asked Bosie to meet her. The sound of her voice "completely finished" him and he went at once to see her. There was a reconciliation and though he and Olive never lived together again they remained friends till her death, which took place shortly before Bosie's. The reconciliation, he said later, was not permanent or complete, but she never again sided with her father against Bosie, indeed, later she appeared with Bosie in the Chancery Court to seek a variation of the original order about Raymond. She had resisted, in those four months, a continuous barrage of persuasion to divorce Bosie. But Custance under-rated her. It was the very evidence he produced of Bosie's infidelity which sent her back to him to oust the interloper.

Bosie's reconciliation with his wife meant the departure of the American girl. They met once more when she came with Crosland to see him in Boulogne, and after she had returned to California she wrote begging him to join her. But his religion gave him a strict rule of life and after those few weeks in London he remained till his death a happily chaste man, and for him this was no contradiction in terms.

Towards the end of 1913 he got rid of the house in Church Row and went to live with his mother in Chelsea, at 19 Royal Avenue, Sloane Square.

4

With his vitality and striking-power resuscitated, Bosie went over to the offensive against both Custance and Ross. His apology to Custance was what Bernard Shaw called Wilde's denials of homosexuality, a legal fiction necessary in the law courts. Bosie felt so far from apologetic, now that he was separated from Raymond for three fifths of the boy's holidays, that after his reconciliation with Olive he wrote to Custance again, this time blaming him for the break-up of his marriage.

The letter was not strictly speaking a repetition of his previous libels but it served the same purpose. Custance showed it to Lewis who advised action.

Meanwhile, since it was for some years a three-cornered fight in which Bosie sometimes provoked charges by both his opponents at the same moment, we must see what was happening to Ross.

I find it strange, or perhaps not so strange, that in her loyal book about her uncle *Robert Ross: Friend of Friends* Miss Margery Ross does not reprint among the hundreds of letters of which the book chiefly consists any that have references to the Ransome case, Ross's unsuccessful actions against Crossland and Bosie, Ross's subsequent disgrace or even the public testimonial with which an attempt was made to reinstate him. There were surely many letters sent to him in 1913 which congratulated him on his triumph which, though it turned out to be a passing one, must have seemed splendid at the time, at least to his friends. Yet except for an oblique reference by Sir George Alexander to Ross's "time of happiness and relief" and by Cyril Holland who was then in Thibet to a "heartfelt cry of joy" that the "last cause célèbre" was at an end, a hope that it will be the last indeed, and a mention of the "glory" that was Ross's, we find no reference to the Ransome case.

Nor do we find reprinted among the letters Ross received from eminent people this one from Crosland which was sent on January 4, 1914:

12 Burleigh Street,
Strand.

Robert B. Ross,

For years past you have been engaged in creating for Oscar Wilde a literary and general reputation which is to a great extent a fraudulent one. With the help of dishonest prefaces and the garbling of the work Wilde wrote in prison you have succeeded in foisting him on the public in the figure of a repentant saint, and incidentally you have obtained for yourself, a literary credit thereby which would not otherwise have come your way. From the public point of view it is the highly respectable Ross labouring generously for the much maligned and greatly suffering Wilde and bringing him into his own. From my point of view, and in the face of the facts, it is one dirty Sodomite bestowing lavish whitewash upon another. You have flooded the book-stalls with Wilde's works to the great detriment of the public mind. If your publishers knew what manner of man you really are their activities in the chase of the useful shilling would in the nature of things come to a somewhat sudden period. You cannot hope to escape from the sharp and inevitable consequences of your own villainies, and you are sufficient of a tradesman to know that when these come within the public knowledge, as they are bound to do, the damage to Wilde will be infinitely greater than the good you are supposed to have done him, and he will at once sink back into the obloquy from which you have dragged him. My own efforts to bring you to book have not been personal to yourself and therefore it is that I propose to you now that you should withdraw your prefaces and other sophistications from publication and resign your executorship of Wilde's literary estate, and that you should further make some public statement which would help in the correction of the false and dangerous conception of Wilde you have been the means of spreading abroad. If you consider what I have said I think you will agree with me that you could not adopt a wiser course. I am told by your friends that, in spite of your notorious vices, you are a man who is not by any means denuded of decent feelings, and though I have never found you conducting yourself in any other than brutish and disgraceful ways I make this present suggestion to you in the hope that your friends are right. As a private citizen, I should wish to see you checked in your courses of foulness, but the great point with me is the irreparable hurt you are inflicting upon letters and the thought of the time by your persistent pushing forward of Wilde as a writer of weight and sincerity and a man whose sins can be overlooked.

T. W. H. Crosland.

When this was ignored, Crosland wrote another letter which stated simply:

A letter nailing you down has been sent by Lord Alfred Douglas to the following persons: Mr. Justice Darling, Mr. Justice Astbury, the Recorder of London, the Prime Minister, the Public Prosecutor, Mr. Basil Thompson (Scotland Yard), Mr. Gwynne (*Morning Post*), Mr. John Lane (Publisher), Sir George Lewis, and the Master of St. Paul's School. If these letters do not contain the truth about you, there can be little question that you would have taken a certain and obvious legal remedy.

The precise terms of Bosie's letter are unknown but between it and two pamphlets which he published at this time he applied, he says, the following flowers of speech to Ross. 'An unspeakable skunk', a 'filthy b——', a 'notorious Sodomite', an 'habitual debaucher and corrupter of young boys right down to the present day', and last, but not least a 'blackmailer'.

These letters were not sent before Crosland and Bosie had what they thought was evidence with which to support a plea of justification. A boy named Garratt, in prison for importuning, at his trial had called Christopher Millard to speak for him.

Now Millard was a picturesque character who had also served a sentence for a homosexual offence and was employed by Ross as a secretary. He was an able if eccentric man who after being in trouble as a schoolmaster had worked on *The Burlington Magazine* and in 1911 published anonymously *Oscar Wilde Three Times Tried*, the first account of the proceedings against Queensberry and Wilde. His *Bibliography of Oscar Wilde*, a remarkable piece of research and editing, one of the most lavish bibliographies to be devoted to a writer in English, was published in this same year (1914). He was unstable and disloyal but clever.

A. J. A. Symons, who knew Millard as I did in the last years of his life (he died in 1927) gives a vivid account of him in *The Quest for Corvo*, for it was Millard who first introduced Symons to *Hadrian the Seventh* and set him on the trail which led to one of the most fascinating biographies in the language. Millard was then living "in a small bungalow hidden behind a Victorian villa in Abercorn Place, reached by descending area steps and walking round the side of the house". Symons saw him as a burly, self-sufficient, lonely man and seems to have liked and admired him. I thought there was something slightly sinister about him and his stock of 'curious' literature, compromising letters and typescripts, his intense yet sly manner and his scandalous conversation.

His love for books was that of a bibliophile and bookseller, but none the less genuine. The work he did for Ross in editing the accounts of Wilde's trials and drawing up his enormous Bibliography was valuable, but his indiscretions helped to ruin Ross when litigation began.

When Crosland, or Bosie, or both, noticed the appearance of Millard in connection with Garratt they jumped to the conclusion that the boy had associated with Ross. They successfully applied to the Home Office for permission to send a solicitor to see him in prison.

Garratt, evidently interested in what there might be for him in this, made a crafty statement in which he said he knew Ross well but would give no further details till he came out of prison.

He was met at the prison gates and made a statement, this time incriminating Ross, and was taken to Scotland Yard, where he repeated and signed it. But the Metropolitan police unlike the more enthusiastic provincial forces, have always sought to avoid prosecutions under Section 11 of the Criminal Law Amendment Act of 1885 and took no steps in the matter.

Crosland then went down to see the boy's mother described as a charwoman of Countesthorpe in Lincolnshire. They went to a pub and over a drink Mrs. Garratt heard about her son in London and agreed to give evidence if necessary.

This, for the moment, seemed sufficient on which to plead justi-fication if the hypothetical action was ever begun by Ross, an unlikely contingency. Ross could easily laugh off Bosie's letters—even to the Master of St. Paul's School who must have wondered at the receipt of it. The Asquiths, who had suffered from Bosie and Crosland in *The Academy* days, were firmly behind him. (Margot Asquith wrote to him in May 1914 saying that she had got to go and dine with the King but Ross was to bring anyone he liked to dinner on Wednesday.) So long as Bosie could be dismissed as too eccentric and vindictive to be taken seriously Ross had no intention of walking into the trap which had been fatal to Oscar twenty years earlier and fatal to Bosie last year. It was very uncomfortable to have Bosie going for him in this way, but if it got no worse he would ignore it. Besides, as Sir George Lewis told him, Bosie was in trouble with Custance and with any luck would be committed to prison for a breach of his recognizances. Time enough then, when Bosie would be behind bars and unable to find justifying evidence, to bring an action for libel.

Bosie *was* in trouble with Custance. On the strength of that letter of what Bosie called 'remonstrance', Custance had gone with Lewis to the Recorder who had tried the previous case and applied for a Bench Warrant to call Bosie up "to show cause why he should not be com-mitted to prison" for a breach of his recognizances.

When Bosie received that summons he "saw in a flash" the dilemma he was in. Lewis was the solicitor for both Custance and Ross. If Custance succeeded in gaoling Bosie, Ross would immediately apply for a writ against him for criminal libel. Locked away, he would be unable to obtain the evidence with which to justify it.

He did the only possible thing in the circumstances. On March 4 he crossed to Boulogne and settled at 102 rue de Boston.

5

At that both his opponents must have rejoiced. Custance had succeeded in getting Bosie out of the country, which to a man of his background and point of view was the same as getting him into gaol, while Ross, on Lewis's advice, felt safe to issue two writs, one charging Crosland and Bosie with conspiracy, the other, of which Bosie in Boulogne knew nothing, charging Bosie with criminally libelling Ross. These, in combination with Custance's Bench Warrant, would keep Bosie out of the country, he hoped.

Crosland was arrested as he was entering his rooms in Mitcham Street late at night on Sunday, April 12. An inspector was invited in and Crosland was shown the warrant. "Why don't you arrest Robert Ross?" he asked. "Lord Alfred Douglas and I have been to Scotland Yard. We gave you all the information about what these fellows did to the boy Garratt. We have been to great expense and trouble to do all that the police ought to have done."

Next morning he was charged at Marylebone.

For that he, being concerned with Lord Alfred Bruce Douglas, did, on September 17, 1913, and on divers other dates between September 17 and February 14 last, unlawfully and wickedly conspire, combine, confederate, and agree together, and with divers other persons unknown, unlawfully, falsely, and corruptly to charge Robert Baldwin Ross with having committed certain acts with one Charles Garratt.

One of Bosie's cousins (Sholto Johnstone Douglas) went bail for Crosland and Bosie's mother undertook to pay his costs and expenses. He prepared for the case with gusto. When Bosie heard of the arrest he wanted to take the chance of being imprisoned by Custance and join Crosland in the dock, but this was the Yorkshireman's scene and he did not mean to be deprived of one glorious exhibitionistic moment of it.

Bosie wrote every day. He had supported Wilde—

So it would be a poor thing if I couldn't do as much and more for you, who are the only real friend I have ever had and especially as you are in all this through me. In view of all you say, I shall not return to England until I can do so with safety. As long as you are clear about my motives and my absolute loyalty to you I don't care a row of pins what anyone else says on that point.

He also wrote to the presiding magistrate offering to return to England

and place himself at the disposal of the court, if he could be assured that no steps would be taken against him in the Custance case until the present case was finished. No such assurance could be given and the trial of Crosland began.

Comyns Carr appeared for Crosland, Ernest Wild, K.C. (later Sir Ernest Wild, Recorder of London) for Ross.

As soon as Garratt appeared it was evident that he had found it more profitable to change his mind. He calmly stated that he had never seen Ross in his life. Well rehearsed, he denied, even when Ross appeared, that he knew him. He described interviews with Millard, Crosland and Douglas, and various occasions on which he had made various statements. Ross and Millard gave evidence and Crosland was committed for trial.

There were several adjournments and the trial did not take place until June 28th, 1914. It was before Mr. Justice Avory and this time Wild had been joined by F. E. Smith, while Comyns Carr had given place to Cecil Hayes.

Throughout the protracted hearings, both in the Magistrate's court and at the Old Bailey, Crosland's John Blunt attitude, his anxiety to give as good as he got, his evident if misplaced sincerity, his belief (which by this time wholly consumed him) that he was a brave man fighting fearful odds for the sake of decency and public morality, were immensely telling and the press as well as the jury appreciated him. He had very little evidence[*] to support him but he shouted and played the wronged man to great effect.

Wild, in the lower court, made reference to an occasion on which Crosland had taken Garratt out to dinner. "I won't have you talk to me like that!" snapped Crosland. "I'm as good as a master of sneers and jeers as you are. Keep a civil tongue in your head." Also in the lower court he refused to be calmed by his own Counsel and said loudly: "I have been ten years trying to bring this thing about and I am here now"—he banged the witness-box—"very happy and comfortable!"

At one point, when it had been shown that Garratt was lying, Crosland was asked whether, if he had known the boy was such a liar, he would have put the same confidence in him. "Well, obviously I

---

[*] Twelve years later Millard, an ageing bookseller living on a legacy from Ross and first editions of Wilde, told me that although Garratt had been with him (Millard) and he had met Ross often, Ross had nothing to do with that boy sexually.

would not, but if he is such a liar, why is he a witness for the prosecution against me now?" The Magistrate said he thought that was very material.

Against F. E. Smith he was even more antagonistic and in his own bulldozer way effective.

"Have you taken it upon you to regulate the private life of Mr. Ross?" Smith asked him.

"Oh no. I don't object to Ross making a pig of himself; what I mind is his making a sty of the world."

When Crosland said he did not want the jury confused, Smith told him: "The jury can probably take care of themselves."

"I dare say they can," said Crosland, "but I want them to take care of me."

This produced loud and prolonged laughter in which the Judge joined, a happy augury. Smith allowed himself a small sneer at his opposing counsel which did not help him. "There is £2,000's worth of counsel against a poor man," said Crosland, to which Smith replied— "You can get Mr. Cecil Hayes."

Crosland was questioned about his taking Mrs. Garratt to a pub.

"Have you ever stood a drink to a charwoman before?"

"I'm afraid I haven't," Crosland said, "but you don't bribe people to commit perjury with a drink. Lewis and Lewis may, but I don't."

Smith appealed to the Judge to know if this was a proper answer.

"I think you provoked the witness by your line of cross-examination. You invited the witness to argue."

"I shall not appeal to your Lordship again," said Smith sulkily.

This parry and thrust between Judge and Counsel was continued, to Crosland's advantage, in Smith's final speech to the jury and Avory's summing-up. The Judge, said Smith, held the scales of justice in these cases evenly between the two parties, but, from some observations which his Lordship had let fall during the hearing, he (Smith) drew the inference that in some parts of the case the Judge had adopted views which were not the views that he (Smith) had put before him. "But," Smith went on, "as the Judge will be the first to tell you, the issue in this case is purely an issue of fact, and of the facts you and you alone are the judges. The law for well-considered reasons, has, in these cases, removed the final and ultimate adjudication from the Bench to the jury-box; and, whatever may be said to you, you must give the final decision on the facts."

"In this case," retorted Avory in his summing-up, "Mr. Smith has undoubtedly overlooked the important fact that we are not here for the purpose merely of determining as to the character of Mr. Ross. We are not here for the purpose of admiring the advocacy of Mr. Ross's learned counsel. And we certainly are not here, you are not here, to convict anybody merely because Mr. Ross has had the good fortune to have secured the services of one of the most eminent and eloquent of counsel at the English Bar.''

After that, Crosland was acquitted, and Bosie gleefully wrote one of his satires, *The Rhyme of F Double E*, which was published by the faithful Sorley Brown in Galashiels.

6

Bosie's greatest mistake in these hostilities was to bring his action for libel against Ransome. Ross now made his. Even after the acquittal of Crosland, which was a disaster for him, he did not take steps to withdraw his charge of criminal libel against Bosie. In fact the whole story persuades one now that anyone's greatest mistake is to resort to the law over anything at any time.

Ross's reasons may be guessed. The Crosland case had produced nothing against him and had not been fought directly on his character but on whether or not Crosland *believed* Garratt. Then the supporting evidence had been thin and he may have thought no more was forthcoming. Again, he may have considered—and perhaps with reason—that his only way of stopping Bosie's attacks was to get him to prison. Or he may have supposed that in view of Custance's Bench warrant Bosie would never return to face his, Ross's charge. Or perhaps he was encouraged by Lewis and other supporters. Or stung by *The Rhyme of F Double E*. At all events the writ remained and although Bosie was still unaware of it a warrant was in existence for his arrest.

Bosie's acquittal on the conspiracy charge was automatic when Crosland won so that, so far as he knew, all he had to face in England was Custance's Bench Warrant. He was considering whether he should return to London when war broke out.

The first troops to land in Boulogne were the Argyll and Sutherland Highlanders and there is no reason to doubt Bosie's envy of them. He wrote to Kitchener, whom he knew, and though in that hectic month Kitchener found time to answer him, it was to say that in spite of his fluent French there was nothing for him at present. (It must be remembered that the Army was still thought of as a gentleman's profession, or, in the ranks, often a resort for those who had been in trouble, could not find work or hoped to elude their wives. The 'citizen army' of Kitchener was as yet unheard-of.)

Bosie had a characteristically crazy and romantic idea—he would join the French Foreign Legion, then unpictured in bad English novels and still considered a remote mysterious collection of beings like the prisoners on Devil's Island or the Mafia. He wrote to a soldier friend of his called Colonel "Taffy" Lewis who had reviewed military books for him on *The Academy* and had been an honorary member of the Foreign Legion mess when *The Times* war correspondent in Morocco. Lewis sent him a letter of introduction but warned him that he could never stand the conditions. Finally Bosie compromised by resolving to return to England to face the Recorder and Custance before joining in the war effort.

He wrote to the Recorder and, rather naïvely, asked for fair treatment in view of the frightful provocation he had received from his father-in-law who had smashed up his home and separated him from his wife. He also wrote to the police and told them the time of his arrival.

His own account of the next week or two is one of the best passages of prose he wrote and I propose to use his own words to tell the story. In his *Autobiography* he broke off all too often to argue and justify himself but this piece of narrative, racy, lucid and moving, is uninterrupted by polemics and gives a vivid picture of his actions and state of mind at the time.

Crossing the Channel, as I had done a hundred times before, always with a certain amount of holiday feeling, seemed now a dismal business. If I had known what was in store for me I would have been even more gloomy. As it was I had a black feeling of impending trouble. I spent the whole time of my crossing saying my rosary. When the boat got in, the captain, who knew what was to happen, politely asked me to go off first. A path was cleared for me, and I descended the landing stairs and was accosted by a nice-looking and smartly dressed detective in plain clothes. He carried my bag for me, and was most obliging. He said I could get my other luggage later on. I thought I was, of course, going to London, but he said I was to go to the Folkestone Police Court to be charged. I did not in the least understand what he meant, as I thought I was being arrested on the Recorder's "Bench Warrant". But he told me I was arrested on a warrant granted on a sworn information to Robert Ross. Even then I did not understand. I thought that this was the old warrant for conspiring with Crosland to bring a "false charge", and that my arrest, as far as Ross was concerned, was a mere formality, and that I would perhaps be brought up before a judge and formally acquitted and discharged.

The detective drove me in a cab to the police station. I was locked in a cell, and told that I would be formally charged when the detective in charge of my case came down from London, which would not be before at least two or three hours. I was given some tea and bread-and-butter and a piece of cake, and left alone.

After two or three hours of waiting in the cell the door opened, and another Scotland Yard man came in. He said: "I will now read you the warrant, and must warn you that anything you say may be used against you." He then read the warrant, in which I was charged with "Falsely and maliciously publishing a defamatory libel on and about Robert Ross". I replied, when he had finished: "All right. I shall plead justification. Every word I have published about Ross is true, and will be proved up to the hilt."

I felt for the moment rather exhilarated, as I always do when the issue is definitely joined in any kind of fight. I found the detective quite friendly. He had already collected my luggage, and we went off in a cab to the station, where he bought two first-class tickets to London. He then offered me a whisky-and-soda, which I was very glad to get. He would not allow me to pay for anything. On the way up to London he opened my dispatch box and extracted a number of my letters, most of which had not the slightest bearing on the case at issue. I did not get these back till months afterwards, and after making an application in open court before a magistrate, asking for an order for their return.

When we got to London I was taken to the police station, I think it was the Marylebone Road, but am not quite sure—at any rate it was the police court at that time presided over by Mr. Paul Taylor, before whom I appeared next morning. The police, as always, were exceedingly kind and friendly. They made me as comfortable as possible in the detention-room instead of locking me up in a cell. I was allowed to send out for dinner, and afterwards went to bed in the detention-room.

Next morning I was brought up before Mr. Paul Taylor. I was represented by a solicitor whose name for the moment I forget. He appeared for me only on this occasion. He was very competent, and I think it was Crosland who had sent him along on my behalf. George Lewis appeared for Ross, and read out various extracts from my printed pamphlets and written letters, on which he asked the magistrate to commit me for trial. The magistrate asked me if I wished to say anything and I said: "I plead justification." He said: "Very well; of course you know that you cannot do that in this court, and I commit you for trial at the next sessions at the Central Criminal Court." I then applied for bail, and the magistrate said: "Oh, certainly. One surety in £500." My cousin Sholto was in court ready to go bail for me. At this point George Lewis rose and said to the magistrate: "You cannot let him out on bail because there is a warrant against him from a superior court, issued by the Recorder, ordering him to come up for judgment in respect of charges of which he has been convicted in regard to another client of mine, for whom I also appear, Colonel Custance."

The magistrate then, with reluctance, and expressing his regret, declared that in that case it was not in his power to allow me out on bail, and I was sent off to Brixton Prison in a taxi. To this extent, therefore, Custance did at last succeed in getting me locked up, although it was only on remand, and for a few days.

When I got to the prison, and was shut up in a small cell on the ground floor, I must confess that my nerve failed. I suddenly realized for the first time that I really was right in the trap which George Lewis had laid for me. Here was I due to come up before the Recorder in a few days, certain, as I supposed, to be sent to prison by him, and thus placed in a position in which it would be utterly impossible to defend myself against Ross. So I took it I was in for six months from the Recorder, and perhaps twelve or eighteen more on the top of that for libelling Ross. I realized, not for the first or last time, that it is very dangerous to tell the truth in England. I felt that I was "done" and the worst part of it all was that I would never be able to prove that I had told the truth about Ross, and he would be vindicated and whitewashed, and be able once more to pose as the pure, noble and disinterested friend of Oscar Wilde, in contrast to my depraved self!

I went through about two hours of mortal agony, during which I called on God, and reproached Him for deserting me.

Though it was a very cold evening, and my cell was far from warm, the sweat actually streamed down my face. At last I looked round in utter despair, and saw a New Testament, the only book in my cell. I snatched it up, and opened it and read these words:

"And when Herod would have brought him forth, the same night Peter was sleeping between two soldiers, bound with two chains: and the keepers before the door kept the prison.

"And, behold, the angel of the Lord came upon him, and a light shined in the prison: and he smote Peter on the side, and raised him up, saying, Arise up quickly. And his chains fell off from his hands," etc.

This struck me then, and strikes me now, as being a supernatural answer to my cry of despair and dereliction. Directly I read the words confidence returned to me. I did not see how I was going to get out of prison and defeat the frightful combination of deadly enemies in front of me, but I felt convinced that I would somehow be saved.

I stayed five days in Brixton, and was then taken first to the police court and then on to the Old Bailey. To my great joy and consolation, Olive turned up, and accompanied me to the Old Bailey. We drove across London holding hands, under the benevolent eye of a warder. Olive accompanied me to the corridor on the first floor, outside the courts, and while we were there together her father and Admiral Sir Reginald Custance suddenly appeared before us. When they saw her with me they were livid with rage, and Sir Reginald rated my wife in a loud voice and quite in the good old quarter-deck and grand old English gentleman (all of the olden time) style, bless him!

However, further bitter disappointments were in store for them, for the good old Recorder (may his soul rest in peace!) merely pretended to be very angry, snorted quite a lot in the most approved style, and spoke to me 'with awful severity', exactly as if I were a little boy who had been caught stealing the jam. At the end of all this by-play, and after saying solemnly, 'The question is now, what is to be done with you?' he bound me over again with two sureties, to the disgust and indignation of the Custances and George Lewis.

I had already provided myself with two sureties, in anticipation of a possible miracle, my cousin Sholto and an Anglican parson, the Reverend James Mills, who came out of the void, evidently sent along by Providence, and offered in the kindest and most generous manner "to go bail for me to any amount". My counsel was Mr. now Sir Henry, Curtis Bennett, who did the apologizing to the Recorder and the court very gracefully, and, as it appears, evidently successfully. Thus the snare was broken and I was delivered quite as effectually as St. Peter was delivered by the angel. Really, from this moment I 'never looked back', except for one relapse which I shall presently describe. For although I was committed for trial, and had only about five weeks in which to get evidence against Ross, with the alternative of anything from six months' to two years' imprisonment, I felt perfectly confident.

Although I had been bound over with two sureties of £200 each, and although my two sureties were waiting to enter into their recognizances in court, I did not, after all, get out that night. Sir George Lewis somehow contrived that the police (that is to say, the detective in charge of the case) should refuse to accept my Anglican friend as a surety without "twenty-four hours' notice" for investigation. Mr. Mills offered to take the police to his bank and show them that his balance there was more than five times as much as the sum for which he had gone surety, but the detective refused, and said he must make inquiries at his domicile next day.

The effect of this was, of course, as was intended, that instead of being let out at once, as was the Recorder's intention, I was kept in custody as a convicted prisoner. My sentence was "to be bound over with two sureties, or in default of producing sureties, six months' imprisonment". So at seven o'clock that evening, after I had been shut up in a cell for several hours I was told that my sureties would not be available that night, and that in the meanwhile I was a convicted prisoner, with nominally six months to serve, and must go to Wormwood Scrubs. So off I went in the "Black Maria", with about a dozen other convicted prisoners, all of whom were handcuffed. I was exempted from this, in consideration of the fact that I was only "bound over", and due to go out next day. On the way to the prison we were allowed to smoke cigarettes and talk. We drove right down Piccadilly. It was a curious sensation to look out through the chinks of the cover of the sort of waggonette we occupied and see the clubs and restaurants and the people going out to dinner. This particular "Black Maria" was not a regular one, divided into cells, but I may say, with satisfaction, that I had then, and have since, been in a proper regulation "Black Maria".

When we got to Wormwood Scrubs the ceremony of "reception" took at least an hour and a half. All our clothes were taken away, and we were sent one by one into three or four bathrooms, which contained warm-water baths. When my turn came the reception officer, a delightful Irishman, full of jokes and good humour, and doing his best, in the most charitable way, to cheer everyone up, looked me over casually and said: "You needn't have a bath; you are quite clean." I was much upset, and said: "Oh, but please let me have a bath. I have been in Brixton for five days without one!" The officer (in prison the warders are always called officers) said: "Well of course you can have one if you like." So I got my bath and enjoyed the hot water, and was lying luxuriously in it when a prisoner in prison clothes, who was helping in the "reception", looked in and said: "Get out quick, kid; you are only allowed five minutes." He gave me a towel. After that I was inspected by the doctor. The same doctor was at the prison ten years later when I revisited the classic shades of Wormwood Scrubs—Dr. Watson, kindest and most considerate of men, who always had a kind word for me and lent me books (with the approval of the Catholic chaplain) when I was in hospital.

All this took much longer than one would suppose. We were also given cocoa and bread (quite uneatable and as hard as a brick,) and then conducted to our respective cells. I was put on the second and top floor of the sinister and forbidding-looking iron and steel house, smelling strongly of gas, with its rows and rows of numbered cells, to which I was destined. I was in the third or hard-labour division, and I must therefore, I imagine, have been in the same building where Oscar Wilde had been confined I thought of him as I "went to bed" (a plank bed and no mattress), and said to myself: "Poor Oscar, however did he manage to stand this for two years?" That was the first time I had had a comparatively soft thought about him since I read the "unpublished part" of *De Profundis*.

I slept like a log, in spite of plank bed and no mattress, being worn out, and was awakened by the ringing of the prison bell at five-thirty. I got up and dressed, putting on the ghastly prison clothes which had been served out to me the night before. I began to have a reaction and to feel frightened and wretched. What if there was some hitch about my sureties and I could not get out? My imagination began to work fantastically, suggesting that the whole thing was a trap, and that once in this prison, a mere number without a name, I was done for, and would be kept indefinitely.

The door was unlocked and left open. I heard the clanking of tins and pails. Two prisoners came along with a sort of tank on wheels and told me to empty my slops. A warder looked in and said something which I did not understand. The door was shut and locked. Then there was a long pause. I remained apathetically sitting on the little backless stool which was all there was in the way of a chair. Uneatable and evil-smelling food was handed in. I looked at it with disgust and put it as far away from me as possible. It was nearly dark; the only window, a small square, was so high up that I could reach it only by standing on my stool. I was faint with hunger, as I had had nothing to eat since breakfast the day before. I had been too agitated to eat my good lunch at the Old Bailey (cold chicken and bread), and owing to the fact that I had expected to get out before dinner-time I had not bothered about food. The bread and cocoa which had been offered me when I got into the "reception-room" I had not touched.

The door was again opened, and my untasted breakfast was removed by a prisoner, who eagerly took possession of my bread and stuffed it into his shirt. I sat on for some time in a dazed condition, hearing the noise of walking and tramping outside. Then a fierce-looking "officer" looked in and shouted angrily at me: "What are you doing here? Why haven't you made your bed? What do you think you are doing? You ought to be in the shed!" I looked at him with wide eyes and then burst into tears. I buried my face in my hands and sobbed. He came up to me in the kindest way and put his arm round my neck: "Here, sonny, this won't do—cheer up, no harm meant. I know it must be very hard on you, first day and all. You needn't go into the shed if you'd rather stay here."

His kindness made me cry all the more, and he tactfully went away and came back ten minutes later, and asked me how I felt. I said I felt all right now and would like to go to the shed, though I had no idea what "the shed" was. He showed me how to fold my blankets and lean my plank bed against the wall. He got a wet towel and wiped my face and dried it, making jokes all the time. May God reward him!

He then conducted me down two flights of iron stairs and out of the dreadful hall into the open air, and so to the shed, a large building, where about a hundred prisoners were working at sewing sacks and picking oakum. I was given some oakum to pick. Either before or after that, I forget which, I had an hours's "exercise", walking round and round a yard, with a hundred and fifty or so of other prisoners.

Then came more revolting food in my cell, the mere sight and smell of it making me sick. Ten years later I starved on it for seven weeks, losing nearly two stone of weight in the process. But at this time I merely looked at it and hoped someone would take it away soon. The editor of *The Tablet* (among others) declares, in contradiction to me, that the food in prisons is really excellent. Of course, never having been in prison, he is bound to know more about it than I do! Perhaps the editor of *The Tablet* likes lumps of stinking meat swimming in lukewarm kitchen grease. There is no accounting for taste. Personally, I do not fancy it, and when the time came I preferred, even starving as I was, not to eat it, and to live for seven weeks on crusts of bread and watery cocoa.

After "dinner" we went back to the "shed", and I picked more oakum. By this time I was in complete despair. I could not understand why my sureties had not come to take me out, and I made up my mind that something had gone wrong and that I was going to be kept in prison. Of course this was childish and unreasonable on my part; but in prison, especially at first, one is not reasonable, and is liable to all sorts of panics and nightmarish ideas. I sat in the shed for about two hours, and at last I heard my number called out—curiously, I forget the number. I jumped to my feet and went up to the officer who had just come into the shed and called my number. He said: "You are wanted by the Governor; come along with me." I said: "Is it my sureties?" He said: "I don't know anything about it. All I know is, you are to go to the Governor."

I followed him into one of the rooms leading into the reception office, where I had been the night before. My heart leapt up, for there was the Governor talking affably to dear old Sholto and my clerical friend and benefactor, who both smiled and shook hands with me.

I was immediately taken into the reception-room and relieved of my prison clothes, my own clothes, watch and money being given back to me. The only thing I had been allowed to keep was my rosary, which I was wearing round my neck.

When I was "clothed and in my right mind" I went back into the other room, and the Governor shook hands and said: "Well, good-bye; don't come back again"; and I went off with my two sureties. Sholto had to rush off somewhere, but Mr. Mills carried me off to a restaurant and fed me sumptuously. Curiously enough, I could hardly eat anything. On my way home to my mother's—she was then staying at Cliveden Place—I thought to myself: "I cannot risk going back to that hellish place." I made up my mind that I would come to terms with Ross, which of course would have been easy enough to do provided I would "climb down" and withdraw my charges.

This state of mind, which had been produced by one night and day in a real convict prison (as distinct from Brixton, a remand prison, where you keep your own clothes and can order in any food that you like to pay for), was of course exactly the state of mind which Sir George Lewis, on behalf of Ross, had wanted to produce in me. If I had been let out the day before, as the Recorder fully intended I should be, I would not have been able to imagine how dreadful it is to be in prison as a convicted prisoner. I had thought it bad enough in Brixton, but Brixton was heaven compared with Wormwood Scrubs.

However, one night's good sleep in a real bed, in a comfortable bedroom, followed by bacon and eggs and toast and marmalade for breakfast, altered all my feelings. I swore to myself that I would spend the rest of my life in an underground dungeon before I climbed down an inch to Ross and Lewis.

Then began the, at first apparently hopeless task of trying to get evidence against Ross. I saw Mr. Comyns Carr and made a statement to him. He said to me: "If you will undertake to go into the witness-box and say there what you have told me I will draw up a plea of justification; but I tell you frankly that unless you can get quite a lot of real evidence, apart from your own, you will not have a chance."

I got most of the evidence myself at the very last moment, as I have already stated. I tried clue after clue, and came up against blanks and brick walls, and people who were "not going to be mixed up" in the affair. At last I got word, sent anonymously, that there was a certain Mr. E., living at some number in a street near Campden Hill (I will not give his name, for obvious reasons), who was the respectable father of a young boy who had been a victim of Ross. When I got this information there were less than ten days to run before my trial was due to begin, and I had no evidence at all, although I had been to Guernsey in one fruitless quest, and to a dozen other places in vain. I went to the address given, and asked for Mr. E. No such name was known there. My heart sank into my boots. I turned away and looked down the street of at least a hundred and fifty houses. What was I to do? I prayed desperately to St. Anthony of Padua, for whom I have always had a special cult. I walked a few yards with my eyes on the ground. A voice said: "What do you want? Can I help you?" I looked up and saw a beautiful little boy about ten years old, smiling at me. I said: "I was looking for someone at a number which was given in this street, and now I am told there is no such name known there." He said: "Tell me the name and the number." I did so. He said: "All right. I know where it is. The numbers in the street have been changed."

He took my hand and led me right down to the other end of the street, stopped in front of a door and said: "You'll get what you want here." I let go his hand and went up to the door and rang the bell. I looked round and the little boy was gone. I looked down the street both ways and saw no sign of him. The door opened and I said: "Does Mr. E. live here?" "Yes, he does. Will you come in?" was the reply.

With great difficulty I got from Mr. E. confirmation of what I had been told. The difficulty was caused by the woman who had let me in, and who, I found, was his second wife, and stepmother of his two sons. She said: "Don't tell him anything. We don't want to have any scandal in the family." I appealed strongly to Mr. E. I said: "If you don't help me I shall be sent to prison. For God's sake, tell me." He said: "Very well. I can't refuse. The boy himself is dead. After what happened when he left home he went to South Africa and died there. His elder brother, who is a private in the —— Regiment, now at Goring, will tell you the whole story." He gave me the name and military address of the brother and I went out.

This is the story to which I have referred as being what I believe to be a supernatural experience. It did not strike me till long afterwards, when I got the evidence which proved to be perhaps the most damning of all the evidence I got against Ross, that the whole thing was mysterious and wonderful. How should a little boy of ten years old know about the change of numbers, and where Mr. E. lived? Why should a child of that age go up to a man he had never seen before and say: "What do you want? Can I help you?" I firmly believe that the child was an angel, or, at any rate, that he was supernaturally moved to help me. He was most beautiful little boy, and he had an angelic face and smile. And how did he disappear in the space of time, a few seconds, between when I let go of his hand and when I looked round again? Perhaps Dr. Barnes or Dean Inge will oblige with an explanation which will satisfy believers in the Darwinian hypothesis and the impossibility of miracles.

Even after this I had a desperate difficulty in getting the evidence. When I got to Goring I was told that the particular unit in which the man I wanted was serving had been transferred to a town in Norfolk. I went there, and went to the headquarters of the colonel of the regiment. It was a house belonging to a man I knew, Charlie Tracey, now Lord Sudeley, but he was not there himself. The colonel was odious. When he heard what I wanted he was insolent and rude, and declared that he would not let me see the man I wanted. I had to have a regular fight with him. In the presence of his adjutant and several other officers I told him that unless he produced the man, for whom I had a subpoena, I would apply to the judge for a "Bench Warrant", and that I would publicly expose him as a man who was trying to shield Ross and what he stood for. He grew red in the face and stormed out of the room, followed by his officers. The door was slammed and I was left alone.

After about five minutes a very charming young subaltern, very much a gentleman, which was not always the case in those days of "temporary gentlemen", came in and told me that the colonel had sent him to say that he had sent for the man, and that I might interview him in his (the subaltern's) presence. A few minutes later the young man arrived. The subaltern told him what I wanted, and said: "You are not obliged to answer Lord Alfred's questions unless you wish." The man was reluctant at first, but I appealed to him and said: "You don't want to shield the man who ruined your brother, and is, indirectly, responsible for his death, do you?" I also told him that unless he told me the truth I would be sent to prison for denouncing Ross. He thereupon gave me the whole story, which was damning for Ross. I wrote down what he said, and he read it through and signed it, after being told by the subaltern that he need not do so unless he wished. I gave him a subpoena and three pounds, and told him he would have to be at the Old Bailey on the date fixed for my trial, early in December. This was a great triumph, and bucked me up considerably.

It never rains but it pours. After that, evidence began to flow in. I got the names of half-a-dozen people who could give me valuable information from a man I went to see at Yarmouth. In the end I had thirteen or fourteen witnesses. They were all respectable people. One was a clergyman of the Church of England, and I had not one single case of what is called "tainted evidence".

7

Comparison is irresistible between Wilde's action for libel against Queensberry in 1895 and Ross's action for the same offence against Queensberry's son nearly twenty years later.

Both were deliberately provoked and both should have been avoided at all costs. Both were against dangerous members of the Douglas family who believed they were in the right. Both the defendants were actuated by hostility, one with only a hypocritical cause, the other with a very real one. Both the plaintiffs were homosexual and therefore in an English court vulnerable.

But there was a very different atmosphere in the court in November, 1914. The devoted efforts of Ross himself had made Wilde remembered more kindly, and with Wilde the man on whom his mantle had fallen. Ross was popular and had the support of a great number of people who, though not in the least homosexual, wanted to show their loathing for the abominable persecution of Wilde and the Blackmailer's Charter of 1885 which had made it possible. Though no one came forward at Wilde's trial to give evidence of his character, there were now in court H. G. Wells, and Edmund Gosse to give evidence for Ross. It was perfectly well known that Ross was homosexual and that the defence would call witnesses to prove it, as Queensberry's defence had been prepared to do, but through Wilde's own martyrdom a saner spirit was abroad and there was a general determination that Ross should not suffer as his master had.

Bosie, on the other hand, as a public figure was almost universally unpopular and even those who had supported Crosland a mere intolerant homosexual-hater, had no sympathy with a man who had been one of the family and now came forward in opposition to a member of it. Certainly his rôle was not an admirable one and few troubled to see what had caused him to assume it. It was easy to forget by what underhand means Ross had previously provoked and then defeated him. It was easier to remember Ross's gentle charm, his encouragement to young writers, his patient work for the Wilde estate in evidence of which he would call Captain Cyril Holland, Wilde's eldest son, who would say that Ross had been a second father to him.

Intelligent opinion, in other words, had come round to at least an attitude of greater tolerance towards homosexuality and with it sympathy for Ross who was seen as an unwilling prosecutor dragged into court by Bosie's jealousy, vindictiveness or fanatical bigotry. He was actually dragged there by Bosie's thirst for vengeance, no more laudable a motive but perhaps a more understandable and virile one.

So to this it had come after all Ross's secretive chicanery with *De Profundis* and the letters, and after all Bosie's implacable vengefulness, that the two men who had loved Wilde faced each other across the court in which Wilde had been sentenced, and knew that their fight was a life-and-death struggle. One or the other would almost certainly go to prison after it. If Ross won Bosie would get two years for criminal libel, for his letter accused Ross not only of being a sodomite but a blackmailer. If Bosie won Ross would be arrested, as Wilde had been, within twenty-four hours and his friendship with the Asquiths could not save him.

Perhaps in all the court Bosie and Ross were the only two who had been present in 1895 when Wilde's case for libel was heard, the only two who realized the fearful precedent. But for neither of them was there any turning back now.

The trial which began on November 19, 1914 was before Mr. Justice Coleridge. With the echoes of the Battle of Ypres still in the air and the country first realizing that it was in for a war of unprecedented ghastliness, it was scarcely likely that this 'unpleasant' libel action could be given much attention in the press, but the blind eye turned on it was caused by something more than the claims of war news. The case could not be "kept out of the papers" altogether, but on the plea of patriotism, and to "conceal British decadence", a good deal was done and even *The Times* reported it scantily. No details were given of Ross in the box or of the various witnesses called by the defence though their evidence was as lurid as that against Wilde.

Perhaps remembering his misfortunes against Crosland, Ross had not got F. E. Smith this time but depended on Sir Ernest Wild. Bosie had Comyns Carr.

The case followed much the same order as the Queensberry case and Ross, like Wilde, went into the box to answer questions about the witnesses who would presently be called. But though he had none of Wilde's arrogance and unfortunate brilliance he had a more difficult task for the evidence which Bosie's witnesses would give would not be tainted and Ross was unsure of himself. There was no 'love that dare not speak its name' to be rhetorical about but a dreary succession of bits of writing and letters which showed poor Ross to be homosexual and could not be explained away. He did not show the indignation that the Judge would have liked. "I waited and waited", said the Judge in his summing up,

but I waited in vain for any moral expression of indignation or horror at the practice of sodomitical vices . . . and, indeed, to be frank with Mr. Ross, when he was asked whether he did not constantly introduce these leprous things into ordinary articles in the magazine, all he could say was that he could not remember. It certainly was not so emphatic a denial as you could expect from a man with no leprosy upon him. Although we have a large literature from Mr. Ross, letters wholesale dealing with all kinds of subjects, yet I do not recollect, and I have carefully been keeping my mind open on the matter, although there are constant allusions to this kind of practice, I don't recollect that there is any copy or extract which has been produced indicating that he disapproved or that he views this kind of vice with disgust. Then that is the man, I would say that is the attitude of the man and his mind towards this kind of perversion of sex.

On the young men to be called Ross was equivocal and hesitant. Asked if he had been to a party on New Year's Eve three years ago at which twenty or thirty men had danced together he rather lamely denied it. On the whole he made such a bad impression that the foreman of the jury, after his evidence, wanted to stop the case and dismiss Ross's action. He had eight of his jurymen with him but one stated flatly that he would in no circumstances find against Ross and the case went on.

Bosie called fourteen witnesses with definite accusations, "with names, dates, etc.", and the effect was devastating. There was not much laughter in Court. A boy named Smith, a member of a dramatic society connected with a London church who testified to his association with Ross admitted "painting and powdering" his face. Asked by Ross's Counsel if this was not quite usual for actors, he said: "Hardly, when they come to church."

The young soldier, who at one point broke down as he recalled his dead brother, told how this brother had disappeared from home when he was sixteen years old and how he and his father heard that Ross was responsible. He described his going to a bar in Copthall Avenue which Ross was known to frequent and asking Ross what he had done with his brother. He said Ross offered him money which he refused then threatened to accuse him of blackmail so that in fear he made off. Comyns Carr asked him if he would recognize the man he had seen in the bar in Copthall Avenue and he said he was not sure, for it had happened some years ago. He was told to look round the Court and after some moments of breathless silence said there was a gentleman at the solicitors' table who, he thought, resembled him. Ross was asked to stand up and he said: "That is the man." Had he been a Latinist and punster he might have made it *Ecce Homo*. The incident was very telling and when a retired police inspector who had volunteered his evidence (his name was West) stated that he had been twenty-five years in the police, had spent fifteen of them in the West End and had known Ross during that time as an associate of "sodomites" and "male prostitutes" the case was virtually decided. Indeed as Montgomery Hyde said,

In the light of the evidence given at this trial it must be admitted that Ross . . . was extremely fortunate in not being prosecuted himself on similar charges to Wilde.

Every attempt was made to discredit Bosie, and those old letters were brought up again. Moreover, because George Lewis was Ross's solicitor all the Custance affair was re-told but to no very great effect. H. G. Wells was asked whether he advocated free love and Edmund Gosse who had known Ross since 1890 gave evidence which was virtually evidence of character.

Wild in his last address for Ross rather dangerously suggested that *anyhow* Ross had not been proved a blackmailer though it was part of the libel. Bosie in the witness-box had maintained that there was such a thing as moral blackmail and that a man who kept old letters of his friends and, after using threats, brought them out against them twenty years after, was as much a blackmailer as one who demanded money and the Judge in his summing up was sympathetic to this view.

The jury was out for three hours and failed to agree. They were sent back and failed again so that the case was adjourned. The foreman and eight members of the jury awaited Bosie outside the Court and told him that they were unanimous but that one man had from the beginning made it clear that he would not agree to a verdict which inculpated Ross. In a letter to Sorley Brown, which must not be treated without reserve, Bosie maintained that he and his solicitor saw George Lewis go up to this man after the case and walk away with him, recognizing him presumably, as the one juryman who had *not* waited with the foreman.

It did not matter, in fact it benefited Bosie in that his costs were paid as they might not otherwise have been. For before the case was due to re-open Ross indicated that he wished to enter a plea of *nolle prosequi*. The case had followed altogether too closely the lines of Oscar's and he did not mean the unfortunate precedent to go farther. Bosie instructed his solicitors, Carter and Bell, to resist this and insist on his right to be tried again so that his plea of justification might be openly established. Forrest Fulton, junior Counsel for Ross, pointed out to Bell, Bosie's solicitor, that a *nolle prosequi*, which meant that Bosie would be acquitted and discharged, and his plea of justification remain on the file at the Old Bailey, was virtually an acknowledgment of guilt by the plaintiff. Only when Wild and Comyns Carr had met and Wild had agreed that Ross would pay Bosie's costs and out-of-pocket expenses (about £600) was the *nolle prosequi* entered and signed by the Attorney General, then Sir John Simon.

"If I could have afforded it," wrote Bosie implacably to Sorley Brown, "I would have refused to make any terms at all . . . But I am absolutely ruined by all this and I could not afford to lose the certainty of making sure of my costs."

It gave Ross, he added, "a sort of hole to wriggle out of" and although the Treasury sent for the shorthand notes of the case, no prosecution of Ross followed. He had to resign his post as 'assessor of picture valuations to the Board of Trade' and retire from what public life he had, but after two or three years was appointed a trustee of the National Gallery.

In the meantime his friends rallied to him nobly and everything was done to re-assure him. A testimonial was prepared by Edmund Gosse and signed by some three hundred well-wishers, many of them distinguished people. This was a somewhat farcical affair. If Gosse had stated frankly its object, to show that people were willing to stand by Ross after an exposure similar to that suffered by Wilde, or if he had even let the testimonial be offered to Ross, as a public dinner had been seven years earlier, for his work as Wilde's executor, one could respect his generosity. But the testimonial spoke of Ross's work as a Man of Letters and this was really too much. It ran:

To Robert Ross

We, whose names are set down below, claim to be counted among your friends, or at least your admirers. We desire in the first place to state publicly our recognition of your services to Art and Literature. You have long been distinguished for the justice and courage of your writings, and you have illuminated the expression of your views with humour and resource. Your work as a Man of Letters, however, is but a small part of the useful energy which you have shown in many directions. You have been conspicuous for the generosity with which you have put yourself at the disposal of all who claimed your sympathy or your help. You have been one of the earliest amongst us to observe new talent and one of the most zealous to encourage it. By these qualities you have earned what we desire to record, our esteem and regard for one who has proved a brave, loyal, and devoted friend.

Bosie selected these to record as signatories: Mr. and Mrs. Asquith, the Earl of Plymouth, Sir Coleridge Kennard, Mr. Agg Gardner, M.P., Mr. More Adey, Mr. Frank Hird, Mr. Bernard Shaw, Mr. and Mrs. Emil Mond, Mr. Schiff, Mr. Schiller, K.C., Miss Schuster, Sir Isidore Spielmann, Mr. Strauss, Sir George Lewis, Lady Lewis (née Marie Hirsch of Mannheim), Mr. Charles Rothenstein, Mr. Heinemann, Mr. William Rothenstein, Mr. Gutenkunst, Mr. Robert Trevelyan, Mr. Arthur Ponsonby, M.P., Mr. Phillip Morrell, M.P., Mr. G. Lowes Dickinson, Mr. J. L. Garvin, Mrs. Leverson, Mrs. Charles Hunter, Lady Ottoline Morrell, Mrs. Carew, Mrs. Allbusen, Miss Lawrence Alma Tadema, Mr. H. G. Wells, Mr. Methuen, Mr. Robert Harborough Sherard, and the Bishop of Birmingham.

The only paper which would print a protest from Bosie was *The Globe* under Charles Palmer, and a few months later this paper was officially suppressed for a fortnight until a new editor had been appointed.

Bosie wrote another, and a far more cutting satire which was again published by Sorley Brown.

Bernard Shaw, who kept his head admirably throughout the whole dissension wrote to Bosie in 1931:

Ross did not get his testimonial for nothing. Only a great deal of good nature on his part could have won over that distinguished and very normal list of names to give public support to a man who began with so very obvious a mark of the beast on him.

It is good to find that things had changed a little since the failure of Wilde's action against Queensberry and that in 1914 a man proved homosexual by no means became an outcast. But Ross never recovered his poise. He was ill for long periods and four years after the case, on October 5, 1918, at the age of forty-nine he died of heart-failure. He was found in his rooms in Georgian House, Bury Street where he had died in his sleep. It was, Sorley Brown points out,[*] only a month or two after poor Chris Millard had been sent to prison again for a homosexual offence.

Ross left many friends, some of them still living, who spoke of him as a genial, intelligent, well-meaning man, a friend to young poets and an honest lover of art and literature. John Lane said he was the most lovable, the most generous, the most stimulating and the most suggestive man he had ever known, and his was only one of many tributes.

[*] In *The Life and Genius of T. W. H. Crosland* (1928).

The pity of it is that the internecine war between Ross and Bosie, like all wars, could have been avoided and there were several occasions on which peace could have been made on terms that would have offended neither of them. "In the early days I was very fond of Ross, and it is difficult for me to realize, even now, that he was the same man who afterwards treated me in so cruel and abominable a fashion", wrote Bosie fifteen years after Ross's death. If Ross had only been honest about *De Profundis*, if Bosie had only understood all that Ross had in his life was Oscar and the memory of Oscar, if Ross had laughed at Bosie's tantrums when they first quarrelled over *The Academy* and Bosie wrote that letter of his, if Bosie had ignored Ransome's book . . the possibilities were endless. But the two men fought and their fighting brought to each of them only anguish and embitterment. By it Bosie made himself detestable to all who loved Ross and Ross ruined himself and saddened his last years, so that in July 1918 Charles Rickett wrote:—

It [the Wilde trial] has been a constant burden to R. Ross, the heroic self-constituted literary executor of Wilde, the man in fact who has helped to negative the iniquitous consequences of the verdict. To this day he is subject to persecution from ignoble quarters, a little uncertain in mental and bodily health, as a consequence an old man before his time.

Nothing was gained by either of them.

CHAPTER XIII

Wartime

I

FROM the moment he entered that *nolle prosequi* Ross was unable to defend himself against any attack Bosie might make. To have allowed to be established Bosie's plea of justification for calling him a sodomite and blackmailer meant that there was no insult or accusation which Bosie could not publicly and with impunity hurl at him. But Bosie behaved better in victory than in defeat and there were no more defamatory letters sent round to people in public life.

True, when the testimonial to Ross was organized he wrote his satire *The Rossiad* but this was a merry piece in the eighteenth century tradition of pamphleteering and derided Edmund Gosse almost as much as its nominal victim. True, he sent a quatrain to the Reform Club which, after the committee had debated the matter, allowed Ross to remain a member. It ended——

> Is the Reform reforming Robert Ross
> Or Robert Ross reforming the Reform?

But these, for him, were mild *jeux d'esprit* and he did no more to kick the unfortunate man when he was down.

What he did was to plan a book which would tell the whole story. *Oscar Wilde and Myself* had been written and published before Ross's action had failed, and Ross had been able to obtain an injunction to prevent Bosie quoting *De Profundis* and other letters, and to prevail on the publishers to insist on certain modifications. This time Ross was not in a position to interfere and Bosie believed he could put his case in his own terms.

He found a publisher who advanced him £200, of which he at once paid £50 to Crosland for his promised assistance in writing the book, which was to be called *The Wilde Myth*. But Bosie and Crosland were not on the same good terms as before, which in the outcome was perhaps fortunate.

When Bosie was preparing his defence for the Ross case he asked Crosland to give evidence on his behalf. Crosland, who was finding himself unpopular in certain quarters in Fleet Street since his acquittal earlier in the year, refused. He said his prospects and his wife would suffer. Bosie wrote reminding him that *he* could have pleaded his material prospects and his wife when he gave evidence for Crosland against Manners-Sutton. "I don't wish to argue with you or even quarrel with you but I shall never feel the same about you."

Crosland, when the case approached, offered to give evidence if he were paid £50. "I told him to go to hell", Bosie wrote to Sorley Brown. But when the Ross testimonial was presented Crosland had a little paper called *The Antidote* in which the occasion could be noticed with Crosland's heavy thunder and Bosie's spitfire invective. The fourth number was devoted to the testimonial, Crosland bumbling that "it is just as important to civilization that literary England should be cleansed of sex-mongers and pedlars of perversity as that Flanders should be cleared of Germans". Bosie had staked Crosland to this number but afterwards found that Crosland had not paid the printer's bill and there was the usual row, with Crosland sending a solicitor's letter and Bosie calling him Ancient Pistol. Neither let such mild thunder deter him when Bosie wanted Crosland's assistance for *The Wilde Myth* and Crosland pocketed his £50.

There, however, the matter stopped. Crosland wrote nothing and gave no assistance and Bosie settled down to write the book himself. He took eighteen months to do it and towards the end of 1916 delivered the manuscript of eighty thousand words to his publisher who had it set up in type.

Years later I read the book in proof—for it was never published. Unfortunately, it is more than thirty years since I did so and I can remember little of it except that it was written in much the same spirit as *Oscar Wilde and Myself* though in very different prose. It was in fact Bosie's rendering rather than Crosland's, but it went over the same ground with the same arguments and it would have done nothing but harm to Bosie if it had been published for once again it overstated his case and was full of noisy self-justification.

The publisher who had commissioned it refused it and Bosie took it to Martin Secker. He writes about it now:

The Wilde Myth was never published. The publisher who commissioned the book wisely decided not to proceed, and Bosie brought me the proofs in the hopes that I would publish it. It was, as you say, *O.W. & Myself* over again, with a great deal of diatribe about Ross.

Several copies of it are in existence. Bosie wrote to me in 1927 that he had sold the manuscript to Foyle's, and later the American purchaser of it wanted to publish it. Bosie refused but it would have been better destroyed.

Crosland's failing him in this was not forgiven for several years and their quarrel was celebrated by one of Bosie's most telling sonnets of invective: "You were a brute and more than half a knave." They came together again in 1920 when Bosie was once more an editor and Crosland could gain some advantage from reconciliation. It is worth noticing that these years, during which Crosland's influence was in eclipse, were free from litigation.

2

Bosie made another attempt to join the Army in some useful capacity. He was now forty-five and retorted tartly to his wife when she suggested, obviously at her father's instigation, that as a last resort he could join the ranks as other poets had done. In all the circumstances his indignation was understandable and the letter he wrote explaining why it was impossible for him to follow her suggestion is reasonable and convincing.

Besides, he had his own wars. Like one of those early kings who had to turn his attention first to the Scots, then the French, while settling an armed revolt at home, Bosie felt free now for a full-scale attack on Custance. Ross was driven back to his fastness in Half Moon Street which for a year or two after the case he scarcely left. Bosie's old ally Crosland was out of action, but for a new offensive against Custance Bosie now had in Olive the auxiliary he had always needed. On June 30, 1915, he applied to the Chancery Court for the full custody of Raymond and Olive joined him in the application.

It was pointed out by Comyns Carr that when the original order had been made two years ago Lady Alfred Douglas had been a respondent with Colonel Custance. She was now reconciled with her husband and joined him in asking for full custody.

On these facts it would seem to be a clear-cut issue. Father and mother wanted their son from grandfather. But P. O. Lawrence, K.C., for Custance read a number of Bosie's more violent letters, including the one in which he explained to Olive his reasons for not enlisting. War fever was raging—conscription had not been introduced and hysterical people walked around with packets of white feathers and talked about 'slackers'. Though Bosie by reason of his age and character was utterly unsuitable for, if not incapable of service in the ranks, this letter must have influenced Mr. Justice Eve who was also deeply shocked by the fact that Raymond's photograph had appeared in "a work dealing with Oscar Wilde" (*Oscar Wilde and Myself*.) He expressed some sympathy with Bosie and Olive but said that he needed strong reasons for varying the order made two years ago and dismissed the application with costs. What stronger reasons there could be than a father and mother wanting their own child it is hard to imagine. Two and a half weeks later he refused another application for a variation of the order, this time from Lady Queensberry.

Bosie was furious and in this he deserves every sympathy. If Bosie and Olive had been given the custody of their son they would certainly have lived together again and Olive's gentle influence with Bosie would have saved him, as it had done before, from his more reckless blunders.

Bosie's reactions to Mr. Justice Eve's decision were twofold. He wrote his satire, *Eve and the Serpent*, and took Raymond to Scotland, out of the jurisdiction of the Chancery Court. They went to Fort Augustus, at the southern tip of Loch Ness, where Olive was to join them as soon as they could move into a house which Bosie found there.

The Rt. Reverend Sir David Hunter-Blair was Abbot of the Benedictine Monastery of Fort Augustus. He had been a friend of Wilde's at Magdalen and figures as "Dunsky", the name of his Galloway home, in many of Wilde's early letters. They visited Rome together and when in 1875 Hunter-Blair became a Catholic he almost succeeded in taking Wilde with him. He was ordained priest in 1886 and was Abbot of St. Augustus from 1913 to 1917. He was a remarkable man and greatly loved.

Bosie put Raymond in his care to be educated by the monks. He then wrote a defiant letter to Justice Eve telling him exactly what he had done. He had no intention, he said, of sending his son to Custance and he and Raymond would stay indefinitely in Scotland, where the English Chancery Courts had no jurisdiction.

Custance, however, rose to this. He first got in touch with Raymond, who was a charming and affectionate little boy, torn between his grandfather, his mother and his father. How the grandfather and grandson corresponded or what was said in the letters is unknown but one may guess that Custance, who probably believed that Raymond in a monastery was in danger of being walled-up at any moment, played on the boy's natural love of adventure to induce him to escape in a motor-car to England. Raymond was to go fishing in the loch by himself and a private detective would come for him. The little boy's life had been so full of alarms and excursions and his elders so unaccountable that this seemed nothing very strange or new and he agreed. So one afternoon Raymond disappeared and Bosie and the monks were distracted, thinking he had been drowned in the loch. Not until two days later did Bosie receive a telegram from Olive saying that Raymond was safely back at Weston Old Hall.

He at once went to the police and applied for a warrant for Custance for kidnapping his son and was referred to the Lord Advocate, an official in Edinburgh who corresponds more or less to the English Public Prosecutor. The Lord Advocate, a Mr. Munro-Ferguson, was, says Bosie meaningly, a 'friend of the Asquiths', and refused a warrant.

But Custance also failed in another of his attempts to get Bosie locked up. He implored Justice Eve to commit Bosie for contempt of court, but that wily and compromising old arbiter refused to do anything of the sort. Bosie was informed that the arrangement by which Raymond would spend two-fifths of his holidays with his father and the rest with Custance would be continued. Eve then handed over the case, with some relief, one imagines, to Justice Peterson.

Bosie who had now discovered that the plot by which Raymond was kidnapped was carried out with the boy's knowledge and consent, washed his hands of the whole affair and did not see his son for eight years.

I was at that time intensely devoted to my son. His loss and the horrible circumstances of it, completed my sense of the cruelty and injustice of the world. I gave up all idea of happiness in this life and clung to Catholicism as my only consolation.

3

"A period of two years then elapsed", said Bosie, unconscious of irony, "in which very little happened." But memorable happenings for Bosie differed from the common conception of the term and his life was not wholly uneventful by less stirring standards than his own.

He lived with his mother first at St. Aubyns, Hove, and then in a house she had taken near Lewes. While they were at Hove Bosie's nephew Bruce, the son of his younger brother Sholto, was killed in action—a Second Lieutenant not quite eighteen years old. Bruce was Lady Queensberry's favourite grandson and had been brought up by her.

On the day after the news was received Sorley Brown, an officer in the K.O.S.B., was due to stay for a few days of his leave and characteristically Bosie and his mother concealed their grief from the young man. Brown wrote for a newspaper published in Galashiels, *The Border Standard*, which he later acquired. Bosie took young Brown to London and introduced him to Crosland and the three went to the Café Royal.

Lady Queensberry and Bosie moved to a house called Shelley's Folly which belonged to Lord Monk Bretton. It was three miles from Lewes and was the favourite among Bosie's later homes.

His reading towards the end of his life was almost exclusively of two kinds, Shakespeare and Shakespearean commentators on the one hand and the lives and writings of the Saints on the other. At this time he was reading St. Augustine, St. Teresa and St. Catherine of Siena besides the whole of the *Summa Theologica* of St. Thomas Aquinas. He wrote his two satires, *The Rossiad* (which Sorley Brown published during the lifetime of Ross) and *Eve and the Serpent*, but apart from these scathing and unworthily directed lampoons he wrote a number of poems which reveal the extraordinary state of mysticism and bitterness of his mind. Most of them, in a harsh and pitiful way, are very fine, but they never transcend the limits of a pathetic *cri de cœur*, never quite achieve the truly tragic. One or two are clearly directed at the woman who only a few years previously had inspired his sonnets "To Olive". "I know you now, Circe and Sycorax" ends one, and in *The Witch* and *Canker Blooms* the theme is little varied. But another sonnet—too 'personal' Wilde would have said—called *Behold, your house is left unto you desolate*, is sad and moving rather than acrimonious. *Lighten our Darkness* and *Before a Crucifix* are perhaps the best sonnets he wrote in these years, though some may prefer the withering *English Benedictines* (later called *The Erastians*) or the exquisite *On a Showing of the Nativity*.

His physical energy was remarkable. From Shelley's Folly he tramped the Sussex downs and occasionally rode in Lord Monk Bretton's park one of the racehorses being trained by Dale, whose stables were nearby. He went up to Caithness-shire for snipe and duck-shooting being unable in wartime to reach the Orkney Islands, where a friend had a snipe bog.

He also went to Newmarket to stay with Bob Sievier who owned that lively and sometimes scurrilous paper, *The Winning Post*. Sievier had always maintained a die-hard "these filthy b——s; ought to be shot" attitude towards everything "decadent" and in the days when Bosie was defending Wilde's work in *The Academy* had published what Bosie called "coarse and offensive" paragraphs about him to which *The Academy* had replied. But when Bosie and Crosland started their campaign, *The Winning Post*, which had considerable influence with a certain kind of reader, strongly supported them, and Bosie and Sievier, instead of glaring at one another when they met at race-meetings, became friends.

Bosie went to stay at Fitzroy House, Newmarket, Sievier's home, and rode both Bath and Tweedledum in early-morning gallops. One visit was at the time of the presentation of the testimonial to Ross which Bosie unforgivingly saw as an attempt by the Asquiths to "rehabilitate and whitewash" Ross at his expense. Sievier agreed to publish Bosie's views and in *The Winning Post* appeared "a slashing article" called "O.H.M.S." The world, as Shaw said, had had quite enough of that squabble but Bosie could never see the Ross testimonial as anything but a direct hit at himself. That Ross was a man with many friends who felt gratitude and wanted to show it, never seemed to occur to him. The "Ross signatories" were always his enemies. But Bosie's Janus nature is revealed by the fact that in one week-end he rode race-horses in gallops (in his later forties) and wrote this unrelenting attack.

Suffering as he was at this time from something uncomfortably like persecution mania, he was grateful for any spontaneous expression of friendship and when he received an invitation to stay with a man named Herbert Moore Pim he went, for the first and (as it turned out) last time to Ireland.

Later when Bosie was editing *Plain English* Pim did for it what Crosland had done for the *Academy*, but Pim's enmities were more simple and sincere than Crosland's. He too was a poet, as most of the odd men of Fleet Street were in those days, he too would find a cause to serve and would worry its enemies like a terrier. But whereas Crosland's opinions varied with his necessities, Pim was an honest fanatic and like so many single-minded and passionate believers he was a convert in both religion and politics.

An Ulsterman of Protestant stock, the nephew of a Judge, he had become a Catholic and an ardent Fenian and was editing a paper called *The Irishman* which supported the Nationalists. He had a small charming home near Dunmurry called Finachy Cottage and here Bosie,

who had originally met Pim through Crosland, stayed for sever
weeks. Pim published *The Unspeakable Englishman*, with a s
appreciation of the title, and the two became fast if incongruous friend

Bosie read John Mitchell's *The Jail Journal* and this and Pim
influence gave him a new interest which he adopted with his usu
whole-heartedness—Irish Nationalism. This was to take an unexpecte
turn later.

4

All Bosie's litigation was within a period of fourteen years and th
time of his resentment against Wilde, so disagreeable to him an
everyone else, was even shorter, lasting from the time he read th
'unpublished portions' of *De Profundis* in 1913 till he came out o
prison in 1924. For the first few years it was a raging fever which can
to a climax in June 1918 when Bosie gave evidence in an affair know
as the Pemberton Billing Case.

This was a libel action brought by a dancer against a Member o
Parliament, but in its course and result it was much more than that, a
expression of mass hysteria, an exploitation of the philistinism an
puritanism of the public, a reaction against 'decadence' and th
re-establishment of Wilde, a wave of McCarthyism such as may strik
any people whose nerves are unstrung by years of war and who play
as English, Americans and Germans do, on the slopes of a volcano o
prejudice and bigotry which erupts at irregular intervals in the
history.

The circumstances were not without interest. In 1891 a Dutchma
named Jack Thomas Grein had copied the idea of Antoine's *Théât*
Libre and created the Independent Theatre in London. Max Beerbohr
wrote of him:

The Ibsen movement became more mobile later on, when a very dynami
and fervent little Dutchman, J. T. Grein, who was not at all content with bein
"something in the City" and being also Consul for Bolivia, rushed in, founde
the Independent Theatre and produced *Ghosts*.

In 1892 *Widowers' Houses*, the first of Shaw's plays to be seen i
London, was produced by the Independent Theatre* and late
organized as a 'theatre club' like those of today, it produced unde
Grein many plays considered 'modern' 'psychological' or 'decadent
most of them translated from the German.

Early in 1918 Grein decided to put on Wilde's *Salome* for which th

---

* It had no special building but rented various theatres for its productions.

Lord Chamberlain had withheld his license in 1892 on the grounds that it introduced biblical characters. Grein could not have chosen a worse moment for the experiment. The war news for most of that year was bad, often frightening, to the home population and there was public exasperation with everything 'foreign' 'perverse' and 'unhealthy'. As a result of the failure of Ross's libel action against Bosie in 1914 Wilde was in eclipse, not among normally intelligent people but with the philistine masses who were just then more than usually vocal. Grein, moreover, seems to have deliberately flouted popular opinion as from the beginning his Independent Theatre had been designed to do. He announced that Maud Allan, who had already caused some sensation and had a reputation for *risqué* dancing, would perform "the dance of the seven veils" in playing the part of Salome. It sounds like and probably was an offence against taste, for *Salome* is a bathetic piece of work and the dance early striptease, but scarcely an offence against morals unless, as Wilde implied, the two are the same.

A character named Noel Pemberton Billing had been elected to Parliament as Independent Member for Mid-Hertfordshire, on a programme of a stronger Air Force and an all-out war effort. He was something of an eccentric, less than forty years old. Son of a Birmingham iron-founder, he had fought in the Boer War and been in the R.N.A.S. since 1914. He wore a monocle and unusual clothes and drove a white Rolls Royce. Like Harris and other 'characters' of the time he claimed to have followed many professions, including the stage and the sea, and he ran a weekly paper of his own called *The Imperialist*. In this he published, on January 28 1918 an article which raised a mighty stink at the time. It was called (parodying Ian Hay's title) *The First Forty-seven Thousand* and it claimed that there existed a Black Book compiled by the German Secret Service of the names of 47,000 people prominent in Great Britain whose sexual views and vices laid them open to blackmail by the Germans—the very line taken by Senator McCarthy thirty years later and exploited in more recent cases in England. The book was supposed to be in the hands of 'a certain German prince'. This piece of nonsense had caught and inflamed popular imagination and the Black Book and the 47,000 names were bywords.

A society had been formed called the Vigilantes for promoting "purity in public life" and Billing made his paper its organ, changing the title to *The Vigilante*. The first number of this (February 28) contained this paragraph:

THE CULT OF THE CLITORIS[*]

To be a member of Maud Allan's private performances in Oscar Wilde's *Salome* one has to apply to a Miss Valetta of 9, Duke Street, Adelphi, W.C. If Scotland Yard were to seize the list of these members I have no doubt they would secure the names of several thousand of the first 47,000.

J. T. Grein and Maud Allan at once brought an action for criminal libel and Billing came up before Sir John Dickinson at Bow Street, where Travers Humphreys for the plaintiffs said: "A more horrible libel to publish of any woman, in my submission, it is impossible to find."

The trial of Billing was at the Old Bailey in the first days of June. It had been stated that Ross was to give evidence for the prosecution, in fact in her book about him already quoted Miss Margery Ross says that he was "called to give evidence" though there is no record of his having done so. But the news was sufficient for Bosie who agreed to go into the witness-box for Billing, an unfortunate decision which put him in the position, false to his nature and to his sentiments before and after this period, of doing what Ross called "kicking Oscar's corpse" and ranging himself with the philistines.

Pemberton Billing decided to defend himself and this made the case a riot. The public gallery was packed and evidence was cheered or boo'd in the most disgraceful way. Justice Darling seems to have quite lost control of his own court, for he was in the difficult position of not being able to order Billing, the defendant, out of it. The trial, says Montgomery Hyde, was probably marked by more disorderly scenes than have ever been witnessed on any similar occasion at the Old Bailey.

Pemberton Billing unsuccessfully objected to Justice Darling's presence on the Bench. He then began to call a collection of extra-ordinary witnesses whose evidence had little or nothing to do with the libel but who succeeded in helping him to create an impression in the minds of the jury of himself as a lonely champion of decent morality with vast numbers of sinister enemies in public life pledged to promote 'the Wilde cult'.

A Mrs. Villiers Stuart claimed actually to have seen the Black Book and began solemnly reading out a list of the names in it. This seems roughly to have corresponded with the signatories of the Ross testi-monial. She began with the Asquiths, mentioned Lord Haldane and

[*] There was much chi-chi about reading out this heading in court and news-papers used a row of stars or a line for the last word.

amid cheers and laughter in the court read out the name of Justice Darling himself. She afterwards claimed that she had received an anonymous letter saying that if she returned to the witness-box she would be shot from the public gallery.

Counsel for the plaintiffs, Mr. Hume-Williams, tried in vain to keep the issue before the jury but the court became more uproarious as Billing called his witnesses to show that the play was a danger to public morality. A surgeon called Sir Alfred Fripp said he was there out of a sense of duty. He had not read the play but knew there were moral perverts in the ruling and governing classes and in all grades of society. A Dr. Leonard Williams said that the play was disgusting and calculated to harm public morals.

When Bosie was called he said he had known Wilde from 1892 to the time of his death in 1900, and described him as a 'good second-rate *litterateur*, tremendously over-rated'. He explained how Wilde wrote his plays and said that he (Douglas) had translated *Salome* from the French. Wilde professed a horror of coarse expressions and clothed the thing in flowery language. He would have been as horrified about the title to the paragraph in *The Vigilante* as Mr. Hume-Williams was.

Pemberton Billing brought out these and other details efficiently, then asked Bosie if he regretted having known Wilde.

"I do. Most intensely. He had a diabolical influence on everyone. I think he was the greatest force for evil in Europe for the last 350 years."

"Do you regard his works as classics?"

"I suppose they have become classics because of the tremendous notoriety they have attained."

"When he wrote *Salome* was he studying Kraft-Ebbing?"

It was explained that Kraft-Ebbing was a German whose study of sexual matters pretended to be scientific. But the word 'German' was sufficient in June 1918.

Billing went a little too far when he asked if *Salome* was 'based on Kraft-Ebbing' but Bosie agreed that it could not have been written by anybody who had not made a study of Kraft-Ebbing.

Billing then recalled that *Salome* had been shown *in Berlin* for 200 nights to enthusiastic audiences. Was it not more in accordance with German Kultur than British ideals? Certainly.

"The moon" came into it. The judge wanted to know if Wilde had intended "perverted morality with regard to the moon" and Bosie said, understandably, that he did not know about that.

There was a good deal more of this sort of thing. "Herod says 'kill

that woman' and Mr. Justice Darling says that's the best thing in th
play", said Billing. "I have already commended Herod" retorte
Darling who had a reputation as a legal comedian.

Then Bosie faced Hume-Williams who made the mistake of bringin
up those wretched letters of Wilde's which had been read to so man
juries over the years. Bosie protested.

"That is a letter written to me," he shouted. "It was stolen from m
and is brought out every time I come here by that German blackmaile
George Lewis.* It is the fifteenth time it has come out. Every time
come here this beastly drivel is produced."

Billing asked why they wanted to drag this muck up and Darlin
told him it was hardly for him to protest about things being dragge
up.

"It is not right to throw mud at a man who has come here in th
public interest," said Billing.

"Be quiet!" ordered the Judge.

"I shall not be quiet, Judge Darling," retorted Billing lightly, wit
the emphasis on the word 'Judge'.

Hume-Williams made another attempt to read the letter.

"It is a letter written by a diabolical scoundrel to a wretched sill
youth," interrupted Bosie.

"Listen to the question and answer," Darling told him.

"I shall answer as I please and not as you please. I am here to give m
evidence and I shall do so as I choose. You bullied me last time but yo
will not bully me again."

"You will do as you are told or you will be removed."

"I don't care if I am removed. It's no pleasure to me to be here."

There was laughter and Darling threatened that if there was mor
laughter he would clear the court.

"May we laugh at your jokes, my lord?" asked Billing sweetly.

"No, you may not!" said poor Darling, more and more in th
position of a schoolmaster being ragged in class.

When Hume-Williams tried to return to the letters Bosie said–
"You wretched lawyers come and spit this all up twenty-five year
later because you are paid to do so."

Then Hume-Williams started to read Bosie's letter to Labouchère o
Truth in 1895 saying that it was an attempt to justify homosexuality.

"That is exactly what you are doing," said Bosie.

* Sir George Lewis had married a German lady, and was, Bosie maintaine
himself of German descent.

Frontispiece to 'The Collected Poems' (1919). Aged 45.

Arriving at the Old Bailey, 1923.

Hume-Williams played into his hand, suggesting that the time he had hoped for in his letter when 'this vice' would no longer be punished had not yet arrived.

"I think it has, if you ask me. It is now approved all over the place. Cabinet ministers, greasy advocates, and everyone holding high positions—Asquith and all those people, they give good posts and send testimonials. The reason they go for me is because I am no longer on their side. If I were I should get a big testimonial and a large sum of money and be told I was a delightful person and a beautiful artist. That is what they did for Ross. They gave him a testimonial simply because he was a pervert."

There were more heated exchanges in which Hume-Williams took no part. Then Billing called other witnesses. G. E. Morrison, dramatic critic of the *Morning Post*, said *Salome* was "diseased but not indecent", Bernard Weller of *The Stage* said that it was "impure, decadent and degenerate", Father Bernard Vaughan more viciously said it was an abomination and that an actress who would perform in it must be a perverted creature, Dr. John Henry Clarke said the only theatre for such a play was a medical theatre and even then it might corrupt the students, Dr. Arthur Everard said it was a repulsive and blasphemous play.

Darling made a wandering and inept summing-up and in the course of it said Bosie had 'written' (instead of 'translated') a certain passage. (Darling had already said that the play was written by Wilde and Douglas in collaboration.)

Bosie who was sitting on the steps at the back of the court, jumped up and shouted: "You have no right to say that. You have no right to say it at all and you know very well you haven't. You can't say I wrote this play. You're a liar. You lie. You're a damned liar, and if you say it outside I'll prosecute you."

According to the *Daily Mail*,

Lord Alfred was immediately hustled out of court but a great storm of clapping broke out in the gallery and at the back of the court. It lasted for a minute and the judge's order for Lord Alfred's removal was drowned in the noise.

The verdict was for Billing with costs against Grein and Maud Allan.

5

Although there had been no quarrel between Bosie and his brother Percy (the ninth Marquess) they seem to have been out of touch (unless

Bosie's syntax is at fault) for Percy, he said, wrote to him unexpectedly and told him of his second marriage.

His wife wanted to give Percy a horse which would revive the racing colours of Queensberry and of his cousin Arthur Douglas, the owner of Old Joe, the colours which Bosie had used when he had his stable at Chantilly—salmon with green sleeves and cap. The idea was to buy a three-year-old which was entered in the Derby.

Bosie knew better and wrote back asking:

What's the use of buying a three-year-old to run in the Derby, when it is quite impossible, even for a great deal more than your wife would be likely to give, to buy one that would have the slightest chance of winning? Why not buy a horse to win a big handicap at the beginning of the year?

Moreover, Bosie knew a horse. Bob Sievier had a horse called Royal Bucks which he believed would win the Lincolnshire. He might sell it because he had not enough money to back it in the way he liked.

Percy, his wife and Bosie went down to stay with Sievier at Newmarket and over dinner on the night of their arrival the horse was bought for £3,000. But Percy could not wait to see it run. His mind was full of certain properties in America which he had marked down as valuable and he went off with all his speculative optimism to invest in them.

Royal Bucks made two triumphant appearances in his absence, winning both the Lincoln Handicap and the City and Suburban. Bosie had not the money to back the horse as it deserved but Sievier sent him £100 of his winnings in the first race and his sister-in-law put a pony on for him in the second so he made what he describes as a few hundred pounds. "It ought to have been thousands, of course."

When Percy returned from America, having lost his investment, he found that as the horse had run in his wife's name the Queensberry colours had been altered. Also that if he had stayed in England and backed his horse instead of going off on yet another of his abortive dashes to make a fortune, he would have been a richer man instead of a very much poorer one. There was a family row in which Sievier was involved but which was settled amicably in time.

Percy died in South Africa a year later and the title passed to his son Francis.

6

But lest it should be supposed that Bosie was growing placid in those years at Shelley's Folly after the Pemberton Billing case it is apposite to recall an exchange of letters, with a most inoffensive and well-meaning person, Sir Arthur Conan Doyle. This happened in 1919 the year in which Bosie's *Collected Poems* was published.

Doyle who had become a spiritualist and devoted not only his time but his fortune to the cause in which he believed, published something about Christianity which seems to have infuriated Bosie who wrote him a letter opening:—"Sir, What a disgusting beast you are with your caricatures of Christ." The letter goes on to say that the proper way to deal with Doyle is to give him a thrashing with a horse-whip and accuses him of "running this spiritualistic business simply to get money and notoriety". Doyle, said Bosie, was an apostate Catholic and there was nothing in the world worse than that. The letter was signed "Yours with the utmost contempt."

Doyle, however, knew an answer worth two of that. It was brief. He was *relieved*, he said, to get Bosie's letter. "It is only your approval that could in any way annoy me."

CHAPTER XIV

Plain English, Trial and Imprisonment

I

IT was indirectly through his brother Percy that Bosie became an editor again. Before he left on his last journey to South Africa Queensberry was staying with a man named James Conchie, who was also a friend of Bosie's. Little is known of Conchie except that he had a house in Great Cumberland Place and Feddal Castle and a grouse moor in Perthshire. He was a Presbyterian and his wife a Catholic. He asked Queensberry why a clever fellow like his brother did nothing and Queensberry told him in the best of good faith that Bosie was boycotted by the papers and could not get an article printed anywhere.

The last part of this explanation was true. Bosie was no Crosland who could turn out articles to order. Though as an editor he had encouraged a good many young or struggling writers and published an interesting because unpredictable weekly he was incapable of writing anything, except poetry, which was likely to be appreciated by other editors. There was no boycott against him and when his *Collected Poems* had been published by Secker in the previous year (1919) they were treated quite fairly by the literary press. It was simply that as a contributor to established daily or weekly papers he had nothing to offer.

James Conchie, one must assume, knew little of journalism but he liked the Douglas brothers and he was rich. He decided to finance Bosie in the venture of starting a new weekly paper to compete with the many, alike in format but differing violently in viewpoint, which were on the bookstalls. Bosie was given an entirely free hand and as may be imagined he took advantage of it.

He called his paper *Plain English* and like the other weeklies which it resembled externally it cost sixpence. Conchie paid £100 for the title of The Academy so it appeared as "*Plain English:* with which is incorporated *The Academy*".

His first step was to send a telegram to Herbert Moore Pim offering him the post of assistant editor. Pim came, but this produced a momentary impasse. Since Bosie had stayed with him at Dunmurry Pim's views had undergone a complete change. He had been then an ardent supporter of Sinn Fein and Irish Nationalism but "when the Sinn Feiners started murdering people, cutting off the noses of donkeys, and dragging the Catholic Church in the mire for political ends" he became as violently opposed to Sinn Fein as he had been in favour of it and at the time when he received Bosie's wire his life was threatened. Awkward, this. Bosie had decided that *Plain English* was to be the only Secular Catholic paper to be published in England since the Reformation and for it to oppose Irish Nationalism would be, to say the least of it, anomalous.

However, Pim, who in spite of his gentle soft-voiced manner was a self-opinionated man, put his point of view to Bosie, and Bosie accepted it. One is tempted to wonder whether it mattered to Bosie what he attacked at this time so long as he had plenty of opponents. He not only accepted Pim's new alignment but put himself beside his sub-editor. "I soon followed him in his change of views", he wrote, and *Plain English* put up a strenuous fight "far stronger than that made by any other paper" against "the iniquitous surrender to Sinn Fein and the betrayal of the Irish Loyalists, which will ever remain the darkest blot on the history of the Neo-Georgian period."

Plain English thus alienated a large proportion of its potential readership, for to appreciate an English Catholic weekly which supported the Ulstermen demanded feats of mental gymnastics that few could achieve. It was, moreover, die-hard Tory, or at least ferociously 'anti-Lloyd-George and Coalition'. But this was not enough and casting round for adversaries Bosie and Pim (who had been joined by Crosland, just then writing his *Fine Old Hebrew Gentleman*) decided to attack a mysterious "clique of rich Jews" whose machinations in the City were responsible for everything wrong in English finance. Although Bosie wrote afterwards that *Plain English* was 'strongly anti-Semitic' it was nothing of the sort, in the sense that we have come to understand the term. He made this admission after *Plain English* had perished and long before Hitler had been heard of. His Anti-Semiticism if it can be called that, was of the Belloc-Chesterton order, a belief in financial conspiracies, not a rabidly racial thing. He lived to see where such attempted witch-hunting led in Germany and in his last years he regretted that he had ever soiled his hands with it, loathing Nazism with a hearty and verbose hatred that comes out in his letters. When Bosie

wrote in *Plain English* of Jews he was not thinking of members of a race
but of Sir Alfred Mond or Sir Ernest Cassel or some other of his *bêtes
noires*. The nearest he came to any generalized attack was when he
published for the first time the quatrain which was afterwards made
famous by *The Week-End Book*:

> *How odd*
> *Of God*
> *To choose*
> *The Jews.*

The reconciliation with Crosland was inevitably one of convenience
for Bosie had never lost his belief in Crosland as a writer of stout-
hearted articles nor Crosland his need for extra guineas for his work. It
brought with it more enmities and in one of the first numbers Crosland
wrote a fulminating attack on J. C. Squire called 'The Tin Whistle'.
This, says his biographer, was a 'Masterpiece' and 'well worth £4'—
the sum which, by special arrangement with Conchie, Crosland was
paid for his articles.

So for sixteen months *Plain English* went its calumnious way, though
Bosie protested when Pim called Robert Bridges a 'humbug'. It
was not without its better moments and some good literary criticism
and poetry was published in its pages, but for the most part it was a
hymn of hate or a scream of patriotism.

Bosie, with a persecution mania raging in him like an abscess, with
no proprietary control, 'went for' anything he believed should be
attacked. Of his honesty of purpose there is no doubt. "I was desperately sincere," he said ten years later, "and quite ready to die or go
to prison for my convictions". But again to quote Shaw, who could
say things to Bosie which no one else could, "Why should you, who
have been so unjust to many good men, expect justice for yourself? Are
you not wise enough yet to pray God to defend you from it? Does your
conscience never reproach you for the reckless way in which you
exploited Crosland's phobia for calumny in *The Academy*?"

He was sincere, but when a man is able to convince himself of bun-
kum and then sacrifice himself and everyone around him for the sake of
it, his sincerity becomes more dangerous than mere time-serving. "It
is a fact", wrote Bosie afterwards,

that the Ulster Defence Council came to us after having been, in vain, to every
other paper in London, including *The Morning Post*, and asked us to give

details of the Sinn Fein outrages which were going on, unreported in the craven London Press, week by week. I saw the President, and agreed to print anything they liked to send in, and we went on printing details of outrages every week in spite of the fact that I was threatened with "reprisals", and warned anonymously that I would be shot.

What kind of sincerity was this? But there were even wilder stories he believed and published in good—but idiotic—faith, one of which was to come home to him later.

The trouble was that Bosie as an editor could never resist anyone with a bee in his bonnet and having adopted him, bee and all, he would fight for him in issue after issue. I used to read *Plain English* as a schoolboy and thrill to the Jack-the-Giant-Killer motif which ran through it. There must have been a few thousand people of all ages with minds as immature as mine who felt like this for the circulation, starting at a few hundreds with the first issue, rose to a steady three thousand copies a week. But no genuine adult—if such a person exists—could read it without amusement or exasperation. As I look through the faded pages now, with their undignified sensationalism and crazy wisecracks, I wonder how *Plain English* can have survived so long or how it can have earned the letters and telegrams of congratulation which Conchie used to send Bosie when 'a particularly good number' came out.*

Mr. Conchie, however, seems to have changed his point of view or perhaps given up his ownership of the paper for after sixteen months there was an 'ignoble intrigue' through which Bosie lost the editorship. What this was, who was responsible, whether Conchie was involved— all these are mysteries. Bosie speaks of 'some people' who engineered it, through whom he lost the paper he had created, the very name of which he had invented. He was succeeded by a Mr. Harold Spencer who was promptly sent to prison for a criminal libel in its pages. *Plain English* then perished.

Bosie decided to start a paper of his own and did so immediately, taking many of his subscribers with him. It was called *Plain Speech* and ran for several months. Pim followed him to *Plain Speech* but not Crosland.

This, at last, ended the friendship which had continued fitfully for

---

* It was only once threatened with an action for libel, however. That was during Bosie's absence in Scotland (shooting with Conchie) when Pim and Crosland libelled a Member of Parliament named Higham and the paper had to pay damages.

fifteen years. "The real character of the man", wrote Bosie to Sorley Brown some years later,

was shown by the fact that the moment I had been done out of the editorship of *Plain English* (my creation and the apple of my eye), he went straight round to the people who had done me out of it and offered to write for them, and did, in fact, write for them. From that day till his death I never saw him or spoke to him again.

2

While *Plain Speech* was still appearing, on February 4, 1921, Bosie saw a newspaper placard announcing his death, a somewhat macabre experience, particularly when he could buy the paper, *The Evening News*, and read his own obituary. It was written, he afterwards discovered, by Arthur Machen whose work he had published in the days of *The Academy*. The wording was not friendly. It was headed "A Great Life Spoilt" and subtitled "How the Evil Genius of the Douglases Dogged Lord Alfred." It ran:

A brilliant and most unhappy career is ended. Lord Alfred Douglas was born, in a sense, under the happiest auspices. He was a Douglas, the son of one of the most ancient families in Britain. He was connected with many of the "best people" in society, he had brilliant capacities, and showed that he was certainly to be numbered among the poets.

He might have done anything, and, his poetry excepted, he did nothing and worse than nothing.

The charity which is fitting at all times, but most fitting when we are speaking of the newly-dead, urges that much should be forgiven to this poor, bewildered man, who, with all his gifts, will perhaps only be remembered by the scandals and the quarrels in which he involved himself.

It is a great thing, in a sense, to be born a Douglas, but the family inheritance had gifts from evil fairies as well as from good ones.

It would not be true to say that all ancient races are degenerate, but there are very marked signs of degeneracy in the House of Douglas.

Many of them are violently eccentric, to put the case mildly.

This was in an early edition of the paper. Before the later ones the truth was discovered and a paragraph inserted to the effect that the report was unfounded. "We regret having given currency to the inaccurate statement," said the editor but added nothing about the inaccurate, not to say highly libellous, obituary notice.

He was soon reminded of it for Bosie, in this case most justifiably, sued for libel.

Nowadays such an action would be settled out of court, 'substantial damages' be paid by the newspaper or its insurance company and when someone on the staff had been rapped over the knuckles for careless- ness the incident would be forgotten. Not so forty years ago. *The Evening News* consulted George Lewis who advised them to plead justification. As solicitor to both Ross and Custance Lewis could, and in fact *did* through Counsel trot out in court all Bosie's letters to Ross and Wilde, all the Custance scandal, a mass of valuable material with which he attempted to 'justify' the *Evening News* state- ment that Bosie had done nothing "and worse than nothing" and the rest of it.

It in no way reflects on *The Evening News* or its proprietors today to call this an impudent and a cowardly plea which could have been made against no one but Bosie, and only against him by reviving things which he had earned the right to consider lived down. 'Justification' could only be pleaded, moreover, by a defendant with Lewis's re- sources to draw on. To libel a man grossly by error and then, instead of apologizing, to say that the libels are true and can be proved in open court from details of the man's past life, is aggravated injury and no solicitor but George Lewis, with his obsessional hatred for Bosie, would have dared to advise it.

A few days before the case came on Bosie was shocked to learn that it would be tried by Justice Darling. He hurried down to the Law Courts and asked to see the Associate, the official who settles the order of cases and the judges for each. The Associate came out and asked Bosie 'stiffly' what he wanted. Bosie became heated and threatened to 'make a row' if Darling tried his case, then explained more calmly that after the Pemberton Billing case Darling was bound to feel prejudice, and surely would not wish to try a case in which Bosie was concerned. The Associate told him that there were only three judges on the rota and Darling happened to have been selected for his case but that it should be given to Mr. Justice Bray.

But this would not do either. Bosie reminded the Associate ,who was now unbending, that Bray had tried the case when Crosland was non-suited in an action against Ross for malicious prosecution and Bosie had recorded this in a lampoon ending—"And down the ages bray and bray and bray."

The Associate pointed out with some amusement that litigants could not come and choose their own judges. "May I ask what judge *would* suit you?"

Bosie said he wouldn't mind the Lord Chief Justice, who was the third judge on the rota and the Associate promised him this.

The case came before Mr. Justice Horridge in the King's Bench Division on November 25th, 1921. Comyns Carr was for Bosie, Douglas Hogg, K.C., for *The Evening News*.

Bosie knew that among other things which Lewis had put in Hogg's brief was the Custance correspondence. He was given valuable support against this by Olive who sat with him in court throughout the case.

At the beginning it seemed that Justice Horridge was hostile to Bosie and Comyns Carr had decided not to put him in the box. Carr pointed out that *The Evening News* had not apologized and was not apologizing now but trying to justify its libel by bringing up details of Douglas's past, even recalling that he had not taken a degree at Oxford. They were quoting the old stories of Douglas's friendship with Wilde, of his friction with his father-in-law and so on, and these were no justification whatever.

He then, to Bosie's dismay, since as usual he longed to get into the witness-box, handed over to Douglas Hogg who made a deadly attack on Bosie. He thought *The Evening News* obituary in the circumstances a very kindly one. He quoted again those stolen letters which had been produced against Bosie so often. He even went back to *The Chameleon* and *The Priest and the Acolyte*. When he began to misquote something from *The Academy* Bosie could stand it no longer and jumped to his feet protesting that Hogg was reading what was not there.

The judge told him sharply not to interfere. Bosie's case began to seem shaky in spite of evidence from a doctor and a Bishop of his state of health and character. Finally Carr saw that his only chance lay in putting Bosie in the box. It was a gamble, as always, for though he thought himself a matchless witness Bosie was unpredictable. He might appeal to the imagination of the jury or arouse their antipathy. He might be cheeky to the judge and would certainly work off some retorts on the opposing counsel. But Carr had to take the chance. The jury would not forgive the prosecution for not giving them the entertainment. He asked leave of the judge to let Bosie go into the box "in rebuttal". The judge hesitated, pointed out that it was entirely in his discretion, but finally decided that "the jury would like to hear him". Perhaps Horridge felt his own curiosity, too.

Hogg cross-examined Bosie who immediately got in a broadside at the defendants' solicitor, Sir George Lewis. Horridge said to Hogg, "I am not stopping this witness because I imagine you would not wish me to," implying that he was letting Bosie cut his own throat. But slowly, very slowly, the judge began to come round and when the case was adjourned for the day Bosie was able to reassure Comyns Carr. He had got the jury already, he said.

His cross-examination was continued throughout the following day. Bosie raised a laugh when he said he had written to the King complaining of Custance and had received a reply saying his letter was 'receiving attention'. "I knew the King was shooting with my father-in-law and I wanted him to know what kind of man he was associating with."

Hogg referred to *Oscar Wilde and Myself*, and the Judge, who was now obviously sympathetic, told Bosie to read any passage he liked. "You put it in, you know," he said to Hogg when Bosie had read several pieces of Crosland's manly prose which were just the thing for a jury.

Later there was a reference to *Eve and the Serpent*, which Hogg called "a disgraceful and scurrilous attack on one of the Chancery Judges." Bosie tried to persuade Horridge that it "was not exactly meant for Mr. Justice Eve" but Horridge, who was chuckling over the satire, told him to 'do himself justice'.

The jury began to get sick of Hogg's repeated harking back to Bosie's past and one of them asked at last if they *must* hear all this. The truth was that the letters had been produced by Lewis once too often and their effect was to rouse sympathy for Bosie.

The jury were out only fifteen minutes and brought in a verdict for Bosie, assessing the damages at £1,000. This, with costs, was considered 'heavy' at that time and indeed was a large sum of money in 1921. The jury added a rider saying that Bosie's letters should be returned to him or destroyed.

The Evening News, said Bosie, relieved its feelings by sacking Arthur Machen who had written the obituary.

3

This was his one unalloyed triumph in litigation. He felt that he had defeated not so much *The Evening News* as Lewis and Custance. Lewis's advice to depend on the story of Bosie's warfare with his father-in-law was certainly foolish and because it had failed in its effect Bosie felt he had scored off Custance himself.

But the strain of his days in the witness-box coming after his prolonged fight to keep *Plain Speech* alive caused a breakdown. He was
subject all his life to bouts of influenza and one now, in his fatigued
state, nearly killed him and he was in bed for several months. *Plain
Speech* which had been kept going only by the faith of a City man who
supported it with a subscription of £50 a week could not survive
Bosie's absence and published its last number.

4

He was living in 1922 with his mother at 16 Draycott Place. His illness
had left him rather frail in appearance but still, at fifty-two, he kept his
extraordinary youthfulness, and his delicate skin could flush rosily like
a boy's. It was now that I met him for the first time.

He was enjoying, in a sense, an interval, a year's break between his
action against *The Evening News* and his fight to keep *Plain Speech* in
1921 and his last fatal appearance in court in 1923, when after being
convicted of criminal libel he would be sentenced to six months'
imprisonment. He was supposed to be resting after his illness but he
asked me, a nineteen-year-old boy who had sent him some verses from
school, to come to lunch in Draycott Place.

Arriving in Kensington an hour too soon, I decided to walk to Tite
Street to see the house in which Wilde lived. I stared curiously at a tall
narrow Victorian house, but since the numbers in the street were
changed then or thereafter, it may have been the wrong one.

I told Bosie this when I reached Draycott Place and for the first time
I heard his high-pitched and quite unforgettable laughter, the laughter
of a small boy deriding a ridiculous schoolmaster.

"I suppose there's a commemorative tablet?" he said. "I wonder
there isn't an equestrian statue at the top of the street."

He did not say this bitterly. I never heard him speak bitterly of
Wilde.

Bosie did not seem, even to me at nineteen, an old man. His hair was
thick and silky, scarcely touched with grey, his face showed lines only as
skin which has been clear and feminine in boyhood becomes wrinkled.
His hands and wrists were white and slender and his voice had an
almost treble pitch when he was excited, delightful when he laughed
but shrill when he was angry. He dressed simply, with a liking for
heavy boots rather than shoes and a habit of wearing battered hats.

He looked like a hurt boy. The eyes were brilliantly expressive, often
merry but sometimes pained and resentful. The features which in

boyhood were so delicately modelled had grown pronounced, the nose formidable, the corners of the mouth turning down petulantly. But I saw only a friendly, eagerly talkative man who treated me at once without patronage or pomposity, as though we were both of an age.

Bosie had a little study behind the dining-room and took me there after lunch. I spent many hours in it during that winter, but all I remember of it is a small fireplace with two arm-chairs facing one another across the hearth. One became mine while in the other Bosie sat in his peculiarly fidgety way, twisting his body, leaning suddenly across the chair-arm, moving his hands not in gesticulation but from natural restlessness.

Of his own work he spoke little except of the nonsense rhymes and satires. I read *The Duke of Berwick*, the story of that 'very upright nobleman':

> *He and the Duchess always turned their backs*
> *On those whose conduct was the least bit lax.*
> *Where'er they went they waved a moral banner*
> *And constantly left rooms "in a marked manner."* . . .

Bosie forgot his resentment as he often did at that time when he remembered Wilde.

"I wrote it to pull Oscar's leg," he said. "Do you remember in *The Picture of Dorian Gray* someone showing their disapproval of Dorian by 'leaving the room in a marked manner'? Poor Oscar, for all his brilliant wit, he had very little sense of humour or he could never have written such a line in deadly earnest. His hatred of being laughed at in even the smallest things was quite morbid. . . ." (In his last published book about Wilde written sixteen years later, Bosie spoke of his sense of humour as 'superb'.)

One form of reading other than Shakespeare was habitual with Bosie though, and he recommended it to me as a challenge to all adversities.

"Whenever things seem really too much for me," he said, "I read the Lives of the Saints. It never fails. Try it when you think you're beaten. I learned that a few years ago when I needed miracles to keep me going. You'll see for yourself."

5

There is a kind of story which gains currency especially in wartime. However far-fetched it may be it has some picturesque coincidence, some flashy detail, which appeals to the credulous. One is reminded of that chestnut of the last war—the church clock story. Usually honest men and women, who had themselves been told it by others, would look you in the eyes and inform you that they had been listening to one of Joyce's broadcasts and he had announced that next week the *Luftwaffe* would bomb this town or village on Thursday night. To prove that he knew what was going on here he had stated in his broadcast that the church clock was ten minutes slow. "And", added your informant dramatically, "when I came out I looked up at the church clock and by heaven he was right!" Every one of Joyce's broadcasts was recorded and in no single one did he threaten a raid on any specific date or mention a church clock. Yet the story was told and believed all over the country. There are, and always have been, others, some of which from time to time crop up in Fleet Street. A young reporter thinks perhaps he is fortunate when he hears about the Russian royal prince who escaped assassination and is living in Pimlico until a more experienced colleague who may have fallen for this thirty years ago tells him not to be silly. The more dangerous ones may have a grain of truth like the 'Marconi Affair' which Cecil Chesterton exposed in *The New Witness* to his own cost.

While he was editing *Plain English* Bosie heard two such rumours which anyone in Fleet Street could have told him to leave alone. Just as he believed he was the only editor who had the courage to print those propaganda stories put out by the Ulster Defence Council so, when he heard these two pieces of circumstantial fantasy, he really thought that no other paper had printed them because no other dared. He swallowed both—hook, line and sinker, and they appeared in *Plain English* in all their calumnious absurdity.

The first dealt with the Battle of Jutland. It was a matter of history that the earliest two reports of this battle were gloomy in the extreme and that later a more reassuring report was made public. The story told to Bosie was that this had been a matter of deliberate policy, that the first statements had been made to lower the value of Government stock and that when certain rich Jews, including Sir Ernest Cassel, had purchased enough of this, the true facts about the battle were published and 'the syndicate' reaped a profit of many million pounds. It was, in a new form, the old legend of the Rothschilds and their carrier pigeon information about the battle of Waterloo. A final touch was added to the story by the fact, also undisputed, that Winston Churchill, who had not been at the Admiralty for months, was asked by Balfour to prepare that third statement to reassure the neutral press. In Bosie's mind

Winston Churchill stood with Asquith and Lloyd George for all the Liberal, anti-patriotic forces in the country, and it was only a step for him to believe that Churchill, in concert with Cassel and others, had taken part in a large-scale conspiracy by which they were all enriched.

Here again were certain details which might appear to be connected but which in fact had nothing to do with the matter, like the church clock. These were sufficient to make the credulous suppose that there was 'something in it'. Lord Balfour who was perfectly capable of preparing a report, had in fact, asked Churchill to do so. Sir Ernest Cassel had been born in Germany. He had been a friend of Churchill's parents and of Churchill himself. He had made a wedding-present to Churchill of £500 and furnished his library for him—in 1905. He had invested, in Churchill's early days, certain sums of money which Churchill had made from his books. All this was totally irrelevant, the sort of hastily accepted nonsense which could only convince someone who, like Bosie, was determined to be convinced.

But Bosie published the story, having no factual support, of course, having nothing but a sensational anecdote such as might be heard at any bar counter in war-time. When Churchill ignored it, as he was advised to do by the Attorney-General, Bosie became more and more convinced that he had discovered a sinister plot which its participants wanted to hush up. In fact it was ignored because *Plain English* was too insignificant to be worth an expensive libel action, but Bosie believed his enemies dared not face him in court.

The second story was even more melodramatic and even more widely told and swallowed during the 1914-18 War. That it should have reached Bosie three years after the Armistice and that he should have accepted it and published it in the form he did, shows a credulousness on his part which is little short of infantile. Those who heard the church clock story will recognize the same dependence on picturesque but totally fictional touches.

It was to the effect that Kitchener had been deliberately murdered. The circumstances of his leaving for Russia are described as follows by the *Encylopaedia Britannica* and are a matter of history:

"Early in May 1916 the Tsar urged that Kitchener should visit Russia, promising that his counsel would be taken to the full even if that counsel included certain transfers of control into British hands. Kitchener was to start from Scapa Flow on June 5 for Archangel.

On the afternoon of the appointed day, Kitchener, having paid a visit to

Lord Jellicoe on his flagship, embarked on the *Hampshire*, which was directed to proceed on what, with the prevailing wind—as reported—would be the lee side of the Orkneys and Shetlands. The arrangements made for the voyage of the cruiser have been, and perhaps always will be, open to question. It is at least certain that an unswept channel was chosen for her passage and that, under stress of weather, the destroyers who formed her titular escort turned about, leaving the vessel, with her priceless freight, to steam to her doom. The *Hampshire* struck a mine, and went down with nearly all hands.

Here, it will be seen, was great scope for the sensation-monger and the story as it appeared in *Plain English* with embellishments showed this. Kitchener was taking with him experts to replace the 'corrupt Bolshevik Jews' in office, so it was *necessary that he should never arrive*. The destroyers which were to accompany the *Hampshire* were *deliberately held back*. The wreck floated for a time but *the lifeboat did not start for some hours* after the news was received ashore and when it had gone a mile or so *was recalled*. Seventy of the crew of the *Hampshire* drifted ashore but only eleven survived and these were taken to London but *had not been heard of since*. The people of the Orkneys had been *forbidden to talk*. *No divers* had been sent down to investigate. In later stages the story acquired supporting evidence from *a German naval officer* who stated that no German U-boat or mine had been anywhere near the spot where the *Hampshire* sank.

It must be admitted that the loss of the *Hampshire* ranks with other mysteries of the sea and some of the circumstances were questionable. For this very reason Bosie's hare-brained publication of the story with no proper investigation may have been a disservice to truth. The details as he gave them could easily be refuted and his attribution of blame to "Bolshevik Jewry" was farcical. But when he published it he got widespread support. There are always plenty of people to believe in dark mysteries in high places and to champion the brave man who dares to expose them. Horatio Bottomley made several fortunes out of this kind of credulity. John Wilkes and other demagogues thrived on it. Bosie, who really believed what he published, went to prison for it.

6

While these stories appeared only in *Plain English*, a scurrilous weekly with a circulation of a thousand or two run by the irresponsible Alfred Douglas, they were ignored. But after his year's rest Bosie began to stir things up again. He had no paper in which to publish his startling theories but a committee was formed to support him and a public meeting planned.

It was called The Lord Kitchener and Jutland Publicity Committee and its object was to communicate to the public the sensational theories of its members on the two wartime events. A meeting at the Memorial Hall, Farringdon Street, was extensively advertised and Bosie, speaking in public for the first time in his life, addressed a large audience for forty-five minutes and was riotously cheered. Members of the committee on the platform included General Prescott-Decie in the chair, Bosie's old friend the explorer Harry de Windt, Bosie's sister Lady Edith Fox-Pitt, Colonel Haines, the Hon. Mrs. Greville-Nugent and a Mr. Cunningham.

The press ignored this, of course, but Bosie sent a copy of his speech, which contained specific accusations against Churchill and others, to Sorley Brown who published it in full in the *Border Standard*. It was then issued as a pamphlet entitled *The Murder of Lord Kitchener and the Truth about the Battle of Jutland and the Jews*. Thirty thousand copies of this were printed and sent to London for distribution.* Six thousand of them had been sold when on November 6, 1923, Bosie was arrested and charged with having libelled Churchill. He said he would plead justification and was committed to trial, bail being allowed.

The trial, which began on December 11 and lasted four days, was fully reported in the press, so fully that it daily filled many columns of most papers. Bosie could certainly not complain, as he did in other cases, that he was insufficiently reported. But almost at once it became pitifully obvious that he had nothing but the most fictitious hearsay with which to back his accusations. So flimsy was the evidence on which his very grave libels had been based that even his sincerity was doubted. It seemed impossible, when the story was brought to the grey light of the Old Bailey, that anyone could have been so credulous as to believe it, so reckless as to publish it and so determined to go to prison that he would plead justification when charged with criminal libel on the strength of it.

The case was heard before Mr. Justice Avory. Bosie had Cecil Hayes to defend him and was prosecuted by the Attorney-General Sir Douglas Hogg with Sir Richard Muir.

---

* His mother, in her late seventies, supported him in this as in everything. She wrote to Sorley Brown: "We have had quite exciting times lately selling the pamphlets and fighting the underhand expedients for stopping the sale and frightening the men who tried to sell."

Bosie had perhaps supposed there would be scenes like those of the Pemberton Billing trial when, with no evidence to justify his libel, Billing had thrown so much unpleasant dust in the jury's eyes that amid resounding cheers he had been given a verdict. But this was a very different situation. Avory was not a man to let the case get out of hand and there were to be no heroics from Bosie. His own counsel was prevented from asking him irrelevant questions and Douglas Hogg confined his cross-examination to seven points which gave no scope for oratory, so that Bosie, deprived of the chance of introducing hares or red herrings, protested to Avory: "I have not been allowed to put my case before the court at all. Every time I tried to present my case to the jury I have been prevented from doing so. I have never been able to tell the jury why I did it or where I got this information. Everything has been stopped. It is an abominable piece of work."

Douglas Hogg opened by calmly giving details of the alleged libel as printed in *Plain English*. The 'false Jutland communiqué' meant that Cassel and his syndicate had made eighteen million pounds out of British stock and thirty-six million out of German stock, on which Churchill had been given forty thousand poundsworth of furniture. There was no plot, said Hogg, there was no false communiqué, there was no profit made by anybody dealing in British or German stocks and Churchill had received no gift from Cassel at the time specified. True, when in 1905 Churchill had taken a house Cassel had furnished one room for him, true also that on the occasion of his wedding Cassel had made him a gift of £500, but that was eight years before the battle of Jutland.

Lord Balfour gave evidence about the Jutland communiqués. Churchill had been called in to write a statement for the neutral press: "As far as I remember the origin of that document is based on an anxiety felt by Admiral Brownrigg and others, myself no doubt included, as to the effect upon neutral opinion which would be produced by the German mendacious communiqué, which, of course, had received the widest publication in neutral countries. It was thought that the bare Admiralty statement which I had drawn up might be very properly supplemented by a less responsible statement on the general maritime situation as disclosed by the telegrams we had received and it seemed to me that there could be no better person for carrying out that useful task than my predecessor at the Admiralty. He is a very good writer, as everybody knows. He was intimately acquainted with the strength and character of the British Fleet. He was perfectly qualified to form an estimate of the real scope of the Battle of Jutland and its effects as then known, and he had what was an additional qualification—impartiality. He was supposed to be a not wholly friendly critic of his Majesty's Government as then constituted. These qualifications seemed to me unique, and I was very glad to obtain his services."

Poor Hayes had little to ask about this. Balfour admitted that when the first Jutland communiqué was issued he was violently attacked over it.

"I did not join in it," said Hayes amid laughter.

"You are having your field-day today," Avory told him on which laughter was 'renewed'.

Churchill was in the box all the afternoon of the first day and the morning of the second. He gave details of the communiqués and his dealings with Cassel. When Hayes suggested that Cassel was not received everywhere Churchill said he was asked to be Master of the Quorn Hunt, a reply to which Hayes returned with gusto next morning.

"Do you seriously ask the jury to believe that there was ever any possibility of Sir Ernest Cassel being Master of the Quorn Hounds?"

"Yes."

"Do you think that the members of this hunt would ever have been likely to have him as master? A German naturalized. You remember how he used to speak. A full-blown German naturalized in England. Do you remember what he looked like when sitting on a horse. Do you think for a moment he could have been Master of the Quorn?"

Avory interrupted but Hayes, who had little enough to make a case out of, returned to Cassel and the Quorn.

"I put it to you as a hunting man who has hunted with the Quorn that this suggestion is grotesque?"

And so on. Hayes cross-examined Churchill on his meeting Lord Fisher at Biarritz while he was Cassel's guest, about Cassel being sent to Germany on a mission, about the Kiel Regatta in June 1914, the Dardanelles, his royalties, about attacks in the *Daily Mail*, but Churchill remained admirably good-humoured and left the box smiling.

A number of senior civil servants and others were called and disposed of any fragments of suspicion that were left. Then Hayes made a fairly effective but quite unjustified attack on Churchill who at this time was, as he had always been, a controversial figure. "Statesman, they call him! God save the mark!" Hayes said, on which there was laughter in court but at whose expense it is difficult to say. On the appreciation Churchill prepared of the naval situation after the Battle of Jutland he said it was a most extraordinary thing that Lord Balfour who was a master of the English language and one of our ablest writers should have called in Mr. Churchill to compose this short and simple document. His book (*The World Crisis*) admitted one hundred times more than Lord Alfred accused him of.

Bosie was not long in the box and made his protest given above, chiefly, one cannot help feeling, because Douglas Hogg (who had been Counsel for *The Evening News* in Bosie's successful libel action and was aware of his gift for breaking out of the bounds of cross-examination) did not choose to question him long.

He was succeeded by his only witness, a certain ex-Captain Spencer. This gentleman had somehow secured the editorship of *Plain English* after Bosie had lost it. In 1919 he had been, he said, prospective parliamentary candidate for Dundee in which city his father-in-law, Sir James Beattie, was a prominent citizen. He gave an account of a conversation he claimed to have held with Churchill at a civic luncheon to Lord Haig, and as he had worked for Bosie on *Plain English* before obtaining the editorship, it began to be revealed whence Bosie's wild misinformation had come. He had told Churchill, he maintained, that he was going to turn him out of Dundee, adding "Your Jutland report was a bit thick, wasn't it?" To which Churchill is supposed to have replied "What do you care? We did it to get the money out of the Yanks."

That may or may not have impressed the jury for a moment, but soon Spencer was under cross-examination. Had he the right to the title of Captain with which he had come to court? He said he had been told there was an order in the *Gazette* depriving him of it. Had he been twice convicted by the civil power? Yes, by jobs Sir Douglas Hogg put up. Hogg had had him watched for three years and spent thousands of pounds on detectives. Spencer had done six months imprisonment for libel in 1922 and been fined 40s. this year for insulting behaviour. He had consulted Sir Richard Muir who had charged him six guineas for telling him that it was no use appealing as the police had been corrupt since the strike. Had he been three times certified as suffering from delusional insanity? He did not remember. The Attorney-General was looking at the jury and 'leering' he said; this conduct was grossly unfair. Spencer considered that the Attorney-General had the manner of an old actor.

Had Spencer been in hospital in Salonica? Yes, because while on a mission to Rome he had reported a plot to assassinate the Czar. He had been confined by the people most anxious that the plot should succeed. He escaped from hospital but on his way home was kept under hatches. Subsequently when the medical board had certified him insane it was a plot to get him out of the Army. He did not say he had been persecuted. "They murdered Lord Kitchener but they have been very gentle with me."

Next morning the prosecution had more fun with the unfortunate Spencer. He had represented himself falsely as a friend of the Duke of Northumberland. He had met Mr. Churchill at Lady Randolph Churchill's flat in St. James's Place. When told that Lady Randolph had not lived in St. James's Place since 1883 (before he was born) he still maintained he had met her there. In 1912 he had met Mr. Churchill coming out of Boodle's Club in an unfortunate condition. (Churchill went back into the box to say he had never entered the club.) In 1915 he had brought from America two machines on which Churchill had based the tank and had received five thousand pounds for them from the Government. He reported that he had information that Lenin and two other Bolsheviks were going from Switzerland to Russia and that another man was to murder the Czar. He reported to Sir Rennell Rodd in May 1917. At Salonica he was, he said, put in a hut with a roaring madman and told that he had hallucinations about Russian Bolsheviks, the result of sunstroke. He escaped from hospital in Salonica by putting a Red Cross nurse's uniform over his pyjamas and cycling to the United States Consulate three miles away. He was there told that it would be all right and was sent back to Salonica. At one time he was employed at 10 Downing Street. Mr. Philip Kerr (Mr. Lloyd George's political secretary) took him to a room there, pointed out a table and writing materials, and told him to make himself at home. His official address at the War Office was "C/o 10 Downing Street", if the War Office wanted him.

The final speeches were moderate. Hayes said that Bosie honestly believed what he wrote and Hogg said Lord Alfred Douglas was 'a writer of poetry' who had written disgraceful fiction about prominent public men. Avory summed up in the only way he could on the evidence and the jury took only eight minutes to find Bosie guilty.

Avory, in passing sentence, said: "Alfred Bruce Douglas, it is to be regretted that your undoubted literary abilities have been degraded to such purposes as this. If I could have taken the view that you could have been honestly deceived into believing the truth of these accusations, I should have taken a different and more lenient course." This was the only unkind cut for it should have been perfectly obvious that Bosie *had* been 'honestly deceived.' Avory then sentenced him to six months in the second division after which he would be bound over for a further six months with a surety of £100 to keep the peace to all his Majesty's subjects, particularly Mr. Churchill.

7

Bosie was able to survive the squalid conditions of prison in 1923, the crass stupidity of the system which was designed to reduce men to Bible-reading beasts, the filthy food and the senseless deprivations, because he was sustained by an inner exaltation of mind. Wilde was not the only British writer who had been incarcerated—he thought of George Chapman, Leigh Hunt, Richard Lovelace, John Bunyan, Daniel Defoe and others who in one way or another had not conformed to standard and had spent, some of them, years behind bars. To no man in prison is his sentence a short one and Bosie's six months, which would be five with remission, seemed at first to be for ever, as all sentences seem. He felt no self-pity; on the contrary, in the very humiliations and horrors that he suffered there was a mystical consolation.

He was unable or perhaps unwilling to explain this in his short account of prison in the *Autobiography*, but in the sonnet sequence he wrote in Wormwood Scrubs, *In Excelsis*, it was magnificently revealed. It was not a thing for him to write of in prose or to talk about, but his poetry was always subjective; his true autobiography is his *Collected Poems*. The very title of *In Excelsis* shows his state of mind.

There was nothing unreal about this, or about the conditions around him. He could not, as Wilde had done, melodramatize the experience or talk of the ruins of his wonderful life. He did not believe himself a martyr but quite simply a man who had challenged forces too powerful for him and was suffering the natural consequences. But he did not minimize the loathsome nature of the experience. In certain ways prison had improved since Wilde's time. The convict with the shaven head and the broad arrow was no more. But from the system as Bosie found it there could be none of the relief given to Oscar in his last ten months. In Wilde's time a sane or humane governor could use his discretion in individual cases and easily obtain the support of the Commissioners, then a more indifferent body, so that, as we have seen, Wilde was given privileges which no prisoner would believe possible today. When Bosie went to prison the whole thing was remorselessly standardized and prison officials had become timid creatures of the Commissioners, afraid to make a decision for fear of losing their jobs. Wilde, for instance, was allowed to walk out of Reading Gaol with the manuscript of *De Profundis* under his arm. Bosie had to commit to memory the whole of his *In Excelsis*, for the exercise book in which he had written it was appropriated and in spite of repeated demands to the Home Office after his release it was never returned to him. Wilde in his last months was allowed visits and letters in almost any number; Bosie's were limited to the statutory allowance in the Second Division of his time, one letter and one visit a month. Besides, Bosie was thirteen years older than Wilde had been.

The food, and the manner in which it was slopped out, was much the same for both of them—it was not until the winter of 1953 that a plastic tray was introduced which was less like a pig-trough than the greasy metal pots of their time. Bosie found it uneatable and for the first five weeks of his sentence subsisted on bread and thin, almost milkless cocoa. He lost weight so alarmingly that he was removed—in fact almost carried—to a cell in the hospital building where he remained for the rest of his sentence. Here the food was less nauseating and the general conditions somewhat better. He was rather proud of the fact that he made no application for this and no complaint to the doctor or anyone else. He was first put in 'the shed' to stitch mail-bags, then given a job in the garden which included coal-heaving. He was anxious, he said, to do the same as everyone else did and believed that if he could have had proper food his hours in the open air, without a hat or coat in winter, would have done him no harm. But he became so weak in his semi-starved condition that a deputy governor noticed it and ordered a medical examination.

He tells a vivid little story of his arrival at the hospital.

It shows what a state of collapse I was in that I remember being filled with horror and apprehension because, when I got to the hospital, there was a cat standing at the door with a mouse in its mouth. I dislike mice very much, and I had never seen a sign of one in my cell in Hall B (No. 69), to my great relief. So when I saw the cat I remembered that someone had told me that there were swarms of mice in the hospital. I said to the officer: "Will there be mice in my ward?" He said: "Well, there *might* be, but you needn't mind them, they won't hurt you." (People never can understand that one's dislike of mice is not connected with any apprehension that they may be liable to bite one!) I was frozen with horror. I thought to myself: "If the place is going to be full of mice it will just about finish me." When I was left alone I prayed desperately to St. Anthony of Padua to keep mice away from me. It is extra-ordinary fact that I never saw one again, or heard the slightest sound of one, the whole time I was in the hospital, though other prisoners told me that the place was full of them.

The mention of St. Anthony is characteristic. Bosie had a special cult for this Saint and in the *Autobiography* frequently attributes small miracles to him. Absolute in all things, Bosie had a faith which may be called childlike, but only in an appreciative sense. It was other-worldly rather than childlike, perhaps, a refusal to compromise with what is called common sense. He wrote his *Autobiography* in a spirit of taking his friends and supporters into his confidence rather than putting his case before hostile or sceptical critics so that his references to his religion are matter-of-fact and humorous as well as earnest. Not surprisingly they have brought sniggers from at least one critic.

The organist in the Catholic chapel 'went out' and Bosie was asked to take his place. This brought him into contact with a number of Fenians who were serving short sentences in the Scrubs and all Bosie's *Plain English* prejudices dissolved as they were "Catholics, gentlemen and political offenders". Some of them, he said, had "frightful" sentences, "as long as twelve or eighteen months".

8

To a man of courage and strength of mind a short prison sentence for some offence of which he need feel no shame can be a great spiritual experience and Bosie's courage never faltered. His self-justification over his libels may have been the merest illusion but it sustained him, and his period of imprisonment during which he wrote *In Excelsis* was the turning-point of his life.

For as Wilde in *De Profundis* rid himself of spleen, Bosie by writing his sonnet sequence exorcised himself of all the bitterness and rancour, the sense of persecution, the fury accumulated in his heart during the years of his suicidal struggles. It is no credit to the prison system that he came out of Wormwood Scrubs a changed man for this was not the kind of reform that penologists desire or understand. He was a poet and only in the medium of poetry was he capable of expressing himself. In the sonnets of *In Excelsis* he said it all, and never wanted to say it again. That he had nothing much else to say and wrote only half a dozen mediocre poems during the remaining twenty years of his life is true, but irrelevant. That *In Excelsis* as poetry is marred in places by that evisceration is also true; it is a fierce and sometimes pyrotechnic poem with scorn and odium in it, but without despair and without self-pity. It brought him peace of mind and tolerance and from this time he walked in pleasant avenues and talked with ease and humour, and lived without enmity. To those who had known only the ferocious litigant of the middle years, the Bosie of his last two decades was an almost incredible figure. Only by the few, like his mother, who had known him before he met Wilde or read the unpublished portions of *De Profundis*, or felt himself betrayed by those about him, was he understandable and understood throughout his life.

Prison seemed to him the culminating self-sacrifice, its disgusting conditions and killing monotony, its deliberate humiliations were the last demands in suffering which would be made of him—as he saw it—for publishing what he had believed was truth. Perhaps in after years he saw that the 'truth' for which he was punished was no more than a wild and calumnious story he had foolishly believed, for one of his last sonnets, during the second world war, was in praise of Churchill. At the time he suffered prison with agony but a kind of triumph and to it he owed the inspiration for *In Excelsis*, while to *In Excelsis* he owed his emancipation from the bitter past.

9

The seventeen sonnets which make up *In Excelsis* considered as a single poem, represent Douglas's fulfilment as a poet and as a man, and by them his name must stand or fall. Individual sonnets of his may be considered better than any one of them but the sustained effort of this long poem was his greatest achievement. He himself believed that he was addressing posterity.

"The whole art of poetry", he had written to me three years earlier,

is to take a genuine emotion and force the expression of it into a strict form. It is *frightfully* difficult, and only one man in a million succeeds in being a real poet. Most of the poetry written nowadays is absolutely worthless.

He had no doubts, it will be seen, and he himself worked within the severest technical limits, choosing the Petrarchan sonnet and never allowing himself the smallest laxity. In others this use of a rigid form becomes virtuosity; he had so mastered it that his metrical perfection has an air of inevitability, and what might be stiff and corseted is easy and natural in the best of his work. As his wayward youth had become a highly disciplined maturity, ruled by an absolute Faith, so in his poetry he rejoiced in the bonds of symmetry.

Through them burst out his vehemence and fervour, his fierce sincerity, his devoutness, his faith and his defiance. The whole poem is charged with such passion that the lesser emotions, some of them unworthy, are forgotten in paean and challenge. It is at once an appeal to God and a counterblast to his own enemies, a shout of healthy pride and a dithyramb of scorn which sometimes descends to spite. It is intricately contrived and at the same time artless in its wild vociferations. Its prosody is impeccable and its argument, though superbly well articulated, is often frenzied, though never hysterical. It takes the intensely personal way to universality which Wordsworth used. It is a great poem by any standards, in spite of its malicious moments. It comes as anomalously into the twentieth century as an archaeological find.

10

Bosie's last visitors in prison were his sister Edith and his nephew Lord Cecil Douglas. During his last week he suffered from a kind of panic which is, if he had known it, common among men serving first sentences—the hellish unreasoning fear that they will not be released. They may know that the prison governor would be laying himself open to serious charges if a man was held an hour longer than his sentence laid down, they may have seen others go out on their appointed days, but nothing can re-assure them.

In Bosie's case there was perhaps a little reason in that he had been ordered by Avory to find a surety in £100 for six months after imprisonment, and failing this surety would serve six further months. His cousin John Sholto Douglas had again offered this but the Governor of Wormwood Scrubs had not received notice that the surety was accepted. He told Bosie to write to the Home Office himself and this was done but he was kept in suspense until the last moment by a piece of malice or bumbledom as typical of the Home Office then as now.

He came out on May 12 1924 and went at once to the office of a friend to write out the whole *In Excelsis* sequence which he had committed to memory during the previous week. Later in the year the sequence appeared in *The London Mercury* at that time the most interesting literary monthly. J. C. Squire may not have forgotten 'The Tin Whistle' but he was too good an editor to miss this chance, though he excluded three of the sonnets which were Anti-Semitic. Nor did the sonnets in their classic and timeless form seem out of place on those large finely printed pages among the efforts of self-conscious young writers, for *In Excelsis* was both ancient and modern, in a high tradition yet sparkling and new as frost. It keeps that quality today.

CHAPTER XV

New Friends and an Old Enemy

I

ALL his life Bosie seemed to attract and be attracted by a certain kind of charlatan. With his wishful idealising of human relationships went trust and gullibility until the inevitable disillusionment.

One of the most improbable and not the least interesting of the odd characters to whom Bosie gave his friendship was a man named Alfred Rose with whom he associated after his own release from Wormwood Scrubs.

It is probable that Rose on some pretext went to see him in prison and Bosie believed that it was through his intervention that he was allowed writing materials. It was certainly to Rose's office that Bosie went on his first morning of freedom, there to commit to paper the sonnets of the *In Excelsis* series which he had memorized.

Rose had a tragic history not unlike that of Frederick Rolfe, whose Anglican counterpart in some respects he was. As a very young man he joined a brotherhood of High Church monks with monastic quarters on the Isle of Dogs. The brotherhood believed that "the vice of private ownership was to be cut off at the roots" and practised a form of communism which they called Early Christian. Rose was known as Brother Oswald and distinguished himself by his learning on the subject of monumental brasses.

He was introduced by a clergyman called (by a coincidence) Douglas, described as an invalid, to a certain Canon Deedes who possessed one of the finest libraries of early ecclesiastical literature in private hands. Dressed in the habit of his order Brother Oswald gained access to the Canon's library and from it not only removed a number of valuable books but cut out certain pages of an illuminated manuscript.

In the meantime his 'Order' was in disfavour. Some members of it belonged to a secret organization called the Society of the Holy Cross. This Society, to some extent protected by the (High Church) English Church Union, had incurred the disapproval of the Archbishop of

Canterbury owing to their private printing of a book called *The Priest in Absolution*. The (Low Church) Church Association wanted to expose this secret society and apparently knowing more of Rose than his associates did, wrote offering him the not very princely sum of twenty-five shillings, not quite thirty pieces of silver, for a report on the society's transactions. Rose accepted the offer and through his agency a list of members was published in *Church Intelligence*.

There was, of course, a crisis on the Isle of Dogs when it was realized that a traitor was among the brethren. Rose was at once suspected and during his absence two of the monks, whose lay names were Green and Drake, broke into his cell and discovered not only the incriminating letter from the Church Association but all the books and manuscripts belonging to Canon Deedes. These they decided to retain.

Canon Deedes, informed of what had happened, sent for Rose. The invalid clergyman Douglas having died in the meantime, Rose at once said that he had been given the books by him, thus accusing the dead man of theft. In spite of this Canon Deedes agreed not to prosecute if his books were returned to him.

But the Canon was not allowed this peaceful way out of the impasse. The monastery authorities, outraged by Rose's treachery, were determined to force Canon Deedes to prosecute and refused to return his books unless he did so. Backed by their fellow High Churchmen they were resolved to bring the traitor to book. Rose went to the Church Association for support and the advice they gave him was to issue a writ against Green and Drake for breaking into his cell and retaining the books they had removed from it. One gets the impression of fierce factional warfare between the two bodies, High and Low Church, in which the wretched Rose, whatever his crimes, was a pawn.

Canon Deedes then prosecuted Rose for theft and Marshall Hall was briefed to defend him. It was, in fact, Marshall Hall's first important case, but his skill and eloquence, afterwards much over-rated, could not save the unfortunate young man. "Behind this prosecution," he said, "is one of the bitterest pieces of religious persecution heard of for many years. I shall show that Canon Deedes was the involuntary instrument forced by others to bring this prosecution." But the only defence he could put up was one of prejudice. There was really no doubt that Rose had stolen the books, on the other hand it seems certain that Canon Deedes would not have prosecuted but for the determination of the brethren to punish their traitor. Rose obstinately held to his untenable defence that he had been given the books by the dead

man and Justice Grantham gave him the brutal sentence of three years
penal servitude. He was just twenty-two years old and "of uncertain
mental balance".

This, of course, wrecked his life. After his sentence he still wanted
to take orders but this was refused and he behaved much as Rolfe had
done. He dressed and spoke like a clergyman without a clerical collar
and wavered between religiosity and a fierce hatred of the Church
which rejected him. The events of his life during the twenty-five years
between his prison sentence and his meeting with Bosie are unknown
but they included, there is good reason to think, another term of
imprisonment. Treatment such as he was given makes the recidivist.

But at some time in the early 1920's a number of influential doctors
came to his aid and purchased for him the right to publish a medical
directory which he turned into a sound, and eventually profitable
business. He kept an up-to-date mailing list of the medical profession
which, by using an addressograph, he could put at the disposal of
manufacturers of drugs and health foods. Sir Arbuthnot Lane nobly
sponsored the scheme and at the time when Bosie came out of prison
Rose was beginning to turn the corner. He kept an office in the region
of Lincoln's Inn and though still hard-up and looking for modest
capital he carried himself with a magisterial air, wore neat black clothes
and with his square-set figure, spectacles and bowler hat looked like a
prosperous lawyer or a bishop incognito.

I do not know whether Bosie was aware of his story, but for nearly
three years the ill-matched friendship continued. Rose had an alert
mind. He was downright and self-possessed, a good if over-assertive
talker. Bosie believed his kindness was distinterested and accepted,
perhaps too readily, Rose's admiration of his work.

Awakening came rudely. "I had already heard", wrote Bosie to me
in 1927,

that Rose had sold some of my manuscripts to Foyles, but did not know the
details. 'The Wilde Myth' I myself sold but all the rest, except the copy of
'The Devil's Carnival' which I gave to Rose, were stolen or appropriated by
him. I really don't know what to do about it, as of course Foyle bought them
in good faith. A friend of mine who knows Foyle personally is going into it
for me. Rose is a dangerous and unscrupulous person.

2

When Bosie came out of prison, he went for a holiday in Bruges, where
he stayed at the Hôtel de Londres which was kept by an Englishman

named Blake-Hales. He had some days racing at Ostend and a few weeks in Brussels. He then returned to his mother's house in Draycott Place and this was his headquarters till they both moved down to Hove a year or two later.

He did not lack friends now.

All of a sudden everyone I met, wherever I went, began to be kind and amiable. This was entirely due to the sympathy which my imprisonment and sufferings aroused. The English are like that. They have very little imagination, and they will go on behaving in a perfectly brutal way for years to a man, not out of ill-nature, for really they are the most good-hearted and kindly people *au fond*, but simply, as I say, from want of imagination and because they have never taken the trouble to find out the facts about the man in question for themselves, but have been hypnotized by parrot cries and mass suggestion. Then one day insensibly the scale tips in the other direction, probably as the result of a long process whose details are hidden in obscurity.

This is a very characteristic way of saying that he himself had become more amenable and was no longer involved in the kind of legal strife which frankly bored most of his friends and frightened others. If 'the English' felt anything about it at all, it was the admiration they always have for a good loser. Instead of coming out of prison spitting venom and swearing revenge, Bosie spoke of his ordeal with amusement. In his *Autobiography* he says it took him two years to get over the effects of his imprisonment but in fact before the end of 1924 he was fit, vigorous and cheerful.

He had been reconciled with his son for two years now for I remember the winter afternoon of 1922 when he was expecting Raymond to call at Draycott Place after the two had not seen each other for eight years. "This action of my son" (asking Bosie's forgiveness) "was a bitter blow to Colonel Custance and he did not long survive it", wrote Bosie pawkily, forgetting that Custance survived it long enough to see others achieve what he had vainly attempted, the incarceration of his son-in-law. Now Bosie and Raymond saw a good deal of one another and later went abroad together.

3

But the past was not dead and Bosie was soon reminded of this by a letter from Frank Harris.

Physically squat, muscular and ugly Harris has been described as a monster. He pushed his way with vociferous effrontery into English life and letters and his noisy ghost refuses to be left out of this story.

His origins have not been certainly discovered even by his most shrewd and pertinacious biographers. "He was supposed to be either a Welsh Jew or a Spanish Irishman", says H. G. Wells, "he spoke with an accent but he had done so much with his accent that I doubt whether Shaw could place it precisely." "Frank Harris", says Vincent Brome in his biography, "was born in two different countries on three different dates and his name was not Frank Harris." He goes on to hazard that "he was almost certainly born on February 14th, 1856, in Galway, the far western seaport of Ireland, and that he was baptized James Thomas Harris". Hugh Kingsmill thinks he was of mixed Celtic and Jewish blood. From the British Isles he emigrated as a boy to America and in the highly-coloured stories he told of his past he was a cowboy, a bell-hop, an advertising canvasser and a sailor. He became a journalist in Chicago and in the eighties came to London where he bluffed his way to the editorship of *The Evening News*. After losing this post, he married a rich widow named Clayton who had a house in Park Lane at which Harris entertained and talked to such effect that he became editor of *The Fortnightly Review*.

In this capacity he met Wilde and through publishing his work had some acquaintance with him before the downfall. He greatly exaggerated this later, indeed throughout his life he greatly exaggerated most things, particularly his own importance. He published a book of short stories and believed he was a great writer. He decided to enter politics and said he would become "the British Bismarck". At the same time he claimed to be a villain on the grand scale who extorted huge sums from financiers by publishing or not publishing details of obscure transactions. "I'm a blackmailer," he announced to Wells on several occasions and when he had obtained control of *The Saturday Review* in 1894 he seems seriously to have supposed that he could make extortions through his city page pay for "literature" elsewhere.

He talked too much. His voice was a roar and he never lowered it or controlled his bombast. He boasted so often of his achievements as an amorist and behaved with such drunken insolence that his rich wife sickened of him and got rid of him. He drank more heavily and shouted louder. He pretended to learning and committed to memory a quotation in Greek (from the *Odyssey*) and repeated it at dinner-parties. He wore an Old Etonian tie and talked of his days at Rugby. But he had a genuine flair for literature, knew and loved Shakespeare and as an editor was in many ways brilliant.

As we have seen he sold *The Saturday Review* and went to France

In his sixties.

The last photograph of Rosie shows him at Old Monk's Farm, Lancing, with Mrs Edward

where he seems to have been fairly generous to Wilde but at the same time appropriated Wilde's play synopsis, *Mr. and Mrs. Daventry*, over which he behaved shabbily. The last words Wilde wrote were to Harris—"I rely on receiving from you the £150 you owe me. Sincerely yours, Oscar Wilde." He started speculations in the South of France, obtaining £2,000 of Bosie's patrimony. He returned to London and ran several papers for short periods. *Hearth and Home*, *The Candid Friend*, *Vanity Fair* and *Modern Society*, but in these later ventures he showed no editorial talent, only publishing or not publishing abuse as it was made worth his while, a practice which nearly approached, if it did not become, blackmail. He was sent to prison for a month for contempt of court, having published in *Modern Society* details of the private life of a defendant in a divorce case while it was still being heard. He spoke of his four weeks in Brixton as a martyrdom. There was another warrant for his arrest when he escaped to France at the beginning of 1914-18 War.

Suspected of dangerous pro-German activities, he had to leave France and went into hiding in England till he could sail for America. Lady Warwick lent a house to him and his second wife, a kindness he repaid by stealing from her a number of letters from "a certain royal personage" and taking them to America. (They were recovered from Harris at considerable cost.) In America he was made editor of a magazine and ran it in the Pro-German interest until the United States declared war.

Then, his funds running low, he set about raising money in the only way he could—by writing a racy and dirty-minded piece of fiction in two volumes—*Oscar Wilde: His Life and Confessions*. As an Appendix to this, Harris printed those portions of *De Profundis* which had been read aloud in the Ransome case to confound Bosie. This must have been done with the collusion of Ross since Harris prints several pages of Ross's commentary on the book. But it meant that his book could not be sold in England during Bosie's life-time for the 'unpublished portions' constituted an obvious libel on him.

It was in order to get over this disability that Harris approached Bosie in 1925. He calmly proposed that Bosie should give his permission for the book to be published in England.

4

Oscar Wilde: His Life and Confessions is one of the curiosities of literature. No one but Harris would have had the impudence to put into a dead

man's mouth a complete apologia for his life which is a shoddy and
ill-contrived invention of the author's own. In the few years during
which Wilde knew Harris he was scarcely ever alone with him for
Wilde, like Wells, was unenchanted by Harris's bombast. "I do not
know what a football scrimmage is", Wilde said, "but I imagine it
must be very like a conversation with Frank Harris." Yet Harris produced two volumes of Wilde's supposed confessions to himself, including long passages of controversy in which Wilde is made to defend
homosexuality with arguments that would not convince a moron and
in words which would have shamed Amanda Ros. "What you call
vice, Frank, is not vice: it is as good to me as it was to Caesar,
Alexander, Michaelangelo and Shakespeare" and so on, pages of
feeble remonstrance and lurid humourless confessions of an affair with
a French soldier, utterly unlike the gay and shameless details Wilde
gives in his letters of his promiscuities with Boulevard boys. Moreover
Harris takes phrases of Wilde's used in letters to others, in court, even
in his published writings, and giving them a twist or a small change of
emphasis prints them as spoken by Wilde to him in one of the
interminable conversations between a manly, understanding 'Frank'
and a maudlin 'Oscar'. Most pitiable are his attempts to make Wilde
profound or epigrammatic. "And so the great romantic passion comes
to this tame conclusion?" suggests Harris at the end of a long admission
by Wilde of his failure with 'a soldier boy'. "What would you,
Frank?" replied Oscar. "*Whatever begins must also end.*" The italics are
mine but the platitude, it is scarcely necessary to say, is Harris's.

However, all this awaits a biographer of Wilde who thinks it worth
going through the book to expose its shoddiness and scurrility. As far
as it concerned Bosie it was no less mendacious and far more spiteful.
Harris starts with a description of Bosie when Oscar met him as
"girlishly pretty", a phrase belied by every photograph and contemporary description. He then produces a paraphrased version of
parts of *De Profundis* as having been spoken to him at the time. "He
frightened me, Frank, as much as he attracted me, and I held away from
him. But he wouldn't have it; he sought me out again and again and I
couldn't resist him." He repeats Wilde's accusations in *De Profundis*
against Bosie as his own observations. He draws a fanciful and offensive
picture of Bosie at a meeting with him and Wilde at the Café Royal
just before the trials, but fortunately Shaw was present and corrected
him on this. Then for the first time we hear of Bosie's 'white venomous
distorted face' which becomes on the next page his 'white bitter face'

and a few lines lower 'that little face blanched with rage'. He gives a wildly fictitious account of the day of Wilde's arrest including a call at the Cadogan Hotel by George Wyndham, whom, it will be remembered, Bosie went to see at the House of Commons. He describes Ross's flight on that day, and Bosie's departure three weeks later in the words "Ross went to the Terminus Hotel at Calais where Bosie Douglas joined him a little later." He goes on to fatuous reproductions of Wilde's conversations with him in prison, so utterly at variance with others and with the character of Wilde at this or any other time that they are almost comic, adding a reference to Bosie invented from his own knowledge, when he wrote his book, of *De Profundis*. He retails these spoony and nonsensical words, supposed to be spoken to him by Wilde in defence of his going to Naples with Bosie after his imprisonment:

I got a letter almost every day, Frank, begging me to come to Posilippo, to the villa which Lord Alfred Douglas had rented. Every day I heard his voice calling, "Come, come to sunshine and to me. Come to Naples with its wonderful museum of bronzes and Pompeii and Paestum, the city of Poseidon: I am waiting to welcome you. Come." Who could resist it, Frank? love calling, calling, with outstretched arms; who could stay in bleak Berneval and watch the sheets of rain falling, falling—and the grey mist shrouding the grey sea, and think of Naples and love and sunshine; who could resist it all? I could not, Frank I was so lonely and I hated solitude. I resisted as long as I could, but when chill October came and Bosie came to Rouen for me, I gave up the struggle and yielded.

He describes Wilde's rejoining Bosie as "soul-suicide" and follows this with another confession in the words of the strange chimera of Harris's creation whom he called Oscar Wilde, this time paraphrasing Wilde's letter to Ross after Naples:

As soon as the means of life were straitened, he became sullen and began reproaching me; why didn't I write? Why didn't I earn money? What was the good of me? As if I could write under such conditions. No man, Frank, has ever suffered worse shame and humiliation. At last there was a washing bill to be paid; Bosie was dunned for it, and when I came in, he raged and whipped me with his tongue. It was appalling; I had done everything for him, given him everything, lost everything, and now I could only stand and see love turned to hate: the strength of love's wine making the bitter more venomous. Then he left me, Frank, and now there is no hope for me. I am lost, finished, a derelict floating at the mercy of the stream, without plan or purpose. . . .

And the worst of it is, I know if men have treated me badly, I have treated myself worse; it is our sins against ourselves we can never forgive. . . . Do you wonder that I snatch at any pleasure?

Then comes the occasion at Chantilly when in fact Harris touched Bosie for £2,000. Again we have 'the strained white face' and a conversation which could never have taken place in which Bosie, flushing angrily, 'jerked out' 'snapped out' 'cried' 'barked', 'whipped out' and 'cried bitterly' a number of incredible remarks about Wilde before Harris lay awake, his eyes, 'prickling with sorrow and sympathy for poor Oscar, insulted in his misery and destitution, outraged and trodden on by the man he had loved, by the man who had thrust him into the Pit'.

As one appendix to his book Harris printed, in open breach of copyright, the two poems of Bosie's which had appeared in *The Chameleon* and which had been omitted from the *Collected Poems* of 1919. Also, in a highly inaccurate form those portions of *De Profundis* which had been read in court. For good measure he threw in, as a footnote, a proven lie that Bosie was sent down from Oxford. He printed an early and inferior version of Bosie's sonnet *The Dead Poet* and added some remarks by Ross in disparagement of Bosie in connection with *The Ballad of Reading Gaol*, and others about Bosie's translation of *Salome*.

It must be remembered that Harris wrote his book after the ignominious failure of Ross's libel action against Bosie and that in order to print in America the 'unpublished portions' of *De Profundis* Harris had to obtain the permission of Ross, who was Wilde's executor. He took the easiest way and faithfully produced the Bosie-driving-Oscar-to-his-doom legend which, when taken from Ross by Ransome, had caused Bosie's action. Harris's book, therefore, was in a sense Ross's parting shot at Bosie before Ross's death in 1918. It could not be sold openly in England but it was fairly sure that Bosie would hear of it and read it and this would be some consolation to the wounded Ross.

Yet it was this book which, in 1925, Harris proposed, with Bosie's permission, to publish in London.

5

The bait was twofold. Though neither Bosie nor Harris ever gave details of it, some financial benefit was offered to Bosie in return for his co-operation and for writing a letter to be included in a Preface to the book. But far more important to Bosie was the promise that he would be given an opportunity to answer seriatim the accusations in *De Profundis* and Harris's own misinterpretations. He had wanted to do this ever since reading the 'unpublished portions' and would have done so if Ross had not prevented him from quoting from them either in England or America. It was not the way he would have chosen to do it, in a letter to be included in the Preface to Harris's book, but it was the only way which offered itself.

Harris was now living in the South of France on the proceeds of the first volume of his pornographic autobiography *My Life and Loves*. When he heard that Bosie was staying in Nice he suggested that Bosie should come to his Villa to discuss the project and in March 1925 Bosie went. Did he remember, perhaps, the last time he had been with Harris in Nice a quarter of a century earlier, and its costly sequel?

The visit was not altogether a success. Harris, who had a villa at this time in the Boulevard Edouard VII, started by sending to Bosie's hotel a copy of *My Life and Loves* of which the first volume had been published in Paris. Bosie read thirty or forty pages of it, then wrapped it up and sent it back by messenger with a note to say he would not keep such a book in his possession, and did not wish Harris to mention it in conversation. Beyond a jocular remark about Bosie's 'prudery' Harris never referred to it again.

When *My Life and Loves* failed Harris tried another of his books. He had started issuing a series of *Contemporary Portraits* some years earlier, sketches of people he had met, chiefly while he was a London editor. He had now reached the *Fourth Series* of these and had been forced to rely less on experience and more on his rather conventional imagination, so that the portraits had become fanciful interviews between Harris and his victim, void of any real knowledge and sketched in with bits of background from *Who's Who*.

Bosie found the first two subjects for portraiture were both cousins of his—Wilfred Scawen Blunt and George Wyndham. Harris pretended to an intimacy with Blunt who had met him once, when Harris went to interview that strange and interesting man for one of his papers. The interview had barely started when Blunt found Harris's loud-mouthed and bawdy asseverations too much for him and asked Harris to leave. In his *Portrait* Harris puts forward some wholly mistaken conclusions he had drawn from the terms of the poet's will. Bosie had been fond of his cousin with whom he had made a memorable pilgrimage to Stratford-on-Avon in the year before Wilde's downfall, and felt some resentment at Harris's intrepid claims of familiar friendship.

Moreover Harris pretended to have been a member of the famous Crabbet Club which met annually at Blunt's house, though he had never been present at one of its gatherings. The conversations he was supposed to have had with George Wyndham were of a piece with this.

Bosie said nothing about these things at the time but the attempted reconciliation with Harris was not made easier by them.

Then Harris took Bosie for a drive in a car he had hired.

"He knew I can't stand heights," Bosie told me a few months later, "I never could and he was perfectly well aware of it. So he drove up to the top of some cliffs and stopped the car on the very edge. Almost hanging over them. It was part of his whole plan for intimidating me. For getting his own way."

Harris got his own way to the extent of persuading Bosie to write him a long letter which was to be included in his own Preface. In this letter Bosie makes a brief retort to the matter of *De Profundis* and deals at greater length with Ross and their litigation. It is not a good defence because it is written with too much indignation and too little considered argument but it satisfied Bosie at the time and he waited to see in what kind of a Preface by Harris it would be embedded.

Harris was expansive about this. He recognized, he said, that Ross had misled him and he would make amends. Bosie need not fear. *Oscar Wilde: His Life and Confessions* would be a credit to him. With that assurance Bosie returned to London.

But before he left Nice Bosie was persuaded by Harris to set down 'once and for all' the truth about his sexual relationship with Wilde and did so in a letter which was carefully preserved afterwards by Harris's lawyers in America. Up to this time he had made no admission —in fact, in court on many occasions and in *Oscar Wilde and Myself* he had expressly denied—that the friendship had been a sexual one. Quite what induced him to tell the truth now it is hard to decide, for the reason he gives Harris is not wholly convincing. He repeated it in more general, and more delicate, terms in his *Autobiography* but this was his first statement of the case and bears the stamp of hard-won truth.

Within a month they had quarrelled again over the terms of Harris's withdrawals of the various libels, which Harris now intended to attribute to Ross. Vincent Brome* says:

* See Bibliographical Notes.

This first revised preface was to be a joint venture. Later, Harris wanted to write the whole preface himself, whereupon Douglas insisted that footnotes should qualify every passage in the book which he regarded as defamatory. Harris, when it came to adding the footnotes, suddenly changed his mind once more.

On this Bosie, to whom Harris had sent a copy of his proposed new Preface, including Bosie's letter, published the thing as a separate book through a small press: *A New Preface to "The Life and Confessions of Oscar Wilde"*, by Frank Harris and Lord Alfred Douglas. It was not until after Harris's death, when Bernard Shaw wrote a Preface to the book which stated the facts fairly, that Bosie consented to its publication for the benefit of Harris's widow.

6

It was in 1925 that Bosie met another baroque character but one with whom he never quarelled. This was surprising because both Bosie and Alphonse James Albert Symons were natural disputants, and because A.J., as he was called, was already associated with several of Ross's partisans.

Symons was a romantic who invested his own humdrum beginnings with mystery and encouraged the legends, some of them far from flattering, which that mystery engendered. There was talk of yachts and racing stables and property deals, there were also darker rumours, one of which he owed to his hobby of amateur forgery. He was at this time running The First Edition Club which was partly financed by Foyles. He was also working—or trying to find time and energy to work left from many more exciting pursuits—on a Bibliography of the Nineties. He was dressy, eloquent and impatiently ambitious. He did not so much want riches as he wanted to be thought a rich man and though he never achieved this he looked and lived and talked like one all his adult life.

He met Bosie after writing to him for some information for his Bibliography. Early in their friendship he proved the sincerity of this though he never told Bosie of the incident. He had just achieved membership of a famous club, a necessary step in his upward advance, and invited Bosie and two other guests to dine there. For this he was called before the Committee and reprimanded for bringing into the club a man who had been in prison. His retort was characteristic. "If I cannot dine here with a major living British poet, I shall resign," he said and did so.

He gathered the few poems Bosie had written since his *Collected Poems* had appeared and made of them a charming little book, published by the First Edition Club, called *Nine Poems*. Whether he discussed Bosie with Vyvyan Holland and Millard, or these two friends of his with Bosie, can only be guessed, but he was capable of both free loquacity and shrewd discretion. At all events he and Bosie became friends.

CHAPTER XVI

Towards Tranquillity

I

THROUGHOUT the beautiful summer and autumn of 1925 Bosie seemed content to bask in freedom, sunlight and the company of many friends, new and old. He had never lost his sense of humour in the blackest days but now he could laugh even at Harris, the nearest he had to a living enemy. Time passed lightly and though he had been out of prison for a year he was still luxuriating in his emancipation from it. He went to Mass daily. He has been described as a "bigoted Catholic". This is an exaggeration though he was apt to seem opinionated on religious matters—to Catholics as well as to others. He had neither the money nor the wish to 'go about' much and as his mother was not well that year he spent much of his time with her in Draycott Place.

He always had a rather Edwardian hankering for Monte Carlo and the roulette table—"Monte Carlo, of all revolting places on God's earth" as Wilde called it in *De Profundis*. Bosie's idea of a good holiday was the conventional one—the Blue Train, warm sunlight, the sparkling Mediterranean and at night the green baize cloth.

In January (1926) he went to Monte Carlo with Raymond. "The weather here has been glorious ever since the first week when it rained all day" he wrote to me, and after describing his winnings and losses at the Casino said:—"However I am still well up on them", a very characteristic remark. 'Them' for Bosie, the vague too potent enemy, might be 'the Ross gang', the Custance family, the Liberal Party or merely the proprietors of a casino in which he chanced his luck. He went on even more in character. "I hear the Preface is selling fairly well though of course it has been boycotted by all the reviewers." This suggests a conspiracy of critics. In fact the book, published obscurely and dealing with a subject just then *vieux jeu*, received little or no attention but it was not 'boycotted'.

Bosie had a small income at this time but his mother's circumstances had been greatly reduced by Percy's disastrous speculations and Bosie's litigious forays, as well as by the 1914-18 war. Percy's son Francis, (the tenth Marquess of Queensberry who during his marquisate became the eleventh) was now a man of thirty-one who was working to retrieve the family fortunes, but these were still uncertain. However the Dowager Marchioness, who all her life was beloved of many people, was seldom without the offer of a furnished house from one of her friends or relatives and that summer, when she had given up her home in Draycott Place, she had the use of a charming house called Horn's Lodge, just outside Tonbridge, which belonged to a relative of hers, Lord Eglinton. It stood in a private lane off the—then rural and wooded—Shipbourne Road. Bosie spent the summer with her there. Raymond was with him and I found them, when I went down to stay, a united and cheerful family.

Bosie's extraordinary good health and energy, his love of the country and his delight in the company of his charming young son, gave a youthful gusto to all he did—riding, playing the piano, working out chess problems with Raymond, walking and talking. His *Collected Satires* was to be published that autumn and it gave him some amusement to prepare the various rhymes and sonnets and to write a preface and dedication for the book.

The dedication has been called by his nephew a hymn of hate. It is to "the whole company of Rosencrantz and Guildenstern in general" and in particular to a catalogue of "false friends", among whom are those "who ended by forcing me to think far better of the average Jew than the average Englishman". He showed me this extraordinary document of 350 words that summer, not as the solemn denunciation it appears to be in print but as what H. G. Wells would call a Lark.

Later in the year, at another house where he was living with his mother (St. Martin's, Limpsfield, Surrey) I found Bosie with a young companion, a bright and very handsome youth who had been sent down from Oxford for neglecting his work. According to one historian of the 1920's this youth had a habit of announcing himself as "the reincarnation of Dorian Gray". He was certainly picturesque and precious.

He had captivated Bosie who for years, among his self-denials, had taken no pleasure in the society of young men of this kind. He loved youth and male beauty and gaiety in a perfectly innocent way but in the sterner times now behind him, and while his litigation had made it essential for him to provoke no misunderstanding, he had grown so ascetic that even radiant company like this had to be foregone, though it of course entailed no departure from Bosie's habitual continence.

It was pleasant to watch them together—the young man 'camping' in a bright and flirtatious but quite decorous way, Bosie flattered and cheered by this butterfly devotion. This swept the last cobwebs of the Old Bailey from his mind, woke the ghost of the young Bosie who had been chaffed by Wilde over the 'Florifer', and to use an inevitable and expressive vulgarism "took him out of himself."

The relationship lasted at intervals for a year, after which the young man left for America where he made a successful career in musical comedy. Bosie saw him and his mother off on the *Aquitania* and was saddened by his departure. Though the relationship certainly involved no breach of Bosie's monastic rule of chastity it was not without emotion and it brought from Bosie one of the very few poems of his later years, *To———With an Ivory Hand Mirror.*

2

The Collected Satires was published that winter. Writing, six months later, to Terence Creagh-Coen, one of a group of Oxford under-graduates he had met at Monte Carlo, Bosie said that not a single review had appeared. This was not surprising in view of the fact given in the same letter that "only one copy was sent out for review—to *The Times Literary Supplement*", whose editor Bruce Richmond had told Bosie that the review was in type. "As it has not yet appeared it looks as if he is going to funk it", Bosie added.

It would not have been altogether surprising if this had happened. The book contained such lines about still-living people as "Bottomley's boy, the dud K.C." for F. E. Smith, "Merry Margot, crowned with Lesbian fillets" for Mrs. Asquith, and snappy alliteration like "Strabismic Strachey's Spectatorial squint." It also contained a Sonnet 'To a Certain Judge', the first letters of the fourteen lines of which spelt out MR JUSTICE AVORY. But *The Times Literary Supplement* did not funk it. Bosie had to wait till June 23, 1927, six months after the book's publication, to find that in a leading article on *Satire* he was reviewed in good company. The review was just, if a little portentous for so irresponsible a book.

He had another small burst of publicity in January 1927 when he demanded possession of the manuscript of *De Profundis*. He had seen, offered for sale by Messrs. Dulau, the only letter known to exist in which Wilde gave explicit instructions about it. This was the letter written to Ross on April 1st 1897 from Reading Gaol. "The copy done and verified from the manuscript, the original should be dispatched to A.D. by More." Apart from all considerations of copyright the MS of *De Profundis* was now a valuable item for as Mr. Hart-Davis's edition of Wilde's *Letters* shows it differs in many respects from the typescript copies made for Ross. Bosie had suffered so much from the wretched thing that at least now, he felt, he should have what recompense there was in it.

On January 27, 1927 *The Daily Express* ran the story on its front page. "Oscar Wilde Manuscript. Lord Alfred Douglas Claims Possession." In an interview Bosie optimistically said "I am sure the Museum authorities will see the justice of my claim. I don't anticipate any difficulty and my request will be made in the friendliest possible way."

But the Museum authorities, having once accepted the manuscript, perhaps illegally and certainly unethically, were not in a position to restore it to its rightful owner and Bosie never obtained it. Nor, for that matter, were his letters to Wilde restored to him.

3

Early in that year (1927) Bosie and his mother moved to Hove, first to a private hotel St. Catherine's Lodge, then to 24 Wilbury Road and afterwards to 35 Fourth Avenue where they remained for eight years, their longest time, in the later years, in any one home.

On October 14 of that year Bosie wrote to me from the second of these addresses with some news which to me was stirring.

I have written 22 chapters of my "Memoirs" which I am doing for Heinemann★ and an American publisher. I only started to write it on the 8th of September. I have written 50,000 words and am still only at 1897-8. It looks as if I shall have to make it into two books.

This was the first I knew of the *Autobiography*, the first published book in prose he would write without collaboration. Crosland, it has been seen, wrote most if not all of *Oscar Wilde and Myself* and *The Wilde Myth*, though sometimes mentioned in Bosie's letters, was never published.

What he was writing now with such facility and enthusiasm would be, one had good reason to hope, a very different book, written by a very different man. He seemed no longer so savagely concerned in all the issues of his earlier life and would be able to see his own story, perhaps, with some detachment.

★ The *Autobiography* was in fact published by Martin Secker.

He was certainly working hard at it. Some friends★ lent him "a fine large room to write in" at 26 Brunswick Square and he hoped to finish the book before the following summer. He did better. When I went to see him late in 1927 he showed me the immense pile of manuscript which was about to be typed.

Two other events of 1927 showed that he could still be bellicose and litigious. Herbert Moore Pim published a volume of poems and printed on its dustwrapper and in the body of the book some praise which Bosie had given to another poem ten years earlier. Bosie was indignant. It made him seem to give a lavish eulogy to the poems which were, Bosie told Sorley Brown, the merest doggerel. He made the publishers withdraw the book till the words were removed and wrote one of his letters to Pim who was in a sanatorium in Norfolk. This quarrel was never fully healed.

He also sued for libel both Hatchards and Harrods for selling (one copy each) of Harris's *Life and Confessions of Oscar Wilde*. He was awarded £200 damages from each.

4

In March 1929 the *Autobiography* appeared, a handsome book of 340 pages in small quarto published by Martin Secker.

At first it really looked as though Bosie had been content to tell his story without polemics. The book opens conventionally enough "I was born . . ." and tells of his childhood at Kinmount. But already on page five the reader is asked to remember his lineage in judging his actions and on the next page, ominously, comes a reference to "my critics, notably Frank Harris". Follows a chapter of straight narrative but at the end of chapter three Uncle Percy Wyndham is recalled and this leads to a premature attack on the Asquiths. By the time we are in chapter four we are growing used to hearing that this is "a true picture of myself to set against the ludicrous caricature that is to be found in such books as Frank Harris's *Life and Confessions of Oscar Wilde* and the equally idiotic outpourings of Robert Harborough Sherard," while by chapter six all pretence of sequence is lost, so eager is the author to reach controversy, and we are faced with "This is what happened to me in 1913", the stolen letters, Ransome, Ross, *the lot*, while chapter seven consists in its entirety of a quotation from that letter of Bosie's which was to have been incorporated in Harris's Preface, including remarks like "The trouble about Ross has always been that what he

★ Mr. and Mrs. Griffiths-Masters.

did was so bad as to be, on the face of it, incredible. Most people simply
will not believe that any man could be such a villain and such a hypocrite."

So on, through this long, lively, energetic and passionately written
book. In conversation Bosie could smile about the past but as soon as
he began to write prose he was caught up by his indignation and the
irresistible urge to justify himself. One is never in doubt, throughout
the book, that he is anxious to tell the truth, that he is sincere and
deliberately self-revealing. He makes no bones about his sexual relations with Wilde and regrets his denials in *Oscar Wilde and Myself*.
He is naïf about his appearance as a young man and his belief that he is
the poet of his generation. His book is of course interesting—how
could writing at once so vigorous, so ingenuous, so virulent and so
dedicated be otherwise? But it is not a life-story and the man it tries
so hard to disclose is not in the least the man who wrote it.

That is the pity of it. Bosie who above everyone else needed—not
arguments and diatribes but a cool straight narrative of the facts,
could only rant when he came to tell his story. The facts were all there
and mostly in his favour. But he was not satisfied to relate them. He
rushes on with disputatious abandon carrying us, breathless, amused,
irritated but never bored to a conclusion which for the first time gives
a hint of the calm he had already, in his own life, found. Small wonder
that those who have written about Bosie with this as their only
source-book have produced sadly distorted portraits.

5

He took seriously the foreign translations of his *Autobiography*. "I have
been over to Paris about the French translation of my autobiography",
he wrote to me on March 24, 1930. "At last I have got it fixed up
after being badly let down by two publishers. I have now got Stock
who is the best publisher in Paris." It was typical of Bosie to be 'let
down' by two publishers and then to find 'the best'. "My autobiography has had a large sale in Germany (German translation) I have
also sold the Spanish rights."

Later that year—"I am probably going to Paris in a few days as my
book (French translation) is due to come out next week. I have got
an advance copy. I shall be rather thrilled to see it spread all over the
Boulevards." I find that admission from a man of sixty, so long after
he had met 'The Florifer' on those boulevards, a touching one. But
although he had an exalted idea of his place in literature he never took

for granted even the smallest success. On November 24, 1930 he wrote to me:

I gave an "address" and a recital of my poems to the Catholic Poetry Society last Tuesday. I had quite an ovation and very nice speeches about me by Padraic Gregory and Shane Leslie. They both called me "the greatest living poet". I was really quite overwhelmed, being more used to abuse than praise!"

Sir Shane Leslie writes of this occasion:

It is difficult to write about Lord Alfred Douglas, whom I only knew as a poet when the Catholic Poetry Society gave him an evening. I was entranced by his nostalgic sonnet about Oscar Wilde—one of the most moving sonnets in English. It was not only because we were sorry for him but because his poetry rang true that we were glad to give him an ovation. Later I lent my house in Westbourne Terrace to the same Society for Abbot Hunter Blair to read a paper on his attempts to convert Oscar Wilde to the Catholic Faith. Lord Alfred was to take the Chair and arrived, but not the Abbot who had been prevented by ecclesiastical prudes. A large crowd had arrived and I introduced Lord Alfred who made a pathetic little speech and disappeared into the night. I never saw him again.

6

It was in 1930, also, that he accepted a long-standing invitation to stay with his old friend and supporter William Sorley Brown in Galashiels.

'Sorley' as Bosie always called him, started writing letters of allegiance and admiration to both Bosie and Crosland when he was a reporter on a newspaper called *The Border Standard* in his native town. Returning from service in the 1914-18 War he acquired the paper in 1920 and thereafter kept up a campaign for Bosie not only in the columns of his paper but by printing satires and pamphlets, risking prosecution in a cause, or a number of causes, in which he came ardently to believe. In 1928 Cecil Palmer published a vast book of his, *The Life and Genius of T. W. H. Crosland*, which showed that although he firmly believed in the genius some episodes of the life were not so easily admired, even by the Scotsman whose proverbial dourness and hard-headedness were a façade for eager hero-worshipping. But in Bosie he could see no wrong and Bosie's madcap enthusiasms and hatreds became his own. He was called as a witness in Bosie's trial for criminally libelling Winston Churchill and might easily have been prosecuted for printing the pamphlet which caused that prosecution had it not been for his palpable honesty of intention and good faith.

Now, their battles over, the two friends spent some happy days trout-fishing. "Lord Alfred is almost as proficient at dry-fly fishing as he is at writing sonnets," wrote Sorley Brown in an article in *The Scottish Field* some years later. "Many a fine basket of trout have we caught from the Tweed at Thornilee, Ashiestiel, Yair, Lowood and Mertown."

Sorley Brown took Bosie to Abbotsford where Sir Walter Maxwell Scott showed them the Waverley treasures. "In the evening, warm and still, we had dinner in the dining-room overlooking the river, and at a late hour were ferried across to the opposite bank, where a car was waiting to take us to Galashiels."

Sorley Brown's son writes of this visit:

I have vague recollections of Lord Alfred myself as I was only eight years old when he was here in 1930. One thing that stands out however is that he always used to insist on his cold bath in the mornings and as it was rather a novelty for me at the time, I used to join him in the bath.

Sorley Brown, in his article, quotes John Buchan as saying of one of Bosie's sonnets to Olive that it was "the finest written in our day". Bosie, on the other hand, always intended that Sorley Brown should be his biographer.

7

In 1933 Martin Secker published Bosie's *The True History of Shakespeare's Sonnets*. As a work of scholarship this is not very impressive; it must be considered as a labour of love. Bosie had always been a passionate Shakespearean and it is no more than a small exaggeration to say that he knew the sonnets by heart.

On the old question, battered by argument, of the identity of Mr. W.H. and his relationship with Shakespeare Bosie had an opinion but it adds very little to knowledge or previous theory on the subject. It was Thomas Tyrwhitt, that extraordinary multilingual eighteenth century scholar and exposer of Chatterton's Rowley forgeries, who in his anonymous *Observations . . . upon . . . Shakespeare* first put forward the theory that Mr. W.H. was Will Hughes (contemporary spelling Hews) and Edmund Malone accepted it. But not much interest was taken in the matter till Oscar Wilde made an ingenious short story from the idea, suggesting that Will Hughes was a boy actor whom Shakespeare knew. Samuel Butler put this in terms of scholarship and brought his own evidence to argue that Shakespeare was in his early twenties when he wrote the sonnets. Butler, said Bosie, "distinctly brings the charge of homosexuality against Shakespeare". The crux of Bosie's case was in one sentence of his: "The present writer, while accepting it as perfectly obvious and indisputable that the great majority of Shakespeare's incomparable Sonnets (which comprise among them the finest poetry that has ever been written in this or any language) were written to, or about a boy whom Shakespeare adored, utterly rejects the notion that Shakespeare was a homosexualist."

The whole argument is shoddy and pointless. To apply the terms of modern sexual psychology to the Elizabethans is a waste of time which would have moved them to hearty laughter. One might as well judge Cain by the forensic standards of the twentieth century. What in the world does it matter whether Shakespeare slept with the boy or merely dreamed of doing so? The beauty of these love poems is unaffected by such issues. Bosie understandably rejects the wishful theorising of other writers, that the sonnets were addressed to a powerful patron, that only the language is extravagant like much poetic language of the time, that the marriage urged on Mr. W.H. was a marriage with his muse. He also smiles at Hallam's prudish absurdity: "It is impossible not to wish that Shakespeare had never written them." But although he prints the whole series of sonnets with a commentary which is often useful, his remarks lack substance and his theory is little more than an individual viewpoint.

It was after the publication of his book that he heard of a reference to a Will Hewes in the Archives of Canterbury Cathedral, a Will Hewes, moreover, connected with Christopher Marlowe. "I did not discover the reference", he wrote to Hesketh Pearson on November 13, 1944,

till after the book was published. The entry in the archives describes him as "Master Will Hewes formerly apprentice to John Marlowe" and records that he "was admitted to the freedom of the City". He is not described as an actor, but as he was the apprentice of John Marlowe (father of Christopher) I surmise that Christopher Marlowe took him to London and put him on the stage to act girls' parts and that he then met Shakespeare. I always intended to write a new chapter about all this in a new edition of my book, but various things have so far prevented the publication of a new edition.

8

In November 1935 after months of painful illness his beloved mother died in her ninety-first year. She had not only made Bosie her first care since his childhood, she had fought with him and suffered with him, given him faith and support in all his battles, and—hardest of all perhaps—befriended those who had believed in him. She had tried to persuade him, in the early days of his friendship with Wilde, that it was dangerous, but when Wilde fell she never wavered in her loyalty to her son. She distrusted Crosland from the first and disliked Herbert Moore Pim but accepted them as Bosie's friends. In her days of wealth she had made Bosie an allowance, in the comparative poverty of her old age she had shared what she had with him. She had followed him into the Church; she had visited him in prison.

Her letters, both to Sorley Brown and to me show how she followed with passionate interest Bosie's turns of fortune and accepted his standards.

I did not much like *The Times* critic; there was an undertone of disparagement all through, but criticism in nearly all the papers is in the hands of a regular set who are demolishing all literature in England at present.

"I hear on all sides" (during Bosie's imprisonment) "that everyone except the fashionable set is on Lord Alfred's side." And so on through all the vicissitudes.

Though her death had been expected for several weeks Bosie was shattered when it came as the letters he wrote then reveal. But he remained Bosie, ready to believe in miracles, almost ecstatic in his grief, and my letter of condolence brought two replies. He wrote at this time:

The pain of losing my darling mother has been simply unbearable, but I feel better now that she is buried in the Franciscan Monastery at Crawley. After the burial Father Walstan the Franciscan monk who performed the final rites, said to me "We have just buried a little saint." He scarcely knew my mother and had not seen her more than twice for a minute or two more than a year ago. But he is a man of marvellous spiritual perception. . . . Indeed no other word describes her. After she died (about an hour later) all her wonderful beauty of face, hands and arms returned to her as if by magic. I never saw anything more beautiful than she looked. All the distortions and disfigurements caused by her long cruel illness, pains and suffering disappeared and she looked about thirty—not a wrinkle in her lovely face which had a faint pink tinge like the face of a girl. Her arms and hands were of surpassing beauty, white as snowdrops. She went on looking like that just as though she was only asleep for 24 hours, and then the colour faded out of her cheeks, but otherwise she remained unchanged to the last. . . . She gave me, all her life, the most wonderful and perfect love that ever mother gave to her son. I feel at present as if I don't know how I shall go on living without her.

CHAPTER XVII

Peacetime

I

EXCEPT to stay for a week or two with friends Bosie did not leave Brighton and Hove until the last few months of his life. He moved about among the Regency avenues and the neo-Georgian blocks of flats, but from 1927 onwards the twin coastal cities were his home.

Olive came to join him there. She, too, had several flats in succession and they did not live together but visited one another almost daily. So the quiet years began to pass. From 1929 to 1939 little change seemed to come to Bosie. His face grew more avian and sharp-featured and his hair lost the lustre it had kept so long and turned a greyish mouse colour but his laugh was not less gay and his walk was energetic.

After his mother's death in 1935 he had a flat on his own for some years. It was on the ground floor of one of the less offensive modern blocks—St. Ann's Court, Nizell's Avenue. From here he kept up an enormous correspondence with old friends and new, with cranks and inquisitive time-wasters, with anybody who cared to write to him about poetry, Shakespeare, Wilde or himself.

He lived alone but passed few days in solitude for Olive lived not far away and the number of people who wanted to call on him in those years, either to make or renew his acquaintance, was vast and at times his flat seemed in danger of becoming the goal of pilgrimages like Flint Cottage or Max Gate. The younger generation who read his poetry and knew the story of his friendship with Wilde were curious and he was preyed on by first edition sharks, autographed copy collectors, idle admirers, columnists, undergraduates to whom he was a ghost from the past, professional acquaintance-makers and people attracted by his story, his reputation or his photographs in youth.

He bore it all with patience and courtesy. "Bosie had the most beautiful manners. I hope you will mention them", wrote John Betjeman to me when I told him I was writing this book. I should not have mentioned them, I fear, for they were so much a part of Bosie that one took them for granted. Yet looking back I see what John Betjeman means. They were not ostentatious and had no flourish about them but they were—beautiful. Particularly when he was with people younger, less thoughtful of others and less intelligent than himself he had a gentleness and a modesty in his behaviour which set any visitor at his ease. He was a splendid example of the truth of the tag that a gentleman is one who is never rude, except on purpose. He could be, in his earlier days particularly, most effectively rude, as his satires prove. But he could not be rude to the merely importunate, the tactless or the dull-witted.

He was noticeably restless of movement. Even in an armchair when perfectly at his ease with his friends, he could not keep still. He twisted from one side to another, leant forward suddenly, gripped the arms of his chair and then released them. He never gesticulated but he was never motionless. This I noticed when I first met him in 1922 and though he grew calmer in spirit his fidgetiness never left him. His voice was high-pitched but not squeaky or effeminate. He grew very animated in conversation, was prone to laugh suddenly and heartily and was never ponderous or self-pitying.

"Do you remember," asks John Betjeman in the same letter,

how good a raconteur he was? Those stories about his father? That high voice and the way he wore a soft felt hat turned up in front and down behind and was always having to run out, after about 4 p.m. when he was in Brighton to buy the *Brighton Argus* to see if one of his doubles had come off? This is a very dull letter about a vastly entertaining man who gave one a sense of holiday and exaltation whenever one was in his company.

He did. But not to everyone, it seems. There were visitors who reported that he was irritable and self-centred. Hugh Kingsmill who went to see him first in about 1936 when Bosie was sixty-six years old is recorded by Hesketh Pearson and Malcolm Muggeridge in *About Kingsmill* as saying:

The first thing that struck me about Douglas was his looks. He is decidedly plain. I cannot imagine that even in his prime his nose meant much to connoisseurs. It has a curious cleft at the base, odd rather than pleasing. His eyes, hair, etc., have all lost their glow and he is too restless and irritable to have acquired any of the dignity of age. In short, not at all impressive, and owing to a stoop he looks hardly more than middle height—say five foot six—I suppose you would call five foot nine low middle.

Bosie was in fact five foot nine inches, and unless he was suffering from back-ache for the only time in his life, carried himself upright. His nose, for some reason connected with the bone structure of his face, became prominent with the years. Pictures of him as a youth show that it was in proportion to his other features. But he was not plain. Kingsmill goes on:

Douglas struck me as really rather simple and unsophisticated . . . but there is something touching and likeable about him. . . . I should say that all the troubles of his life were due to his never having grown beyond a juvenile idea of what a combined poet-aristocrat ought to be like and having tried to realise this idea in spite of being really a timid and unworldly-wise person.

The thing that appealed most to my imagination during the afternoon was our walk along the front. A bitter east wind; Douglas wizened and bowed; his nose jutting out from beneath his soft hat. If anyone had been told by God (he would not have accepted it from lesser authority) that one of these two men had been the handsomest man in England in his youth, he must have picked me out. We struggled along, left the promenade, and made for a bun shop to get some cakes for tea. I thought of the world-wide hurricane that had raged over Douglas and here he was lamenting in the most ordinary tones that Wilde "never could get any work done after he left Naples. . . . You know he really did all his best work with me, all his comedies. Why even *De Profundis* was written to me. By Jove, that never occurred to me before!" he laughed, "when he wasn't with me he couldn't work except in the form of a letter to me. By Jove, I never thought of that before! He either had to have me with him, or if I wasn't there he couldn't do any work except. . . ."

This part of Kingsmill's picture, at least, is incredible since Bosie had made this 'discovery' before writing his *Autobiography* ten years earlier and in this, after listing the work Wilde had done while they were together, wrote: "Even *De Profundis* is a letter written to me!" Kingsmill concludes:

Best touch of all which much endeared him to me, was as we neared the bun shop. I said something about Harris having made out Wilde was heartless. "He was the kindest chap", said Douglas, "the kindest chap."

Kingsmill went to see him again, with Malcolm Muggeridge and Hesketh Pearson, after he had moved into his flat in St. Ann's Court. Hesketh Pearson describes the occasion in an Appendix to the Penguin edition of his *Life of Oscar Wilde*.

Tea was ready for us when we arrived, but it was more like a meal for lads of fourteen or fifteen than for men, two of whom were nearer fifty than forty.

We sat up to the table, just as we had done in our teens and faced a spread of buttered toast, scones, cream cakes, jam puffs, tarts and all that class of confectionery which we had viewed with satisfaction as schoolboys; so we could only guess that the usual gatherings at Douglas's flat were juvenile, especially as we three were grouped round one end of a long table with the housemaster sitting at the other. The conversation, between mouthfuls, was agreeable but uninspiring, and we were relieved when, no longer in front of the pastry, we sat by the fire and discussed poetry.

Douglas was amiable and urbane, though he showed irritation when a theory he had put forward about Shakespeare's Sonnets provoked Kingsmill's disagreement. He talked chiefly about himself and his poetry, as indeed we wished him to do, though he made a few friendly references to Shaw and Wilde and some less friendly ones to Robert Ross and Frank Harris. I did not think it opportune to remind him that he had once written me a violent and menacing letter because I had described Ross in print as a pleasant little man. . . .

His self-absorption was curiously illustrated after the tea-party I have described. He accompanied us to the street, shook hands, waved a farewell, and as he turned away to re-enter the block of flats both Kingsmill and myself experienced the same odd feeling that, for him, we had completely ceased to exist. So strong was the impression that each of us took several seconds to recover the consciousness of his own identity.

To others, Bosie seemed too interested in too many things to be self-absorbed. He delighted in good food and wine and was an excellent host. He played the piano well, though his taste in music was narrow and his repertoire limited. He talked about pictures, horses, shooting, fishing, people and poetry. He had a huge range of anecdote, and never, in my hearing, repeated himself. He took pleasure in old and beautiful things and though only odds and ends of family possessions had come to him, what he had in his flat was faultless and the silver was superb.

It needed a man like A. J. A. Symons to appreciate these minor characteristics of his. Symons who was now running the Wine and Food Society visited Bosie from time to time and they wrote to one another as 'Bosie' and 'Ajaccio'. Bosie stayed with Symons at Finchingfield and A.J.'s young brother Julian Symons recalls that they played chess together. "A.J. who was really no chess player," writes Julian Symons to me, apologizing for this 'gossipy nonsense',

was greatly impressed by Douglas's use of the Muzio Gambit. I remember that when I said to him that this rather flashy 19th-century Gambit was now altogether out of date and discredited he was rather annoyed—on Douglas's behalf, as it were!

When A. J. A. Symons planned to write a Life of Oscar Wilde, Bosie was interested and helpful. In the *Autobiography* he refers to Symons as his friend and in *Oscar Wilde: A Summing-Up* (1940) he says—talking of Ross again—

He was, in this, as in everything else connected with Wilde, the villain of the piece. I believe this fact will emerge more clearly when Mr. A. J. A. Symons publishes his book on Wilde which is due very soon.

It was 'due' for many years but was never completed. As Julian Symons says, parts of it were written "but the calls of wine and food and Victoriana and dinner-parties and country weekends (and the constant need to make money to pay for these things) were too strong" and *The Quest for Corvo* was Symons's last completed book.

For several years however, Bosie and Symons talked and corresponded about it, only once nearing a serious dispute. This was when Symons showed Bosie the typescript copies of letters he had written from Biskra (see page 112) and said that he would like to quote from them in his study of the relationship between Wilde and Bosie. Bosie replied sorrowfully but obviously quite seriously that if A.J. used this material he would have to bring an action against him. "Why must you rake up all this stuff now? Can't you leave it until I'm dead?"

"The disagreement", writes Julian Symons "didn't affect their friendship, but the difficulty of dealing with this phase of Douglas's life was undoubtedly one reason why A.J. gave up the book."

2

Only once during the last sixteen years of his life did Bosie threaten litigation. This was in May 1933 when he read the first volume of Lord Birkenhead's biography of his father. In it he found this statement: "Lord Alfred Douglas proposed to write a book called *Oscar Wilde and Myself* but was prevented by an injunction obtained by Robert Ross in the interests of Wilde's family." Now although Ross had in fact obtained an injunction it was to prevent Bosie quoting from *De Profundis* and could not, and did not, (more's the pity) prevent him writing and publishing his book. To anyone else this would have seemed a harmless inaccuracy but in Bosie it awakened all the old indignation. The mere mention of Ross's name in connection with his own was sufficient, and to have Ross once again, by implication, made the protector of the Wilde interest against him, Bosie, infuriated him.

He threatened to bring an action for libel and may even have started proceedings for Lord Birkenhead and Thornton Butterworth the publisher took Counsel's opinion. They were advised to settle and Bosie was paid two or three hundred pounds.

"I was extremely annoyed at the time," writes Lord Birkenhead, "as there was nothing whatever injurious in what I said." Well he might be, for this litigious ghost from the past was scarcely expected to rise and claim damages for a statement which almost anyone else would have ignored. Nor was Bosie altogether happy about his action, I think, for although I saw him frequently that year he never mentioned it and in a letter he told Sherard that what had angered him in the book was a repetition of the story that F. E. Smith had met Wilde in Bosie's rooms at Oxford.

3

He made many friends in those years. In fact he went on making friends up to his last months, as we shall see.

John Betjeman wrote to him first in 1924 when as a boy at Marlborough he had discovered the poetry of the Nineties. Bosie replied at once saying that he had just come out of prison and was going to Belgium to recover from prison food. They carried on a long correspondence on how to write sonnets and who was a good poet and who wasn't, Bosie giving Betjeman the name Moth, that of Armado's page in *Love's Labour Lost*, a 'well-educated infant.' But when Betjeman's parents discovered this they were so shocked that they confiscated and doubtless destroyed all Bosie's letters.

It was not until 1930 that they met and then, ironically enough, through a shooting friend of Betjeman's father, Sir Frederick O'Connor. Bosie heard the sad story of the letters and of how John's father deplored his decadence and told him to be an open air man. Bosie replied by a copy of his *Collected Poems* inscribed: "Get out into the open air!"

They became good friends after that and when *The Importance of Being Earnest* was produced by the boys of Westminster School, (Angus Wilson was in the cast,) Betjeman took Bosie to the performance and to a party after it at the flat of one of the masters who passed out on a bottle of Champagne, an event which Bosie treated with a calm "Poor fellow, he's ill," before discussing the play and Wilde as a playwright.

Betjeman noticed, as I did in the same years, an extraordinary resemblance in voice and manner of speech between Bosie and Sir Compton Mackenzie, a piece of observation at which, perhaps, neither would be flattered. "Sometimes when I'm listening to Monty its like hearing Bosie again—the same gift for narration and the same way of pronouncing words—it must have been Magdalen in the 'nineties'," Betjeman writes.

He used to motor over from Brighton with Frederick O'Connor and stay with Penelope and me when we were first married at Uffington, [Betjeman continues] I remember I often used to dine with him and his wife Olive in the various flats she inhabited. They got on very well and he was very fond of her and was always so pleased to come and see her. She was a most amusing person—quite as witty as Bosie. I remember her telling us about how she walked outside Cromer with her father Colonel Custance who was an enormous man and had sold some of his land to a speculator who had erected bungalows on it. The Colonel, who seemed bigger than the bungalows, leaned down and peered into one of them and said to his daughter—"Do you mean to say people *live* in these things?"

Betjeman adds:

Olive lived at Bembridge in the late twenties then moved to Westbourne Terrace where I used to lunch with her and Bosie in the early thirties, and I should think she moved to Hove in about 1932. She was round-faced, plumpish, with enormous round eyes and was extremely vivacious and funny. She must have been very beautiful in a curly-headed way, rather like a Hilda Cowan watercolour of a schoolgirl. She was devoted to the poetry of Byron and could quote him at length.

Her devotion to Byron was, I think, to more than his poetry. Perhaps she saw in him a forerunner of her own idealized 'Prince', for it is easy to find parallels between the two. If so, it was, in the later years, with humour and common sense. There was nothing in the least mawkish about her.

Another friend was Richard Rumbold, also the offspring of parents who recommended the open air to a son already dedicated to less hearty pursuits. Bosie wrote to me on October 20, 1932—"I am going to Oxford on Monday to stay with young Richard Rumbold. There is a dinner and an 'address' on Tuesday at the 'English Club'".

Richard Rumbold who was as highly-strung as Bosie up to his tragic death in 1961, recorded this meeting, as he recorded most things in his book *My Father's Son*, to show its precise relationship with his own character and development. He seems to have at first regarded Bosie as a convenient stalking-horse who attracted him "because of his association with Wilde" and his own "early passion for Dorian Gray". He goes on: "He stayed with me in College where I gave a party for him—a bold thing to do but in tune with my desire to shock my relations and to put myself at any cost in the limelight."

Rumbold was aware "of course" of "the bad side of his character" and repeats the constantly reiterated myth which always puzzles Bosie's friends—"he would fly into a temper at the slightest provocation." But as the acquaintance progressed Rumbold, who had some acute perceptions, came to understand him better and do him more justice. "[He] was a magnificent story-teller", Rumbold wrote in *My Father's Son*,

with a sense of the ridiculous, which brought out all the rich fantastical quality of life; and he would talk of himself and his adventurous, chequered career with immense gusto, often interrupting the narrative with fits of irrepressible laughter. There was a great deal of the child in him; his mood and the expression of his features would change in a flash from anger to joy, from blank despair and depression to merriment. There was also about him a kind of charming, whimsical naïvety—the whimsy of the ballads and the *Pongo Papers* —combined with a childish belief in angels, daily occurring miracles, and all the simpler aspects of Catholicism.

It was on religion that they argued. Rumbold did not mind Bosie's hatred of the Left and even of all modern poetry which Bosie believed to be empty and formless, but about religion, he says, he felt as deeply as Bosie did, and never renounced his point till he saw Bosie "trembling with agony and rage." Rumbold was a kind and honest man but he had unfortunately little sense of humour and did not see that if Bosie indeed 'trembled' when Rumbold talked of the Zen Buddhism which attracted him it was with helpless suppressed laughter.

They continued to meet till the last months of Bosie's life but Rumbold "grew embarrassed by his improvidence and pathetic appeals for money". This remark can perhaps be explained by Rumbold's own peculiar mentality. He had a large income and although by no means ungenerous he sometimes suspected those about him of coveting his wealth and seeking to take advantage of him. Bosie probably grumbled about his poverty, as he often did, and Rumbold mistook this for a direct appeal.

Writing about this, Richard Rumbold's friend and literary executor William Plomer says:

You are quite right in believing that Richard did not view Bosie unsympathetically. As you know, many people, whether they knew Bosie or not, were (and are) disposed to judge him as harshly as possible, but Richard's attitude to him was not a critical one. I believe his own sad heredity and bad upbringing gave him a special understanding of Bosie, which came into being when Richard asked him to speak to the English Club at Oxford.

He seems to have kept intermittently in touch with Bosie, occasionally saw him in his declining days at Hove and once took me to see him. I know that he occasionally gave Bosie money either to meet his needs or to back horses with, and I expect you will agree that he did Bosie a particularly good turn by introducing him to Edward Colman and his wife.

My own impression of Bosie (in case it is of any interest) was of his distinction in appearance and manner. He showed me much civility, gave me one of his books, and was not ostentatious about his evident poverty.

Edward Colman and his wife, to whom Plomer refers, were the friends in whose home Bosie spent his last days, and Colman became Bosie's literary executor. But when Richard Rumbold planned to write about Bosie after his death, Colman discouraged him.

I never felt about Richard Rumbold that he would be the ideal person to write about Bosie. So many of the things that Bosie stood for, the established order, the monarchy, the value of an aristocracy, and above all his devotion to the Catholic faith, were all anathematized by Richard whose views tended to become after the end of the war, more and more socialistic.

4

With his family Bosie was on the friendliest terms before and after his mother's death in 1935. His sister, Lady Edith Fox-Pitt was a staunch friend to Bosie all their lives, present at his wedding and with him on the Jutland Committee. His nephews Queensberry and Lord Cecil Douglas also came frequently to Hove and it was Queensberry who gave him his flat in St. Ann's Court. Bosie had the greatest admiration for his nephew's business acumen and looked forward to his visits.

But in those pacific years before the war it was not enough for Bosie to make new friends and renew old friendships, he wanted to bury a number of rusty hatchets. It was not only the Christian compulsion to forgive his enemies, though this perpetually disturbed the last years of one who had never found it easy. When Custance was dying he wanted to be reconciled with him, but Custance 'remained implacable', though he seems to have expressed some regret to his daughter about his behaviour over Raymond. Then, confiding in his reader in a way that sometimes lays him open to ridicule and scepticism, he says in the *Autobiography*, "I also wish to put it on record that I forgive George Lewis, and it is a fact that for at least twelve years I prayed for him and Colonel Custance by name as my greatest enemies every day of my life."

There is no mention, it will be seen, of the man who, one would have thought, was considered an even greater enemy. Yet I believe that if Ross had lived there would have been a reconciliation at this time.

Long before Reggie Turner's death in 1938 he and Bosie corresponded amicably, after this kindly man had written Bosie 'a very touching letter' about his *Autobiography*. But Turner had never been much involved in the litigation and since he lived abroad had not 'taken sides' as openly as Adey had done. In one of Bosie's last letters, written on November 13, 1944, he spoke of Turner as 'a charming fellow'. Bosie also wrote, in a matter of mutual interest, to Wilde's son Vyvyan Holland. For some reason which I cannot understand, in *Son of Oscar Wilde* Holland describes Bosie's olive branch as 'an infuriated letter' then reproduces it in the same book as an Appendix, showing that it was reasonable and friendly, even appreciating Holland's 'feelings of loyalty towards Ross'.

I feel very sorry that you should persist in carrying on a feud against me. I was your father's greatest friend and I was also a great friend of your mother's. I knew you as a child. The legend you have imbibed about me in relation to your father is almost entirely false. It is true that I attacked him in my book *Oscar Wilde and Myself*, but I did it under frightful provocation, and I have now repudiated the book. Could you not manage to get out of your mind the ill-feeling which you appear to cherish? I have only good feelings towards you.

Vyvyan Holland replied saying that he did not think any meeting between Bosie and him could serve any useful purpose "since we seemed to be in diametrically opposed camps, so far as Robert Ross was concerned".

Robert Sherard became a regular correspondent of Bosie's. He himself took the initiative after the publication of Bosie's *Autobiography*, sending a letter, in the third person, on some points connected with the book. Bosie replied that he really could not undertake to answer Sherard in the third person and before long they were going hammer-and-tongs over their old quarrel, its causes and effects, who was right and wrong, the sort of thing that both of them loved doing. The result was a complete reconciliation, though Bosie was always a little exasperated with the blind chivalry of Sherard who after carrying a lance for Wilde all his life wanted to believe that Bosie too had been immaculate. Sherard in his last years changed from an ardent Rossophil to a devoted Bosie-ite, just as though they were all back at their preparatory schools supporting rival secret societies. In 1937 Sherard published the last of his books about Wilde, *Bernard Shaw, Frank Harris and Oscar Wilde*, and in it proclaimed his new alignment.

5

With George Bernard Shaw it was another matter. The two only met once—on the momentous occasion in the Café Royal when Frank Harris was trying to persuade Wilde to leave the country. But they corresponded for years, the first recorded exchange being in 1931, after what Bosie described as a 'twenty-year-old feud' between them, a feud of which Shaw was, it seems, wholly unaware. Bosie wrote to Shaw to complain of his references to him in Shaw's footnote to the American edition of Harris's book on Wilde, and Shaw replied with friendly good-nature.

It is inevitable that you should appear in these biographies as a sort of *ame damnée* beside him, not in the least because you were a beautiful youth who seduced him into homosexuality (how enormously better it would have been for him if you had: you might have saved him from wretched debaucheries with guttersnipes!) but because you were a lord and he was a snob. Judging from the suppressed part of *De Profundis* (Carlos Blacker lent me his copy) I should say that you did one another far more harm socially than you could possibly have wrought by any extremity of sensual affection. You had much better have been at the street corner with me, preaching Socialism. However, you need not worry. Your autobiography and your book anticipating the publication of *De Profundis* in full (I have read both of them attentively) have made your position quite clear; and you need not fear that any biographer will be powerful enough to write you down.

After Harris's death in 1931 it was hoped to issue his book on Wilde in Great Britain, for the benefit of his widow, and Shaw appealed to Bosie to allow this, offering to write a preface which would protect Bosie from Harris's misrepresentations. Perhaps nothing showed the change in Bosie so much as his permitting the publication of a book which had caused him so much grief and anger in the past but in response to Shaw he agreed and the book appeared. Thereafter they corresponded assiduously till a month or two before Bosie's death.

The fate of their letters, in manuscript, is not without irony. When Queensberry and Colson were preparing their sensational book they wanted to include the whole correspondence and wrote to Shaw who sent them all the letters he had received from Bosie and gave them permission to print his own. But they could only find one of Shaw's, dated 30 November 1944, for the good reason that Bosie had sold the remainder. When I saw him on the eve of war, Bosie showed me a thick packet of Shaw's letters and explained that a bookseller had heard of the correspondence and made a standing offer for every letter Shaw had written or would write. Bosie was hard up as usual and took the surprising but at least honourable step of writing to Shaw to ask his permission to sell his letters. Shaw, characteristically, was delighted at the idea. He had already underwritten an overdraft of £100 for Bosie at his own suggestion and now agreed readily, in a long letter which itself added considerably to the total value of the collection, only insisting that Bosie should demand double the price offered—which Bosie successfully did. Thereafter Shaw wrote at even greater length and more frequently. It amused and pleased him to know that the correspondence, which he enjoyed, gave Bosie a small income.

Baulked on this account of publishing Shaw's letters, Queensberry and Colson intended to include only Bosie's, but again they met insuperable opposition. Bosie's literary executor, Edward Colman, refused categorically to allow anything by Bosie to appear in a book called *Oscar Wilde and the Black Douglas* and they had to content themselves with saying rather sulkily that Bosie's letters "except for their bigoted intolerance and violence are not very interesting".

It was however a charming correspondence on both sides as will be seen when eventually it is published. Shaw, said Bosie, spent a great deal of his time in "the St. Christopher-like employment of carrying forlorn children over deep rivers", and in all his letters wrote to him as "Dear St. Christopher". Shaw called Bosie "My dear Childe Alfred". "You know", Bosie said smiling to me when he showed me Shaw's letters, "I think he pictures me as he saw me last, half a century ago."

6

He was appealed to for an introduction to a collection of the literary remains of Richard Middleton who had been one of his discoveries when he edited *The Academy*.* He wrote this well, though he could not resist a dig at Harris who had claimed the credit—not a very important one for Middleton's merits were obvious—of having been the first to accept Middleton's work though Bosie had in fact sent the bearded poet, so proudly a 'Bohemian', to Harris when he edited *Vanity Fair*.

* *The Pantomime Man*, by Richard Middleton (Rich and Cowan, 1933).

Bosie quoted in his Introduction a phrase of Middleton's—"It was natural that two adults, marooned in a turbulent sea of children, should exchange confidences and criticisms," and his remarks about this are illuminating, for they suggest that Bosie still thought of heaven as a place in which he could be a child again.

Middleton was preoccupied with children, and he suffered that nostalgia of lost childhood which is shared by many poets who, at the back of their hearts, regret the fact that, against their will, they are obliged to "grow up". This feeling has nothing in common with the arch sentimentalities of "Peter Pan". It is, on the contrary, a sad and wistful feeling. It reaches back on the one hand to the vanished kingdom of childhood, and on the other hand it makes a fierce spiritual effort towards another world "beyond the stars" where childhood may perhaps be recaptured.

Bosie also wrote in 1938 his somewhat raucous *Without Apology* and followed it, in 1940, with his last book on Wilde, appropriately called *Oscar Wilde: A Summing-Up*. This is the coolest and best of his prose works, written with clarity and a resolute respect for truth. He sees Wilde, at the last, as neither a superman nor a gross sensualist, as neither "a martyr to progress" whose place was "at the very summit of English literature" nor "the greatest force for evil in Europe during the last three hundred and fifty years," but as a dear friend and a considerable artist.

He sees homosexuality as "simply a sin of the flesh . . . no worse than adultery or fornication" and he was perhaps the first in England to point out, what has been reiterated since, that

Sooner or later the criminal law will have to be revised on the basis of admitting this fact, which involves the principle that the law is not concerned with sin but merely with crime. Sometimes a sin is also a crime (for example, a murder or theft) but this is not the case with homosexuality any more than with adultery.

All his polemical skill, which had developed over the years till he could argue without falling into fits of indignation or self-justification, is used in the first chapters to demand a little common sense for the whole vexed subject.

The law in England against homosexuality has no justification in religion. It is in fact in itself a gross sin against charity and directly traverses the law of Jesus Christ who intervened to save the adulterous woman from being stoned to death as she was properly and legally condemned to be.

He does not condone vice but he asks finally and unanswerably:

How can it ever be justifiable for a judge and jury to send a man to the torture and horror of two years' hard labour (there is no such sentence now) for an offence against morals? If they were all sinless saints they *wouldn't* do it, and if they were (as they would be) ordinary human beings and sinners they *couldn't* do it without staining their own consciences.

He goes on to consider Wilde with affection and with admiration for his finer qualities and achievements. He pays tribute to Wilde's gifts as a dramatist and—in *The Ballad of Reading Gaol*—as a poet, and he quotes E. F. Benson's fine exordium which ends with:

Behind the brilliance of his talk, behind and infinitely more charming than his poses, in those days before his bitter ruin came on him, was an extraordinarily amiable and sunny spirit which wished well to everyone, and the sense of that gave him a charm that many of those who distrusted him or found him sinister were unable long to resist.

Bosie was paid a small advance for this book—in a letter to Sherard he said it was £30. He was originally commissioned to write it as one of Duckworths' short "Great Lives" series but the publishers did not find it suitable for this and published it as an independent volume. But he was happy to have written it, as indeed he might be. More than any repudiation of *Oscar Wilde and Myself* which he could make, and he made several, this celebrated the most important of all his reconciliations, that with the memory of Wilde. It is a mellow and chivalrous book.

Bosie, who had a calm certainty of his survival as a poet which has infuriated his critics, always wrote for posterity. "I am glad I've written this," he told me. "It will set things right for ever."

7

Though he wrote no poetry in these years he kept a disdainful eye on his contemporaries. As in 1919 he had spoken of the 'puerilities' of Rupert Brooke and expressed his contempt for the Georgians, so in 1938 he wrote in *Without Apology*, that T. S. Eliot and W. H. Auden were "simply not poets at all". He always had a particular dislike for the work of writers who are over-rated for short periods, and a hard-working poet like T. S. Eliot, who was just then bowing to hysterical applause, was certain to rouse Bosie's scorn and he expressed it in conversation, in letters and in his books.

When W. B. Yeats edited the *Oxford Book of Modern Verse* he did not include a Douglas sonnet. He was an unenterprising anthologist with a bias in favour of the school he is sometimes thought to have founded and the classic form and discipline of Bosie's poetry made no appeal to a man of misty visions and Celtic fantasy. But to Bosie the absence of his work from the book after the inclusion of three of his Sonnets in both *The Oxford Book of English Verse* and *The Oxford Book of Victorian Verse* seemed a deliberate insult and he hurried round to the post office to send one of his liveliest telegrams:

W. B. Yeats, Abbey Theatre, Dublin. Your omission of my name from the absurdly named Oxford Book of Modern Verse is typical of the attitude of the minor poet to the major one. Had Thomas Moore been editing such a book he would have omitted Keats and Shelley. Incidentally why drag in Oxford? Why not Shoneen Irish? Alfred Douglas.

He had a hundred copies of this printed and sent them to the press and his intimate friends. *The Daily Express* reproduced it with relish. This was typical of Bosie who was modest enough to have been delighted when Quiller-Couch included him in the more general *Oxford Book of English Verse*, but was ready, as always, to take offence at Yeats's omission.

Although he added almost nothing to the sum of his own poetry, Bosie had the satisfaction of seeing it frequently reprinted. In 1935 a firm which was then cutting a dash in publishing, Rich and Cowan, wanted to issue a collection of his poems which would be truly complete and include the two which had appeared in *The Chameleon*. Bosie agreed and two volumes, one of *Sonnets* the other of *Lyrics* were published. Even this cannot be recorded by Queensberry and Colson without a gibe.

Several of these poems are homosexual [they say]. These poems he suppressed after he became a Catholic but he allowed them to be included in the 1935 edition, when assured by the publisher that they would help the sale.

Bosie had never 'suppressed' the two poems. They appeared in the *Mercure de France* edition in 1896 but were not included in the English edition *The City of the Soul* which was published in 1899, twelve years before he became a Catholic, nor in the collections of 1909, 1919, or 1928. Now that he had made clear his attitude to the whole question of homosexuality in his *Autobiography* there was no reason, he felt, why the two poems should not appear, dated, among the rest. Later, when the firm which published these books like other firms of its kind had been dropped into the hold-all of the late Walter Hutchinson,

Martin Secker took over the remaining quire stock and re-issued them with a cancel title-page.

8

Bosie's vanity, which had amused Wilde during their early friendship and vexed him in retrospect when he was writing *De Profundis*, was not tiresome or aggressive, and in his last years it was a humorous wistful quality which let him hang in his flat a portrait of himself as a beautiful child and remember with amusement the days when he had been flattered and spoilt by many people, including the most successful and spectacular literary figure of his age. All links with that time gave him artless pleasure and he responded quickly to any of those—decreasing quickly in number—who remembered him in youth.

A school-friend of mine, Lincoln Torrey Brown, whom I had introduced to Bosie in 1925, met him by chance on the Newhaven-Dieppe crossing one summer day in the thirties. He gives this pleasantly verbose account of it:

Douglas was in excellent form and the journey passed all too quickly. I had planned to break my journey for one night in Paris and he suggested we dine together. "How about Maxim's?" he asked me. "I haven't been there for thirty years." As we entered the once-renowned establishment, still echoing with names made increasingly famous with the passing of time, made even greater because of the literary famine which has since overtaken us, the *maître d'hôtel* advanced towards us to shepherd us to a table, paused, drew back, hesitated, then came at us as it were in a sudden spurt of delighted recognition. "*Mais oui! Mais ci! C'est Lord Alfred Douglas lui-même!*"

The complete and absolute success of our evening was assured. Thirty long and all too tragically eventful years had passed since the *maître d'hôtel* had last seen our sadly aged friend. He had been a waiter at the time and had remained on, slowly to ascend to his present pinnacle. And how richly he deserved to do so! Where was Lord Alfred's beauty now, where the gay and pleasing but doubtless arrogant charm? Gone, but something compulsive, some absolute quality of worth and distinction undoubtedly remained very much alive and the one-time waiter had not failed to recognize it and in doing so paid fitting tribute no less to the art of the *restaurateur* than to the personality of the possibly too blue-blooded poet. Lord Alfred beamed with pleasure and talked brilliantly of Wilde in Paris for the rest of the evening.

Bosie, a life-long Francophil, had been a restaurant and café man all his adult life. Once the family home was lost in his childhood neither he nor his mother had remained in any home for long, as this book has shown, and though their homes were never makeshift they were impermanent and sometimes under-staffed. So from his early meals with Wilde at Kettners, Willis's, the Berkeley, the Café Royal, the Solferino, and the Savoy, and their dinners together in Paris, at Maire's, the Café de la Paix, Paillard's and the rest, Bosie had spent an appreciable proportion of his life in restaurants from the magnificent to the excellent little bourgeois eating-houses of France and Belgium and restaurants of every kind in England. Some of the happiest meals I remember with him were in the most unexpected places, the gloomy Dickensian dining-room of the Bull Hotel at Rochester, the Grosvenor Hotel at Victoria Station, the Metropole and St. James's at Brighton and a little pub scorned by tourists in the centre of Ostend. He had the facility, given only to the most skilled of gourmets, of getting more from an uninteresting-looking menu than would have been thought possible. He dealt with waiters with charm but with brevity, he had an inspired rather than a bookish knowledge of wine, he had luck in ordering, which seemed to me then and still seems more important in restaurants than a statistical knowledge of vintages. He was the best table-companion I have known.

He took a mild and passing pleasure in scenes such as Lincoln Brown describes and was known by name in a great number of hotels and restaurants, of cafés and bars, in London, Paris, Belgium and the South of France, his chief stamping-grounds. As he could eat economically in small restaurants he never went to the more luxurious unless he had plenty of money so that succeeding generations of waiters in these places knew him and were attentive to him. He never fussed or complained but knew how to get good food and drink without doing either.

His whole being responded to it. He was not greedy and was never drunk, but even as a man in his sixties he flushed like a boy with good food and wine and became loquacious and exultant over a fine brandy with which he liked to end a meal. But he was not a wine or food bore, rarely discussing either away from the table and never discursive there.

There was an element of vanity it is true, in his liking for being recognized by waiters and such, but it was no more complicated than his pleasure in being recognized in another sense, as a poet, as a horseman, an editor, a gambler, an Adonis in youth, a critic, a litigant, or, in the last years, as the loyalest friend Wilde had. It was the elation of a boy congratulated on winning an event in the school sports.

9

Everything came late to Bosie, who had been a schoolboy at Oxford and an undergraduate in more than appearance till he reached his forties. It is not fanciful to describe the decade of his sixties, that is from 1930 to 1940, as his prime. As far as he was capable of it he had grown up, as far as it was possible to one of his nature and upbringing he lived within his means—at least he left no debts except the ancient bankruptcy from which he had always refused to get himself discharged. Though often hard up he was able to be extravagant in his own way, too. His nephew had given him his flat, his wife made him an allowance, he earned a certain amount by writing, and there were still remnants of family money which came to him. He could live and entertain and back horses with only occasional brief embarrassments and he did all these with gusto.

He was not a conspicuous figure in Hove. He dressed conventionally with a taste for bow-ties and tweed suits and a countryman's liking for boots, shabby mackintoshes and battered hats. No one, in that city of retired gentlefolk, would have looked at him twice as he walked resolutely along the front in winter or lunched with Olive in one of the restaurants, each lunch with her, though it might be repeated on the next day, an 'occasion' like their meals together in Paris forty years earlier. He never called attention to himself and though one of the most absurdly misleading accounts of him published since his death describes him as providing a diversion for children in the public gardens by making a show of tearing his hair in impotent rage, he never gesticulated. He was far too well-mannered for exhibitionism and whatever his writings had been he had too much humour to show rage.

If he talked much about himself and his past it was, after all, what most of his visitors wanted him to do; he would have preferred to talk about Shakespeare's sonnets on which he was, to me at least, almost a bore at times. The subject was for some years dangerously near to being an *idée fixe* with him and though his liveliness and enthusiasm saved it ultimately from dullness one could have wished he had chosen something less supposititious for research and commentary.

Once he had thought and spoken of his 'ruined' life—it was largely owing to Shaw that he saw his past in happier and more romantic colours. Shaw almost miraculously restored his self-confidence, a quality which, despite his vanity and defiance, was for a long time lacking in him. Shaw started by lecturing Bosie as though, (as Bosie believed,) he thought of him still as a young man. "Why has heaven afflicted me with that infantine complex of yours? You remind me of Mrs. McStinger's baby who was constantly making a low-spirited noise." But when Shaw began to investigate the tiresome facts for his introduction to the English edition of Frank Harris's book, he became more and more impressed with the Douglas story and at last wrote to Hesketh Pearson:

Mr. W.H. was evidently one of those rare persons whose personal beauty enchanted lovers of their own sex, *not* sexually. The only living W.H. as far as I know is Lord Alfred Douglas (now in his seventies); and his edition of the sonnets is the only book about them worth your reading. He was an amazingly pretty youth, not a pederast; and nobody who understands that the infamy brought on him by his association with Wilde was the work of his crazy father, and that there was not a scrap of evidence against himself, has anything to fear from his perfectly justifiable and mostly successful litigiousness in the matter. I am now on very friendly corresponding terms with Lord Alfred, whose reputation was cleaned up by my Preface to Harris's *Life of Wilde*.

With his enemies forgiven, Bosie had a great many friends (including one as eminent as Shaw) who saw his life as the quest of a knight errant or a subject for Border Minstrelsy, so that he could afford to smile at the humiliations of the past and at his own variations of loyalty and purpose. This relieved him of the need for self-defensiveness and he no longer had to shout about his victories in the law courts because the memory of his defeats no longer rankled. That physical restlessness of his robbed him of outward serenity but he was during those years gay, talkative, and for the most part contented and although he was threatened with the loss of sight in one eye his health remained robust and his physical energy unimpaired.

10

Few men, in the years between the wars, aroused more personal curiosity, especially among those to whom Wilde and his tragedy was a legend of perennial fascination. His friends became accustomed to being asked, and not only by the superficial and inquisitive, "What is he *like*?" This kind of interest among intelligent homosexuals, people of the theatre, writers, artists, readers of fashionable books, namedroppers or admirers of those with out-of-the-run reputations was excited in one who typified most of these, James Agate, then a man of noisy repute as a vigorous dramatic critic and miscellaneous writer in popular newspapers.

When in 1936 Agate found that a novel of mine which he was reviewing for the *Daily Express* was dedicated to Bosie he sought me out to ask a number of glib questions about him, his present whereabouts, his manner of life and the possibilities of meeting him, after which he wrote to Bosie and of course received a reply, thus beginning a correspondence which continued in a touchy and not always very civil way for some years. In one of the later of his *Ego* books he records that he received a letter from Bosie telling him that his article on Bernardette was "peculiarly but typically, revolting". In the meantime at Christmas 1936 in *Ego 3* he says that he has received a 'delightful' letter from Lord Alfred Douglas whom he had never met. The letter

is about Wills who wrote the play of *Charles the First* in which Irving was so unbearably moving and how he has a painting by Wills of himself at the age of three sitting up in bed in a frilled nightgown, and being at that age an infant of surpassing beauty.

This refers to William Gorman Wills, a strangely versatile Dubliner, novelist, portrait painter and dramatist. The portrait hung in Bosie's flat in Hove.

Agate followed this up with a visit to Hove in January 1937 but could not see Bosie who had one of his recurring attacks of influenza. But on February 12 they met.

Lunched at Hove with Lord Alfred Douglas, whom I met for the first time. A very gracious and pleasant meal, with A.D. obviously best side out. Plenty of lively talk and still more lively listening (me). I thought that after the war the old story would die down. But it doesn't. Sherard has just produced an enormous pail of whitewash. I came away with the notion that, as between Ross and Harris, there was precious little to choose. My impression of A.D. was that he has mellowed. I think I should like a little of him very much.

CHAPTER XVIII

Last Years

I

PERHAPS unaware of the precedent for her action in Bosie's early life, an unknown poetess sent him, in 1938, some of her verses. Unknown, that is, to him, or by the name with which she signed her letter, 'Marie Carmichael'. In fact the sender was Marie Stopes. She offered these, entreating the advice of 'a great poet', in much the same spirit as Olive Custance had written nearly forty years earlier, for although she had made her startling career as the author of *Married Love* and the founder of birth control clinics it was only recently that she had felt herself at liberty to indulge in verse-writing. She had published a book *Man, Other Poems and a Preface* in 1914, but she now intended to take poetry seriously.

Wisely, in view of Bosie's dislike of all she stood for, she intended in a well-planned and decisive way which was characteristic of this strange woman, to gain his confidence before revealing herself. This she did without much difficulty. Bosie always answered letters from strangers particularly when they addressed him as a poet. He believed he was corresponding with a young married woman with one small son.

In his first reply Bosie said that his own sonnets had been refused by editors, on which "Mrs. Carmichael" said she yearned to discuss poetry with him. Bosie told her that if he had received one of her poems *Out of the News* when he was editing *The Academy* he would have published it, adding ominously that he liked it better than her sonnet.

The correspondence continued for several months and when Bosie fell ill that winter his new correspondent sent him a gift, probably of money, since he replied that he ought to refuse it with hauteur, but on the contrary would accept it with the greatest gratitude because he was as usual hard-up. To this Marie Stopes—still as Mrs. Carmichael—suggested that she should approach the Royal Literary Fund.

Bosie replied that he was not eligible for a grant as he had £400 a year. (This was a voluntary allowance made him by Olive.) His nephew had so far paid the rent of his flat.

It was not until February 1939 that Marie Stopes revealed her identity and Bosie was 'astounded' to see the signature. It must have been a shock for him for not only had he attacked her violently in his weekly papers, but he can scarcely have been unaware of her eventually unsuccessful action for libel against Dr. Halliday Sutherland, a Catholic who had condemned her propaganda for birth-control, an action which had roused strong feelings among other Catholics. He told her that he disliked her views but after her kindness to him and interest in his poetry and health and worldly condition he felt remorseful that he had ever had unkind thoughts about her.

She came to Hove; the meeting was a great success and was the beginning of the most anomalous of all Bosie's unlikely friendships. Indeed it was the very improbability of it which appealed to both of these rebellious characters, each of whom had a taste for shocking and surprising the world. They grew fond of one another in an oblique and volatile way. "It was a strange spectacle", says Marie Stopes's perceptive biographer Keith Briant, "the author of *Married Love* mothering the tiring, ageing, disillusioned partner in the great Wilde scandal." But they also took pleasure in other people's astonishment at their relationship. I remember the merry yet rather shy smile with which Bosie told me he had become friendly with Marie Stopes. "She really does write rather good verse," he said, as though trying to convince himself.

Bosie went for a week-end to Norbury Park, her Surrey home. She warned him that her husband and son had no interest in poetry to which Bosie replied, doubtless with some amusement and with considerable truth, that he had spent much of his life among hunting people and was accustomed to an environment in which poetry was despised. A Mrs. Monro, however, nearly wrecked this diplomatic preparation by losing her temper in defence of T. S. Eliot who was dismissed by Bosie as 'not a real poet'. But when Bosie was alone with his hostess on the last morning he had one of those cloudy storms of depression which came up suddenly in his last years and said there was nothing for him to do but die—his life was done. "Look what rubbish Tennyson wrote in his last year. You would not have me do the same?"

Back in Hove he wrote to her in an almost pitiful way about his money troubles. Shaw was a mutual friend of theirs and Bosie believed that if Shaw knew how things were with him he would do something.

Would it be possible for Marie Stopes to tell him? Bosie's chief cause for worry was that his nephew Francis (the eleventh Marquess of Queensberry) could no longer pay the rent of his flat after March and Bosie did not know what was to become of him. "I look at my rather pretty things and it is a nightmare to think I shall have to store them and clear out of here and go into lodgings."

This roused a very resolute woman to action. She became determined to obtain for Bosie a Civil List pension whatever the opposition might be. Almost immediately she came up against the difficulty, pointed out by Shaw, that a man with an income of £400 a year, whether voluntary allowance from his wife or not, could scarcely be considered to be in 'straitened circumstances'. She was undeterred and began an immense correspondence with a variety of people before approaching the Prime Minister. John Betjeman added his efforts and sent a list of names of suggested signatories to a petition. Bosie erased two of these but said that Jack Squire was a great friend of his and would certainly sign—also, he thought, Rothermere. Marie Stopes got Clonmore but although Bosie was touched he thought it better not to have 'any Dukes or merely social figures'. St. John Ervine, John Gielgud and Edmund Blunden were roped in and, with a flourish, Hugh Walpole who wrote to Bosie characteristically that he was lunching that week with the Prime Minister and would speak to him if he got a chance.

On June 21, 1939, Marie Stopes eventually sent her petition to the Prime Minister (Neville Chamberlain). It was signed by James Agate, Edmund Blunden, Clonmore, Arthur Quiller Couch, St. John Ervine, John Gielgud, Christopher Hassall, Harold Nicolson, J. C. Squire, Hugh Walpole, Evelyn Waugh, Humbert Wolfe, Virginia Woolf and Marie Stopes. Chamberlain replied that the pension list was drawn up every March and the case would be considered then. In the meantime war was declared.

2

Bosie continued to meet people who interested him, for he kept a lively curiosity about men and women particularly in relation to himself. He had refused his permission for a play by Maurice Rostand in which he figured with Wilde to be produced in London but went to the Gate Theatre where another play about Wilde and him, by Leslie and Sewell Stokes, was being performed. He also saw its revival at the Arts Theatre and lunched with Francis Sullivan, who played Wilde, afterwards going with him and his wife to see *The Importance of Being*

Earnest. He was delighted that John Gielgud whom he met at this time played Ernest Worthing and, as Wilde intended, as a man of twenty-nine and not as Alexander had played it.

This play had always been the one with which he was most intimately connected, written as it was in that long-ago summer at Worthing. He decided to go back and find the house in which Oscar and he had stayed—'The Haven', 5 Esplanade. The name of the street had been changed but Bosie discovered the house through an old fisherman who remembered its previous name. He found that the large room with a balcony overlooking the sea, in which he and Oscar had worked and laughed, had been divided into two but that otherwise the house was much the same.

Other acquaintances were made, Isobel Jeans and Ivor Novello who were acting at the Theatre Royal in Brighton, and then, just after the outbreak of war, Hugh Walpole.

This was an occasion on which anyone, with normal human curiosity, would like to have been present. Walpole with his obsessional yearning to be loved, the pawky little belief on which he nourished his ego that he was the most enviable of men, set out to captivate Bosie, to add one more to his visionary circle of admirers and debtors. It was not a success. "What a pleasant fellow Hugh Walpole is", wrote Bosie to his hostess after the week-end at Norbury Park in which the two had been fellow-guests, "though I cannot see many signs in him of being really interested in the great issues of either life or literature"—an acute piece of observation which could serve as an epitaph to Walpole and all his works.

Walpole, could not, of course, consciously recognize his failure to impress and be liked, and in his journal afterwards created a wholly imaginary occasion to demonstrate his success. "When I went to bed on Sunday evening not very well, he [Douglas] came in to see me with most tender solicitude." Keith Briant, who was present, recalls—"In fact, Douglas retired to sleep while Walpole and I remained to talk with Marie Stopes," and adds that during the week-end Walpole was aware that Douglas had not formed any great opinion of him. This brought out all poor Walpole's sub-conscious dissatisfaction and prodded his malice.

"How astonished was I", he wrote in his journal,

when this rather bent, crooked-bodied, hideous old man came into the room. How could he ever have been beautiful, for he has a nose as ugly as Cyrano's, with a dead-white bulbous end? . . . He talks ceaselessly on a shrill almost-broken note, agitated, trembling. He is so obviously a gentleman, full of little courtesies, delicacies, that, as gentlemen are now as rare as dodos, he seems remarkable. He loves to talk of his ancestors fighting in border raids, of Oscar whom now he always defends. When someone he hates, like Wells, is mentioned, he gets so angry that all his crooked features light up and his nose achieves a sort of sombre glow. In the afternoon he had before all of us a first-class row with young Briant about the Russians, listening to no argument, screaming like a parrot, repeating phrases again and again. At last he shrieked, "Oh, go to Hell!" He is a real poet (witness "the ribs of Time", one of the finest lines in all English poetry) but has a streak of craziness running through his charm and talent.

So uncharacteristic was that outburst—"Oh, go to hell!"—that I asked Keith Briant whether it had in fact come from Bosie who in conversation was the most courteous of men, however excitable. Keith Briant says: "To the best of my recollection, I would say that Walpole somewhat titillated his diary here, to heighten the effect. When Rupert Hart-Davis first produced this book I was surprised to find the remark 'Oh, go to hell', because the bell did not seem quite to ring. Alfred Douglas certainly ended the argument very heatedly, but not, I think, in these words."

3

My own last meeting with Bosie, two or three days before the outbreak of war, was one of the happiest. I was travelling with a family circus and writing a book about it, and we had reached Lewes. I arranged with Bosie that I would come into Brighton in the morning, lunch with him and in the afternoon bring him over to see the show. We would dine at the White Hart at Lewes and I would take him back afterwards. This could have been settled by a telephone call but knowing his distaste for the telephone and his lifelong liking for telegrams I exchanged several with him in making plans.

I force myself to recognize now that he was in his sixty-ninth year but it is only by arithmetic—for the mysteries of which I share with him the awe of the ignorant—that I can do so. The weather in that last week of peacetime was, it may be remembered, superb and Bosie always responded to the sun.

We had a cheerful, almost I think a hilarious lunch and it was then that he told me about his correspondence with Shaw and showed me a batch of letters soon to be despatched to the bookseller for what Wilde used to call 'gold". They were love-letters of the intellect, full of sentiment, sometimes open, sometimes concealed by astringent phraseology and rich humour.

At lunch Bosie spoke of *Oscar Wilde: A Summing-Up*, though he had not yet decided on that title. At last he was saying the things that for years he had wanted to say.

This led him to talk at some length of Wilde—one of the very few occasions during our long friendship. When I first met him I was impelled, either by unconscious tact or because I was more interested in Bosie himself, to avoid the subject and this created a sort of convention which persisted through the years. He would occasionally recall an anecdote or remember a remark of Oscar's but I seldom asked questions about their relationship.

"What I have never sufficiently brought out," he said that day, "was the *fun* of being with Oscar. Not his epigrams or more studied humour but his continuous light-heartedness and love of laughter. Everyone felt gay and carefree in his company. He wasn't a 'funny man' looking for chances to make jokes, he bubbled all the time with frivolous, happy humour, and he encouraged it in those with him. Everyone talked a little better with Oscar than with anyone else.

"The worst of *De Profundis* is that it makes our friendship seem a solemn sort of thing, crossed with terrible quarrels. But we were laughing most of the time—often at one another. There were whole days we laughed our way through. I remember once at Torquay going into a hotel for breakfast—I forget why now—and being told by the waiter that there was some nice fish. 'If you knew the breeding habits of fish you would scarcely call them *nice*', said Oscar. Not a remark to treasure perhaps, but it led us into endless absurdities. I don't think I owed much in my poetry to Oscar but I did owe much in the nonsense rhymes to him. *The Duke of Berwick* reflects his influence far more than any of my sonnets.

"That's what people, simple unintellectual people, loved about Oscar—he could make them laugh. Even the wretched young men who gave evidence against him. Far more than cigarette-cases and meals at Kettner's. He made the dullest of them gay and amusing. He brought out oddity and humour in them which they never knew they possessed."

I hoped he would show this in the book he was writing.

"I hope I can. But that kind of humour is incommunicable. It's like trying to convey the qualities of a great actor. You can record a man's most brilliant remarks and *say* he was a marvellous conversationalist, but you can't really show him as he was. It's all on the passing moment, spontaneous, fleeting . . . not to be set down in words. . . ."

4

Neither on that day, nor at any time while I knew him, did Bosie talk to me about his money difficulties. Cynically it can be supposed that he knew I could do nothing to relieve them, but I do not think this is the explanation. His letters to Marie Stopes seem to dwell on them, but Marie Stopes was engaged in a struggle to obtain a Civil List pension for him. He was by nature the least money-loving of men, generous and spendthrift, and it was only after his mother's death and with the onset of old age that he thought of trying to find security. I had seen a good deal of him during his correspondence with Marie Stopes and remained wholly unaware, as he intended that I should, of any financial anxieties. He did not even tell me that a petition for a Civil List pension had been sent in or that his nephew could no longer pay his rent. On the contrary he appeared to be flourishing and at no time in that long August day showed any sign of even momentary depression.

We drank a sound Burgundy. "A friend sent me a couple of dozen."

I had become used to hearing of friends who gave him things—no man surely had more friends than Bosie in his last years. I could remember when I met him in 1922 the only friend I saw or heard of was Herbert Moore Pim. Perhaps his gift for making enemies was a gift for friendship, too.

We set out for Lewes in my little Opel car with my yellow Alsatian Dingo on the seat behind us, Bosie having instantly gained the favour of that most reserved creature. On the way out of Brighton we were stopped for speeding, an incident which rather distressed Bosie. (The summons eventually reached me when I was in the Army and could ignore it.) "Were you *really* breaking the speed limit? You shouldn't have done that. There was no need to," he said but not querulously.

On the circus field what chiefly interested him was the liberty horses which he discussed with one of the family. He recalled that on his last visit to Paris he had gone to the Cirque d'Hiver and remembered some acrobats he had seen with Wilde in Algiers. Though not that dangerously boring character a circus fan with a knowledge of performers and acts, circus genealogies and famous clowns, who has become all too buttonholing of recent years, he showed a friendly curiosity in my circus acquaintances and their hard nomadic life and was cordial with everyone down to the young man I employed to clean my trailer. The circus people with their curiously mixed knowledge of men and things and their quick appreciation of character, liked him at once and he sat through the show with open enjoyment.

That night we dined together at the White Hart, which Bosie had known when he lived at Shelley's Folly. We ate trout, I remember, and drank champagne.

"I don't know why you should think there is going to be a war," Bosie said. "I can tell you there won't be. Last year at the time of the Munich crisis I told my nephew Francis Queensberry the same and if he had listened to me he would have made a lot of money on the Stock Exchange."

This was on the Thursday or Friday evening and war was declared on Sunday, but Bosie was backing peace, yet another, perhaps the last, of his life-long series of losers.

5

Another was the pension. On the approach of March 1940, in which the matter was to be decided, Marie Stopes wrote again to Neville Chamberlain and on March 12 received his decision that no pension was to be granted.

Bosie who had been sceptical at first had come to believe, during these long delays, that a pension would eventually be given him. He was deeply distressed by the news and, a little of his old persecution mania lighting up again, began to look for the enemies who had caused his disappointment.

He did not have to look far. "I have been badly treated all my life," he wrote to Marie Stopes,

(though I don't deny that it is partly my own fault) but I began to think that the hostility and unfairness had practically died down. Now I find it is still there, and I feel in my bones that Walpole double-crossed me. If it were not so, surely he would reply to my last letter, in which I told him that I found it hard to reconcile his studied and marked neglect of my poems, and his abuse of Osborn merely because he called me a great poet, with his professions of sincere friendship. I don't like Walpole and I know he is a man of detestable private life. My belief is that he deliberately did something to "queer" my pension.

He may even have been right. Walpole could be unforgiving towards those who were guilty of the cruelty of not loving him. But there is nothing beyond Bosie's instincts to make us think so, and Keith Briant says:

I have no reason to believe that Hugh Walpole did anything which could have prejudiced his chances of a pension. At this stage in Alfred Douglas's life I think he had developed a propensity for finding a victim to blame when something went wrong.

Bosie's literary executor, Edward Colman, gives a simple and credible explanation for the refusal:

Here I think the Establishment should be vindicated and cleared of any charge of prejudice or victimisation in the matter. Bosie naturally thought that the old forces were at work against him and charges of treachery were made against all and sundry—and Walpole was singled out as the seller of the pass, with vituperation flying in all directions. But the explanation is really quite simple. If he had been granted a Civil List pension at that time, it would have been immediately sequestrated by another state department—the Official Receiver. Bosie had omitted to apply for and obtain, as he could quite easily have done any time within the previous 30 years, his Discharge from Bankruptcy. It is said that he did this deliberately out of childish petulance at having been adjudicated. It would be clearly out of the question that the Prime Minister could advise the grant of a pension in such circumstances.

But still the indomitable Marie Stopes did not give up. With the help of Duff Cooper and Lady Diana she gathered her forces again. Bosie met them for the first time that year during a week-end at Summerfold, the Duchess of Westminster's home in Surrey. Lady Diana thought he was 'delightful' and Duff Cooper admired his poetry. It was suggested that Brendan Bracken's aid should be enlisted. But St. John Ervine shrewdly assessed the situation. "It will be useless to petition for a Civil List pension for Lord Alfred Douglas if he is still in receipt of an allowance . . . from the Marquess of Queensberry . . . especially now when there are authors who are destitute. My recollection is that Lord Alfred thought the allowance would be stopped. If it has been, then a pension should be easy to obtain for him. His distinction as a poet is indisputable, and he requires no certificate from anybody: his work is his certificate. But until this question is settled, it is pure waste of time to try to organize an appeal, and you will do Lord Alfred himself more harm than good. I will most gladly sign an application, but only when I hear what the financial position is." Harold Nicolson thought that there would be much criticism in the House by which Bosie might be wounded.

When at last Marie Stopes gave up hope she set on foot a movement by which a few people should make Bosie an allowance of £25 a year, to bring the amount up to the rent of his flat, setting an example by doing this herself and being followed by Lord Tredegar and others. Like Bosie she had fought for strange causes all her life and ironically found in him, who had opposed most of them, a last cause to champion.

6

After that day at Lewes I saw Bosie no more, but while I was in the army his letters continued to reach me and curiously irrelevant they seemed in Madagascar and India. They contained the news—to him, and at other times to me, all-important—that he was writing poetry again. He blandly ignored the implication of APO addresses and there was often a hint of reproach that I did not come to see him though in fact I was many thousand miles away.

On August 21, 1941, he wrote to me from his flat in St. Ann's Court a characteristic letter which I received while training in Combined Operations on Loch Fyne:

My dear Rupert,

Very glad to hear from you and very sorry you weren't able to come and see me. Don't apologize for being sentimental. I have always been inclined that way myself! I enclose a sheet torn out of a new publication at Oxford. It contains a copy of my sonnet about Winston Churchill which appeared in the *Daily Mail* on July 4th. This was the first sonnet (or any poem) I had written for seven years! I don't think it is anything out of the way, but its not *too* bad and its had a great deal of praise. I have written 2 more sonnets since— one of them called *The Old Soldier* was in the *Evening Standard* on July 21st. I had a letter about it from Capt. Margesson the Minister of War and he says: "it is full of sadness and truth". But as its almost all in defence of "Colonel Blimp" most people took it for a mere joke. The Minister of War had the acumen to see that it is quite serious poetry. I have written another sonnet which I believe to be *really good*, much better than the other two. I haven't done anything about it yet, but I'm going to send it to Peter Page of the *Daily Mail*. I don't suppose they'll publish it because it contains a "kick in the pants" for "Democracy". Don't forget to come and see me whenever you get the chance. Life remains quiet here. My only news is that the BBC are going to broadcast a lot of my sonnets. I don't know the date yet.

Yours ever affect'ly,

Bosie.

The first of the sonnets mentioned was given a brave display by the *Daily Mail*. The naïvety of the opening line was characteristic of the poet who had started one of his *In Excelsis* sonnets "Not I, alas, at any rate, not yet;" But the lines here were strong and apposite and made sincere amends for the foolish calumnies of twenty years earlier.

Not that of old I loved you over-much
Or followed your quick changes with great glee,
While through rough paths of harsh hostility
You fought your way, using a sword or crutch
To serve occasion. Yours it was to clutch
And lose again. Lacking the charity
Which looks behind the mask, I did not see
The immanent shadow of "the Winston touch".

Axe for embedded evil's cancerous roots.
When all the world was one vast funeral pyre,
Like genie smoke you rose, a giant form
Clothed with the Addisonian attributes
Of God-directed angel. Like your sire
You rode the whirlwind and outstormed the storm.

When this was published Bosie's nephew sent a copy to Churchill who found time, in 1941, to answer: "Thank you very much for the sonnet you sent me which I shall keep and value. Tell him from me that 'Time Ends All Things'."

The two other sonnets, the last poetry that Bosie wrote, appear in *The Sonnets of Alfred Douglas* published by the Richards Press in 1943. Bosie was immensely gratified, both in pride and pocket, when *The Evening Standard* paid him twenty guineas for the one published.

7

Bosie, in his seventies, was at first far from acknowledging defeat at the hands of advancing age. He was brisk in movement and his gusto was undaunted. He kept in touch with a great number of friends and went up to town from time to time.

On one occasion in 1942 after he had lunched at Scott's with Martin Secker, now a friend of thirty years' standing, they passed the Phoenix Theatre at which there was a revival of *The Importance of Being Earnest*. As people were going into a matinée they joined them and Bosie saw once again the play Wilde had written while they were together at Worthing. It was the only one of the plays of which he had missed the first night—for he had been still in Algeria—but he had seen it on that memorable evening, just before the opening of Wilde's case against Queensberry, when he sat with Oscar and Constance Wilde in a box as a gesture of solidarity. He enjoyed seeing it again but disagreed with Martin Secker about the performance of Cyril Ritchard who played

z

Algernon. Secker thought it was very good—Bosie dismissed it as 'common'.

In 1943 he was invited to address the Royal Society of Literature on any subject he chose and decided to do so on *The Principles of Poetry*, attacking what he called 'the modern heretical "poets" such as T. S. Eliot, Auden and Co.' There was a fee of forty guineas for this and Martin Secker agreed to publish his paper afterwards. Marie Stopes wanted him to 'be a dear magician' and work into his lecture a reference to the fact that there was no memorial to Shelley in Westminster Abbey, as (needless to say) she was interested in a 'movement' which had been 'set on foot'. Bosie refused, giving as his reason the fact that it would be wholly irrelevant to his subject. (Did it occur to either of them, one wonders, that Shelley had no need of the smiles of the Establishment and would not have thanked anyone for setting him in that memorial zoo?)

The lecture was given on September 2 with Lord Tredegar in the Chair.

Bosie started mildly enough by remembering that only thirty years before "there was a fairly general agreement among educated people as to what was poetry and what was not". Walt Whitman was an isolated phenomenon, "Yet . . ." Here it comes, his audience must have thought with relish. "Yet he was a serious writer and not a mere mountebank playing the impudent fool with words, like some of our alleged modern poets."

Thereafter he began to enjoy himself in a dashing young man's attack on the vulnerable—and one hopes absent—T. S. Eliot and his 'besotted admirers'. Ingeniously he took a piece of prose from a leading article in *The Daily Telegraph* and by cutting it up into 'lines' made it a modern poem, then, taking the opening lines of a modern poem, he ran it as a continuous paragraph as prose. Thus the article:

> We are clearly in the presence of something
> Very different from what the allies
> And the enemy alike used to try
> In the way of strategic bombing.

And thus the poem (T. S. Eliot's):

> Miss Helen Slingsby was my maiden aunt and
> lived in a small house near a fashionable
> square, cared for by servants to the number
> of four.

What was there about this, he asked triumphantly, that makes it any more poetical than the words in the leading article?

If the words of Mr. Eliot are poetry then the words of the leading article must be poetry. . . . It is a frightful reflection on the miserable and abject state to which criticism has sunk in England that this pitiable stuff has for years been accepted without protest as poetry.

He then turned to W. B. Yeats. "Unlike Mr. Eliot he *did* write poetry, sometimes fine poetry", though he had a defective ear for rhythm.

But his long address was not all attack, nor the attack itself ill-humoured, however sweeping. There was some honest erudition in the thing and an enthusiasm, sometimes a little breathless, which seems to have communicated itself to the audience. "I was pleased and gratified to find my attack on T. S. Eliot so well received. I quite expected some people would object but apparently the feeling of the audience was unanimous." This in a letter to Marie Stopes. Yet one feels that the audience was unanimous in only one thing—their admiration for his septuagenarian spirit and his obvious sincerity. He was speaking for something more than himself or his prejudices. He was defending what he saw as the temporarily lost cause of classic form in poetry. It was a plucky defence, not without occasional brilliance and humour and not wholly without effect.

8

In those years of war many of his old friends died, also one or two of his antagonists. "Freddy" Benson whom he had quoted enthusiastically in his last book, died in 1940, 'Ajaccio' (A. J. A. Symons) with whom he was in correspondence to the last, in 1941, and his staunch friend and supporter W. Sorley Brown in 1942. More Adey, with whom he had kept the promise made thirty years earlier that he would never speak to him again, also died in 1942 and in 1943 Bosie lost his intimate friend Sir Frederick O'Connor. O'Connor was Bosie's contemporary to a year; although he had a distinguished career he attributed his failure to reach the highest distinction to his own nature which resembled Bosie's in more than one respect. The two saw a great deal of one another in the last years and until the outbreak of war continued to enjoy an occasional day's shooting.

Also in 1943 died Robert Sherard. Bosie had corresponded with him in the friendliest way for several years, and lunched with him in London, their first meeting since Wilde's death, a year earlier.

But in 1944 he suffered a series of blows which broke him in heart and body, though not in spirit. In February his wife died. He had not lived with her since she deserted him for her father in 1913, but they had become intimate, even loving friends and few days passed in which they did not see one another. Bosie was greatly distressed because although Olive 'of her own free will' had become a Catholic twenty years or more earlier, she had lapsed after about three years. Five weeks before her death she told Bosie that she bitterly regretted having left the Church and had had nothing but ill luck and misery since she did so. She intended, she said, to 'do something about it' as soon as she felt well enough, but during her last weeks she was in a very weak mental state and for much of the time was incoherent or semi-conscious.

Bosie wrote to Marie Stopes who had suggested that the point was not important:

Under these circumstances I felt it would be a mere piece of humbug to bring a priest in. Besides which I had no right to do so unless she asked me to. So I confined myself to praying for her and hoping that some miracle would occur. I found what hopes I have for her in what she said to me about her bitter regret at having left the Church. For all I know she may have made an act of perfect contrition. God's mercy is infinite, and of course millions of souls outside the Church are saved. But it is easier for someone who has never been in the Church to be saved because of his or her "invincible ignorance" (which is the theological term for your state, my dear Marie) than for someone who has had the light and then deliberately rejected it as my poor wife did. She was cremated yesterday here. . . .

The death of Olive was closely followed by another tragedy. Bosie's son Raymond had been confined for many years in a mental home. It is possible that the stresses and quarrels of his childhood and Custance's obstinate determination to separate him from his father, had affected his mind. This was a constant grief to Bosie, particularly as Raymond, in his calmer moments, kept all his charm and gentleness of character and when Bosie went to see him appeared almost normal, going out with his father to lunch or dinner, full of affection and humour.

His doctors now decided that he might occupy Olive's flat on the sea-front at Hove, and since his income was increased after his mother's death, he offered to make Bosie an allowance of £300 a year, in place of that which he had lost on Olive's death. (Olive's fairly substantial income was derived from Custance trust funds.)

Raymond's stay at the flat was an experiment and his doctors hoped that he might take it over if all went well. But, writes Bosie's literary executor Edward Colman, "before a week was up Raymond had a brain storm, and thanks to Olive's maid Eileen, to whom Evan Tredegar always referred as 'the Irish giantess' (she was truly enormous) tragedy was narrowly averted."

This affected Bosie deeply and he talked of "possession" by evil spirits.

9

But he continued throughout the summer months of 1944 to make new friends and keep in touch with old ones. He saw a good deal of Lord Tredegar and at Lady Tredegar's home he met young people who interested him. Hector Bolitho recalls seeing him there "walking in, slowly, with a sad face and quick lively eyes."

Not everyone found him sad. Richard Blake Brown, for instance, then Chaplain of H.M.S. *Vernon*, the Torpedo School which had taken over Roedean, saw him several times and himself an exhilarating person found Bosie no less so. They met in the flat which had been Olive's and Blake Brown describes it:

A charming flat with white glass-doored cupboards, with glass and china; blue was the predominant colour of cushions and curtains but it seemed to be all painted or papered with white which gave it a light and cheerful air in which Lord Alfred was completely at home. He spoke most affectionately of Olive and seemed thoroughly to enjoy living in the flat she had occupied. He talked vivaciously and happily, never growing angry over his memories. His face seemed sharper, the nose almost ugly. I had re-met him by running into him when I had been dining with a woman friend at the Norfolk Hotel (where Charles Dickens used to stay.) I ordered three Green Chartreuses and we had an animated chat in the lounge, but the friend I was with later told other people that I knew scandalous and undesirable people. On the last time I had tea with him Lord Alfred was particularly charming and showed me his wife's Byron books, while a big fat Irish servant who had been I fancy with his wife bustled about, red-faced, merry and with sparse black hair. She no doubt looked after him magnificently, even dotingly. His talk was fascinating as ever.

10

But in the autumn his health broke down and he could no longer afford to keep his flat in St. Ann's Court, while the furniture in Olive's flat, left to Bosie with a sum of money in her will had been seized by the Official Receivers. Edward Colman says of this:

His wife Olive had died a short time before and left him such money as she had in her banking account together with a good deal of valuable furniture which she held in her own right (her fairly substantial income was derived from Custance trust funds). The whole lot was swept into the maw of the Official Receiver, there to await the claims and identity of as heterogeneous a collection of creditors and their successors in title, as was ever seen! As his executor I was faced with the seemingly impossible task of protecting his copyright which had become vested in the O.R., and assisting the authorities to determine and settle claims against his estate dating back to 1912. I settled the former by taking an assignment by purchase, and the latter by two years work in sorting out most of the claimants or their survivors so that their claims could be met. The officials concerned deserve the highest praise for their consideration, co-operation, and general attitude of helpfulness in this difficult task.

Bosie decided to go into rooms and in order to pay for these and for two weeks' rest cure in a nursing home he sold the furniture of his flat. Before he moved, in one of those moods of destruction in which he had burnt Wilde's letters long ago, he threw out an enormous number of letters, manuscripts and other material. Edward Colman writes of this:

As soon as he told me what he had done (a day or two after) I immediately tried to retrieve the sacks full of 'rubbish' he had thrown out, but although the refuse disposal department were as helpful as they could be, I was just too late to save it from the pulping machines, which owing to the urgent necessity at that phase of the war, stood waiting for every scrap and morsel of salvage the authorities could lay their hands on.

He felt much better for the rest cure but a few days after he was up and about he was 'as bad as ever'. "Honestly", he wrote to Hesketh Pearson on November 13,

I don't expect to recover at my age (74 last birthday) as I expect my heart is pretty well worn out after all the troubles and fights I have had. But if you will come and see me here [i.e. in his rooms at 16 Silverdale Avenue, Hove] I will tell you all I can by word of mouth as I can still talk!

He could still write, too, and in the long letter which followed, answering points put to him by Pearson who was writing his *Life of Oscar Wilde*, he argued vigorously about the identity of W.H. and the "perfidy" (long forgiven) of Robert Hichens.

Pearson went to see him but instead of talking about Wilde they became involved in an argument about Shakespeare's sonnets. At last Bosie made Pearson feel remorseful.

"My heart is paining me," he said. "Let us talk some other time." Murmuring sympathy and regret, I rose to go. He again invited me to tea the following week, and I promised to bring him some eggs and brandy, both of which he lacked and needed. I asked whether he wanted any money, but he replied that his son had been very kind to him and that he was in no anxiety on that account. I then withdrew, and on my way to the station cursed myself heartily for letting my interest in Shakespeare drive everything else out of my head.

A week later Pearson called again.

Sternly reminding myself, as I stood on the doorstep of Douglas's lodgings that if Shakespeare were mentioned I must count ten slowly before speaking and then change the subject. I rang the bell and concentrated my mind on Oscar Wilde. A dozen eggs and a bottle of brandy made a pleasing impression; once more I found myself sitting at a table with Douglas and doing justice to the wartime cakes and scones; and whenever the conversation drifted away from Wilde I resolutely brought it back again. He answered all the questions I wished to ask him, and remembered something that he had forgotten to record: the remarkable incident of Wilde being held up by apaches in Paris and delighting them so much by his conversation that they paid for his drinks instead of stealing his watch. At last he tired of talking about Wilde and got on to the topic of his health, concerning which he had so much to say that I advised him to think of something else. "Brooding on one's ailments is the surest way of intensifying them", I said. "Why not"—I thought hard, and then blurted out the fated suggestion—"why not re-read Shakespeare's plays and study the Sonnets with a clear knowledge of the man who wrote them?" The last syllable was scarcely off my tongue before I wanted to bang my head against the wall. "Oh, damn Shakespeare!" he exploded. I did my best to restore harmony; but the word was spoken; we were both agitated; and I parted from him on a note of muted discord.

He continued to write to Marie Stopes, though he did not go out at all but just 'sat in a chair and read and drowsed'. He knew he would die soon, "but I don't mind at all and am quite happy because I have complete faith and trust in darling Jesus", a simple statement of faith. He must have said something of the sort to his nephew who interpreted it as—"being in such high favour with the heavenly powers, he was under no apprehension as to his future state."

Then Bosie, always ready to believe in miracles, believed that yet another had happened to him. He was suffering what he thought was the approach of death—a feeling of suffocation which caused him to send for a priest who gave him Extreme Unction. He had heard of miraculous recoveries after this sacrament but was expecting nothing of the sort and only hoping for relief. The whole thing lasted about five minutes during which he was overcome with 'terrific emotion'. "The tears rained down my cheeks." When it was over the suffocation was completely gone and though he feared it was only a temporary relief by the evening he felt perfectly well. He had a boiled egg and some sherry and after a good night's sleep wrote to put off his nephew and sister who were coming to his deathbed.

His last letter to Marie Stopes that December was characteristic. The miraculous recovery had been no more than a dying flicker—he was worse than ever now and he 'couldn't write'.

Couldn't he? The letter continues: "Did you see Agate's idiotic remarks about your poems and my Preface in the *Express*? I wrote a 'stinker' in reply but of course they did not print it."

Then, as more than once in his life by the intervention of others he was given complete relief from all his cares, financial and domestic. "Colman wants to cart me off to Lancing and give me good food and wine", he had written in a previous letter. This is what happened.

II

Early in the war he had met Edward Colman and his wife who lived at Old Monk's Farm, Lancing. Their home was filled with the comings and goings of young friends who soon began to disappear into the services, but would come back on leave. Bosie, who always enjoyed the company of the young, delighted in staying at the farm for week-ends and holidays. As the stringencies of rationing tightened the Colmans would encourage him to come more often for they thought he looked frail. His response to good food and wine with congenial friends was, as ever, immediate and his hosts knew how to avoid, or adroitly handle, the controversial issues which could still cause him to be downright and peremptory, though not discourteous. He was an ideal guest and told good stories of the past in his high-pitched voice, bringing laughter with him and unquenchable gusto.

The Colmans now persuaded him to give up his rooms and stay with them. Critics who have depicted Bosie as a sour unlovable man have never explained the fact that all his life he found devoted friends and never more than in these years of poverty, illness and the approaching victory of old age over his shrinking frame. He accepted the offer with gratitude and the last four months of his life were, in spite of his heart trouble ("a leaky valve," he said) some of his happiest. He was resigned to the approach of death but had not lost his enjoyment of living and responded as always to kindness.

In the last days of November (1944) he was driven out to Old Monk's Farm.* Here he was able to rest and talk, to eat and drink, to make small bets every day, often to laugh, and above all to see the many friends who wanted to visit him.

His first visitor (on December 1) was his nephew Queensberry who writes in *Oscar Wilde and the Black Douglas*. "He asked me to send him a bottle of old brandy, as a bottle for which he had paid five guineas was undrinkable. He also told me that he hated brandy, which showed a remarkable change in his tastes."

Another visitor was Lord Tredegar. "He was indeed a good friend to Bosie", writes Edward Colman,

and came frequently to see him with succulent titbits such as oysters and champagne to tempt his failing appetite, and often brought with him a somewhat strange entourage of youthful admirers whom Bosie enjoyed immensely.

But before Bosie's last weeks Tredegar's own health began to fail and he was not able to go to Lancing.†

From Lancing, just a month before he died, Bosie wrote to Hesketh Pearson who had sent him in typescript chapters 15 and 16 of his *Life of Oscar Wilde*, those dealing with Wilde's trial and imprisonment. His letter was written in pencil and the script was halting but the sentiments were still sturdy and in his own tradition.

I read the chapters you sent this morning. They are admirable and moving (in fact I found it exceedingly painful to read once more the dreadful story of cruelty and hypocrisy and humbug). Your book will be far the best written on the subject. I can't write at length, I am far too ill, but hope you will come

---

* Among the malicious or merely clumsy inventions of his chroniclers is one that at this time he arrived at the Hampstead home of 'his old friend Miss Mary Grosvenor' but that a discussion with his sister made him change his mind. There was no Miss Mary Grosvenor and no discussion with his sister. He had once thought of staying with his friend Poppea Vanda in Hampstead but nothing came of it. The same writer says with no more truth that he was granted a Civil List pension.

† Thus contradicting another absurd story in which 'just before he slipped into the long merciful oblivion which preceded the end' he handed Tredegar a bundle of letters from his mother.

and see me *any afternoon* between 3 and 4. My hosts the Colmans, quite charming, will give you tea after we have had our talk. I really have no criticisms to make except that the last few pages about the *De Profundis* letter are less than fair to me. You do not sufficiently make clear how monstrous and ridiculous O.W.'s charges against me were. "Refusing" to give him lemonade when he was ill! Is that really a serious charge! He was in his own house and only had to order what he wanted. His statements about money also are fantastically untrue. I gave him far more money than he ever gave me, including the many hundreds I gave him in Paris after he left Naples when I myself was by no means wealthy. However perhaps you will put this right when you come to that part of the book.

His mind was clear till the last few hours. The Saturday before he died was St. Patrick's Day and he was sufficiently alert to give Mrs. Colman a long explanation of why the Irish take their saints' days more seriously than the English, because there has been no break in the continuity of Catholicism, as for instance, by the Reformation in England.

He was visited every day, and sometimes twice a day by the local (Irish) priest, Fr. Corley. He was given mild sedatives, but on the afternoon before he died he made a game and characteristic rally to give Mrs. Colman instructions for his bookmaker and "Mixed bark doubles—Nicholson's mounts" may well have been his last articulate words. It would be pleasant to think that this, 'the other side of his nature' as he called racing and all sporting activities, asserted itself in the last sentence he framed.

In the early hours of March 20 (1945) the night-nurse called the Colmans to his room when she noticed the onset of the final stages. They held his hand in turn but it is doubtful if he was aware of any presence in the room and he died peacefully at about 4 a.m.

He was buried on March 23 in the cemetery of the Franciscan Friary at Crawley beside the grave of his mother who was buried there ten years earlier.

H. Montgomery Hyde, who was present, writes of the funeral:

Father F. Herbert celebrated the requiem mass. The attendance would be what the newspapers sometimes describe as "modest". Of the family and relatives present there were Francis Queensberry and his third wife; Lady Edith Fox-Pitt; Lord Cecil Douglas; Lady Jane Douglas and Lord Leconfield. I should say there were not more than thirty present in all. Among the others, I remember Lord Tredegar, Colman and his wife, Donald Sinden, Adrian Earle and

Mrs. Fabienne Hillyard, who as "Francis D'Avilla" translated Bosie's poems into French. Most of us lunched together in the local pub in Crawley. Evan Morgan [Tredegar] and several others came down by train from London, and I remember Evan carried a large wreath: he was the only one to do so. The date was Friday 23 March 1945.

Of his immediate relatives he was survived by his sister, Lady Edith Fox-Pitt, and his son Raymond.

12

Almost immediately the clamour broke out, and the old controversies were revived, by both those who had feared his aptitude for litigation too much to abuse him in his life-time, and those who saw in him and his part in the Wilde scandal, a chance for that kind of retrospective sensation-mongering which had become popular. Occasionally, as in Percy Colson and others the two combined. "It was natural enough, I suppose", writes Edward Colman

that on Bosie's death all the old hacks who had been waiting to have a go at him should seize the opportunity of giving their version of one of the greatest of all *causes célèbres*. It was equally natural that they should approach the then head of the family Francis Queensberry for permission to obtain the material required which would enable them for the first time to give their view of what they thought Bosie's life had been like, without finishing up in the law courts. Unfortunately for him, and perhaps fortunately for Bosie, the chief of the Douglas clan had no mandate to give any such thing, and as Bosie's literary executor I had to deal with some of these persons in a rather peremptory way.

As to the others, those who had merely held their fire, the thing became a massacre. "Alfred Douglas died in 1945", wrote Vyvyan Holland in introducing a book printed from Ross's typescript of *De Profundis* which he described as the first complete and accurate version, "and the last objection is thus removed." So that all the *De Profundis* libels could be read without commentary. In the same introduction Vyvyan Holland—doubtless in loyal but futile defence of his friend Robert Ross—revived the old and totally incredible story that Bosie received a typescript of *De Profundis* from Ross during Wilde's lifetime and thinking that this carbon copy was the only one in existence, destroyed it. Surprisingly, Rupert Hart-Davis in editing *The Letters of Oscar Wilde* was in danger of falling into the same

error. At least his account of the matter seemed to suggest that
he was.

This long letter was not posted from Reading but on the day after Wilde
left prison he handed it to Robert Ross, who had two typed copies made.
Ross then sent Douglas, not the original manuscript, as Wilde had instructed, but one of the typed copies, which Douglas always denied having
received.

On this I wrote to Rupert Hart-Davis:

I don't want to enter the interminable debate about *De Profundis* but I am
convinced, after reading and hearing everything available, that Bosie did *not*
see the unpublished portions till his libel action against Ransome. When *could*
he have, in fact? To suggest that Bosie destroyed a typescript thinking there
was no original is ridiculous. Would it never have been discussed in any letter
if he had seen it? Would he have lived with Wilde at Naples without mentioning it? Would he have favourably reviewed the published portion (as he did)
when it came out? Would he have *brought* the Ransome action if he had known
of it? No. Oscar never made up his mind what should be done about it after
it was typed and he was friends again with Bosie. There was no money in it
at the time. So there it stayed with Ross or among Wilde's papers which
Ross sorted on his death. I am not a blind champion of Bosie but I can't understand you flatly taking the other view and saying that Ross sent Douglas a
copy when there is *nothing* but Ross's word for this and a vast amount of evidence against it.

Rupert Hart-Davis generously replied:

The more I read what you say and think about it, the more sure do I become
that you are right and that I was wrong to be so categorical. If Bosie never saw
the letter, many things are explained which otherwise are hard to understand.
I think the simplest way for me to correct my mistake in the next impression
is to rewrite the second sentence of the footnote to read 'According to Ross
he then sent. . . .

But not all writers on the subject are so unprejudiced. In the same
introduction to the 1949 edition of *De Profundis* above quoted Vyvyan
Holland remarks that when Bosie claimed the original manuscript,
"No doubt he thought he would be able to get a handsome sum of
money for it, as indeed he did from all other letters which Wilde
wrote him." No doubt he did—and who had a better right to? *De
Profundis* was a letter addressed to him and Wilde's only known written

instructions were that the manuscript should be handed to him; moreover it was his by right of his suffering from it, if for no other reason.

There is some excuse for Vyvyan Holland's view; there is none for the host of lesser detractors for whom abuse of Bosie has been a fashionable and much applauded pastime.

When Wilde wrote that prison letter to Bosie, he wanted to explode a myth. ("Your father will always live among the kind pure-minded parents of Sunday-school literature, your place is with the Infant Samuel, and in the lowest mire of Malebolge I sit between Gilles de Retz and the Marquis de Sade.") He did this most effectively, but in doing so he created another, of Bosie as a vicious and selfish creature who had 'ruined' and 'abandoned' him. It is no less false, but nurtured for twenty years by Ross, and since then by the friends and adherents of Ross, many of whom are still living, it is in danger of passing into perpetuity.

For it still goes on. People who in his last years met Bosie out of curiosity and expected, apparently, to find him still the youth whom Wilde had loved, make venom of their disappointment, and people who never knew him accept the fable of his infamy with a glee that matches that of his jealous contemporaries when he seemed to have everything the world could offer.

In the book *Oscar Wilde and the Black Douglas*, nominally by Bosie's nephew the eleventh Marquess of Queensberry 'in collaboration with Percy Colson' there are other jeers, chiefly at Bosie's religion. Of these the present Lord Queensberry writes:

I think you are right in supposing that my father left the majority of the text to Colson. My father was, at the time he wrote the book, somewhat opposed to the Roman Catholic Church and although I doubt him writing the jibes it is possible he did not object to them. He did, however, subsequently become a Roman Catholic and died with the rites of the Church.

In both the films of Wilde's life, made and released at the same time, Bosie figured as a brainless and treacherous Giton, and as a fair proportion of the population depend on the cinema for their history, the myth is kept alive.

More worth answering is a remark by Rupert Hart-Davis in his introductory note to Part Five of *The Letters of Oscar Wilde*, a remark which has been seized on by the more biased reviewers. It is disturbing to find this level-headed and scrupulous editor, who moreover, as he says, makes a point of not butting in with his own opinions, writing of Bosie that he was the man who was to be in some sense Wilde's inspiration and "in every sense his evil genius." The only basis this accusation has ever had is Wilde's letter from prison, a letter on which he recanted scores of times by word and action when he was released, a letter which (once he had worked off his spleen in it) he never wished to reach its addressee. He did, in that letter, accuse Bosie by implication of being his evil genius but at the same time he was writing to accuse More Adey, Robert Ross and Ernest Leverson of being wrong, unkind, deceitful, heartless, stupid, offensive, outrageous, fraudulent, dishonest, utterly incompetent, foolish; he was saying that he had been unjust to Bosie and telling Ross that Bosie would have shown up very well beside him. If these epithets and accusations are not to be taken at their face value, why are all the no less frenzied denunciations of Bosie, simply because these have been common property for years while those against his other friends have had to await Rupert Hart-Davis's publication of the letters?

There is no other foundation for this myth of Bosie as the evil genius except later enlargements on the theme of *De Profundis* by Ross and Harris. One may search in vain through the whole wretched story for evidence that Bosie 'ruined' or 'abandoned' Wilde during his lifetime—on the contrary his loyalty and forbearing, his selfless love and quixotic attempts to defend Wilde when he himself was a young man of twenty-four who found his life destroyed in a few weeks of agony, are plain to see for anyone free of sick prejudice. That later, after the events of 1913 which I have described, he wrote *Oscar Wilde and Myself* and for twelve years tried to disentangle himself from that loyalty, is not to be denied. But he returned to it, and died with it fully proclaimed in his last book.

By what, then, can this prejudice be answered? Many of the more flagrant lies can be disproved as—I venture to hope—earlier chapters of this book have shown. But the more subtle and malicious can only be disputed by two things, neither of which will make much appeal to lawyers, logicians and controversialists, Bosie's personality and his poetry.

His personality, except to a small and quickly diminishing number of friends, can only be judged from the printed word, and it is here that Bosie suffers for both in his own books and in those that concern him by most writers from Wilde onwards, he appears with none of the radiance, generosity, humour and charm which in truth were his. It is of little use for me or any other of his friends to say Bosie was this or the other when there are his own writings to suggest that he was vengeful and obsessed with self-justification. It is of little use to say that he was gay and engaging in conversation and companionship, that he gave one a sense of holiday and exaltation, as John Betjeman puts it, when the prose of his books is so often either flat or excitable, with no light and shade and little humour or grace. All one can do is to point to the number and the diversity of people who loved him and the greater number of those who, throughout his life, found happiness and inspiration in his company.

There remains his poetry and here the ground is safer and the doubts dissolve. As a poet he was out of date; it may be as Spenser was out of date, but also it may be as Shelley was, a challenge to his time, not merely a reaction against it. To quote *The Times* obituary:

He has left much more than elegant fancies and fragrance. His conversion to the Church of Rome in 1911 gave his mind stability and substance. With that background and support he could relax his distrust of "art for art's sake". But there must be no relaxation of the rules of poetic form. To take him literally would be to condemn half the lines in English poetry as irregular, and he intended to be taken literally. This impossible correctness he not only pre-scribed, he also practised it. He was happiest within the most rigid limits that he could impose upon the most strict of forms—the Petrarchian sonnet. Thus he kept his poetry too small in volume for his powers, but as pure and firm as he could have desired.

He worked within a strict form at a time when the fashion was to liberate poetic diction not only from form but from sense, and he achieved, in his sixty years of writing poetry, perhaps six sonnets which will live as long as the language. For these he went, in a more literal sense than Dante did, through hell; for these he expended his peace of mind, his natural trust in the kindness of life and mankind, his good name and his liberty. But he was the last to grumble at the economics of that, economics common to all poets, many of whom have thrown in their health, their sanity, and what domestic happiness they may have hoped to secure. "What a deal of ruined life it takes to make a little art", said an American writer flippantly but for Bosie the words are coldly and tragically true.

But what may prove his greatest merit has not yet come to fruition, and perhaps is an article of faith to only a few. It is that he wrote words to make him remembered—not for his part in a tragedy which will seem merely preposterous to saner generations—but as a poet of small but superb achievement, a poet in his own right to whom the triumphs and reverses of an eventful life were no more than the stuff of a few sonnets.

Bibliographical Notes

THERE is no need here for a large bibliography. My obligations, though heavy, are to very few books. No book of any significance has been written about Douglas himself and information has had to be drawn from books which primarily concerned other people.

Hesketh Pearson's *Life of Oscar Wilde* (1946) and Rupert Hart-Davis's *The Letters of Oscar Wilde* (1962) are the chief of these. I have drawn on the information in H. Montgomery Hyde's *The Trials of Oscar Wilde* (1948) supplemented with a few details from *Oscar Wilde Three Times Tried* (1911) which Christopher Millard anonymously edited. The same author's extraordinary *Bibliography of Oscar Wilde* by "Stuart Mason" (1914) has been useful in a number of unexpected ways. I have also used, with great caution, Frank Harris's *Oscar Wilde: His Life and Confessions* New York 1916 and Shaw's preface to the English edition of this book. Also in connection with Wilde there is *A New Preface to the Life and Confessions of Oscar Wilde* by Frank Harris and Lord Alfred Douglas (1925). The bulk of Robert Harborough Sherard's work is too biased and quibbling to be reliable but there have been passages of some value particularly in *The Real Oscar Wilde* N.D. (1916). Two letters from Douglas appear in Vyvyan Holland's *Son of Oscar Wilde* (1954).

Some details about Douglas appear in biographies of others, most vividly in Keith Briant's *Marie Stopes: A Biography* (1962), W. Sorley Brown's *The Life and Genius of T. W. H. Crosland*, and *About Kingsmill* by Hesketh Pearson and Malcolm Muggeridge (1951). There are also *Robert Ross: Friend of Friends* by Margery Ross (1952), André Gide *Si le grain ne meurt* (1924), Vincent Brome *Frank Harris* (1959), Julian Symons *A. J. A. Symons His Life and Speculations* (1950), Richard Rumbold *My Father's Son*, Augustus John *Chiaroscuro* (1952), Robert Hichens *Yesterday* (1947), James Agate *Ego 3* (1938), Hugh Kingsmill *Frank Harris* (1932).

By Douglas himself there are many editions of the poems and nonsense rhymes and one of *The Collected Satires* (1926). There are also his five books and one pamphlet in prose, *Oscar Wilde and Myself* (1914) almost entirely written for him by Crosland, *The Autobiography*

(1929), *Without Apology* (1938), *The True History of Shakespeare's Sonnets* (1933), *Oscar Wilde: A Summing-Up* (1940), and his pamphlet *The Principles of Poetry* (1943). He also wrote an Introduction to *The Pantomime Man* by Richard Middleton (1933). Articles and reviews of his appeared in his *Academy* and *Plain English*.

Other books to which I have referred for details usually of minor characters in the story of Douglas are: *Oscar Wilde and the Black Douglas* by the Marquess of Queensberry in collaboration with Percy Colson (N.D.). This has elementary inaccuracies but contains some details about the 8th Marquess of Queensberry not to be found elsewhere. *The Quest for Corvo* by A. J. A. Symons (portrait of Millard), *Marshall Hall* by Edward Marjoribanks (details of Alfred Rose), *An Experiment in Autobiography* by H. G. Wells (1934) (portrait of Frank Harris), *L'Exile de Capri* by Roger Peyrefitte (1959).

Biographical Notes

TO avoid breaking the text with details of those who have been in some way associated with the story of Douglas, I add them here, excluding those whose lives are already given in the book or are well known or easily available.

ADEY, William More. 1858-1942. Translated Ibsen's *Brand* under the pseudonym of William Wilson. Joint Editor of *The Burlington Magazine* 1911-1919. Inherited a house at Wotton-under-Edge, lived at 24 Hornton Street, Kensington.
* *Originally a friend and ardent admirer of A.D. who wrote him many revealing letters. Gained the confidence of Lady Queensberry. Later became partner and neighbour to Ross and failed A.D. over his evidence in the Ransome case.*

ALLAN, Maud, died 1956. Born Toronto, daughter of Dr. William and Dr. Isabel Allan. Educ San Francisco, Vienna (Royal Academy of Music) Berlin. Worked "to revive the lost art of classical dancing." Debut Vienne 1903, Palace Theatre London 1908 with classical dances and *The Vision of Salome*. Appeared St. Petersburg, and Moscow. 1910 America. Toured World. Returned to U.K. 1928. Devoted much time to teaching poor children. Played the Abbess in *The Miracle* at the Lyceum 1932. Pub. *My Life and Dancing* 1908.
* *A.D. appeared as witness for Pemberton Billing in her libel action against him.*

ANGLESEY, Marchioness of. Lillian Florence Maud. Died 1961. Daughter of Sir George Chetwynd, 4th Bart. and Marchioness of Hastings. She married Lord Anglesey in 1898 and after his death in 1905 a banker named John Gilliat.
* *Aided A.D. and Olive Custance to meet in Paris.*

ANTROBUS, Colonel Sir Edmund "Strobus" 4th Bart. 1848-1915. Commanded 3rd Batt. Grenadier Guards. Served Saukin Expedition of 1885. Owned 8000 acres including Stonehenge.
* *Friend of A.D. when living in Wiltshire.*

BENSON, Edward Frederick. (1867-1940.) One of three famous sons of Archbishop of Canterbury. Ed. Marlborough and King's College, Cambridge. First novel *Dodo* 1893 had a popular and 'society' success. Wrote a school novel called *David Blaize* and eventually a number of cattily amusing novels about 'Lucia' and 'Miss Mapp' which still have their devotees.

* *A.D. met him in Egypt and stayed with him in Athens.*

BILLING, Noel Pemberton. (1880-1948.) b. in Hampstead the son of Charles Eardley Billing, iron-founder. Fought in Boer War 1899-1901. R.N.A.S. 1914-16, retiring with rank of Squadron Commander. M.P. (Independent) 1916-21. Play *High Treason* produced 1928. Founder and editor of *Aerocraft* 1908-1910.

* *A.D. gave evidence for him in his famous 'Black Book' case.*

BLOXAM, Rev. John Francis. 1873-1928. Ed. Winchester, Exeter College. Chaplain to the Forces 1917-19 MC and Bar, Vicar of St. Saviour, Hoxton 1922-27.

* *Acquaintance of A.D. at Winchester and Oxford. Edited Chameleon.*

BOURKE, Hon. Algernon Henry. 1854-1922. Younger son of sixth Earl of Mayo. Famous as Edwardian man-about-town and owner of White's Club. Member of the London Stock Exchange.

* *Cousin to A.D. Acted as go-between with Queensberry.*

BRAMSTON, Rev. John Trant. 1843-1931. Ed. Winchester and New College Oxford. Ordained in 1867 he became an assistant master at Wellington 1866-68, Winchester 1868-1914. Housemaster 1869-1908. Chaplain 1877-1914. Wrote *Sermons to Boys* 1899 *Fratribus* 1903.

* *A.D's housemaster at Winchester.*

BUSSELL, Rev. Frederick William. 1862-1944. Ed. Charterhouse and Magdalen. Was M.A., B.D. and B.Mus. and D.D. Fellow Brasenose 1886, Chaplain 1892, Tutor 1895, Vice-Principal 1896-1913. Composed music and wrote on the classics.

* *A.D. had 'lively recollections' of him at Oxford and described him as a fine musician.*

CANTERBURY, 5th Viscount. 1879-1918. Henry Frederick Walpole Manners-Sutton. Succeeded 1914.

* *Brought libel action against Crosland. A.D. gave evidence.*

CHAMBERS, John Graham. (1843-1883.) Ed. Eton and Trinity College, Cambridge. Athlete and oarsman at the university. Contrib.

The Standard. Collab. Queensberry in drawing up the Queensberry Rules of Boxing. Edited *Land and Water.*
★ *Friend of A.D's father.*

CLARKE, Sir Edward George. 1841-1931. b. London. Barrister 1864. Q.S. 1880. Counsel for Patrick Staunton in the Penge murder case 1877, for Mrs. Bartlett 1866, for Sir W. Gordon-Cunning in his action for slander (the Tranby Croft case,) 1890, for Oscar Wilde 1895, for Dr. Leander Starr Jameson after the 'Jameson Raid' 1896. He was a conscientious and altruistic lawyer and (consequently, perhaps) an ineffectual politician.
★ *A.D. wrote to him appreciatively for his defence of Wilde but afterwards blamed him for not calling him (A.D.) to give evidence.*

CLIFTON, Arthur Bellamy 1862-1932. Solicitor son of an Oxford don. In partnership with Ross and Adey in Carfax gallery. Used pen-name Arthur Marvell. Wrote for Wilde in *Woman's World.*
★ *A.D. never an intimate friend of his, but Clifton appears to have kept out of the various Ross intrigues against A.D.*

COMYNS CARR, Sir Arthur Strettell, Q.C. 1882—Son of a dramatist father and novelist mother. Ed. Winchester, Trinity College, Oxford. Labour M.P. 1923-4. Has collaborated in various books on National Insurance, Currency, etc.
★ *Counsel for A.D. in Ross's unsuccessful libel action and in A.D.'s successful action against* The Evening News.

CROFT, William Bleadon. 1851-1928. Ed. Pembroke College, Oxford. Mathematical and Natural Science Master at Winchester 1874-1915.
★ *A.D.'s maths master at Winchester, known as 'The Bleeder'.*

CURRIE, 1st Baron. 1834-1906. Son of Raikes Currie M.P. for Northampton, his name before he was raised to the peerage being Philip Henry Wodehouse Currie. He married Mary Montgomerie (Violet Fane the Novelist) widow of Henry Singleton. Ed. Eton. Ambassador at Constantinople 1876 Rome 1898-1902.
★ *Cancelled arrangement for A.D. to be his attaché in Constantinople.*

CUSTANCE, Admiral Sir Reginald Neville G.C.B. 1848-1935. Cousin to Colonel Frederic Custance. Son of General W. Neville Custance C.B. A.D.C. to Queen Victoria. Director of Naval Intelligence 1899-1902. Hon. D.C.L. Oxford.
★ *Supporter of A.D's father-in-law in court action.*

DODGSON, Campbell. 1867-1948. Winchester and New College with Lionel Johnson. Keeper of Prints and Drawings, British Museum 1912-32.
* *Tutor to A.D. at Babbacombe.*

DOWNSHIRE, 6th Marquess of. 1871-1918. His full name Arthur Wills John Wellington Blundell Trumbull Hill. Succeeded at the age of three. Ed. Eton.
* *Friend of A.D. at Bracknell, known as 'Artie'.*

FEARON, Rev. William Andrewes D.D. Was Informator (i.e. Headmaster) of Winchester 1884-1901, having come from Durham School.
* *A.D's headmaster at Winchester, known as 'The Bear'.*

GLENCONNER, Edward Priaulx Tennant, 1st Baron. 1859-1920. Ed. Eton, Trinity College, Cambridge. Son of Sir Charles Tennant 1st Bt. and brother of Margot Asquith. Barrister. M.P. for Salisbury (Lib.). Owned 7000 acres.
* *Married A.D's cousin Pamela Wyndham and financed A.D's Academy.*

HORTON, Rev. Robert Forman M.A., D.D. 1855-1934. Ed. Shrewsbury, New College, Oxford. Fellow New College 1879. Congregational Minister Lyndhurst Road Church, Hampstead 1888-1930. Chairman of Congregational Union of England and Wales 1903. Wrote many theological books.
* *A.D. sued him for libel with* Daily News.

LEWIS, Sir George Henry. 1833-1911. Solicitor. Knighted 1893, Bart 1902. Friend of Wilde for many years. Wilde said: "He knows all about us and forgives us all."
* *Settled A.D's trouble (probably blackmail) at Oxford.*

LEWIS, Sir George James Graham. 1868-1927. "George Lewis II." Succeeded father as head of firm of Lewis and Lewis. Married, in Douglas's words, 'Marie Hirsch of Mannheim'.
* *Acted as solicitor against A.D. in almost every case.*

LUDOVICI, Captain Anthony M. 1882——. Ed. privately and abroad, but chiefly by his mother. Started life as an artist and book-illustrator. Secretary to Auguste Rodin. Left art for literature. Lectured on Nietzsche. European War 1914-18. Wrote on many subjects.
* *Illustrated A.D's Duke of Berwick.*

MACHEN, Arthur. b. 1863 and died in the 1940's. Writer. Novel *The Hill of Dreams* had some success, also *The House of Souls* 1906, *Hieroglyphics* 1902, *The Great Return* 1915, *Things Near and Far* 1923. Wrote on the supernatural including a book on the Angels of Mons. High Churchman, journalist and stylist.

★ *Contributed to* Academy *and wrote libellous obituary notice in* The Evening News *which was subject of A.D's libel action.*

MARSHALL, Ernest Theodore. "Frank." 1866—. 'Academical Clerk' of Magdalen College Chapel.

★ *Friend of A.D. at Magdalen.*

MIDDLETON, Richard Barham. (1882-1911.) b. Staines. Ed. various London schools and afterwards Cranbrook Grammar School. Insurance Clerk. After six years threw up his job to make a living by writing. Contributed to *Academy, English Review*, etc. After four years of penury, living in a small room in Blackfriars, went to Brussels where he committed suicide. None of his work was published in book form during his life-time. *The Ghost Ship and Other Stories* is his best-known book.

★ *A.D. first editor to accept his work (for* The Academy.)

O'CONNOR, Lt.-Coln. Sir (William) Frederick (Treves) C.S.I., C.I.E., C.V.O. 1870-1943. Ed. Charterhouse. Resident and Envoy in Nepal 1918-1925. wrote some songs.

★ *Friend of A.D. who introduced John Betjeman to him.*

PAUNCEFOTE, Julian. 1st Baron. (1828-1902.) Ed. Marlborough, Paris and Geneva. Permanent under-secretary at the Foreign Office. Delegate to the Suez Canal International Committee. Minister at Washington 1889. Successful, particularly during Venezuelan crisis and Bering Sea fishery dispute. Negotiated Hay-Pauncefote Treaty on Panama Canal.

★ *Entertained A.D. at Washington and supported him in the Metropolitan Club scandal.*

PHIPPS, Edmund Bampfylde 'Sal', 1869-1947. Ed. Winchester and Oxford. Became tutor to the children of the Duke and Duchess of Connaught 1893-96. Board of Education 1901, General Secretary Ministry of Munitions 1916-17. C.B. 1916. Kt. 1917.

★ *Co-editor with A.D. of* The Pentagram.

PRESCOTT-DECIE, Brigadier-General. D.S.O. 1865-1953. Clifton and R.M.A. Severely wounded in France during 1914-18 War.
★ *Chairman of A.D's Jutland Committee.*

RANSOME, Arthur S. 1878. Son of Professor of History at Leeds University. Ed. Rugby. Had written *A History of Story-Telling* (1909), *Edgar Allen Poe* (1910) and *The Footmarks of the Fawn* (1911) before his *Oscar Wilde* (1912).
★ *A.D. unsuccessfully sued him for libel on account of his book on Wilde.*

REID, David Kenneth "Tyler". 1870-1907. Ed. Winchester and Magdalen College, Oxford. Died at San Remo.
★ *Friend of A.D. who pulled him out of frozen Thames.*

RICHARDS (Thomas Franklin) Grant. 1872-1948. Ed. City of London School. With W. T. Stead for some years then set up as a publisher in his early twenties. Published Housman's *Shropshire Lad*, etc. Wrote *Author Hunting* (1924).
★ *Published A.D's* City of the Soul.

ROBERTS, John Varley. 1841-1920. Mus.D. Succeeded Sir Walter Parratt at Magdalen and was organist there 1882-1919. To a visitor who tried to join in a hymn—"You're mistaken, my dear sir. This isn't the House of God. It's Magdalen College Chapel."
★ *A.D. 'on terms of great friendship with' at Magdalen and had run of his organ loft.*

RUMBOLD, Richard William John Nugent. 1912-1962. Ed. Christ Church, Oxford. Wrote autobiography *My Father's Son* under pseudonym Richard Lumford 1949. Re-issued 1958 under his own name.
★ *Friend of A.D. from 1932.*

SANDWICH, George Charles Montagu, 9th Earl of, 1874-1962. Ed. Winchester, Magdalen College, Oxford. M.P. 1900-1906. Published books on Locomotives and medals.
★ *Encombe's fag and A.D's young friend at Winchester and later. Was engaged to Olive Custance.*

SHEPHERD, Edward Francis. Was entered at Eton by Mons. H. E. Leavitt of Paris and was there 1883-87. Subsequent life has proved untraceable.
★ *A.D's American friend at Wixenford Preparatory School.*

SIEVIER, Robert Standish. 1860-1939. Married Lady Mabel Emily Louisa Brudenell-Bruce, sister of 4th Marquis of Ailesbury. Ed. France. Served Kaffir, Zulu and Basuto War. On the stage. Journalist. Founded *The Winning Post* 1904.
★ *First attacked later became friendly with A.D.*

SMITHERS, Leonard. 1861-1900. B. Sheffield, became solicitor, later publisher. Issued books considered pornographic at the time. Died 'of drink and drugs', it is said.
★ *Met A.D. on several occasions in Paris in 1894. Published A.D's* Duke of Berwick.

SOMERSET, Lord Henry Richard Charles. 1849-1932. Second son of the 8th Duke of Beaufort. M.P. for Monmouthshire 1871-1880. Comptroller of H.M. Household 1874-1879. In 1889 was involved in the Cleveland Street Scandal, when the editor of the *North London Press* published an article saying that premises at 19 Cleveland Street were used as a male brothel, and gave names of those who frequented it. The editor was given twelve months imprisonment for criminal libel because he had included the name of the Earl of Euston but could not justify it. Others accused, against whom the evidence was stronger, were allowed to leave the country. Among these was Lord Henry Somerset who remained abroad and died in Florence. He composed many popular songs.
★ *A.D. proposed to visit him during Wilde's imprisonment but was dissuaded by his mother.*

SYMONDS, John Addington. 1840-1893. b. Bristol. Ed. Harrow and Balliol. Elected Fellow of Magdalen. Pulmonary disease took him to Davos Platz in 1877 where except for journeys to Italy he spent the rest of his life. Chief work *The Renaissance in Italy* (7 vols. 1875-86).
★ *Wrote curious letters to A.D. at Oxford.*

TAPSFIELD, Rev. Hugh Alexander. 1870-1945. Ed. Bradfield. Choral Scholar of Magdalen College, Oxford. Afterwards 1929-34 Chaplain to the Bishop of Guildford.
★ *Friend of A.D. at Magdalen. Identical life-span with A.D.*

TREDEGAR, Evan Frederic Morgan. 1st and last Viscount. 1899-1949. Ed. Eton and Christ Church. Friend of Ronald Firbank. Founded Tredegar Memorial Lecture at Royal Society of Literature.
★ *A good friend to A.D. in his last years.*

WARREN, Sir Thomas Herbert. 1853-1930. Ed. Clifton and Balliol. Fellow Magdalen. President 1885. Vice-Chancellor 1906-10. Professor of Poetry 1911-16. K.C.V.O. 1914. Retired 1928.

* *Gushed over A.D's first poem but after Wilde scandal refused to accept gift of his first book.*

WASON, Leighton Sandys. 1867-1931. Ed. Westminster School, Christ Church, Oxford. Started *The Spirit Lamp* at Oxford. Ordained 1894. Vicar of Cury-cum-Gunwalloe, Cornwall 1905-19. Was deprived of this living on refusal to abandon High Church practices.

* *Passed on* The Spirit Lamp *to A.D.*

Correspondence with W. Sorley Brown of Galashiels

WILLIAM SORLEY BROWN, then a young journalist, wrote to Douglas first in 1912 and from then till his death in 1942 their correspondence continued, 237 letters from Douglas existing. After the first world war Sorley Brown became editor and proprietor of *The Border Standard* which gave Douglas a medium of publication for anything he wished. The paper was alone in publishing details of his many cases and Sorley Brown was a staunch friend and supporter.

Brown first wrote on July 25, 1912. He had read of Douglas's tiff with *The Saturday Review* over a review of Masefield's poems. Douglas replied that he was not surprised that the Editor of *The Saturday Review* had refused to print a letter—"he is a shuffling sort of person". Later in the year Douglas, again writing on crested notepaper from 26 Church Row, Hampstead thanks Brown for some trout and his article on angling.

The next year saw Douglas's loss of the Ransome case. "I cannot but think I have been most unfairly and shamefully treated." Brown published a booklet *The Genius of Lord Alfred Douglas* for which Douglas is much obliged, but points out that the spelling of Baudelaire's name is *not* Beaudelaire'. He would like copies of the pamphlet sent to a list of relatives and friends which he gives scrupulously with the correct manner of addressing them, the Very Revd. Lord Archibald Douglas, Miss Mabel Montgomery, the Hon. Mrs. Mure, the Dowager Countess of Mayo, the Dowager Lady Leconfield, the Hon. Mrs. Percy Wyndham, Lady Glenconner, Lady Elcho, Lord Leconfield, Percy Wyndham, the Countess Grosvenor, Wilfrid Scawen Blunt, Arthur Johnstone Douglas, Douglas Dixie, Colonel Guy Wyndham, the Duke of Hamilton, the Duke of Buccleuch, Colonel Lewis, Lady Antrobus, Harry de Windt, the Ranee of Sarawak, General Lord R. D. Kerr, Lord Lovat, Rt. Rev. Sir David Hunter Blair, the Hon. Gervase Beckett, Randal Charlton, Very Rev. Monsignor Hugh Benson, Rt. Rev. Monsignor Bickerstaffe Drew, the Duke of Marlborough, Lord

St. Ledgers, the Earl of Clonmell, John Stirling, Lord Curzon of Keddleston, Rev. Father Mathews. The only surprise in this list is perhaps, Robert Hugh Benson with whom Douglas had recently become friendly. Brown received answers from most of these and communicated them to Bosie. Benson thought it was disgraceful that Bosie's genius was not more widely recognized.

By March 2nd 1914 Douglas has sublet his house in Church Row and is staying with his mother at 19 Royal Avenue, Sloane Square. His book *Oscar Wilde and Myself* has been delayed as the publishers feared Ross might sue for libel, but would be out soon. By July Douglas has crossed to Boulogne for "I have had a dreadful time lately. The persecution has been awful, what with my father-in-law, Ross and George Lewis. Thousands and thousands of pounds have been spent in the effort to ruin me." During the next month Brown publishes an article in defence of Douglas who advises sending some copies to 'the enemy', and gives details of these including his wife. "Not that she admits herself an enemy". As an afterthought (he writes on August 2) "This war business is rather appalling isn't it? . . . If we could smash the Germans once and for all it would be worth it, all the same."

There were sixteen letters from Douglas to Brown in 1915 some of them extremely long. By April "Mr" and "Lord" were dropped. The 'Ross Testimonial' has been presented and both are very concerned about this. An attack on Asquith based on this "from the political point of view might be made the greatest scoop of modern times if only these idiots on London newspapers could see it."

Brown made his first personal appearance at Hove where Douglas was staying with his mother, and on returning to Galashiels printed a hundred copies of Douglas's sonnet *To a Certain Judge* ("And down the ages bray and bray and bray"). "I have circulated them freely among the judges and the bar." Crosland has "behaved abominably," in the matter of *The Antidote*. "It's simply a blackmailing action." In July Douglas has another reverse in the Chancery Court over his son Raymond. "My mother is very indignant about it and went to see Eve the Judge and told him what she thought of him." Later in the month he is staying at St. Benedict's Abbey, Fort Augustus.

I need a rest and plenty of open air to get back to my normal state of health and nerves after three years of worry and persecution. . . . I am going trout fishing today on Loch Tarve with Father Placid, one of the monks, who is a great fisherman and sportsman.

But his mother has found a home for them at last—"a place in Sussex. It is called Shelley's Folly and it was built by the poet's grandfather and has the Shelley arms over the front door . . . a very pretty house date about 1710".

That September was the time of Douglas's escape with Raymond from the jurisdiction of the Chancery Court. "Raymond and I were very sorry to lose you." But after Raymond has returned to Norfolk, and Custance has issued a summons, Douglas writes—"If it were not for my poor mother I should not mind a bit, but it is cruel to see how all this injustice to me affects her and bears her down."

In 1916 Douglas is writing *The Wilde Myth* which was never to be published. It is "utterly different from the last book, but then there was a certain amount of Crosland in that." Douglas sent Brown his satire *Eve and the Serpent* in May 1917 "I wrote it yesterday afternoon and last night." Douglas hopes Brown can get it printed in Scotland. "If I had it printed in London, Lewis would certainly send a private detective round to the printer to hypnotize or terrorize him into dropping it." As an afterthought: "You know my wife became a Catholic and that we are in consequence reconciled." Ross reappears in a letter of July 3. "He simply goes on as usual. He has been made a trustee of the National Gallery . . . The things that were actually proved against him would make your hair stand on end."

Siegfried Sassoon has written some very good poetry. I published one or two of his things in *The Academy*. One I remember called 'The Goose Boy' was very good indeed. However he apostasized and figured in the Ross testimonial as one of the signatories.

A letter about *Eve and the Serpent* from Father Watt the Catholic chaplain at Aldershot has greatly pleased Douglas. Father Watt was Robert Hugh Benson's greatest friend and lived with him. He wrote of the "cads in cassocks" at Ampleforth for the Benedictine fathers there were siding with Custance, it seemed, in the matter of Raymond. Douglas writes, too, of Rupert Brooke: "His sonnets are all wrong in form and the best one can say of them is that they are not so repellent as most of his other work. He was one of the Ross gang and hence the boom."

"The Ross gang" seem to have suffered another reverse in March 1918 for Douglas sends Brown a cutting from *The Times* showing that poor Christopher Millard had been given twelve months (his second sentence) for an offence with a boy. He had been, Douglas recalls, the principal witness against him and Crosland in 1914. Douglas has been staying with Pim and "a month in Ireland has converted me to Sinn Fein. And I have joined the Scottish National Party". He also, in April meets Pemberton Billing, presumably in view of Billing's approaching litigation. "I liked him and think he is a genuine man."

In August Douglas is staying at Invercauld, Braemar and the party has shot 350 brace of grouse, and on September 4 his host, Mr. Scott, caught five salmon 16, 12, 10, 10, and 8 lb. respectively. Back at Shelley's Folley he reflects that the owner of the house, Lord Monk Bretton "is a rotten sort of a chap and has never asked me to shoot or shown any civility to my mother or me."

In 1919 Douglas wrote chiefly about the reception of his *Collected Poems*. There were no reviews for a time which made him cry Boycott! but they soon began to come in, and the *Sunday Times* and *Universe* were 'good' and 'very fine' respectively and in November the book went into a second edition. Early in 1920 Henry Savage brought a libel action against Douglas which was dismissed. "I am in the wars again," he comments to Brown. A month or two later he gives the news that James Conchie is putting up the money for him to start a weekly paper which is to be called "*Plain English* with which is incorporated *The Academy*". At the same time Brown gets a rocket for supporting "that poisonous person Saleeby's" views on Prohibition.

Prohibition is simply a manifestation of Manicheism, a heresy which devastated the Church in the 3rd and 4th centuries. It can of course be bolstered up by specious and plausible arguments (like spiritualism and other madnesses) but it is essentially anti-social and anti-Christian. . . . No Catholic country would tolerate it . . . (it) is an outrage on christian liberty and at the back of the movement there are some of the darkest forces of humanity including Bolshevism.

Letters for the next year are from the offices of The North British Publishing Company Ltd. "*Plain English*," 38 Great Ormond Street, but they are sparse during Douglas's fight for the survival of his paper.

In July 1922 Douglas congratulates Brown on the birth of a son and sends him yet another of the satires. "I miss my paper dreadfully," he says. Brown has written to the *New York Times Book Review* about the appearance of a line of Douglas's poetry there. "As to the unspeakable Untermeyer" writes Douglas. "I suppose I must regard his impudent theft of my line as a sort of back-handed compliment." Nearer home, Douglas is attacking *The Morning Post* by letter, leaflet and litigation and Brown supports him. "You made a fine show of that *Morning Post* business and I gather that Lady Bathurst is *foaming*. *The Morning Post* is certainly run by the meanest and most contemptible people. They make a point of treating me with every possible incivility and petty insult, and yet they have stolen and appropriated to themselves all the ideas I promulgated in *Plain English*, needless to say without a word of acknowledgment. Now that *Plain English* is no longer there to give them a lead they are relapsing again into their former dullness, snobbishness and stupidity, but for the last 6 months they have simply lived on re-hashing my old articles. Now that they have exhausted all those, they have nothing to fall back on but their own brainlessness."

There is only one oblique reference to Douglas's successful libel action against *The Evening News*. By April 1923 Douglas is beginning to defend himself against the charges of criminally libelling Winston Churchill which eventually put him in prison. "I am overwhelmed with work over my forthcoming case which is going to be a very big affair", he writes, apparently with relish. He encloses hand-bills of his forthcoming public meeting, at which General Prescott Decie was to have taken the chair. "He is a fine chap—he commanded the much-maligned Black and Tans in Ireland. . . . He is running a society called The Loyalty League and I have more faith in him than in most of the others." "I am thinking of going round the country and having a series of meetings." He complains that men selling his pamphlets were cleared off the streets by the police along with all the other hawkers. "I immediately went to the Commissioner of Police at Scotland Yard and demanded to know by what right he interfered with the sale of my pamphlets." He was told that what was done was in no way directed against him or his pamphlet—hawkers of German Marks, etc. were causing an obstruction in the Strand. "What a tale!" he comments. The pamphlet's distribution is being organized by Reuben Bigland, the man who caused Bottomley's downfall. It was printed by Brown's printers in Galashiels and the bill for this, £46-19-6, was not paid until long afterwards. "We sold over 6,000 in the Strand. I then telegraphed for 30,000 more and there is no doubt that in a few weeks I should have sold half a million." When the hearing approaches Douglas tells Brown that the Plea of Justification drafted by Cecil Hayes is a "corker". "I don't think the other side will relish it." Brown came to London for the case and stayed with Douglas and his mother at 12 Draycott Place, to which they had moved in the previous year. When the sentence was pronounced, Brown was able to follow Douglas to the cells and afterwards published in the *Border Standard*—"Lord Alfred was in great spirits and remarked 'Tell all my friends I am absolutely all right and never was in better fettle. I expected a heavier sentence.' "

Brown failed to send Douglas a line of congratulation on his release five months later and Douglas complains of this. He is occupied with arranging the press publication of his *In Excelsis* sonnet sequence. "It was offered to all the papers and they all turned it down." But the next letter to "dear old Sorley" apologizes for his complaint. "What ever happened to me in prison didn't do me any harm and certainly on the contrary was for my good. If I hadn't been to prison and been 'put through it' I shouldn't have written *In Excelsis*." A few days later:

I hear no news of my poem and I am feeling rather depressed. After going through such a lot it seems rather blank now. It is hard to think that all I did and suffered may count for nothing as far as any tangible results are concerned.

From Belgium in August Douglas asks Brown to cash a post-dated cheque, and offers him the right to publish the whole *In Excelsis* series immediately after it has appeared in *The London Mercury* (J. C. Squire having bought first serial rights for £30). From Bruges in September he writes in a fit of ill-humour:

I am wretchedly ill and have been in bed for two days. I have never got over the awful time in prison and don't suppose I ever shall. Damn the blasted English. I have given the best years of my life and a vast amount of blood and sweat to try to help them and this is what I get in return. But they have always been the same. They have always hated and persecuted poets. Though they will doubtless slobber over me after I am dead as they do over Keats and Shelley and Byron all of whom they howled down. . . . However I am bound to believe that from a Christian point of view the way of suffering and obloquy is the way to heaven.

A month later his mother has joined him in Brussels: "The weather is heavenly. Cloudless blue sky and as warm as June. I have been a good deal better since I left Bruges." As for *In Excelsis*, "I feel now as if someone else had written the poem, for to tell the truth I can't think how I ever did it."

In January 1925 Douglas writes from Bormes where he is staying with Harry de Windt. *In Excelsis* has been published and he is busy replying to reviewers, in the *TLS*, "A good review but I replied to certain criticisms," in the *Spectator* "a most awfully rotten and dishonest review," and in the *New Witness* whose editor he informed that his reviewer was "probably one of the late Robert Ross's 'young friends' who having outgrown the purposes for which Mr. Ross used to employ him, has taken to literary journalism." A rich man called Steedman had asked Douglas to stay at his villa but later put him off. On March 11 from Nice, Douglas writes: "Frank Harris who is here is making desperate efforts to get at me. . . . So far I have declined to have anything to do with him. But it may be good policy for me to see him."

Later that summer he writes from Horn's Lodge, Tonbridge and in October is back in Draycott Place, still worrying about the printer's bill for the pamphlets which had sent him to prison. "I have just heard that as a consequence of my father-in-law's death I am to have an allowance made to me which will rescue me from my present state of utter impecuniosity." He goes to stay in Norfolk "with my wife and boy." His allowance of £500 a year will not begin till January. In January 1926 he goes again to Norfolk "to see the last of the Old Hall before it is sold." He writes some very violent remarks about the late Sir James Dunn who had just married his nephew's ex-wife. He goes to the South of France again with his son and in July is leaving for Ostend.

I must get away partly for financial reasons and partly because I am bringing out a Collected Edition of my Satires including *F Double E* and a pretty hot preface and I think it wiser to be across the Channel.

The lease of 16 Draycott Place is sold and Douglas and his mother move to Limpsfield where they have a furnished house called St. Martins. During 1927 much of Douglas's correspondence is full of Brown's Life of Crosland which is about to be published. The Queensberry family seem to have invested in an attempt to salvage a Spanish galleon from Tobermory bay and Brown is told about it. Raymond's mental health broke down while he was in France and Douglas hurried across to bring him home. Before the end of the year Douglas is working on his *Autobiography*.

Herbert Moore Pim has turned up again and is staying with Brown. He shows Brown a letter Douglas had written him in order to make mischief between the two friends. Douglas had apparently "doubted" Brown and told Pim so.

It is no use being angry with me because I had a momentary doubt of you.

You must blame my cruel experience of life. Friend after friend on whom I have lavished love and affection has betrayed me and I admit there was a moment when I nearly, but never quite, believed that you were going to play me false. Both my mother and I were deeply distressed at the line you were taking in your book in which you seemed to be deliberately sacrificing me to make a hero of Crosland. . . . I am deeply sorry. . . . I ought to have known better than to doubt you.

Just before the end of 1927 Douglas writes from Hove, to which town he and his mother have now moved, that he has just finished his book (the *Autobiography*) 120,000 words. "Secker is going to do it. Also Philip Morrow in New York." "I have got £200 damages from Hatchard's the Piccadilly bookseller for selling one copy of Frank Harris's *Life and Confessions of Oscar Wilde*.

In March 1928 Douglas writes to congratulate Brown on his *Life of Crosland*, which he considers masterly. He follows it in June with a letter over a thousand words long for publication in the *Border Standard* commiserating with, or congratulating Brown on "the complete boycott" of his book by the London press.

Douglas's *Autobiography* is to come out on March 14 1929 and on March 2 he writes to Brown to tell him it is dedicated to him. Douglas is then drawn into a correspondence in the *Border Standard* over theology with a Mr. Ratcliff who "would be well advised to refrain from writing pernicious nonsense about the 'darkness of Romanism' and to make an attempt to emerge from the darkness of his own ignorance and bigotry." But soon "I really can't go on with this prize idiot Mr. Ratcliff. He writes such utter rot that I have hardly patience to read it."

In 1929 Douglas's friends in Hove, who lent him a writing room in their house in Brunswick Square, a Mr. and Mrs. Griffiths-Masters, died within six weeks of one another, "a dreadful tragedy. They were the dearest and kindest people and their loss to me is irreparable." One of them had left Douglas a thousand pounds. In a later letter he thinks he is having the whole of the £1,000 on Hunter's Moon in the St. Leger but adds that this is intended to be a joke. The American owner of the MS of the unpublished book *The Wilde Myth* wants to publish it, but Douglas has rather changed his views since he wrote it and it would clash with his *Autobiography*. He sends Brown a letter he has written to *The London Mercury* in reply to a young critic's review of his *Autobiography*. Squire had refused to print it, but Brown does so.

"I suppose you saw" writes Douglas from Spa on September 4 1929,

that Desmond MacCarthy in *The New Statesman* in the course of a peculiarly offensive review of my Autobiography called me a "minor poet" and says that no serious critic placed me higher than that. Of course he is a mere little s——t and has no qualifications at all. He has made his way by toadying and log-rolling.

In 1930 Douglas has at last arranged for the French publication of his *Autobiography* by Nouvelle Revue Française who are also to publish a French translation of his poems by 'Francis d'Avilla'. (This was Mrs. Fabienne Hillyard and fifteen years later she was one of the friends who went to his funeral.) "I shall be the only living English poet who has a French edition. So it is a great honour." A fortnight later he writes from a Paris nursing home to say he has had an operation. "Please understand that this is quite a secret. My mother does not know anything about it." He goes to stay with Brown in Galashiels in July—taking a trout rod. In September "It is amusing to note that Squire who professed to be shocked at my Autobiography swallows Lawrence's lunatic obscenities without the slightest mental inconvenience. I see tonight that Birkenhead is dead. . . . Poor man he must have suffered a lot in these last few months. He was almost the last of the gang that Crosland and I fought and beat in 1914. Ross, George Lewis, F. E. Smith, Millard, all dead, and More Adey in a lunatic asylum."

In 1931 Douglas finds Baldwin "a sloppy sentimental Socialist though for obscure reasons best known to himself he calls himself a Conservative." That year Patrick Braybrooke's book on Douglas appeared.

I did not want Braybrooke to write my life at all. But I did not like to refuse permission when he asked me as he is a poor man and depends entirely on his pen. I said I had no objection but could give him no more information than is already contained in my Autobiography. He has merely re-hashed my Autobiography. . . . Braybrooke I hardly know but he seems a very nice chap, gentle and unassuming.

Douglas is still living with his mother at 35 Fourth Avenue, Hove in 1932. He writes feelingly about the suicide of Edward Marjoribanks.

He was a friend of mine and junior counsel for me in my case against Harrods Stores when I got damages for Harris's book. I was dining in his home in Victoria Square only a month or two ago. He was going to try to get the

MS of *De Profundis* for me and said, "I can almost promise that you shall have it." He was a most brilliant and charming fellow. It is dreadful.

A fortnight later a horse called Sorley Boy was tipped for the Scottish Grand National and Douglas backed it at 14-1. "The wretched animal disgraced its name by being nowhere".

Brown wishes to publish something about the past, perhaps *The Wilde Myth* but Douglas decides against it.

I think everyone must be sick of the eternal O.W. and myself business, and I think it is a pity to start it all up again. I don't mind ... from the literary point of view but I think the other part is now a closed chapter. Nobody now believes the Harris-Ross lies.

Sherard is now a friend by correspondence. "He says that in his book he demolishes Ross as well as Harris." So much demolition!

Douglas has some correspondence with Beaverbrook in 1933, since Brown has published a story that Beaverbrook recited Douglas's poetry at tea-parties. Beaverbrook wrote: "I do recite snatches of your poetry but not at tea-parties for I am always working at tea-time." Not long after he is outraged by "this man Megroz, whoever he may be." (R. L. Megroz) has told "deliberate lies about my sonnets" and accused Douglas of "echoing Rossetti so plainly that it was impossible to give me credit for any originality." He is then involved in his threat of litigation against Birkenhead on account of his biography of his father (see page 343). But the end of the year he is at grips with James Douglas of *The Sunday Express* and that paper heads the controversy "Douglas *v.* Douglas." "Evidently a bloody fool," Douglas tells Brown, "he is also a liar." "He may be a Douglas, (though I doubt it very much) but he is certainly not a gentleman."

In 1935 Douglas moved into his flat at 1 St. Ann's Court, Nizell's Avenue. His eye is failing him so much that he postpones a visit to Scotland for he fears it would prevent him from fishing. Early in November his mother died and he wrote most movingly to Brown of his grief.

For the next three months Douglas writes on none of his usual topics but in January 1936 he is congratulating Brown on an article "getting at that appalling bunk of Basil de Selincourt about Edith Sitwell in the *Observer*". A strange confusion, reviving the boy friend who had been with him in Paris during Wilde's trial, occurs when he refers to *The Daily Express* column as *Charles* Hickey's. "His real name is Tom Driberg, a brilliantly clever young chap."

That November Brown gets a rap over the knuckles.

I have been grieved to see what Crosland would have called 'canting slop' you have lately been publishing about war and pacifism. Everyone, (including all the best soldiers,) hates war, but to say that all war is wrong and immoral is simply an abominable poisonous and dangerous anti-Christian heresy.

Douglas sends Brown a copy of his telegram to Yeats (see page 353). From Quiller-Couch it brought: "You should take it as a high compliment that you are not in Mr. Yeats' galley. He was a poet once, but adulation has turned his head, and Lord! *what* an anthology and what a Preface!" Brown, however, did not publish the telegram. "You missed the boat," Douglas tells him. "The *Express* prints it this morning (Nov. 30, 1936) in a prominent way." Brown is also in trouble for publishing "ignorant nonsense" about Spain, and this reproof is repeated vehemently in varied terms during the early months of 1937. Douglas himself becomes involved in correspondence in the columns of *The Border Standard* with someone who signs himself 'D.K.' and poor Brown bears the brunt of it. "There is no editor in England who would allow me to be insulted and abused as I have been in your paper by this man. One looks to editors to protect one from vulgar and offensive abuse. The case is aggravated when, as in your case, the editor is supposed to be one's friend. . . . Of one thing you may be certain, that never again will I write anything for publication in your paper." In the next letter from Douglas (March 29, 1937) 'Dear Sorley', after twenty-five years has become 'Dear Sorley Brown'.

As you have ignored everything I wrote to you (in at least three letters) and as in spite of my protest you have once more published an outrageous and ill-mannered attack on me from the pen of your friend Mr. Kennedy, I take it that you definitely wish to pick a quarrel with me.

He thinks it would be best if Brown ceased sending him his paper. "You are no longer the man I used to like and respect so much." A week later:

Please do not send it again. I do not forget that in the past you have shown me great kindness and that you stuck up for me when I was being attacked unjustly. I will endeavour to keep a pleasant memory of you, but it is impossible for me to go on feeling about you as I did, after the way you have treated me. . . . I am afraid I must say that our friendship is at an end and you are responsible for breaking it.

Not until September was Brown 'Dear Sorley' again, but an olive branch is still not wholly accepted. "I try to remember your good qualities but the blow you dealt me when you allowed that unspeakable person to insult me in your paper has left a mark which does not disappear." In November, however, Douglas is again 'Yours ever' and the quarrel is not referred to, though there was only one letter written by Douglas in 1939.

In 1940 Marie Stopes and Herbert Moore Pim become involved, the latter apparently being employed by Brown. "It is really intolerable!" opens a letter in February when Brown has printed in his paper without permission a ten-year-old letter from Douglas.

I *strongly* object to raking up again all that Robert Ross business. As you know I have completely changed my views about Wilde (though not about Ross) and to stir up all that mud is pointless. After I am dead I suppose I shall not be able to prevent everyone rushing in to dissect my memory but at present I lead a quiet life and I loathe all that sort of thing. For God's sake drop it.

A breeze with James Agate in *The Daily Express* over Clerihews and Sonnets happened in March and Douglas sends Brown his reply to the Editor, which was not printed, for Brown to use. In October Douglas is advocating the forcible seizing of bases in Ireland and issues a pamphlet *Ireland and the War against Hitler*. Douglas is very surprised that Brown does not notice it. Ireland and de Valera become the theme of much indignant writing throughout 1940. In 1941

I suppose you didn't listen to the broadcast of my sonnets from Manchester on September 4th? The broadcast was called 'Modern Poets who have kept the classical tradition.' A. E. Housman, Belloc and myself. I went to Manchester for the occasion as the guest of the BBC.

The last letter to Brown is dated May 26, 1942 and there are two letters of condolence to Brown's widow in August. "I have lost my most faithful and constant friend whose sympathy and support in all my troubles were an unfailing source of comfort to me."

Index